Electoral Systems and Political Context

How the Effects of Rules Vary Across New and Established Democracies

Electoral Systems and Political Context illustrates how political and social context conditions the effects of electoral rules. The book examines electoral behavior and outcomes in countries that use "mixed-member" electoral systems – in which voters cast one ballot for a party list under proportional representation (PR) and one for a candidate in a single-member district (SMD). Based on comparisons of outcomes under the two different rules used in mixed-member systems, the book highlights how electoral systems' effects – especially strategic voting, the number of parties, and women's representation – tend to be different in new democracies from what one usually sees in established democracies. Moreover, electoral systems such as SMDs are usually presumed to constrain the number of parties irrespective of the level of social diversity, but this book demonstrates that social diversity frequently shapes party fragmentation even under such restrictive rules.

Robert G. Moser is Associate Professor of Government at the University of Texas, Austin, and the author of *Unexpected Outcomes: Electoral Systems, Political Parties, and Representation in Russia* (2001). He has co-edited (with Zoltan Barany) *Russian Politics* (2001), *Ethnic Politics after Communism* (2005), and *Is Democracy Exportable?* (2009). His articles have appeared in *World Politics*, *Comparative Politics*, *Comparative Political Studies*, *Legislative Studies Quarterly*, *Electoral Studies*, and *Post-Soviet Affairs*.

Ethan Scheiner is Professor of Political Science at the University of California, Davis. He is the author of *Democracy without Competition in Japan* (Cambridge University Press 2006). His articles have appeared in the *American Political Science Review*, *Annual Review of Political Science*, *British Journal of Political Science*, *Comparative Political Studies*, *Electoral Studies*, *Journal of East Asian Studies*, *Japanese Journal of Political Science*, *Journal of Japanese Studies*, and *Legislative Studies Quarterly*.

Electoral Systems and Political Context

How the Effects of Rules Vary Across New and Established Democracies

ROBERT G. MOSER
University of Texas, Austin

ETHAN SCHEINER
University of California, Davis

CAMBRIDGE
UNIVERSITY PRESS

CAMBRIDGE UNIVERSITY PRESS
Cambridge, New York, Melbourne, Madrid, Cape Town,
Singapore, São Paulo, Delhi, Mexico City

Cambridge University Press
32 Avenue of the Americas, New York, NY 10013-2473, USA

www.cambridge.org
Information on this title: www.cambridge.org/9781107607996

First published 2012

Printed in the United States of America

A catalog record for this publication is available from the British Library.

Library of Congress Cataloging in Publication Data
Moser, Robert G., 1966–
Electoral systems and political context : how the effects of rules vary across new and established
democracies / Robert G. Moser, University of Texas, Austin, Ethan Scheiner, University of
California, Davis.
    pages   cm
Includes bibliographical references and index.
ISBN 978-1-107-02542-4 (hardback) – ISBN 978-1-107-60799-6 (paperback)
1. Proportional representation.   2. Comparative government.   I. Scheiner, Ethan, 1968–
II. Title.
JF1071.M67   2012
324.6–dc23   2012013908

ISBN 978-1-107-02542-4 Hardback
ISBN 978-1-107-60799-6 Paperback

Additional resources for this publication at www.ethanscheiner.edu

To our families:
Linda, Sam, Jake, and Zach Moser

and

Melanie Hurley, and Casey and Serena (aka, Percy) Scheiner

Contents

Tables and Figures	*page*	ix
Abbreviations		xiii
Glossary of Key Terms		xv
Acknowledgments and Note on the Online Appendix		xxi

Introduction: Why Don't Electoral Rules Have the Same Effects in All Countries? — 1

1 When Do the Effects of Electoral Systems Diverge from Our Expectations? — 13

2 Mixed-Member Electoral Systems: How They Work and How They Work for Scholars — 42
  Appendix 2. Cross-National Analysis of the Number of Parties at the SMD Level: SMDs in Mixed-Member Systems Do Not Have More Candidates than SMDs in Pure Systems — 67

3 How Democratic Experience and Party System Development Condition the Effects of Electoral Rules on Disproportionality and the Number of Parties: Theory, Measurement, and Expectations — 70

4 How Democratic Experience and Party System Development Condition the Effects of Electoral Rules on Disproportionality and the Number of Parties: What We Actually See — 89
  Appendix 4A. Effective Number of Parties and Disproportionality for Each Country/Election — 109
  Appendix 4B. Multivariable Analyses — 112

5 Political Context, Electoral Rules, and Their Effects on Strategic and Personal Voting — 121
  Appendix 5. OLS Models of the SMD–PR Vote Gap in Mixed-Member Systems — 141

6   How Democratic Experience and Party System Development
     Condition the Effect of Electoral Rules on Strategic Defection   149
     *Appendix 6A1. Histograms of SF Ratios (First and Most Recent
         Election for Which We Have Data): Established Democracies*   173
     Appendix 6A2. Histograms of SF-Ratios for New Democracies   174
     *Appendix 6B. Multivariate Analysis of SF Ratios in Mixed
         Systems*   175
7   Social Diversity, Electoral Rules, and the Number of Parties   180
     *Appendix 7. Quantitative Analysis of Social Diversity, Electoral
         Rules, and the Number of Parties*   203
8   How Political Context Shapes the Effect of Electoral Rules on
     Women's Representation   208
     Appendix 8. Quantitative Analysis of Women's Representation   230
9   Conclusion: Why and How Political Context Matters for
     Electoral System Effects   236

References   259
Index   273

Tables and Figures

TABLES

I.1 Japan vs. Russia – Average Effective Number of Candidates in SMDs at the District Level and Election Rates of Women under Different Electoral Rules   *page* 3

2.1 Description of 18 Mixed-Member Electoral Systems, 1953–2007   48

2.2 Multilevel Model of the (Logged) Effective Number of Parties Getting Votes in SMDs in 37 Systems that Use Either Pure FPTP or Mixed-Member Rules   68

4.1 Relationship between System Characteristics and (1) Disproportionality (LSq) and (2) Effective Number of Candidates at the SMD level (N_{cands})   92

4.2 Mean Effective Number of District Candidates (N_{cands}) – Broken Down by Rules and Party System Context (number of country cases in parentheses)   98

4A Effective Number of Parties and Disproportionality for Each Country/Election   109

4.3 Impact of Electoral Rules and Democratic Context on Disproportionality (LSq)   113

4.4 What Shapes the Effective Number of Candidates at the SMD Level (N_{cands})?   115

4.5 What Shapes the Psychological Effect ($N_{parties} - N_{cands}$)?   118

4.6 What Shapes Projection of the Number of Parties from the District to the National Level (N_v SMD $- N_{cands}$)?   119

5.1 Correlates of the Gap between Parties' Share of SMD and PR Votes (Germany and New Zealand)   144

5.2 Correlates of the Gap between Parties' Share of SMD and PR Votes (Japan, Scotland, and Wales)   145

5.3 Correlates of the Gap between Parties' Share of SMD and PR
    Votes (Lithuania, Russia, and Ukraine)   146
5.4 Correlates of the Gap between Parties' Share of SMD and PR
    Votes Based on Margin of Victory in the Previous Election   147
6.1 Multilevel Model of Correlates of the SF Ratio   177
7.1 Diversity, Electoral Rules, and the Number of Parties   204
7.2 New Zealand Pre- and Post-Reform in SMDs   206
8.1 Women's Representation in PR and SMD Tiers in 49
    Elections in 18 Mixed-Member Systems   218
8.2 Percentage of Respondents Who Agree with the Statement,
    "Men Make Better Political Leaders than Women Do"   223
8.3 Correlates of the Difference between the Percentage of PR
    and SMD Seats Held by Women (by Country/Election)   232
8.4 Multilevel Probit Model of Correlates of Legislators Being
    Female   235
9.1 Electoral System Outcomes, Expectations, and Alternative
    Findings   241

FIGURES

1.1 FPTP rules and the number of parties   26
1.2 Interaction between electoral rules and social diversity in
    shaping the number of parties   31
1.3 Potential relationship between electoral rules, number of
    parties, and the election of women   35
2.1 Geographical representation of mixed-member electoral
    system   43
2.2 Comparing the (mean) effective number of candidates in
    select FPTP and mixed-member systems at the SMD
    level   56
2.3 Mean effective number of candidates at the SMD level across
    multiple FPTP and mixed-member systems   57
4.1 Rules and democratic context shape disproportionality   95
4.2 Democratic and mixed-system experience shape the effective
    number of candidates at the SMD level   99
4.3 The average effective number of parties in SMDs and PR
    (SMD level)   102
4.4 Democratic experience and tier linkage shape the
    psychological effect (the effective number of PR parties
    [$N_{parties}$] minus the effective number of SMD candidates
    [N_{cands}])   103
4.5 Democratic and mixed-system experience affect the extent of
    SMD party projection from the district to the national level
    (N_v SMD minus N_{cands})   105

5.1 Evidence of personal and strategic voting – relationship
between SMD margin of victory (1st place vote – 2nd place
vote) and the SMD–PR vote gap 132

5.2 Evidence of personal and strategic voting – relationship
between SMD margin of victory (1st place vote – 2nd place
vote) in the *previous* election and the SMD–PR vote gap 138

6.1 District-level SF-ratio patterns suggest greater strategic
defection in SMDs in Germany than in Russia 156

6.2 SF ratios patterns in (post-1996) Japan suggest that there is
greater strategic defection in close races 162

6.3 Relationship between each major variable and the SF ratios
in SMD balloting 166

6.4 The SF ratios we can expect to see in established democracies
are much lower than those in new democracies 168

6.5 Relationship between each major variable and the SF ratios
in SMD balloting, based on margin of victory in the *previous*
election 169

6A1 Histograms of SF ratios (first and most recent election for
which we have data): established democracies 173

6A2 Histograms of SF ratios for new democracies 174

7.1 The most common view of the relationship between social
diversity and party fragmentation 182

7.2 If social diversity affects the number of parties even under
FPTP 186

7.3 Diversity and the number of parties (district and subdistrict
level) 193

7.4 Effect of ethnic diversity on party fragmentation in New
Zealand – pre- and post-reform (1987–2005) 198

8.1 Factors hypothesized to effect women's representation under
PR and SMD rules in postcommunist states 216

8.2 Average percentage of seats won by women 220

8.3 Expected difference in share of seats held by women (PR seat
percentage minus SMD seat percentage), country-level
analysis 221

8.4 Public attitudes toward women in politics and the election of
women 223

8.5 Public attitudes toward women and the probability of
legislators being female 225

8.6 Number of parties and the probability of legislators being
female 226

8.7 Combined effect of the number of parties and public attitudes
toward women on the probability of legislators being
female 227

8.8 Effect of institutions and party ideology on the probability of
legislators being female 228

Abbreviations

AV	Alternative vote
ENEC	Effective number of electoral candidates
ENEG	Effective number of ethnic groups
ENEP (N_v)	Effective number of electoral parties
FPTP	First-past-the-post
LSq	Least-squares index of disproportionality
M	District magnitude
MMD	Multimember district
MMM	Mixed-member majoritarian ("unlinked system")
MMP	Mixed-member proportional ("linked system")
N_{cands}	Mean effective number of candidates per SMD
$N_{parties}$	Mean effective number of PR parties per SMD
N_s	Effective number of legislative parties (i.e., parties winning seats)
N_v (ENEP)	Effective number of electoral parties (i.e., parties winning votes)
PR	Proportional representation
SMD	Single-member district
SNTV	Single nontransferable vote
STV	Single transferable vote

Glossary of Key Terms

Alternative vote (AV): a single-member district electoral system (used primarily in the Australian House of Representatives) in which voters rank the different candidates on a single ballot. Candidates who are ranked first by the smallest numbers of voters are removed from the competition and their votes are redistributed to other candidates according to the voters' rankings. Vote transfers of this kind continue until one candidate has a majority.

Closed-list PR: proportional representation electoral system in which parties control the rank order of their nominees on their party lists.

Compensation seats: seats allocated in mixed-member systems to parties to reduce or eliminate disproportionality (typically emerging as a result of seats won in the SMD tier).

Controlled comparison: a research design that uses cases that differ with regard to the variables the researcher wants to investigate, but are similar with regard to all other important variables that may affect the dependent variable(s). As a result, the research can isolate the influence of variables of interest by holding constant other potential causes.

Disproportionality: the extent to which parties' seat shares deviate from their share of the vote.

District magnitude (M): the number of seats available to be won in an electoral district.

Duverger's Law: the expectation that first-past-the-post electoral systems will tend to have two principal candidates per district.

Duvergerian: having the character and quality of two-party or two-candidate competition, driven by strategic defection from smaller parties to larger ones in reaction to incentives provided by restrictive electoral systems (especially first-past-the-post systems).

Effective number of candidates: an index for measuring the number of candidates within a single-member district that is weighted by the share of votes each candidate receives.

Effective number of ethnic groups: an index for measuring the number of ethnic groups that is weighted by the share of the population made up by members in each group.

Effective number of parties (N): an index for measuring the number of parties that is weighted by the share of votes or seats each party receives.

Effective threshold: the percentage of votes at which a party or candidate can expect to win seats.

Established democracy: a democracy that experienced its democratic transition before 1978.

First-past-the-post (FPTP): a single-member district electoral system in which the candidate with the most votes – even if less than a majority – wins the seat. Also called a *plurality system*.

Gender quota: rule that promotes the election of women by mandating that parties follow specific nomination patterns. Gender quotas may be established by law for all parties in a country or established by individual parties in their own bylaws.

Institutionalized party system: a party system in which parties structure the vote; parties dominate the nomination process and independent (i.e., non-party-affiliated) candidates receive few votes.

Least-squares index of disproportionality (LSq): an index for measuring the degree to which parties' share of the vote deviates from their share of seats.

Legal threshold: a legally mandated vote percentage required for a party to win seats in a proportional representation election.

Linked tiers system: a mixed-member electoral system that provides seats from the PR (or compensation) tier of the system to parties to overcome disproportionality created by the SMD tier of the system. "Linked tiers" might be used by some analysts to refer to any mixed-member system (such as Italy's) in which outcomes in the SMD tier affect outcomes in the PR tier. However, our definition of linked tiers is founded on the presence of compensation seats in the PR tier (see Chapter 2).

M + 1 rule: the expectation that the effective number of parties that will emerge in an electoral contest will be equal to the district magnitude plus one.

Mechanical effect: the formulaic translation of votes into seats.

Mixed-member electoral system: an electoral system that provides voters with two ballots, one for a candidate in a single-member district and one for a party in a proportional representation contest. (This definition of mixed-member systems is narrower than that promoted by some scholars; see Chapter 2.)

Mixed-member majoritarian (MMM) system: a mixed-member electoral system in which no compensation seats are used to make up for disproportionality created by results in the SMD tier. Also called an "unlinked" system.

Mixed-member proportional (MMP) system: a mixed-member electoral system that provides seats from the PR (or compensation) tier of the system to parties in order to overcome disproportionality created by the SMD tier of the system. Also called a "linked" system.

Multimember district: a district in which more than one seat is up for election.

Multiparty system: a party system with more than two parties.

New democracy: a democracy that experienced its democratic transition in 1978 or later.

Noninstitutionalized party system: a party system in which parties do not structure the vote; parties do not dominate the nomination process and independents (i.e., non-party-affiliated candidates) receive a large share of the SMD vote.

Open-list PR: a proportional representation electoral system in which, in addition to a vote for a party, voters are allowed a preference vote for a candidate that determines the rank order of the nominees on party lists; may also refer to systems (such as that of Brazil) in which voters may cast ballots for individual candidates, rather than the party, to determine both the share of votes won by parties and the candidates that win the seats for those parties.

Party magnitude: the number of seats a party wins in a multimember district.

Party system institutionalization: the degree to which political parties are well developed and dominate the electoral process.

Permissive electoral systems: electoral systems that tend to allow even parties with a small share of the vote to win office – typically through the use of high district magnitudes and low legal thresholds of representation.

Placement mandate: a gender quota that requires that female candidates be nominated in particular ("winnable") slots on a party list.

Plurality system: electoral system (usually single-member district) in which the candidate with the most votes – even if less than a majority – wins the seat. Also called a *first-past-the-post system*.

Preference vote: an electoral rule that provides voters with the opportunity to rank their preferences for more than one candidate. In open-list PR systems, preference votes allow voters to change the rank order of candidates on a PR party list.

Proportional representation (PR): electoral system typically designed to give each party a share of seats that roughly matches its share of the vote. For example, in its ideal form, a party that wins 10 percent of the vote will also win roughly 10 percent of the seats. District magnitude and legal thresholds of representation can affect the extent to which PR systems allow parties' share of seats to match their share of the vote.

Psychological effect: electoral behavior by voters, parties, candidates, and other elites in anticipation of the mechanical effect of the translation of votes into seats.

Pure electoral systems: electoral systems with only one tier and thus only one ballot using a single electoral rule, be it PR, FPTP, AV, STV, SNTV, etc.

Restrictive electoral systems: electoral systems that tend to allow only parties or candidates with a larger share of the vote to win office – typically through the use of low district magnitudes or high legal thresholds of representation.

SF ratio: an index calculated by dividing the vote won by the *S*econd loser by the vote of the *F*irst loser in an electoral district. (In first-past-the-post SMD districts, this is the third-place vote divided by the second-place vote. In two-round majority SMDs, it is the fourth-place vote divided by the third-place vote.) The SF ratio index is used to explore the existence of strategic defection from lower-placing candidates to higher-placing ones. SF ratios approaching zero suggest high levels of strategic defection, whereas SF ratios significantly different from zero suggest the absence of strategic defection.

Single-member district (SMD): a district with a district magnitude of one; only one representative gains election.

Single nontransferable vote (SNTV) system: electoral system in which each voter casts a ballot for a single candidate, and no votes are redistributed as they are under STV. The seats then go to whichever candidates receive the most votes – or, more specifically, the number of candidates who receive the most votes, up to the number of seats in the district. When district magnitude equals 1, SNTV simply refers to first-past-the-post systems. Most commonly, therefore, SNTV refers to the multimember district context.

Single transferable vote (STV) system: a multimember district electoral system in which voters rank their preferred candidates on their ballots, low-ranking candidates are dropped, and their votes (along with the "excess" votes of winning candidates) are redistributed according to rankings expressed by the voters until all the seats are allocated.

Strategic defection: voters and elites shifting their support from their most pre-ferred electoral contestant to a more competitive alternative in order to affect the outcome of the race. (Strategic defection can include parties or candidates dropping out of unwinnable races.)

Strategic voting: voters shifting their votes from their most preferred electoral contestant to a more competitive alternative in order to affect the outcome of the race – typically, to try to help the "lesser of two evils" to win.

Two-party system: a party system with only two major parties.

Two-round majority system: a single-member district electoral system that requires that the winner obtain a majority (rather than plurality) of votes to win the seat. If no candidate wins a majority in the first round of balloting, a second round runoff is held between the top vote getters from the first round.

Unlinked tiers system: a mixed-member system with no compensation seats to overcome disproportionality created by the SMD tier of the system. In this book, we usually use the term "unlinked" to describe even systems (such as in Italy) that penalize parties for seats won in the SMD tier by taking away votes in the PR tier, even though there is some linkage between the tiers. (See Chapter 2.)

Acknowledgments and Note on the Online Appendix

Before acknowledging the generous contributions and support of family, friends, and colleagues, we would like to highlight the book's supplementary online appendix, which can be found by following the links at www.ethanscheiner.edu. To shorten the book, we cut a number of pieces of less directly relevant analysis and responses to potential counterarguments and placed them in the online appendix.

Now, the fun stuff! This book is the culmination of a collaboration between the two authors that began (more than) 10 years ago and was brought about by the happy coincidence of a common interest in electoral systems, complementary area specializations in two very different countries (Russia and Japan) that came to adopt remarkably similar electoral systems, and the fact that we overlapped briefly in the PhD program at the University of Wisconsin and thus vaguely knew each other. Over the years, our joint efforts evolved and expanded from a few co-authored papers to this book project. It is sort of a running joke that we have actually seen each other in person only a handful of times over these years, mostly at conferences, which is probably the secret behind our long-running collaboration. Whatever the reason, we both have benefited from the countless e-mails and phone calls working and reworking the arguments presented in this book. One thing is certain: whatever the flaws of our analysis, it is truly the joint and integrated effort of the two of us, as we grappled with the issues of the effects of electoral systems operating in decidedly different political contexts.

Along the way, we have benefited enormously from the work and input of many colleagues. We were extremely fortunate that many were willing to read and provide detailed comments on parts of the book. A number of colleagues and friends saved us from numerous embarrassing errors through their comments on our first chapter – most notably, Jo Andrews, John Carey, Bill Clark, Mark Jones, Ken Kollman, Scott Mainwaring, Matthew Shugart, Kharis Templeman, and Frank Thames. Andy Baker, Barry Burden, Gretchen Helmke, Shigeo Hirano, Cindy Kam, Ken Kollman, Rick Matland, Steve Reed, Matt

Singer, and Heather Stoll commented on various other parts of the book. Mike Thies read the entire manuscript and provided his always-trenchant suggestions.

We are particularly indebted to the scholars who provided data. Matt Singer graciously shared the data from his comprehensive study of single-member district elections and offered insightful comments on our analyses. Kathy Bawn, Alessandro Chiaramonte, Ken Kollman, Raul Madrid, and Steve Reed also generously shared electoral data.

A number of students (many of whom are now colleagues) provided superb research assistance. Thanks especially to Caitlin Milazzo for all her help and insights, especially with our work on social diversity, electoral rules, and party fragmentation. Greg Love, Jennifer Ramos, Shawn Southerd, and Jen Wilking at the University of California at Davis and Mike Dennis, Julie George, and Regina Goodnow at the University of Texas provided instrumental assistance at various times during the development of this project.

We very gratefully acknowledge the outstanding methodological suggestions of Andy Baker, Brad Jones, Cindy Kam, and Caitlin Milazzo. We want to thank Kyle Joyce for his suggestions on graphics in R.

We were fortunate to present our work in various formats at Duke, Harvard, Stanford, Rice, the University of Michigan, UC Berkeley, UC Davis, and the University of Texas, where we received extremely helpful feedback. In particular, Barry Burden, Royce Carroll, Bill Clark, Anna Grzymala-Busse, Gretchen Helmke, Allen Hicken, Mark Jones, Ken Kollman, Danielle Lussier, Lanny Martin, Kenneth McElwain, Rob Salmond, Randy Stevenson, Kharis Templeman, Rick Wilson, and Jason Wittenberg provided extremely important suggestions.

We are grateful to have our book published by Cambridge University Press under the expert guidance of Lew Bateman. Two anonymous reviewers of the full manuscript provided the type of encouraging and insightful assessments of the strengths and weaknesses of our original manuscript that one always hopes for but rarely receives. (We now feel the unpleasant pressure of wanting to try to provide others with the same sorts of serious and constructive reviews we received.) These comments gave us much to think about in our final revisions and made the book *much* stronger.

On the production side, Anne Rounds provided excellent and professional editorial assistance at Cambridge. Robert and Cynthia Swanson were first-rate indexers. Brigitte Coulton did a terrific job of overseeing production of the book. Deborah Wenger's copyediting improved the quality of the prose.

We were both greatly aided by institutional support from our home departments. At the University of Texas, Rob wants to especially thank Gary Freeman, the chair of the Government Department during much of the time we were writing this book for his steady and unflinching support. Zoltan Barany, Wendy Hunter, Stephen Jessee, Patti Maclachlan, Raul Madrid, Pat McDonald, Brian Roberts, Daron Shaw, and Kurt Weyland were great colleagues and friends who were always willing to listen to my updates but polite enough not to ask about progress on the book. Wonderful staff members Annette Carlile, Amy Chi, Katie Beth Lane, Nancy Moses, and Stuart Tendler provided much needed encouragement and chocolate. Rob is also grateful for vital funding for fieldwork for this book in Russia and Ukraine from a University of Texas Special Research Grant and an IREX Short-Term Research Grant.

Our collaboration began while Ethan was still in graduate school at Duke, and then continued during his postdoctoral fellowships in the Program on U.S.-Japan Relations at Harvard and through the Japan Fund at Stanford, and, finally, since he became a faculty member at UC Davis. Ethan gratefully acknowledges the support of all those institutions (and especially discussions about mixed-member electoral systems with Herbert Kitschelt, Meg McKean, and Scott Morgenstern). At Davis, Ethan benefited immeasurably from an extraordinarily collegial department, filled with wonderful personalities and exciting discussions. He especially expresses gratitude to Jo Andrews, Amber Boydstun, Erik Engstrom, Ben Highton, Bob Huckfeldt, Bob Jackman, Brad Jones, Kyle Joyce, Cindy Kam, Debra Leiter, Caitlin Milazzo, John Scott, Cindy Simmons, Randy Siverson, Walt Stone, Liz Zechmeister, and Jim Adams (although any errors in the book – as well as any other shortcomings in Ethan's life – are clearly Adams' fault).

Portions of some chapters borrow heavily with permission from our previously published work: "Strategic Voting in Mixed-Member Systems: An Analysis of Split-Ticket Voting," *Electoral Studies*, Vol. 28, No. 1 (2009): 51–61; "Strategic Ticket Splitting and the Personal Vote in Mixed Systems: A Reconceptualization with Data from Five Countries," *Legislative Studies Quarterly*, Vol. XXX (2005): 259–276; and "Mixed Electoral Systems and Electoral System Effects: Controlled Comparison and Cross-National Analysis," *Electoral Studies*, Vol. 23, No. 4 (2004): 575–599. Although some of the ideas and arguments are similar between the chapters in this book and our previous articles, there are important differences that inspired the writing of this book. First and foremost, we have developed a larger framework in the book, in which we seek to highlight our central point about how context conditions electoral rules. We have also refined the theorizing about party institutionalization and new democracies much more in the book, fleshing out these concepts and the causal connections between these crucial variables and electoral system effects. Finally, we have new data, better variable measurement, and better methods that mark a significant improvement in our analyses and findings.

Finally, and most important, we want to thank our families for their love and support throughout the years we were working on this book. Rob says, "Thank you to my wife, Linda, who has willingly and lovingly put up with the countless long nights at the computer. She is the best thing in my life. My two older sons, Sam and Jake, have grown up with this book. I can't explain how much it meant to me that I usually had one of them as a partner in the computer room at home as we worked late on our "homework." Zach, my youngest, has always been my best reminder to keep my work in its proper perspective. Whenever I started taking this project and myself too seriously, I could always hear his voice in my head asking me why I was allowed to play so much on the computer but he wasn't. I am very thankful for my parents, Paul and Kathy Moser, and my brother Joe and sister Lori for providing unconditional love and support from up north."

Ethan says, "Thanks to my family for offering more love and support (and child care!) than any person has reason to expect. Great thanks to Irv Scheiner, Betsey Scheiner, Margaret Chowning, Dick Hurley, Nila Hurley, Jessica Scheiner, Joe Rois, Polly Bowser, and Sarah Bowser for being their incredible, loving selves – and did I mention the child care? Dida, Boo Boo, and Buela, thank you for understanding – roughly – what I do, and for always being there for me. You are wonderful. Dad (Dida), your example is the single greatest reason that I became an academic and have the intellectual drive that I do. Mom (Boo Boo), you have taught me nearly all I know about how to write. Special mention to the West Siyeeed Fantasy Football league (which I won twice while writing this book – did I mention that I wrote a program in Stata to help me draft?), in particular, Matt 'Sporto' Brown, Vince Chhabria, and Amy Krause. Thank you to my wife, Melanie, for her patience and willingness to do whatever she could to support this project. I love you, Melanie. And, most of all, thank you to my children, Casey ('Dada, are you done with that voting book yet?') and Percy (Serena), for existing. As I write these words, you are screaming at each other in the next room, and, yet, you still make my life complete in a way that nothing else ever could."

Introduction

Why Don't Electoral Rules Have the Same Effects in All Countries?

In the early 1990s, Japan and Russia each adopted a very similar version of a "mixed-member" electoral system. In the form used in Japan and Russia, in elections to a single house of the legislature each voter cast two ballots: one for a candidate in a single-member district (SMD) and one for a party under proportional representation (PR). In the SMD races, both countries used first-past-the-post (FPTP) rules, meaning that the candidate winning the largest number of votes in the district wins the race, even if tallying under a majority of all the SMD ballots cast. In PR, parties win shares of seats roughly in proportion to their share of the party vote. In both Japan and Russia, the PR systems used closed-list rules, meaning that prior to each election central party leaders put together a rank-ordered list of candidates to determine which individuals would win seats if the party won representation in PR. In PR in both countries, voters were only given the chance to choose a single pre-set party list.[1] Both countries used mixed-member-majoritarian (MMM) electoral systems, meaning that the SMD and PR components of the system were "unlinked" – seats won by a party in one tier (e.g., SMDs) did not affect the number of seats allocated to the party in the other tier (e.g., PR).[2] In short, both Russia and Japan adopted very similar forms of mixed-member electoral systems.

In both countries, it was widely expected that the different rules would promote particular outcomes: The SMD tier was expected to lead to a small

---

[1] As we explain in Chapter 2, prior to elections in Japan each party could rank multiple candidates at a single position on the party PR list (as long as these candidates also competed in an SMD race), but voters could not pick and choose among the PR candidates. Evenly ranked candidates received a final ranking based on how well they performed in the SMD race. (Evenly ranked candidates who won their SMD were removed from the PR list.)

[2] The mixed-member-majoritarian system can be contrasted with the mixed-member-proportional (MMP) system, in which the PR and SMD tiers of the mixed-member system are "linked" and seats from the PR half of the system are used to compensate for the disproportionality that typically arises when votes are translated into seats under SMD rules. See Chapter 2 for additional discussion.

number of large, catchall parties, especially at the district level. The PR tier was supposed to promote the proliferation of political parties, greater proportionality, and more female representation – especially when compared with results in the SMD tier.

However, the effects of the rules proved to be very different across the two countries. Despite disappointment over the absence of other improvements expected from electoral reform, the mixed-member system in Japan produced the principal outcomes that scholars tend to expect from such rules (Scheiner 2008; Scheiner and Tronconi 2011). District-level competition in single-member district races produced an average effective number of candidates – a measure that weights the number of candidates/parties according to their share of the vote (see Chapter 3) – that hovered around two, especially after Japanese voters and politicians gained experience under the new system. Moreover, compared with rates in other advanced industrial democracies, the proportion of the legislature made up of women remained low, but the women who did gain office in Japan were much more likely to have won election under closed-list PR than in SMD races. Indeed, the percentage of female legislators was more than twice as large under PR as in SMD contests. In the 2009 Japanese election, there were more women elected in PR seats (29) than in single-member districts (23), despite the fact that there were nearly twice as many SMDs as PR seats overall (300 to 180).

The results in Russia were starkly different. In Russia, there was significant candidate proliferation in elections in the SMD tier, with an average effective number of candidates per district score of just under five across the four elections from 1993 to 2003.[3] SMD seats were often won with vote shares around 30 percent or lower, as the electorate within each district often split its vote across literally a dozen different candidates (Moser 2001a; Belin and Orttung 1997).

Meanwhile, Russia's PR tier regularly produced high levels of disproportionality, meaning that there were significant disparities between parties' share of the votes and their share of the seats won. Under its mixed-member system, Russia used a 5 percent legal threshold, meaning that any party with less than 5 percent of the proportional representation vote was ineligible for PR seats. As a result, dozens of small parties that competed in elections went unrepresented in PR. In the 1995 election, only four parties out of 43 on the PR ballot managed to overcome the legal threshold to win PR seats. Moreover, women were no more likely to win seats in PR than in SMDs. Even in the 1993 election, in which a successful women's party won 8 percent of the vote in the PR tier and secured 21 PR seats (compared with only two SMD seats), women tended to fare roughly as well or better in the SMD tier in Russia. Put differently, women in Russia tended to gain *less* representation under PR rules than in Japan but *more* representation in SMDs (see Table I.1).

---

[3] Russia changed to a pure PR system for legislative elections beginning in 2007.

TABLE I.1. *Japan vs. Russia – Average Effective Number of Candidates in SMDs at the District Level and Election Rates of Women under Different Electoral Rules*

	Effective Number of SMD Candidates	Pct. of Legislators Who are Women When Elected in:		Pct. of Women Elected in PR Minus Pct. of Women Elected in SMDs
		PR	SMD	
Japan				
1996	2.95	8.00	2.33	5.67
2000	2.77	12.22	4.33	7.89
2003	2.41	11.11	4.70	6.41
2005	2.40	13.89	6.71	7.18
2009	2.26	16.20	7.69	8.51
Average	2.56	12.28	5.15	7.13
Russia				
1993	4.72	14.98	11.66	3.32
1995	5.91	6.67	13.78	− 7.11
1999	4.64	5.80	8.29	− 2.49
2003	3.52	10.86	8.44	2.42
Average	4.70	9.58	10.54	− 0.97

Why did a similar electoral system produce such starkly different results in Japan and Russia?

STUDYING MIXED-MEMBER SYSTEMS TO UNDERSTAND THE EFFECTS OF ELECTORAL RULES

In fact, the differences between Japan and Russia extend systematically to many other countries as well. In this book, we highlight such differences across an array of countries (including Japan and Russia) that use mixed-member systems to elect representatives to a single house of the legislature, and look to explain the reasons for these differences. In short, the aim of this book is to develop an understanding of when electoral rules will – and will not – have the effects typically expected of them.

Types of Electoral Rules

A variety of electoral systems are used in legislatures throughout the world. One key element that differentiates systems from one another is *district magnitude*, or the number of seats being contested within a district. Single-member districts, of course, have a district magnitude of one – and most voters cast a single ballot for a candidate under such systems – but the single seat being contested is not allocated in the same way in all SMDs. The most common type of SMD system is *first-past-the-post*, which, as we noted earlier, simply awards the seat to the candidate with the largest number of votes, but FPTP is certainly not the only type of SMD election. The second most common type of SMD electoral system mandates that, to take the seat, a candidate must receive a majority of the vote. In *two-round majority* SMD systems, if no candidate wins a majority in the first round of balloting, the top candidates in the district compete in a second round to determine the final winner.[4]

Proportional representation is the most common type of electoral system that has a district magnitude greater than one,[5] but there is variation in the way PR works. District magnitude varies widely across different PR systems. The *legal threshold of representation* – the share of the vote legally mandated for any party to win representation – is nonexistent in many countries, low in others, and quite high in others – such as the 10 percent threshold in Turkey. Some PR systems are *open-list*. In some cases, open-list PR involves voters casting a ballot for a party, but also maintaining a *preference* vote, which allows them to rearrange the ranked list of candidates presented by the party. Brazil uses a different type of open-list system. In Brazil, each voter casts a ballot for a candidate (although voters also have the option, instead, to simply cast a ballot for a party). Votes for all candidates from a given party are then summed together to determine the party's vote and seat shares. Candidates are then ranked within each party according to the number of votes they individually received, and the most highly ranked candidates (i.e., those with the most individual votes) within the party win the seats. All that being said, the most well-known form of proportional representation is *closed-list PR*: Voters cast ballots for parties, and parties rank their candidate lists prior to the election.

Electoral rules can be divided into permissive and restrictive types. *Permissive* rules – such as PR with high district magnitudes and low legal thresholds – allow even parties that receive a small share of the votes to win representation. *Restrictive* rules – such as FPTP, two-round majority SMDs, and PR with low district magnitude and/or high legal thresholds – can make it more difficult for small parties to win seats.

---

[4] The *alternative vote* (AV), which is used in Australia's House of Representatives, is a third approach to electing representatives under SMDs. Under AV, voters rank the different candidates on a single ballot. Candidates who are ranked first by the smallest numbers of voters are removed from the competition and their votes are redistributed to other candidates according to the voters' rankings. Vote transfers of this kind continue until one candidate has a majority. See Reynolds et al. (2005) for additional details.

[5] The single transferable vote (STV) and the single nontransferable vote (SNTV) systems are among the most well-known multimember district systems that are not principally aimed at party-level proportional representation. STV is essentially the same as AV, but with more seats per district. SNTV is the same as FPTP, but usually with more seats per district. Under SNTV, each voter casts a ballot for a single candidate, and no votes are redistributed as they are under STV. The seats then go to whichever candidates receive the most votes – or, more specifically, the number of candidates who receive the most votes, up to the number of seats in the district. So, for example, in a three-seat district, the three candidates with the most votes win the seats. See Reynolds et al. (2005) for additional details on both STV and SNTV.

The Types of Rules We Examine in this Book

The end of the 20th and beginning of the 21st centuries witnessed a surge in the adoption of mixed-member electoral systems. Mixed systems emerged as the electoral system of choice in many new democracies, particularly among postcommunist states in Eastern Europe and Eurasia but also in countries in Latin America, Asia, and Africa. Moreover, popular discontent with politics led reformers in the established democracies of Italy, New Zealand, and Japan to promote electoral system change as a means to address a range of problems. The new parliaments of Wales and Scotland adopted mixed-member systems, and a Royal Commission suggested introducing the same system for all of Great Britain. What was once the peculiar system of West Germany appeared to be on the verge of becoming the wave of the future and the electoral system of the 21st century.

In this book, we use this newly popular electoral system as a laboratory of sorts to examine the effects of the two most well-known alternative forms of electoral systems in operation in the world today. Many different varieties of mixed-member electoral systems have been introduced (see Shugart and Wattenberg 2001b), but the analysis in this book focuses on mixed-member systems in which (a) voters cast two ballots, (b) one of the ballots is for a candidate in an SMD (either FPTP or two-round majority), and (c) one of the ballots is for a party under closed-list PR.

How Mixed-Member Systems Are Useful to Analysts: Controlled Comparison

Mixed-member electoral systems offer a unique opportunity for *controlled comparison* – that is, the ability to examine the effects of different electoral systems under identical sociopolitical conditions. A major problem with the study of electoral systems is separating their effects from other possible influences on party systems and representation, such as social cleavages, socioeconomic development, history, or culture. Large cross-national studies may, for example, show strong correlations between electoral systems and the number of significant parties, the level of disproportionality between votes and seats, and the number of women elected to office. However, many such studies can be criticized for not controlling for nonelectoral system factors that may be the true causes of the outcomes found in these studies. Mixed-member electoral systems in which voters cast two votes, one for a party in a PR system and one for a candidate in a single-member district, offer a potential remedy to this problem: mixed-member systems represent a social laboratory, in which two electoral contests are conducted simultaneously in the same country under two drastically different electoral systems. Viewed in this way, effects of different types of electoral systems can be studied in isolation from influences of the social context, such as social cleavages, socioeconomic development, and culture, because these other factors are held constant. Consequently, the study of

mixed systems can offer valuable insights, not only for an increasingly important type of electoral system (the mixed-member system generally), but also for
pure PR and SMD systems.

Although there were numerous motivations behind the adoption of mixed-
member systems around the world, there existed a common inspiration. Many
advocates of mixed electoral systems hope and expect that the combination
of PR and SMD electoral rules – which, in their pure form, have been found
to have very different effects on a range of political outcomes – will produce
some measure of balance between two types of desirable outcomes: (a) the
proportionality and small group representation commonly associated with PR
and (b) the geographic representation of a particular locale and the large,
catchall parties that are characteristic of SMD systems. In the words of Matthew
Shugart and Martin Wattenberg, the great promise of mixed systems is that
they could provide "the best of both worlds" (Shugart and Wattenberg 2001a:
581–595).

This "best of both worlds" view of mixed-member electoral systems is hardly
universal. As Giovanni Sartori warned, mixed systems might actually generate
outcomes that combine the *defects* of PR and SMD systems (Sartori 1994: 75).
From a different perspective, some scholars (e.g., Ferrara et al. 2005) argue that
in mixed-member systems, the SMD and PR components do not act as they
would under "pure" systems, in which the other component is not present.
Instead, such scholars argue, the existence of the two tiers leads to "contamination," so the presence of PR balloting affects behavior and outcomes in the
SMD tier and vice versa. As a result, these scholars argue that the controlled
comparison approach cannot work, as it is impossible to separate out the true
independent effects of each type of electoral rule.

However, as we argue in this book (see especially Chapter 2), claims about
the importance of contamination within mixed-member systems are overstated.
There is good reason to believe that the controlled comparison approach allows
us to draw useful inferences about (a) the separate effects of different types of
electoral rules, and (b) the effects of electoral rules separate from the effects of
the sociopolitical context in which they operate.

Studying Many Types of Countries to See When Electoral Rules Have Their Expected Effects

Mixed-member systems have been introduced in many types of democracies.
This fact allows us to explore how sociopolitical context can shape the effects
that electoral systems have: by analyzing the differences in outcomes between
the SMD and PR tiers within mixed systems in a variety of different contexts, we can consider the conditions under which electoral systems have their
expected effects. If different types of countries – for example, new and established democracies – have systematically different patterns in their electoral
outcomes under SMD and PR rules, then there are good reasons to suspect that
these contextual differences have an impact on electoral system effects.

Thus, a controlled comparison of the PR and SMD tiers of mixed-member systems around the world provides two crucial analytical benefits. First, controlled comparison allows analysts to isolate the effects of electoral systems from other factors, such as culture, economic development, and so on. If outcomes differ systematically between SMD and PR rules in a variety of countries, we can be confident that the electoral rules are the reason why. Second, comparison across countries provides the opportunity to study the conditionality of electoral system effects. If certain types of countries experience stark differences between SMD and PR tiers and other types do not, we can assert that the context in which the electoral rules operate is conditioning their effects.

The Importance of District-Level Analysis

An additional noteworthy aspect of this book is that we use data at the district level to examine and test relationships between electoral rules and different electoral outcomes – party system fragmentation, strategic defection from weak parties to stronger ones, the personal vote, and the election of women – as well as the interactive effect of social diversity and electoral rules on party systems. The use of district-level data is important because many of the core theories of electoral system effects are cast at the district level; thus, analyses of electoral system effects must be analyzed at the level at which we expect the causal mechanisms to operate. Whereas many examinations of the impact of electoral rules on the number of parties use district-level data, other relationships – most notably, the interaction between social diversity and electoral rules, but also analyses of women's representation – usually use data aggregated at the national level.[6] It should not be surprising, therefore, that many of our district-level analyses produce new findings that challenge previous research.

THE ARGUMENT IN BRIEF

We argue that variation in the effects of electoral rules is due to specific differences in political context that *systematically* condition the effects of electoral rules.

If our explanation were merely that "context matters," the analysis would be both unsurprising and trivial – but the argument is more subtle. First, our emphasis on context conditioning rules stands in contrast to much work on political institutions: one of the core principles of scholarly analysis of political institutions is how rules condition the effects of context. Indeed, the idea that electoral institutions affect electoral outcomes by producing incentives for certain types of behavior, and thus changing the way other contextual

---

[6] At the same time, some very important theories of electoral systems and their effects focus on national-level considerations. For example, Lijphart's work (e.g., Lijphart 1984) concentrates on national level outcomes, as does Taagepera's (2007), and Cox (1997) examines projection from district-level to national-level party configurations.

factors affect these same outcomes, lies at the heart of how we view the impact of electoral rules (see Grofman et al. 2009: 3). For example, most analyses highlight how social diversity is likely to be expressed in the party system under permissive electoral rules, but restrictive rules such as FPTP constrain the number of parties, irrespective of the level of social diversity (see, e.g., Clark and Golder 2006). We certainly do not quibble with the idea that rules can condition the effect of context. However, our argument in this book is the reverse – context mitigates the way that electoral institutions affect outcomes.

Of course, the electoral system literature has not ignored the impact of context on institutions. Most notably, Gary Cox's (1997) classic work highlights the underlying conditions necessary to promote strategic behavior. However, the role of context in conditioning rules has certainly not been the central message of the voluminous work on electoral system effects, especially the literature emphasizing the prospect for institutional engineering. Moreover, the role of context in conditioning rules is hardly the common understanding among policy makers on how electoral systems affect politics (Reynolds et al. 2005).

Second, in our focus on context, we do not argue that every country is so unique that it must be studied in isolation from all others. Rather, we argue that differences in context are equivalent to variation in the values of important variables, and in this book we highlight a small number of contextual variables that vary in limited – but important – ways. This variation in context leads to systematic differences in the effects of electoral rules across different countries. In this way, this book is not a critique of existing theories for an inability to predict outliers. Rather, we seek to emphasize the importance of outliers and the reasons for their divergence. As Bernard Grofman, Shaun Bowler, and Andre Blais (2009) highlight, recognizing many of the outliers from what is expected in electoral system theories is important because it forces us to consider the mechanisms that explain how electoral systems affect outcomes. Ultimately, then, this book is a call to expand theories to pay greater explicit attention to the contextual foundations that make the predicted outcomes of electoral systems possible – and recognize how other conditions might lead to systematically different outcomes.

In short, we argue that context conditions the effects of electoral rules, and – at least as important – context does so in systematic ways. Electoral rules do not have the same effects in all contexts. Moreover, if armed with knowledge about a small number of key features of a particular country's sociopolitical context, we can make well-informed predictions – which sometimes diverge substantially from what is commonly expected – about the likely effects of electoral rules in that country.

This general argument extends to a set of specific findings:

1. In established democracies, it is common for voters and elites under restrictive electoral rules such as FPTP to transfer support strategically from their most preferred candidate or party to a more competitive

alternative in order to affect the outcome of the race. As a result, in established democracies, restrictive rules constrain the number of competitors in district races. In contrast, in new democracies – especially those with poorly developed parties – strategic "defection" is less common. As a result, the constraining effect of restrictive rules becomes tempered, leading to many more contestants that compete for and receive electoral support.[7]

2. In contexts with substantial social homogeneity, FPTP rules constrain the number of parties and candidates, especially in established democracies. However, there is greater variation in the number of parties in contexts of greater social diversity, irrespective of the electoral rules used (and also irrespective of the amount of democratic experience).

3. In established democracies in which there is (a) significant support for the idea of women as political office holders and (b) a limited number of candidates who contest FPTP races, women are more likely to win legislative office under PR rules than in SMDs. In contrast, in postcommunist societies – which witness many candidates per district in SMDs and demonstrate less public support for women as political leaders – there is little difference in the likelihood of women holding office under SMD and PR rules.

Scholars have long noted the different varieties and levels of democratic consolidation between the so-called third wave (new) democracies and established democracies, and among new democracies themselves, but have rarely shown concrete political repercussions of such differences. This book highlights, for example, that new democracies – especially those with poorly institutionalized party systems – experience great party fragmentation in SMD elections, more personal voting, less strategic defection, and even significant differences in the election of women. Moreover, for new and established democracies alike, scholars argue that increased social diversity tends to promote party fragmentation only under permissive (e.g., PR) electoral systems. However, our analysis challenges this central conclusion about the interaction between electoral rules and social context.

Specific Examples

For example, Japan's established democracy provided the conditions necessary for strategic behavior by elites and voters, which, in turn, produced the effects commonly associated with both PR and SMD elections. Similarly, incentives for the greater nomination and election of women commonly associated with

---

[7] Critics of this analysis might argue that the problem in new democracies is simply that they are not yet in equilibrium. In some cases, this point is correct, although we believe that the presence or lack of equilibrium may itself also be a variable to consider. However, more important, as we argue in Chapter 6, new democracies in countries such as Russia may, in fact, be in equilibrium – but an equilibrium different from that expected according to most work on electoral rules.

PR rules led to greater female representation through PR party lists than in SMDs. In contrast, Russia's newly democratic structures and noninstitutional-ized party system created an environment in which the same electoral rules had very different results. Uncertain information on likely electoral outcomes led few voters and elites to withdraw their support strategically from their most preferred electoral options, especially in local SMDs where there were little or no reliable polling data on individual candidates. In such an atmosphere, additional candidates and parties had an incentive to throw their hats into the ring, further fueling a dynamic that pushed candidate proliferation even in the plurality (SMD) system. The party fragmentation in both the PR and SMD contests in Russia also created a very different environment for the election of women. In SMDs, the crowded field of candidates provided an opportunity for women to run for office and gain election because one of the main obstacles to women's representation in plurality elections – the high vote share typically needed to gain election – was notably absent. Consequently, contrary to expec-tations and global patterns, women were no more likely to win office in PR than in SMDs.[8]

This is not to say that institutions do not matter. PR and SMD electoral rules had discernible effects in both Japan and Russia. However, those effects were not always what scholars expected them to be. It is important to emphasize that we argue that the electoral system effects we find in mixed-member systems around the world are not random, even when they run counter to expectations, as was the case in Russia. Rather, the effects we find are consequences of sys-tematic and discernible differences in the conditions under which elites and voters navigate their electoral environments. It is therefore important to dis-cern how electoral rules and different political and social contexts interact to produce different outcomes. In so doing, we can expand our understanding of electoral system effects and know better what to expect when specific electoral systems are introduced in divergent political environments.

NOTE TO THE READER ON HOW WE PRESENT THE ANALYSIS

Analysis of electoral results lends itself to quantitative analysis, but we want all people interested in parties, elections, and electoral rules – irrespective of their level of technical expertise – to be able to follow the meaning of our findings. For this reason, in each chapter we present and explain the main findings with the aid of simple tables and graphs that demonstrate the relationships. After each chapter, we include appendices that offer detailed explanations of the quantitative models and findings. In addition, for space reasons, we have cut from this book a number of pieces of less directly relevant analysis and

---

[8] We should note, though, that in contrast to other countries that are more supportive of the notion of women as political leaders, in neither Japan nor Russia were many women elected to legislative office under either SMDs or PR.

responses to potential counterarguments. We have placed this material in the online appendix, which can be linked from www.ethanscheiner.com.

PLAN FOR THE BOOK

In this book, we take a broad view of electoral system effects. In Chapter 1, we present our theoretical approach, laying out what we see as the fundamental assumptions underpinning the major arguments of electoral system effects on the number of parties, strategic and personal voting, the interaction between social diversity and electoral rules, and women's representation. We then explain how electoral systems may not have their expected effects on these outcomes if certain conditions are not met. Chapter 2 provides a detailed discussion of the workings of mixed-member electoral systems, and contains an extended explanation of our controlled comparison approach: how we apply the approach to mixed-member electoral systems and how using this approach to compare PR and SMD tiers across a large number of mixed-member systems helps us to understand how political context may alter the effects that electoral rules have. In Chapter 2, we also discuss in detail the contamination critique of the controlled comparison approach, and highlight the lack of grounding for such critiques of our approach.

In Chapters 3 through 8, we test our arguments about how context conditions the effects of electoral rules. In Chapters 3 through 6, we use the controlled comparison approach to examine the impact of electoral rules and democratic experience on party fragmentation and strategic electoral defection. Chapter 7 examines the link between social diversity and the number of parties under PR and SMD rules in mixed systems. Chapter 8 examines the effect of electoral rules on descriptive representation, specifically the election of women. Finally, Chapter 9 summarizes our principal conclusions and fleshes out some of the most important implications.

IMPLICATIONS

Many readers are likely to disagree with our analysis. Even so, we believe that attention should be given to the systematic variation we find and theories we present to explain this variation. These findings have repercussions for scholars and policy makers for the study of electoral systems and beyond. Institutional engineers who presume that electoral systems will have the same effects in every context will be sorely disappointed.

On one level, this book suggests the limits of institutional engineering. The analysis suggests that electoral rules will not function as scholars often portray them if a democratic system is still developing and not yet in "equilibrium." In other words, if electoral behavior is not sufficiently stable, certain political actors will behave quite differently from how they will act once the political system becomes more settled. In this way, institutional engineers ought to be prepared for a period in new democracies in which electoral outcomes do not match those in more established democracies. Indeed, this is one of the crucial differences in the way that electoral systems work in new democracies compared with established ones – it takes much longer for new democracies to reach an equilibrium that makes possible the expected constraining effects of plurality elections. As we show in future chapters, in general, even after a few elections, new democracies such as Russia still had more contestants per SMD than established democracies – and certainly more than expected by most theories of the effects of electoral rules. Moreover, as we discuss later, in some cases, the lack of certainty about outcomes can become self-reinforcing, leading to an equilibrium that makes it difficult for political actors to behave in ways that are consistent with most theories of the constraining effects of electoral rules.

On a different level, though, the analysis also suggests great potential for institutional engineering if the engineers consider the role of political context as a conditioning force. This book argues that contextual factors such as democratic development and social diversity need to be integrated into any general model of the likely effect of electoral institutions. When institutional engineers – especially those in new democracies – do in fact consider context carefully, they can better anticipate the systematically and predictably different outcomes that they may see under the electoral rules that they choose.

1

When Do the Effects of Electoral Systems Diverge from Our Expectations?

It is widely agreed that electoral rules matter. When polities adopt new rules to govern their elections, they usually have a specific effect in mind. At the most basic level, when electoral system engineers choose electoral rules, they do so with the understanding that first-past-the-post (FPTP) single-member district (SMD) systems tend to constrain the number of parties and perhaps even promote a competitive two-party system. When electoral rule designers want to encourage the presence of multiple parties – which, ideally, will provide clear, distinct representation to many different groups in society – they usually institute proportional representation (PR) rules, which allocate to parties a proportion of the total seats that matches their proportion of the total vote. It is also widely believed that electoral rules matter in numerous areas beyond simply the number of parties. Among the most important is the type of people who get elected to office – for example, it is presumed that a side benefit of closed-list PR rules is that they tend to help elect women to public office.

In many cases, political outcomes match the expectations electoral rule designers have for their systems – but often they do not. The recent experience of countries that have adopted mixed-member electoral systems offers very clear examples of FPTP and PR electoral rules having their expected effects under certain conditions, but also other instances when electoral rules fail to promote those outcomes. In the early 1990s, numerous countries instituted mixed-member system rules, with the most common type being electoral rules that offered voters two ballots – one for a candidate in an SMD and one for a party in closed-list PR. In countries such as Germany, Italy, Japan, and New Zealand that used these mixed-member systems, SMD balloting constrained the number of parties competing, whereas under PR, votes and seats were spread more evenly across a larger number of parties. There was also a difference in the types of people elected under the different types of rules in Germany, Italy, Japan, and New Zealand. Most notably, larger numbers of women were elected under PR rules than in SMDs.

However, the outcome was markedly different in countries such as Bolivia, Russia, Ukraine, and Venezuela. In these countries, a relatively large number of parties gained both votes and seats under PR rules. What is surprising, though, is that many different parties competed under SMD rules as well. In these countries, SMD rules produced dramatic candidate proliferation, with, on average, four, five, and sometimes nearly six viable candidates competing for office. Moreover, in postcommunist countries such as Russia and Ukraine, PR rules appeared to offer little benefit to women. Compared with SMD rules, women were not noticeably more likely to get elected under PR. Furthermore, in a number of cases, female representation was even greater under SMD balloting.

The differences in electoral outcomes that we see across these countries raise significant questions about the influence of electoral rules. Perhaps the biggest question is: Under what conditions will electoral systems affect politics in the way that we usually expect? At first glance, the obvious answer is that electoral rules work as expected in well-established democracies, but that they have different effects in new democracies, particularly those in postcommunist countries that transitioned to democracy in the late 1980s and early 1990s. However, such an answer really begs the question. What is different about established and new democracies, or at least particular countries within these two broad categories, that brings about such dissimilar outcomes?

This book examines the impact of electoral rules in both established and new democracies to try to understand when electoral systems will have the effects that we tend to expect from them and when their effects will diverge from our expectations. We focus on both kinds of democracies because much of the variation that we find in political outcomes occurs between new and established democracies. However, as we will discuss in detail, the unusual electoral system effects that we see in many new democracies are not only, or even necessarily, a direct result of their "newness." We speculate that there exists a range of underlying conditions that are found much more regularly in new democracies rather than in established ones. We pay extra attention to one of these factors – party institutionalization. Indeed, the most exceptional newly democratic cases maintain characteristics – such as poorly established party systems – that distinguish them not only from most established democracies, but from many other new democracies as well.

By comparing the effects of electoral systems in a wide variety of cases – including both established and new democracies – we find that one of the greatest limits to the generalizability of many of the most hallowed electoral system theories is that they are founded on assumptions that simply do not hold in all contexts. By examining electoral rules under different political contexts, we see that many factors that most studies of electoral systems do not examine explicitly and systematically are, in fact, potentially powerful variables that shape the ways in which electoral systems affect politics. That is, the factors we discuss are features of political life that vary across different cases and, in turn, affect political outcomes in systematic ways that are not usually accounted for in studies on electoral systems. Put simply, our central argument in this book is that specific contextual factors condition the effects of electoral rules.

WHY STUDY ELECTORAL SYSTEMS?

The study of electoral systems has spawned one of the most extensive and well developed literatures in political science. William Riker (1982) held up the study of electoral rules as an example of how political science can produce an accumulation of knowledge, and thus at times approximate the norms of the natural sciences. Rein Taagepera and Matthew Shugart (1989: 5) similarly praise the study of electoral systems as potentially supplying a "Rosetta Stone" for the development of political science, arguing that votes could be a basic measurable quantity of the field, similar to money in economics or mass in physics.

A useful feature of electoral system scholarship is that it works with data that are comparable across differing political and cultural contexts and commonly available for many countries. Votes and legislative seats are basic units of democratic governance that are more easily compared than attitudes, cultural identities, social classes, or civil society, which may differ substantially in different social contexts. Most electoral data are also easily quantifiable, allowing for more precise measurement of causal relationships.

As a result, work on electoral systems has produced a body of scholarship that is amenable to empirical verification – that is, we can test the hypotheses relatively easily. And through much of its history, the study of electoral systems has found, on average, strong empirical regularities at the district level (Cox 1997; Singer forthcoming).

However, is the empirical record as solid as commonly assumed, even in Western democracies on which much of the literature is based? Do these findings extend past the Western experience? Studies of exceptions in new democracies (and some well-established ones) provide a basis to question whether electoral systems' effects are uniform under all contexts (see Clark and Golder 2006; Diwakar 2007; Grofman et al. 2009). If electoral system effects are contingent on other factors, such as democratic experience, the attainment of a certain level of socioeconomic development, or possibly the amount of social diversity, then how important is the electoral system as an independent causal variable? Ultimately, we argue, our ability to understand the limits of electoral system theories depends on recognition of: (1) the assumptions that underpin these theories and (2) the conditions under which these assumptions do or do not hold.

SOCIAL SCIENCE AND THE USE OF ASSUMPTIONS

The aim of social science is to draw inferences about human behavior, usually from a limited number of real-world observations (King, Keohane, and Verba 1994: 7). Sometimes social scientists focus on description, but for many scholars the principal goal is explanation – ideally, explanation that can be expanded to a wide universe of cases. Speaking for many social scientists, Robert Jackman explains that "we are concerned with identifying and establishing regularities and causal mechanisms" (1985: 166). However, to develop studies that can provide explanations – especially generalizable explanations – it is important to introduce assumptions. Jackman notes that the effort to develop such explanations

> requires simplification of a given research problem into a manageable form, which occurs as the relevant variables are selected. There is a trade-off between simplifying assumptions and descriptive accuracy: if the former become too severe, analyses can quickly lose any meaningful empirical referents. Nonetheless, without simplifying assumptions, the problems of interpreting empirical results become overwhelming (1985: 166).

Indeed, underlying most social science studies is the (usually unstated) assumption that the variables included in the analysis are the most important factors explaining the outcome of interest and that other variables can safely be excluded from the study. The ideal is to create a balance between, on one hand, comprehensive analysis (fully specified models) and, on the other, parsimony (i.e., simple models that emphasize only a small number of key variables). However, much work tends to either examine, in a large number of cases, as many variables as possible that may affect a particular outcome, or isolate a specific potential causal variable by examining cases that are alike in other important ways.

Of course, both approaches have costs. It is usually difficult to measure and collect data on large numbers of variables for large numbers of cases, but it is also difficult to find cases that are alike in every way except one crucial factor. It is for this reason, as Jackman points out, that the practice of social science is founded on simplifying assumptions: social science studies typically assume that the units being analyzed are alike in many important ways, and that the variables not included in the analysis do not require additional consideration.

To put it differently: Social science confronts an infinite number of features of the human world. To try to explain the way things work, it is necessary to focus on the few that are most plausible and omit the rest from the analysis. In the process, social scientists implicitly assume that most of the omitted variables are less important and would not substantially change the impact of the key variables under observation.

To be able to claim more credibly that the omitted variables are not driving the outcomes they witness, social scientists often compare countries within the same geopolitical region that are, as Arend Lijphart writes, "similar in a large number of important characteristics (variables) which one wants to treat as constants, but dissimilar as far as those variables are concerned which one wants to relate to each other" (1971: 687). However, this narrowed focus introduces constraints on our interpretations of the studies' findings by limiting generalizability. It is impossible to know whether the findings of a study examining cases only in Latin America or East Asia are due to a pattern of behavior that exists in all cases or are simply due to features of politics that exist only in that particular set of cases. In fact, it is a misnomer to suggest that these variables were omitted; rather, as Lijphart suggests, their values were assumed to be constant. Only by seeing what happens when these variables actually vary – typically by increasing the number and type of cases under consideration, but also by dropping the assumption of the variables being constant – can we know whether the study's findings are generalizable.

Ultimately, all of this is a problem to some extent in any social science study: All social science research must make assumptions to get any sort of traction in trying to understand the relationship between different variables. It therefore is important to be aware of what these (usually unstated) assumptions are. It is also important to consider when such assumptions might not hold, and what the accompanying consequences would be for political outcomes.

DIFFERENCES AMONG AND WITHIN DEMOCRACIES

We argue that many studies of electoral systems have not adequately taken into account contextual factors; thus, the issue of unstated assumptions, omitted variables, and generalizability across divergent cases has been an important and relatively neglected problem for the literature on electoral systems. There are, of course, an infinite number of ways that context can vary within and between different democracies. In this book, we highlight a small number that we believe play a central part in shaping the way electoral systems affect political outcomes. Some of these differences require little explanation. Most obviously, different contexts contain different levels of social and ethnic diversity, variation in cultural attitudes (such as patterns of support for women in politics), and varying strengths of attachments to particular candidates and parties. However, we would do well to offer greater detail to clarify the most important distinction between democracies that we raise in this book – democratic experience and the accompanying level of party system development.

Established versus New Democracies

There are many important differences between new and established democracies. Compared with established democracies, new democracies tend to be less developed economically (Przeworski et al. 2000) and have weaker civil societies (Howard 2003) and less well-developed media institutions (Mickiewicz 1997, 2008). Nevertheless, for our purposes, the most important differences between new and established democracies relate to the degree to which the political system conveys clear and reliable information to political actors about likely patterns of support for the various contestants in elections.

In this way, an important difference between established and new democracies relates to the stability and certainty of voters' and elites' likely electoral behavior. Typically, established democracies provide more stable and certain political environments than do new democracies: the major parties do not usually change markedly over the short to medium term, and there is widespread knowledge about the rough level of support and prospective electoral fortunes of the principal electoral contestants. More specifically, when contemplating the impact that context has on electoral system effects, we argue that the most important differences that distinguish new democracies from more established ones include (a) a more fluid political context, especially greater party volatility between elections (Mainwaring and Zoco 2007), (b) less-developed opinion polling (Oates 2005, 2006), and (c) parties with less-developed ties to social groups, less well-defined programmatic appeals, and weaker connections to stable, reliable core constituencies (Mainwaring 1999; Mainwaring and Torcal 2006).

Differences in Party System Institutionalization

Of course, there are differences in the stability and certainty of information even among new democracies – most notably, in our view, new democracies differ in the degree to which their party systems are "institutionalized" (Mainwaring and Scully 1995; Mainwaring 1999; Mainwaring and Torcal 2006). Party system institutionalization is a complex process involving different components, including organizational continuity of parties, the relative stability of party support, ideological consistency over time, party legitimacy, and party control over nominations (Mainwaring 1999: 27–39). Most simply put, party institutionalization refers to whether a given polity's parties structure the vote.

In this way, the differences that we highlight among democracies can be viewed as a continuum ranging from, on one end, established democracies with well-institutionalized parties, to new democracies with less-developed party systems, and finally, at the other extreme, new democracies with noninstitutionalized party systems. As Mainwaring and Zoco (2007) demonstrate, most new democracies have weaker, more volatile party systems than established democracies do. However, there is a qualitative difference between new democracies with party systems that structure the vote – meaning that parties dominate the nomination process and serve as the predominant vehicle through which candidates are nominated for election and attract votes – and those with noninstitutionalized party systems in which independents rival political parties in the electoral process.

We can illustrate the difference between a new democracy with a more institutionalized party system and one with a noninstitutionalized party system through a comparison of Hungary and Russia.[1] With democratization, Hungary's party system formed quickly around specific groupings of parties (Kitschelt 1992). By the country's second postcommunist election in 1994,

---

[1] Both countries used mixed-member systems.

these parties structured electoral competition, leading to relatively low electoral volatility between elections, clear and stable governing coalitions comprised of major parties with like-minded ideologies, and little change over time in the form of existing parties "dying" or new parties emerging (Bertoa ND).[2] Independent candidates in Hungary were rare and almost never gained election.

Conversely, Russia's party system was initially inchoate and unstable in its first postcommunist election in 1993 and remained so throughout the 1990s.[3] Unlike Hungary, Russia faced great party volatility. Parties exited and entered the system at such high rates that every new election witnessed a very different array of electoral choices (McFaul 2001; Moser 1997, 1999a, 2001a). Independents in Russia were a predominant electoral force, attracting more votes and seats than any single party through three elections until a major party, United Russia, emerged in the final election held under the mixed-member system in 2003 (see Moser 1999b). Even in 2003, parties structured only a portion of the vote, as independents continued to win more seats than any party except United Russia.

---

[2] In Mainwaring and Zoco's cross-national study of electoral volatility, Hungary had the lowest mean electoral volatility of all postcommunist countries included (2007: 159–60).

[3] It is beyond the scope of this book to consider in detail why some new democracies have more institutionalized party systems than others, but we will note some key factors identified by scholars that explain why party system development proceeded at a much faster pace in East Central Europe than in post-Soviet states. On one side, a number of scholars argue that institutions, most notably constitutional structures of presidential or parliamentary systems, affected party development by creating incentives or disincentives for party building (Bielasiak 2002; Bertoa ND). In part, this argument asserts that the establishment of a strong presidency and weak legislature reinforced the detrimental social environment for party development by undermining incentives for party building, especially under President Boris Yeltsin, who resisted partisan affiliation himself (McFaul 2001; Fish 2005). From a different perspective, Hale (2006) argues that Russia's federal system and political economy produced powerful "party substitutes" such as regional governors' political machines and politicized financial–industrial groups that allowed the candidates they supported to avoid partisan affiliation.

However, much analysis highlights other factors over formal political institutions of the democratic period. With respect to postcommunist countries' democratic development, Horowitz and Browne (2005) find that social forces were more important than institutions in shaping party systems, and Kitschelt (1992) also argues for the preeminence of social and economic bases of party system institutionalization over political institutions. More specifically, many argue that pre-existing nascent party structures formed during the communist period, democratic transitions that were more hospitable to party development, and cleavage structures that provided a stronger basis for the formation of stable parties all contributed to more developed parties in Eastern Europe (Kitschelt 1995; Kitschelt et al. 1999; Bielasiak 2002). As a result, Hungary, in particular, witnessed stable patterns of party competition earlier than other postcommunist states (Kitschelt 1992: 30–31; Bertoa ND). Contrary to the experience in many East European countries, post-Soviet states such as Russia and Ukraine had no previous usable experience with parties or party-like organizations in the communist or precommunist eras (Hough 1998). Indeed, a longer and harsher period of totalitarian communist rule created societies with less-developed social groups and economic interests, thus providing fewer ideological and social bases for stable party identification (Evans and Whitefield 1993; Hough 1998).

THE CONDITIONALITY OF ELECTORAL SYSTEM EFFECTS

Let us now bridge our separate discussions of electoral systems, social science assumptions, and context. In this book, we highlight that many important theories of the effects of electoral rules implicitly assume certain basic underlying conditions. However, we argue, with variation of the sorts that we discussed in the previous section, these assumptions often may not hold. Most important, we argue, if the underlying context is different from what is usually assumed in electoral system theories, electoral rules may not have the effects that are commonly expected of them.

A few scholars, such as Giovanni Sartori (1994), Gary Cox (1997), Rein Taagepera (2007), and Bernard Grofman, Shaun Bowler, and Andre Blais (2009), regarding Duverger's Law, and Richard Matland (1998), discussing electoral system effects on women's representation, identify conditions necessary for electoral systems to have their expected effects and acknowledge the role of contextual factors in mitigating electoral system effects.[4] Recent work by William Clark and Matt Golder (2006: 700–2) indicates that electoral systems have different effects in new democracies than they do in established ones. These analyses provide an excellent starting point to tackle the issue of underlying assumptions and generalizability, but we think that the literature has not adequately probed the impact that political context has on electoral system effects; in addition, contextual factors such as the level of party institutionalization have, in our view, received less empirical attention than they deserve.

To be sure, the importance of political context is hardly specific simply to the realm of electoral rules. As Robert Franzese points out, "The central tenet of modern comparative politics is ... that *context* – structural, cultural, institutional, and strategic; social, economic, and political; international, domestic, and local – matters" (2007: 29; emphasis in original). Context can matter in many different ways, but our focus in this book is the importance of what Franzese calls "context-conditionality" – that is, the effects on an outcome of a given explanatory variable can depend in part on the value of another variable. In this vein, Franzese highlights how institutions can condition the impact of contextual factors on political outcomes.

In this book, we emphasize the reverse relationship: political context also conditions the impact of institutions. For example, electoral rules can constrain the proliferation of parties that would otherwise emerge as a result of a polity's lack of experience with democracy – but factors emerging from a country's lack of experience with democracy and a system of poorly institutionalized parties can dramatically weaken the constraining effect of electoral rules. Franzese (2007: 49) notes with disappointment the lack of attention that empirical

---

[4] Also, see, for example, Shugart and Carey (1992), Mainwaring and Shugart (1997), and Cheibub (2007) for terrific work on ways in which political context can shape the effects of other institutions – most notably, constitutional structure.

analysis of political institutions has given to the interaction between institutions and political context, but the work that has been done on this interaction is usually founded on the ways in which institutions constrain context.[5] We certainly agree that electoral rules mediate the impact of political context, but less work systematically examines – or even considers – the reverse relationship.[6]

For this reason, in this book we consider the conditionality of electoral system effects and seek to uncover systematic ways in which context conditions the impact of rules. We examine factors such as democratic experience that we believe help to explain when electoral systems have their expected effects and when they do not. We also offer new insights that seem to apply to both new and established democracies alike. For example, we reexamine the common assertion in the literature that FPTP electoral systems undermine the relationship between social diversity and the number of parties. In these ways and in others, this book provides a reexamination and rethinking of some of the fundamental arguments regarding electoral system effects.

Assumptions and Electoral Rules

It is widely agreed that political institutions affect behavior. When rules are enacted and enforced, they affect behavior by rewarding or allowing certain actions and penalizing or disallowing others. Actors who best adapt their behavior to the incentives created by the rules tend to grow stronger; whereas those who do not are marginalized. Consequently, when rules are applied uniformly, they are expected to have relatively uniform effects. Indeed, the "new institutionalism" within political science has been built around the premise that institutions matter and have predictable consequences, and the study of electoral systems has been one of its chief sources of inspiration and practitioners. (See, for example, Duverger 1954; Taagepera and Shugart 1989; Lijphart 1994; Cox 1997.) The terminology of this literature – institutional "design" and electoral "engineering" – connotes a sense among politicians and scholars that institutions can be used to shape outcomes and realize certain goals much like architects and engineers use building materials and physics to design sturdy and functional physical structures. In this way, Giovanni Sartori famously asserted that electoral rules were the "most specific manipulable instrument of politics" (1968: 273).

There is much to support such a view of institutions. Indeed, the evidence marshaled in this book will put on display systematic effects of electoral systems on a wide range of political outcomes. Institutions do, indeed, matter.

---

[5] See, for example, analysis of the interaction between social diversity and electoral rules (Amorim Neto and Cox 1997, Clark and Golder 2006, Ordeshook and Shvetsova 1994, Singer and Stephenson 2009).

[6] Most work that does examine how context constrains electoral rules focuses on a narrow set of cases (usually a single country), which limits our ability to make general statements about the systematic impact of variation in contextual conditions. See, for example, Moser (1999a) on postcommunist states and Moser (2001a) on Russia.

We also accept the fact that electoral system effects denote generalizations based on *average* outcomes. Consequently, exceptions to these expected average outcomes are bound to occur and do not necessarily undermine the validity of the arguments based on a probabilistic theory (Taagepera 2007: 101–105).

However, we posit that the variance we find in the effects of electoral systems is *systematic* and, therefore, dependent on identifiable variables that should also be taken into account. We emphasize how the impact of electoral systems is contingent and variable depending on the political and social context in which electoral rules operate.

In the remainder of this chapter, we examine a number of the major theories regarding electoral system effects, the conditions necessary for these effects to be realized, and the extent to which these conditions vary across cases. Ultimately, we argue, this variance in the political context in which electoral rules operate explains why electoral system effects commonly found among established democracies often go unrealized in many new democracies. In other realms – specifically, the relationship between social diversity and the number of parties – we show that the expected mitigating impact of FPTP systems on the relationship between social diversity and party fractionalization does not necessarily hold in either new or established democracies.

ELECTORAL SYSTEM THEORIES AND THEIR ASSUMPTIONS

The literature on electoral systems is actually a series of distinct but overlapping bodies of scholarship that covers a wide range of electoral and political outcomes. Scholars have argued that electoral systems are a primary factor shaping a swath of features of political life, including the number of parties operating in a country, voting behavior (in the form of strategic and personalistic voting), the election of women, and even the degree of clientelism and corruption in the political system.[7]

However, typically, analyses of the effects of electoral rules are most compelling when focused on outcome variables that flow directly from the incentives created by the electoral system (i.e., *proximal* effects). Electoral system explanations are less convincing when they require multiple steps to get from the electoral rule incentives to the predicted outcomes and behaviors (i.e., *distal* effects). In such cases, the electoral system is at best only part of the explanation, and attention needs to be given to other factors (Scheiner 2008).

In this book, we examine non-mechanical effects that can be conceived as most directly affected by electoral rules, rather than outcomes that are, at best, indirect effects such as political corruption or clientelism. The most direct effects of electoral systems are mechanical – the formulaic translation of votes into seats. Analysis of the mechanical effects of electoral rules has led to a

---

[7] Still others have argued that electoral rules affect public policy in realms such as the environment (Rosenbluth and Thies 2002), banking (Rosenbluth and Schaap 2003, Rosenbluth and Thies 2001), and defense (Nagahisa 1995).

consensus about the relationship between electoral systems and disproportion-ality (e.g., higher district magnitude with low legal thresholds of representation improves the correlation between parties' vote and seat shares). As Taagepera writes, "the study of the largely mechanical effect of electoral systems on the distribution of seats... is now largely closed" (2007: 112; see Shugart [2005: 51] for a similar statement). Moving beyond mechanical effects, electoral sys-tems continue to shape politics, but do so less directly – that is, by giving individuals incentives to behave in certain ways, rather than simply translating votes into seats. The influence of electoral systems on some political outcomes, such as the types of policies politicians choose to pursue, may be quite indirect, requiring multiple steps from the formulaic workings of the electoral rule to the ultimate outcome. However, electoral systems require fewer steps to shape other non-mechanical outcomes.

We see three types of non-mechanical outcomes that much scholarly work points to as both substantively important and flowing relatively directly from the mechanical effects of electoral rules:

1. *Incentives to reveal one's preferences – "sincere" vs. "strategic" behav-ior*: Scholars regularly argue that, through the mechanical effects of district magnitude, different types of electoral systems create different incentives for voters and elites to engage in "sincere" (e.g., voting for their top choice) or "strategic" behavior (e.g., voting for a candidate they prefer less in order to affect the outcome of the race).

2. *The number of parties*: Scholars therefore widely agree that, by shaping the amount of strategic behavior (or the amount of "preference revela-tion"), electoral systems affect the translation of societal preferences into the party system, thus shaping the number of parties in the system.

3. *The type of people elected*: Different electoral rules permit voters to cast different types of ballots – that is, for either a candidate or a party. Scholars argue that this difference in the target of voters' ballots alters the types of candidates that parties are likely to nominate. Moreover, through the mechanical effects of district magnitude, it is presumed that electoral rules vary in the opportunities that they present for members of historically marginalized groups to win office.

Along these lines, in this book, we examine three generally accepted broad theories of the effects of electoral rules:

1. *The effect of the electoral system on strategic behavior and the number of parties*: FPTP systems tend toward significant "strategic" defection from less competitive parties to more competitive ones (by both voters and elites) and thus promote the emergence of two parties; PR systems tend toward less "strategic" behavior and multiparty systems.

2. *Electoral rules, social diversity, and the number of parties*: The number of social cleavages in society provides the building blocks for the number of parties. Electoral rules, then, either permit these social cleavages to

help produce an array of political parties or constrain the number of parties without regard to level of social diversity. Put differently, social cleavages shape the number of parties under "permissive" rules, but few viable parties compete under "restrictive" rules, irrespective of the level of social diversity.

3. *The representation of traditionally underrepresented groups*: Closed-list PR electoral rules help promote the election of individuals from historically marginalized groups (e.g., women). As we explain later, scholars expect to see differences between PR and FPTP systems in the amount of representation of marginalized groups, in large part because of differences in district magnitude (the number of seats in a district) across the two types of systems. In addition, scholars expect that the ballot structure of closed-list PR, which forces voters to vote for a party rather than a candidate, also affects the election of marginalized groups such as women.

Nevertheless, as non-mechanical effects, even these outcomes are not direct effects of the electoral system; therefore, other factors may mediate the impact of electoral rules on them. Indeed, as we discuss throughout this book, each of these theories is founded on key (generally unstated) assumptions. That is, for each of these theories, scholars generally assume that particular variables will maintain a specific value (remain constant), or simply be unimportant. However, if the values of these variables vary, it is likely that outcomes will emerge that differ from those that scholars most commonly expect.

More specifically, we argue that these outcomes are conditioned by the following factors:

1. *Democratic experience:* New democracies typically are characterized by a less stable and predictable political environment than more established democracies are. Due to this greater political uncertainty, political actors in new democracies are less likely to have the information necessary to defect strategically from their top electoral choice. Consequently, FPTP systems will constrain party proliferation less in new democracies than in established ones.

2. *Levels of party institutionalization:* Not all countries are founded on well-established party systems that structure candidacies and the vote. Where parties do not structure the vote, voters lack an important cue to candidates' likely competitiveness. As a result, strategic defection by voters and elites becomes more difficult, thus making it less likely that the number of parties will become constrained – even under FPTP rules.

3. *Social diversity and the willingness of voters to cast a "strategic" vote*: Not all voters choose to behave strategically, even when they support a likely loser. When many voters are unwilling to try to affect the outcome of the race by shifting their vote from their preferred option to a more competitive one, restrictive electoral rules will not constrain the number of parties – even in established democracies – to the extent usually expected in the literature. Given that many voters choose not to cast

strategic ballots, variation in social diversity should lead to variation in the number of parties even under FPTP rules.

4. *The number of parties*: The number of parties (and candidates) varies across countries (in part because of differences in democratic experience and party institutionalization). In FPTP districts with large numbers of candidates, fewer votes are needed to win election. Under such circumstances, all candidates have a greater chance of victory, including "riskier" candidates (such as women) from historically marginalized groups.

We turn now to exploring in greater detail how these different factors condition strategic behavior, the number of parties, and women's representation. First, we introduce the prominent theory associated with each electoral system effect, the key assumptions undergirding the central arguments found in the literature, and the shortcomings of these assumptions.[8] We do not pretend that our discussion covers all the important potential effects of electoral rules, that the assumptions we point out are the only ones made, or that all our critiques here are original to us. Nevertheless, collectively this discussion raises important questions about the generalizability of the current models of electoral system effects and highlights the potential pitfalls of omitting variables based on the implicit assumption that they do not vary (or are unimportant). Indeed, in this book we find that when we reintroduce these variables into the analysis by allowing their values to vary, we see outcomes that are very different from those suggested by leading theories.

ELECTORAL SYSTEMS, STRATEGIC VOTING, AND THE NUMBER OF PARTIES

Maurice Duverger (1954) is typically credited with the central theories about the effects of electoral rules. The most famous is Duverger's Law, which holds that SMD systems that operate according to a plurality rule tend to have only two parties. Many have interpreted Duverger's work to mean that FPTP would lead to two nationally competitive parties. But analyses – especially Cox (1997) – since Duverger have, correctly, made the Law more specific, pointing out that FPTP tends toward "two-partism" – or, more accurately, two candidates – *at the district level*.[9] (See the left-hand figure in Figure 1.1.)

---

[8] We discuss each electoral system effect in greater detail in the corresponding empirical chapters throughout the book.

[9] Three important points should be included here. First, Duverger's Law at the district level does not mean that only two actual candidates will appear. In many cases, many non-serious candidates run for office in SMDs. We can account for these candidates and those that are really viable using the "effective number of parties" measure. Second, as Cox (1997) points out, we need not expect precisely two candidates per district. Rather, the logic of Duverger's Law suggests a *maximum* of two viable candidates. Third, factors beyond SMDs are necessary to lead to the projection of two candidates/parties at the district level to two nationally competitive ones. On this last point, see, for example, Cox (1997) and Chhibber and Kollman (1998).

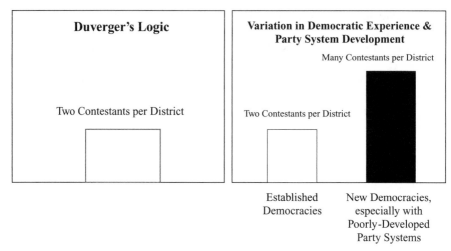

FIGURE 1.1. FPTP rules and the number of parties.

Two effects of FPTP drive the logic behind Duverger's Law. The first is the *mechanical effect*, which is a direct result of the low district magnitude (combined with the fact that the election is a one-round contest) of SMDs: only parties (or candidates) that receive a large number of votes – or, more precisely, the largest number of votes in a given district – gain representation. The second, the *psychological effect*, flows directly from the mechanical effect: the mechanical effect means that parties (or candidates) that receive a relatively small number of votes do not gain representation, making any vote cast for them a "wasted" vote. Seeing this mechanical effect, voters who prefer smaller parties but also wish to affect the election will vote strategically, casting ballots for candidates other than their most preferred, and potentially weak candidates and parties who wish to avoid wasting resources on a losing race will choose not to run. With SMDs being winner-take-all contests, this strategic winnowing-down process should continue until there are only two candidates, candidate #1 (the ultimate winner) and candidate #2, on whom all those opposed to candidate #1 strategically pin their hopes. In short, strategic defection by elites and voters is central to the most hallowed of electoral system theories.

Despite its intuitive logic and canonical status in the subfield, some (see, e.g., Taagepera 2007) question the accuracy of Duverger's Law, in particular the psychological effect of plurality systems on the number of electoral parties. For example, Grofman et al. (2009) argue that only one long-standing plurality system – that of the United States – has had a consistent Duvergerian, two-party outcome, whereas Canada, India, and Great Britain have all experienced significant deviations from two-party competition at the district level (Diwakar 2007; Gaines 1999; Grofman et al. 2009). Moreover, Pradeep Chhibber and Ken Kollman (1998, 2004) find that even in the United States, which has averaged two significant electoral parties, a relatively large share of SMDs diverged significantly from this outcome. Singer (forthcoming) provides the most comprehensive cross-national study of the number of electoral parties in SMD systems, examining more than 6,500 SMD contests in 53 countries around the world, and finds significant variation in the number of parties at the district level in SMD elections.

After controlling for certain conditions such as concurrent majoritarian presidential elections and postcommunist countries, however, Singer finds that the average effective number of candidates (measured by using the weighted vote shares of each of the candidates at the district level) emerging out of plurality elections is 2.20, thus hewing closely to a Duvergerian outcome. Singer's finding suggests that under many circumstances the psychological effect of plurality elections does constrain the number of parties toward a two-party dynamic "such that the top two candidates get over 90 percent of the vote – something that rarely happens in other systems" (Singer forthcoming). In short, this most recent and comprehensive study of the district-level outcomes of FPTP elections supports the notion that plurality elections have a strong constraining effect on the number of parties, leading Singer (forthcoming) to conclude that "strategic behaviour by elites and voters under plurality rule do seem to reduce legislative fragmentation in a way that penalizes small parties and approximates two-party competition."

In summary, despite noteworthy exceptions, the average result of plurality elections tends toward two-party competition, but the winnowing effects of plurality elections are contingent on certain conditions.

Information Is Assumed to Be Widespread

As we noted earlier, Duverger's Law is founded in large part on the mechanism of strategic defection by voters and elites, and evidence of strategic voting in established democracies is abundant and persuasive – see, for example, Barnes et al. (1962), Fisher (1973), Bawn (1993, 1999), Niemi et al. (1992), Cox (1997), Alvarez and Nagler (2000), and Alvarez et al. (2006) – but we really ought to expect such strategic behavior only if we make a series of assumptions. Perhaps most important, as Cox (1997: 79) points out, the strategic defection that underpins the winnowing effects of FPTP elections requires certain preconditions, particularly information that allows voters and elites to determine accurately and reliably the relative support of competing parties.[10] For example, Cox indicates that many cases of divergence from Duvergerian (i.e., two viable candidates per district) outcomes are a result of a close race between the second- and third-place candidates – thus, making it impossible for voters to know for whom to cast a strategic vote in order to best compete with the frontrunner.

Of course, strategic voting is relatively common in established democracies, in which the assumption of widespread accurate information is a reasonable

---

[10] For discussion of additional conditions necessary for Duverger's Law to hold, see Cox (1997: 79) and Chapter 3 in this book.

one. Typically, in established democratic countries, public opinion is tracked closely and established political parties provide cues to elites and voters about how best to channel their strategic behavior. However, reliable information is not a constant, particularly in new democracies. In many new democracies, public opinion is difficult to gauge accurately for a number of reasons (Filippov et al. 1999). Among the biggest reasons for low levels of information in many new democracies is the lack of well-established parties that have strong roots in society and reliable constituencies.[11]

Well-established parties shape voters' level of information about candidates' likely viability and the absence of such parties in some polities produces a formidable obstacle to strategic defection by voters and elites. In well-developed party systems, candidates' party affiliations give voters their best clue as to candidates' likely competitiveness. Without such cues, it is more cumbersome for voters to determine who the likely strong competitors are, thereby making it more difficult to know which candidates are, in fact, viable. The transitory nature of party organizations in unstable new democracies promotes great volatility between electoral periods and provides little opportunity for voters to cultivate lasting preferences for one party or another (see Mainwaring and Zoco 2007; Ames et al. 2009; Baker et al. 2006). In the absence of widespread, concrete party preferences, many voters are left with no partisan cues to help them cast their votes and must instead rely on patronage, incumbency, and the personal characteristics of candidates.

Moreover, the resulting behavior can also become self-reinforcing. With less clear information about voter preferences and few strong parties to help voters coordinate strategically around likely viable competitors, larger numbers of elites have incentive to contest elections. If no one knows with substantial accuracy what the distribution of the vote is likely to be, many candidates will have no reason to exit the race strategically, and additional candidates may even choose to run, because anyone can win (Filippov et al. 1999).[12]

Less Information, Less Strategic Defection, Less Duverger

This discussion does not mean that voters and elites in new democracies can never behave strategically, but it does suggest that strategic defection is less likely in such contexts. Moreover, in the absence of widespread strategic

---

[11] The weakness of parties in new democracies has been widely documented, in particular in Scott Mainwaring's work on party institutionalization (see, especially, Mainwaring 1999). For other examples of the importance of weak parties, see Ames et al. (2009), Baker et al. (2006), and Hale (2006).

[12] As Clark and Golder (2006) suggest, the lack of strategic defection and proliferation of candidates may be due to countries not yet reaching a state of party system equilibrium. However, as we discuss in later chapters, a severe inability by voters and elites to distinguish between the likely electoral success of a number of candidates can also lead to a multicandidate equilibrium founded on little strategic defection by voters and elites. See Cox (1997) for a discussion of "non-Duvergerian" equilibrium.

defection, FPTP elections may no longer produce two-candidate competition at the district level (much less two large parties at the national level). As we depict graphically in the right-hand figure in Figure 1.1, there are likely to be many candidates per district – even under FPTP – in new democracies (especially those with poorly established party systems).[13]

THE INTERACTION BETWEEN ELECTORAL SYSTEMS AND SOCIAL DIVERSITY

Of course, the literature on electoral systems does not suggest that electoral rules work within a vacuum. It is generally agreed that electoral rules interact with the social context in which they operate. More specifically, the level of diversity within society provides the raw material for the number of parties found in a country. In part, this conception is based on the social-cleavage theory of party origins (see Lipset and Rokkan 1967), but Duverger (1954) also noted the idea in his theories of electoral system effects (Clark and Golder 2006). According to this view, social cleavages – which are founded on divisions within society, such as class or ethnic differences – become channeled into the party system. At the most basic level, this theory suggests, for example, that when class is a key dividing point within society, we will be likely to see class-based parties, and when ethnic differences are central there will be ethnic parties.

It is widely agreed that the electoral system, then, serves as a filter on these social cleavages. More "permissive" electoral systems, such as PR with larger district magnitudes (i.e., more seats per district) and low legal thresholds, permit parties to win seats with a smaller share of the vote. As a result, the supporters of many small parties can cast ballots for them without fear of wasting their votes, and these supporters therefore have incentive to vote in line with their true party preferences. In this way, permissive PR systems should allow more social cleavages to be represented by distinct parties.

On the other hand, electoral systems with smaller district magnitudes (especially FPTP systems) raise the vote share needed to guarantee office and, thus, make it more difficult for smaller parties to capture seats. As a result of this mechanical effect, elites and voters become more likely to abandon uncompetitive candidates and parties in order to support those with a greater chance of affecting the race. As shorthand, throughout this book we refer to this behavior as "strategic," but the implication in this language is that it is somehow "unstrategic" for supporters of a candidate to cast votes for him or her

---

[13] Of course, candidate proliferation under FPTP elections is not always the outcome in new democracies. Particularly in situations with dominant ruling parties, and thus little electoral competition, FPTP can lead to outcomes approximating single-party competition, as witnessed in FPTP systems in African countries such as Zambia and Ghana. However, such an outcome is not inconsistent with Duverger's Law as presented by Cox (1997), who argues that FPTP should lead to a *maximum* of two candidates per district.

if the candidate is already competitive. It is probably more accurate, therefore, to say that restrictive rules – such as FPTP – reduce the incentives for "preference revelation" – voters and elites have less incentive to reveal their true party (or candidate) preferences in the electoral process.[14] By reducing the incentives for preference revelation, restrictive rules make it less likely that social cleavages will map onto the party system. In this way, restrictive rules such as FPTP constrain the number of parties. Cross-national studies by scholars such as Ordeshook and Shvetsova (1994), Cox (1997), Clark and Golder (2006), and Singer and Stephenson (2009) provide empirical support that has solidified this interactive model as the most common view within the literature.

Figure 1.2(a) represents the most common view of the interactive relationship between social cleavages and electoral rules in shaping the number of parties: as diversity increases – that is, the number of social groups grows – the number of parties should increase as well. However, if large numbers of voters from all types of groups, including minority groups, strategically defect from their first preference when that party is unlikely to win representation, then the correlation between social diversity and party system fragmentation should be weak or nonexistent under FPTP rules.

Not Everyone Votes Strategically

The core assumption of the literature on the electoral system/social diversity interaction is that under FPTP most supporters of weak parties and candidates will act in accordance with electoral system incentives to withhold support from their top preference and instead attempt to affect the outcome of the race. However, in contrast to the mechanical effects of electoral rules, voters and elites' decision to move away from their top preference is not automatic. As Taagepera notes, "The largely strategic ('psychological') impact of electoral systems on the distribution of votes . . . still remains wide open . . . Institutions are bound to impact votes in a fuzzier way than seats. An electoral system can block the seventh largest party from getting any seats, but it cannot prevent people from voting for this party" (2007: 112). Indeed, analysis of voting behavior under FPTP rules indicates that only a subset of all voters who face a competitive context in which it would make sense for them to cast a strategic ballot actually do so (see especially Alvarez et al. 2006).

There may be many reasons for voters not to cast strategic ballots, even under FPTP (see, e.g., Cox 1997: 79), but, whatever the reason, a lack of widespread strategic defection from uncompetitive to competitive parties would undermine any interactive effect between electoral systems and social diversity on the number of parties. We illustrate this dynamic in Figure 1.2(b): if (1) increases in social diversity tend to lead to larger numbers of parties, and (2) a nontrivial subset of supporters of small parties (or their candidates) refuse to

---

[14] We thank William Clark and Ken Kollman for this important insight.

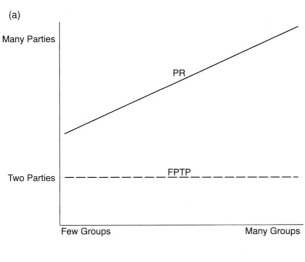

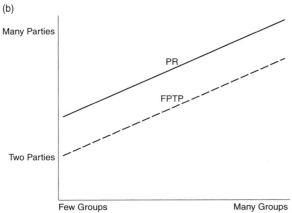

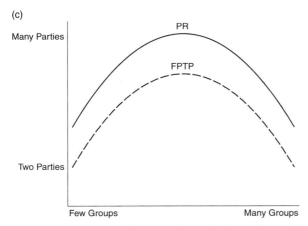

FIGURE 1.2. Interaction between electoral rules and social diversity in shaping the number of parties: (a) most common view; (b) if many voters and elites do not withdraw support from likely losers under FPTP; (c) if curvilinear relationship between groups and parties exists, and there is only limited strategic withdrawal of support from likely FPTP losers.

transfer support to more competitive alternatives, then the presence of larger numbers of distinct societal groups ought to have an impact on the number of parties, even under restrictive rules like FPTP.[15]

Another Possible Pattern

In addition, there may not always be a uniformly positive relationship between social diversity and party fragmentation. Based on the choices available to parties and variation in groups' voting patterns, we can conceive of a number of different ways by which increases in social diversity will not lead to monotonic increases in the number of parties. For example, Heather Stoll (ND) cogently highlights a common scenario in which there are more social groups than parties: in moving from relatively homogeneous environments to greater diversity, there will be an uptick in the number of parties because each group will be large enough to play a meaningful governing role – even as the head of a minority government or part of a coalition government. That is, under this scenario, political entrepreneurs seeking to develop parties will have incentives to create parties founded on the divisions between the large societal groups, as those groups each have sufficient numbers to be competitive actors in the party system. However, after a certain point, further increases in diversity – when there are larger numbers of (especially small) groups – actually lead to a decline in the likelihood that any of the groups will play a meaningful governing role. Under such conditions, political entrepreneurs have an incentive to create parties that can reach out beyond a single group, which in turn leads to a greater concentration of the party system and a decline in the number of parties. In visual terms, Stoll argues that the relationship between diversity and party fragmentation is likely to have a curvilinear upside-down U-shaped pattern to it, similar to that in Figure 1.2(c). Increases in diversity lead to larger numbers of parties up to a point, after which greater diversity leads to smaller numbers of parties. Furthermore, if large numbers of voters do not strategically defect from their most preferred party – even if it is uncompetitive – we might see a curvilinear relationship between social diversity and party fragmentation not only in PR but in SMDs as well, as depicted in Figure 1.2(c).[16]

---

[15] At the same time, from countless scholarly works, we know that strategic behavior (i.e., defection away from a preferred choice in order to affect the outcome of the race) is a common process (see also Chapters 5 and 6). It is unlikely that all voters and elites will be immune to the strategic imperatives of restrictive rules, so there still ought to be fewer parties under restrictive rules than under permissive ones.

[16] We expect this dynamic of diversity affecting the number of parties under even restrictive rules to hold in both new and established democracies. However, it is useful to study this question across both types of democracies, since the number and type of groups often varies substantially between new and established democracies, especially in the role that ethnicity plays in the electoral process (see Chandra 2004; Birnir 2007).

ELECTORAL SYSTEMS AND THE ELECTION OF WOMEN

Electoral systems affect more than just strategic voting and the number of parties. Among the most direct non-mechanical effects of electoral systems is their impact on the type of people who get elected to office. Indeed, a distinct body of scholarship has developed theories of how electoral systems affect the election of historically marginalized social groups – in particular, women.

Dozens of cross-national analyses, regional comparisons, and individual case studies of the determinants of female representation show a consistent relationship between the type of electoral system and the proportion of women elected to the legislature, particularly in Western democracies. Study after study shows that, on average, many more women get elected under closed-list PR than under SMD electoral rules (see, e.g., Matland and Montgomery 2003; Matland and Studlar 1996; Moser 2001b; Kostadinova 2007; Rule 1987, 1994).

Scholars have suggested a whole range of advantages that exist for women contesting elections under proportional representation. Generally speaking, though, two main features of closed-list PR are expected to benefit women. First, the fact that voters cast their ballots for a party (rather than a candidate) is expected to reduce the focus on individual candidacies in elections, undermine incumbency advantages that lock in gender inequalities, provide greater incentives for parties to balance nominations by gender, and encourage parties to centralize control over nominations – all of which serve to mute cultural biases against female candidacies.[17] Second, differences in district magnitude between PR and SMDs suggest significant advantages for women under PR or, to make the argument from the opposite direction, SMDs – especially FPTP – provide substantial disadvantages to female candidates because of the large share of the vote needed to win the single seat.

Not *All* Parties Perceive an Advantage to Nominating Women

One perceived advantage of closed-list PR for women is that voters cast party ballots, rather than voting for candidates. Clearly central to the most basic view of women's representation under different electoral rules is the assumption that parties choose to run women on their PR lists in part because they perceive an electoral advantage from doing so. A common view is that parties have an incentive to put forward a balanced PR-list ticket that can appeal to a wide audience, particularly when they control the nomination process through closed-list PR.[18]

---

[17] Closed-list PR also produces more left-leaning parties and governing coalitions (Iversen and Soskice 2006), which tend to be more likely to nominate women.

[18] A perceived advantage for women under most closed-list PR systems is that nominations for PR lists are usually more centralized in the hands of party leaders than nominations in SMD elections. It is generally assumed that party leaders will be more inclined to nominate women than local leaders who are more likely to control SMD nominations, so closed party lists and

However, as Matland (1998) suggests, in many cases it may not be an advantage for a party to place female candidates on its PR list. For example, in some cases social or cultural norms may be indifferent to or run against the promotion of women. Along these lines, there may be less pressure for gender balancing in new democracies than in established ones because of a lack of socioeconomic development and weaker civil society, which in turn might weaken societal pressure on parties to nominate women. This does not mean that when there is little societal push for women's representation, ambitious female candidates will derive no benefit from closed-list PR rules. However, it does suggest that PR will be no panacea to aid in women's representation under such conditions.

SMDs Do Not Always Require a Large Percentage of the Vote

The first-past-the-post/winner-take-all aspect of single-member districts provides good reason to think that SMDs should be a disadvantage for women. Gender balancing is not usually as important in SMD elections because SMDs isolate district contests from one another and parties are not judged by their full slate of nominations to the same degree that they are in PR. Rather, as a result of FPTP rules, the incentive for parties in SMDs is to run a candidate who is likely to attract a large vote share. To some extent, the problem for women in SMDs, therefore, is undoubtedly a prejudice against female candidates in portions of the general voting population (Valdini 2006). In part, it is that the most likely successful candidates under FPTP rules are those with substantial career experience – whether it be in lower-level offices or positions that help generate political or financial connections – that give them a better chance of winning a large number of votes. For numerous reasons, fewer women than men tend to have such backgrounds, and childbirth may interrupt the careers of many women who start on career paths that might aid their success as candidates (Iversen and Rosenbluth 2010).

However, SMDs – even FPTP – do not always require that the winner receive a large vote percentage. The more viable candidates competing in a single-member district, the smaller the vote needed to win office. As a result, as we illustrate in Figure 1.3, party fragmentation may actually work in favor of women getting elected in SMDs relative to PR. When many viable candidates are running in SMDs – as is common in many new democracies – the vote threshold necessary for victory is lowered and therefore the "risk" of nominating female candidates diminishes, because victory no longer requires attracting nearly half the district's votes. In contrast, party fragmentation under PR is likely to constrain the election of women because women tend to occupy middle- and lower-range positions on party lists. As a result, women may be

centralized party nomination processes are seen as more conducive to women's representation (Norris 1993). Indeed, Valdini's (2005, 2006) analysis of women's representation under different PR rules in established democracies supports this view.

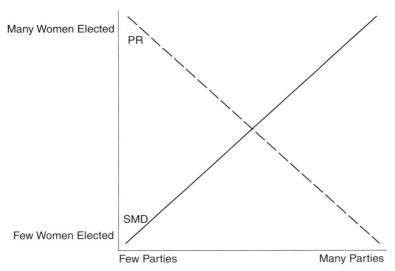

FIGURE 1.3. Potential relationship between electoral rules, number of parties, and the election of women.

more likely to gain election if a few large parties elect many representatives per PR district than if many parties elect a small number of representatives per district (Matland 1993; Matland and Taylor 1997; Reynolds 1999).

Differences between New and Established Democracies

In brief, the level of popular support for women in political leadership positions and the number of viable parties contesting elections are likely to play a significant role in shaping women's representation; variation on these dimensions should be particularly great between established and new – especially postcommunist – democracies. In established democracies, because of greater popular support for women as leaders and smaller numbers of parties, women should be much more likely to hold office under PR rules (relative to SMDs). In postcommunist democracies, in particular, there should be far less disparity between women's success under PR and SMD rules, because the large numbers of competitive candidates in SMD races in postcommunist democracies ought to permit candidates to win district races with a much smaller share of the vote.

SUMMARY – CONTEXTUAL REQUIREMENTS UNDERPINNING ELECTORAL SYSTEM EFFECTS

To summarize, many theories of how electoral systems affect political outcomes presume certain conditions embedded in the political context in which these institutions operate. Looking at many different types of countries, including both established and new democracies, highlights how changing the conditions and context can lead electoral rules to affect political outcomes very differently from what we usually expect. In this book, we address directly this condition-ality of electoral rule effects.

The most commonly expected effects of electoral systems on both the strate-gic behavior of voters and elites and the number of parties depend on the existence of significant information about voters' electoral preferences and support patterns – information that tends to be less available in new democ-racies, especially those in which parties are not well developed. Voters and elites need to know who is out of the running to be reasonably secure in a decision to defect from their preferred electoral option or give up on a bid for political office. Without such information, it is less likely that voters will defect strategically from their top choice under FPTP rules; under such conditions, therefore, plurality elections will be less likely to have their winnowing effect on the number of parties. In established democracies, in which reliable electoral information is typically more widespread, there should be a relatively small number of parties, even if not perfectly matching Duverger's two candidates per district.[19] However, in new democracies, where solid electoral information is often less available, there may be an explosion of candidates competing at the district level in FPTP elections and votes that are widely distributed across these candidates.

The commonly accepted view that electoral systems condition the impact of social cleavages on the number of parties, allowing social diversity's fuller expression in the party system under PR (in contrast to FPTP), rests on the idea that a large proportion of all voters and elites will defect strategically from their top party choice under FPTP rules when that top choice is uncompetitive. If strategic defection is more limited, social diversity may affect party frag-mentation in similar ways under both permissive (PR) and restrictive (FPTP) rules. Most scholars' expectation is that electoral institutions put a brake on the proliferating effect of social diversity, but, we argue, social diversity might also undermine the constraining effect of electoral rules.

Finally, the notion that, compared with SMDs, closed-list PR is more con-ducive to the election of women is based on assumptions about parties' incen-tives to create gender-balanced party lists and the number of candidates who contest SMD elections. It is typically assumed that parties have incentives – growing out of a push by society – to create some level of gender balance in their party lists, but not all societies are equally likely to push for women to be political leaders. In addition, women are seen as less likely to win office in SMDs because of the large number of votes needed to win such races, but if a large number of candidates run as viable contenders in SMDs, the vote share needed for victory will be lower and women should be far less disadvantaged. This brings our analysis full circle. The party fragmentation we witness in SMD elections in new democracies has an impact on the propensity of women

---

[19] Again, see Cox (1997) for conditions under which the number of candidates might stray from two.

to get elected in SMD elections – a larger number of viable candidates in SMDs increases the likelihood of women holding office.

APPROACH AND SPECIFIC FINDINGS OF THE BOOK

In these ways, this book seeks to probe the limits of electoral system explanations by considering the conditional and contextual basis for many of the most well-known theories of electoral rule effects. In our emphasis on variation in political context, much of our focus is on the differences between postcommunist cases and others. Much of the reason for this focus is the larger numbers of postcommunist countries – relative to other new democracies – that use mixed-member systems and the greater availability of data for these postcommunist cases. To be sure, our empirical analysis gives short shrift to non-postcommunist new democracies, and future analysts will undoubtedly want to do as we have done with those that came before us: question the assumptions underlying our analysis, and examine more closely a wider set of cases, especially other examples of new democracies. Nevertheless, with our substantial attention to the postcommunist cases, we believe that we are able to take important steps to understand the limits of current theories of the effects of electoral systems and develop more generalizable models of the impact of electoral rules.

Mixed-Member Systems and Controlled Comparison

To carry out our analyses, we focus on electoral behavior in mixed-member electoral systems, in which voters cast one ballot for a candidate in an SMD and one for a party in PR. As we explain in Chapter 2, we focus on mixed-member systems in order to pursue a "controlled comparison" approach, in which for any given country we can see the impact of different electoral rules while controlling for countless other social and political factors.[20]

To Understand the Impact of Electoral Systems, We Should Do District-Level Analysis

Theories of the effects of electoral rules usually rely first and foremost on a district-level logic (Duverger 1954; Cox 1997; Singer and Stephenson 2009).[21] For example, Duverger's Law is founded on the logic that voters *within a*

---

[20] Analyses such as that by Ferrara et al. (2005) raise concerns about how "contamination" between the SMD and PR tiers leaves analysis of elections under mixed-member rules unable to gauge properly the likely effect of pure SMD and PR systems. We address these concerns in Chapter 2, most notably demonstrating that there is no statistically discernible difference in the number of candidates at the district level between pure FPTP and mixed-member systems.

[21] Of course, national-level analyses make more sense in trying to understand outcomes such as the number of legislative parties, which is a result of the translation of votes into seats in a national legislature.

district seek to affect the outcome of that district's race. However, the aggregate number of parties at the national level is the sum of all the different individual districts and is also affected by factors beyond the district-level context. At the most extreme, elections could work just as Duverger's Law suggests, with only two parties in each FPTP single-member district, but each district could have entirely different parties from all of the other districts. In a country with 435 SMDs, for example, Duverger's Law could, in theory, lead to 870 parties nationally! In other words, district-level outcomes are a much more proximal (i.e., direct) effect of the electoral system than nationally aggregated outcomes; in this way, the electoral system is a more reliable predictor of district-level outcomes (Scheiner 2008).

Unfortunately, until recently, district-level data were difficult to acquire for large numbers of countries, and, as a result, cross-national work on the effects of electoral rules has most commonly used data aggregated at the national level. However, as district-level data for many different countries have become more widely available, important cross-national work by scholars such as Allen Hicken and Heather Stoll (2011) and Singer and Stephenson (2009) has emerged that focuses explicitly on district-level outcomes. One of the most important contributions of this book is that we continue along Hicken and Stoll's and Singer and Stephenson's path and focus nearly all of our analysis on the district level.

Our discussion of Duverger's Law highlights the importance of studying strategic defection and the number of parties at the district level, but district-level analysis is perhaps most important in studying the interaction between social diversity and electoral rules. Nearly all literature on this interaction is founded on nationally aggregated data that are assumed to represent the impact of district-level electoral rules. That is, the most prominent work on the diversity–electoral rules interaction (Amorim Neto and Cox 1997, Clark and Golder 2006, Ordeshook and Shvetsova 1994, Singer and Stephenson 2009) uses nationally aggregated measures of diversity, but the true interactive effect between social structure and electoral rules occurs within districts.[22] The observed relationship between ethnic diversity, electoral rules, and party system fragmentation may be quite different at the national level than at the district level (see Riker 1986, Cox 1997) – especially if national minority groups tend to be concentrated geographically, thus making them majorities in certain districts. To develop greater insight into the relationship between diversity, rules, and the number of parties, in Chapter 7 we analyze data from a handful of countries at the district (and even subdistrict) level.

It is also important to conduct district- and even candidate- or legislator-level analysis in studying women's representation. Single-country studies commonly focus on district or candidate characteristics underlying the election of women to legislative office (see, e.g., Smith and Fox 2001), but, to our knowledge, all

---

[22] A small portion of the literature looks at diversity at the district level, but the generalizability of these analyses is limited. See, for example, Jones (1997) and Madrid (2005a).

cross-national analyses of women's representation focus on nationally aggregated outcomes such as the share of total seats held by women. However, as with other electoral system effects, the incentives to promote (or not promote) female candidacies exist at the district level, and the nationally aggregated measure of women holding seats is simply the sum of all district-level seats. In cases of PR in which there is a single national district, the district and the nationally aggregated measure are the same thing. However, when PR is broken into multiple districts, or when there are smaller district magnitudes (such as SMDs), many different districts contribute to the national aggregate. In short, to get at the mechanisms underlying the election of women, it is important to focus on the district level. In Chapter 8, we begin by confirming key differences between electoral rules and different countries' aggregate share of seats held by women. Then, to address the mechanisms linking electoral rules and the election of women, we turn to an analysis of the gender of individual legislators based, in part, on the electoral rule under which they were elected and the effective number of parties competing in their district.

What We Find

We find, first, that, in many new democracies – especially those lacking well-developed party systems – FPTP rules promote relatively little strategic defection by voters and elites and, therefore, do not constrain competition to two major candidates. Instead, plurality contests in many new democracies include many contestants, with average effective-number-of-candidates scores (based on candidates' weighted share of the vote) of as high as nearly 6.0 per district. It may be the case that, in part, this increased district-level candidate proliferation is due to the fact that new democracies have not yet reached a stable equilibrium, which scholars typically argue is necessary for electoral systems to have their expected effects. However, we find that, although new democracies do eventually experience greater defection and constraining effects on the number of parties over time, the results of elections in established democracies are typically closer to equilibrium Duvergerian outcomes than the results in new democracies such as Russia, even after a number of elections. In other words, it appears that new democracies can take longer to reach the stable equilibrium that is expected of FPTP rules.[23]

Second, we find evidence for a new view of the relationship between social diversity and the number of parties – even under FPTP rules. Despite looking at five very different democracies on this issue, we find consistencies across most of them in the relationship between social diversity and the number of parties. When districts vary substantially in their level of diversity, we find an upside-down U-shaped relationship between diversity and the number of

---

[23] In addition, Chapter 6 even suggests that in certain cases – most notably, poorly institutionalized party systems – the system may actually be in a state of equilibrium that helps promote and maintain a large number of candidates competing under FPTP rules.

parties. Moreover, in all our cases, we find that diversity shapes the party system in similar ways under both PR rules and FPTP: despite the fact that FPTP offers greater incentives for strategic behavior, social diversity does not appear to affect party fragmentation in significantly different ways in SMDs relative to PR. These findings are different from most expectations about the translation of social diversity into the party system and, especially, the mediating effect of electoral systems in the process. Because of the small number of countries we study on this topic and the general lack of variation in the patterns that we find in the relationship between diversity and party fragmentation, we cannot pinpoint empirically the specific conditions that lead to the outcomes that we see. However, our findings diverge so dramatically from general expectations that, at the very least, they suggest that a general rethinking of work on the topic may be in order.[24]

Third, several features of postcommunist states – most notably, party system fragmentation and the general lack of societal support for women as political leaders – undermine the advantages of closed-list PR for the election of women. Indeed, we find that, all else being equal, in postcommunist states women are more likely to hold office under SMDs – relative to their chances of holding office under PR – because the large number of candidates running in single-seat districts in such countries reduces the share of the vote needed to win office.

A CONCEPTUAL FRAMEWORK

Because of our emphasis on the conditionality of institutional effects, some critics might argue that we overstate the deterministic nature of the social science conventional wisdom that we critique. That is, in reality most work on electoral systems is *probabilistic*, indicating that particular types of electoral arrangements make certain outcomes more likely, but not inevitable. In this way, real-world examples that do not match general expectations are not necessarily a problem for the major electoral system theories. We certainly agree that social science need not be able to explain all cases and that the existence of counterexamples does not necessarily suggest overwhelming flaws with a particular theory. Any analysis that could explain all cases would undoubtedly lack parsimony.

On the other hand, the "counterexamples" that we discuss in this book are not merely outliers; they are cases that differ from existing theories in systematic ways. The failure of electoral systems to behave as expected in the cases that we discuss is not random or indecipherable. Rather, the divergent

---

[24] Unlike our analysis in the other areas of this book, we find no evidence of an interaction between context (social diversity) and rules here. We find that rules and diversity each *independently* affects the number of parties, which means that context (social diversity) conditions outcomes even under electoral rules such as FPTP that are usually believed to be immune to such conditioning.

patterns that we discuss can be traced to particular aspects of their political contexts.[25]

Moreover, our argument is not that each country's political context is so different from others that we cannot develop generalizable theories. To the contrary, the analysis in this book includes a small number of variables that we use to characterize different contexts, and these contextual variables shape the effects of electoral rules in important areas. In this way, the aim of this book is to make the systematic study of electoral system effects even more generalizable.

Put differently, electoral systems have important consequences, but these consequences may not be uniform across all countries. Instead, they may be variable and contingent on identifiable factors. This idea is not new to electoral studies. Cox lays out specific conditions (assumptions) that are necessary for electoral systems to promote strategic behavior and adds, "Although closely approximated in some empirical instances, enough to make the theory interesting, these assumptions are certainly not universal" (1997: 32). Matland (1998) shows that electoral system effects on women's representation, which are so prevalent in established democracies, may not hold in developing countries. Furthermore, several recent studies have argued that the correlation between ethnic diversity and party system fragmentation is variable (Birnir and Van Cott 2007; Mozaffar et al. 2003; Madrid 2005a). The aim of this book is to continue along the path of these analyses and provide a more comprehensive understanding of the limits of electoral system theories and the reasons why electoral systems may often have very different effects from what we have usually come to expect.

---

[25] Interestingly, though, outcomes such as the limited impact of electoral rules on the relationship between social diversity and party fragmentation appear to be consistent across a number of different contexts that we examine. This finding suggests that it would be valuable to rethink the assumptions underlying previous work on the subject.

2

Mixed-Member Electoral Systems

How They Work and How They Work for Scholars

In Chapter 1, we suggested a number of ways that we believe electoral rules may affect politics while also being conditioned by other factors. In this chapter, we discuss how studying mixed-member electoral systems with an approach that Arend Lijphart labeled "controlled comparison" can help us investigate these electoral rule effects.

In the first part of this chapter, we describe the basic workings of "two-vote" mixed-member systems and explain how these systems make the controlled comparison approach possible. We highlight how this approach to the study of mixed-member systems offers a number of advantages in studying the differing effects of SMD and PR electoral rules. In the second part of the chapter, we discuss "contamination" between the PR and SMD tiers – the chief misgiving offered by critics of the controlled comparison approach to studying mixed-member systems – and explain why we believe that contamination does not cause significant problems for the analysis in this book. In the third and final part of the chapter, we describe the defining characteristics of mixed-member systems, outline the major variations found within this classification of electoral system, and discuss how these variations may have important consequences of their own.

THE BASICS OF MIXED-MEMBER ELECTORAL SYSTEMS

A central aim of this book is to investigate the extent to which SMD and PR rules lead to differences in behavior in elections to a legislature. For this reason, we focus on two-vote mixed-member systems – that is, systems that give voters two separate ballots to elect representatives to a single house of the legislature. The details of mixed systems vary widely. Numerous important nuances distinguish different mixed-member systems from one another, but

We are grateful to Matthew Singer for sharing his cross-national data set of district-level electoral results for SMD elections.

FIGURE 2.1. Geographical representation of mixed-member electoral system.

for the type of systems we examine in this book, these rules basically work as follows.[1]

In every election to the designated house of the legislature, each voter casts one ballot for a *party* in a PR race (what Shugart and Wattenberg [2001b] call the "list tier")[2] and one ballot for a *candidate* in an SMD (what Shugart and Wattenberg call the "nominal tier"). To distinguish the electoral system in which we are interested from others, such as Israel's that briefly allowed voters a PR vote for a party and a separate but direct vote for the national prime minister, we add the criterion that multiple seats be contested not only in the PR tier, but in the SMD tier as well. In other words, we focus on systems (1) that elect politicians to a single house of the legislature, (2) in which voters are given two ballots, one each under SMD and PR rules, and (3) in which seats to the house are an aggregation of multiple seats that are allocated through proportional representation rules and multiple seats that are filled through single-member district elections.[3]

Figure 2.1 offers a simplified geographical representation of how this system works in practice. In the simplest mixed-member systems, the list tier covers

[1] We are interested in comparing the separate effects of SMD and PR rules, so our focus is narrower than the two most well-established definitions of mixed-member systems. Shugart and Wattenberg (2001b: 10), for example, define mixed-member systems as ones in which "seats are allocated in two (or more) overlapping sets of districts, such that every voter may cast one or more votes that are employed to allocate seats in more than one tier." And Massicotte and Blais (1999: 345) "consider an electoral system to be mixed if its mechanics involves the combination of different electoral formulas (plurality or PR; majority or PR) for an election to a single body." In contrast, we are most interested in seeing how a given group of voters casts votes differently under different sets of rules, so we avoid the preceding definitions in part because they include electoral systems (such as Mexico's) that do not provide separate votes for the SMD and PR tiers. In addition, we are interested specifically in considering the differences between SMD and PR rules. We therefore also avoid the preceding definitions because they include electoral systems outside of SMDs and PR.

[2] This differs from the open-list PR arrangements in Brazil, where voters have the option to instead cast ballots for individual candidates, and then votes for all candidates of a given party are summed together to determine the vote share won by that party.

[3] As we explain later, the "PR" seats may instead be "compensation" that makes up for disproportionality created by the SMD part of the system.

the entire country. All PR votes, which are cast for *parties*, are aggregated to determine the proportion of the total vote won by each party, and each party then is allotted a share of the seats in the list tier that is roughly equal to its share of the PR vote. Prior to the election, each party compiles a ranked list of candidates. Seats are awarded to these candidates according to their ranking on the list and the total number of seats the party wins based on the results of voting in the list tier. If a party wins three seats in the list tier, the top three candidates on that party's list win its PR seats.

At the same time, the entire country is also divided into multiple SMDs. In this way, each voter is simultaneously a resident of both the larger PR/list tier and one single-member district (which is distinct from all other SMDs in the country). SMD (or nominal) votes, which are cast for individual *candidates*, are aggregated within each SMD separately. Whichever candidate – irrespective of his or her party affiliation – takes the largest share of these votes becomes the sole SMD representative from the district.

What this means, then, is that each voter – no matter what SMD he or she resides in – casts a vote for a party, which helps determine the total number of seats won by each party in the large PR/list tier. However, each voter's SMD ballot determines the single candidate winner only from his or her district. To put it differently, party PR votes from SMD 1 are added to the party PR votes in every other SMD to help determine the total number of votes and seats won by each party in the large list tier, but each nominal tier vote from SMD 1 is added only to other nominal tier votes in SMD 1 to determine the single candidate who wins the SMD 1 seat.

We discuss the specific features of these rules in greater detail later in the chapter. Among other things, some countries contain multiple list-tier districts; in some countries, candidates can run in both PR and SMDs; and rules vary substantially from country to country with respect to how results in the PR and SMD tiers affect one another.

No matter the nuances in the rules, however, our main point here remains: at the most basic level, the PR (list tier) and SMD (nominal tier) ballots that voters cast within a given mixed-member system directly promote different outcomes from one another.

CONTROLLED COMPARISON: MIXED-MEMBER SYSTEMS AS A
LABORATORY FOR STUDYING ELECTORAL SYSTEM EFFECTS

For decades, West Germany was the only well-known example of the mixed-member electoral system, but in the 1990s numerous countries around the world seemed to see in mixed systems a potential to combine the best elements of PR and SMD elections in a single system (Shugart and Wattenberg 2001a). Once an oddity that attracted relatively little attention outside of Germany, mixed-member systems were introduced in new democracies in Eastern Europe and Eurasia, Bolivia and Venezuela in Latin America, and Lesotho in Africa, as well as in consolidated democracies such as Japan, Italy, and New Zealand.

Mixed-member electoral systems gained much greater scholarly attention as their use spread quickly during the 1990s. As others did, we found the increased use of the system to be fertile ground for scholarly inquiry. However, our interests go beyond studying a relatively new and unique way of organizing elections.

We believe that the study of mixed-member electoral systems offers a powerful analytical environment for the study of institutional effects on politics. The combination of very different electoral rules in the same country provides a unique opportunity to study the effects of separate electoral systems as they operate under identical social, political, and economic conditions. Because mixed-member systems involve the simultaneous use of the world's two dominant forms of electoral rules – proportional representation and single-member district elections – they allow us to better isolate the impact of institutions on political outcomes by holding constant other important noninstitutional factors such as social cleavages, socioeconomic development, and culture.

It is this approach to studying mixed-member systems that Lijphart (1994) calls the "comparative method" or the method of "controlled comparison." As we discuss in Chapter 1, this approach is at the heart of social science. Controlled comparison uses "cases that differ with regard to the variables one wants to investigate, but similar with regard to all other important variables that may affect the dependent variables; these other variables can then be treated as control variables" (Lijphart 1994: 78). This approach is useful for the researcher because political outcomes are typically determined by a number of important factors (and usually interactions among multiple causes) that are difficult to disentangle from one another. Thus, we gain great analytical leverage if we can compare cases that are similar with regard to all factors except the one under examination. The biggest drawback of the approach is the difficulty of finding comparable cases that differ along only one important factor (Lijphart 1994: 79).

For this reason, many electoral system scholars argue that mixed-member systems are uniquely suited to the researcher seeking to understand the impact of electoral rules. Matthew Shugart (2005: 34) notes that the "recent wave of countries adopting mixed member systems has afforded researchers 'crucial experiments' – case studies in which the effects of specific electoral rules can be isolated from other variables." In this book, we use district-level data from a large number of mixed-member systems to conduct a variety of such experiments.

Controlled comparison has been used to provide valuable insights both in electoral studies and other subfields of political science. In his groundbreaking study of social capital, Robert Putnam (1993) holds constant the institutional context – Italy's nationwide introduction of regional governments – to isolate the influence of environmental factors on democratic performance. Putnam argues that because regional governments in Italy all had the same structure, any variation in the degree of governmental performance could be traced not to institutional design but rather to some aspect of the environment in which institutions operated. Lijphart's influential study of electoral systems covering the period from 1945 to 1990 also uses controlled comparison when he focuses on electoral system changes within individual countries. Lijphart argues that studying the results of electoral system reform – that is, different electoral rules employed successively in the same country – allows the researcher the advantage of holding all other explanatory factors constant because, although the electoral systems changed, one is still dealing with "the same country, the same political parties, the same voters, and so on" (1994: 79). Finally, for many years, researchers have used the controlled comparison approach to study strategic voting in mixed-member systems. Scholars have long compared the PR vote for parties with the SMD vote for candidates in Germany (and now other mixed systems), claiming that vote gaps between the two tiers represent comparable differences in voting behavior among voters acting simultaneously under two different electoral systems (see, e.g., Bawn 1999).

Our approach to mixed-member electoral systems follows and extends this line of research. In a sense, we turn Putnam's approach on its head. By simultaneously employing PR and SMD electoral systems, the mixed-member electoral system allows us to hold the environment constant and isolate the effects of different electoral rules. Following Lijphart, we find much value in studying the effects of different electoral arrangements on the same countries, voters, and parties, and our approach even offers advantages over Lijphart's design. Because countries do not change electoral systems very often or very dramatically, Lijphart was able to examine only a relatively small number of examples.[4] Also, in contrast to Lijphart, by using mixed-member electoral systems we are able to control for time: in considering a given mixed-member system, we are able to see the impact of SMD and PR rules in the same country at the same time. In addition, because Lijphart's cases come primarily from advanced democracies, his analysis is more limited to differences in factors such as electoral formula and district magnitude within the broad class of PR systems – which are the norm in advanced democracies – rather than systemic differences between PR and SMD electoral systems. Our analysis uses controlled comparison to investigate the effects of electoral rules based on the most important and debated difference within electoral system analysis – proportional representation versus single-member district systems.

THE USEFULNESS OF WIDE VARIATION

The proliferation of mixed-member electoral systems around the world adds geographic, socioeconomic, and political diversity to the data in our analysis. With the introduction of mixed systems in developed democracies around the world (Italy, Japan, and New Zealand), as well as new democracies in East Europe, Eurasia, Latin America, and Africa, the controlled comparison

---

[4] See Tables 4.1, 4.2, and 4.3 in Lijphart 1994.

approach to mixed-member electoral systems takes on a truly global, comparative dimension. This diversity of country cases is important because it allows us to isolate differences between PR and SMD electoral systems within vastly different political contexts, which permits us to investigate the conditionality of electoral system effects and the importance of context.

The fact that mixed-member electoral systems now exist in a wide variety of contexts, from well-developed and prosperous Western democracies to new democracies in developing countries, further strengthens the value of comparing differences between the effects of the PR and SMD parts of these systems. We compare the results of the PR and SMD tiers within each country to each other and also compare such results across countries to assess the impact of different political, social, and demographic contexts on electoral system effects. As a result, we can discern whether common patterns exist among different types of countries, under different political contexts, or under different varieties of mixed-member systems. If we find that differences typically occur between political regime types (e.g., established democracy versus new or postcommunist democracy) or the type of party system (institutionalized versus noninstitutionalized) it will suggest that such factors explain these different outcomes better than other explanations, such as cross-contamination between the two halves of the system.

In our analysis, we include all countries for which we could acquire data. Table 2.1 provides greater detail on the cases, but, more generally, we examine mixed-member electoral systems in 18 countries. Six – Germany, Italy, Japan, New Zealand, Scotland, and Wales – are consolidated democracies with long experiences of competitive elections under various systems.[5] One – Venezuela – had a long history (particularly when compared with other Latin American countries) of stable democratic rule, but in recent years has seen a major implosion of its party system. The remaining countries – Albania, Armenia, Bolivia, Bulgaria, Croatia, Hungary, Lesotho, Lithuania, Macedonia, Russia, and Ukraine – are (or were) democratizing states recently emerging from a long period of communist or authoritarian rule. These cases provide a wide range of party systems, varying greatly in the rules governing their mixed-member system and their levels of party institutionalization.

When possible, we collected data at the lowest level of aggregation – usually the district level – to test hypotheses at their appropriate level of analysis. For the number of parties and voting behavior, we analyze data from the single-member district level and even, occasionally, the smaller municipality level. When examining women's representation, we begin by studying the share of seats under SMD and PR electoral rules won by women in each country. Then, we use data on individual legislators to control for factors such as partisanship and incumbency (as well as the number of parties in the district) that might shape women's representation. Such data collection lends itself to a quantitative

---

[5] For Scotland, we examine elections to the Scottish Parliament. For Wales, we analyze elections to the Welsh Assembly.

TABLE 2.1. *Description of 18 Mixed-Member Electoral Systems, 1953–2007*

Country	# of MMS Elects.	Linked Tiers	SMD Formula	SMD: PR Ratio	Avg. PR District. Mag.[a]	PR Legal Threshold	Dem. Exp/ Pty. Inst.[o]
Albania[l]	3	Linked	Plurality	100:40	40	2.5%	New Dem.
Armenia[n]	4	Unlinked	Plurality	75:56	56	5%	Non-Inst.
Bulgaria[m]	1	Unlinked	Majority	200:200	7.14	4%	New Dem.
Bolivia	3	Linked	Plurality	68:62	6.9	3%	New Dem.
Croatia[f,g]	2	Unlinked	Plurality	28:80	80	5%	New Dem.
Germany[b]	15	Linked	Plurality	299:299	299	5%	Est. Dem.
Hungary[e]	5	Unlinked/ partial comp	Majority	176:210	7.60	5%	New Dem.
Italy[d]	3	Unlinked/ partial comp	Plurality	475:155	155	4%	Est. Dem.
Japan[c]	4	Unlinked	Plurality	300:180	16.36	none	Est. Dem.
Lesotho	2	Linked	Plurality	80:40	40	none	New Dem.
Lithuania[h]	5	Unlinked	Majority	71:70	70	5%	New Dem.
Macedonia	1	Unlinked	Majority	85:35	35	5%	New Dem.
New Zealand[b]	4	Linked	Plurality	65:55	55	5%	Est. Dem.
Russia[j]	4	Unlinked	Plurality	225:225	225	5%	Non-Inst.
Scotland	3	Linked	Plurality	73:56	7	none	Est. Dem.
Ukraine[k]	2	Unlinked	Plurality	225:225	225	4%	Non-Inst.
Venezuela[i]	2	Linked	Plurality	88:119	8.3	none	Est. Dem.
Wales	3	Linked	Plurality	40:20	5	none	Est. Dem.

[a] With fully linked tiers (e.g., Germany), one could come up with two different measures of the average PR district magnitude. On one hand, it might be simply the total number of PR seats in the region. On the other, given the linkage, it could be the sum of the SMD and PR seats in the region, so that, for example, in Germany the magnitude in 1998 was in fact 598.

[b] In Germany and New Zealand, the seats a party wins in the SMD tier are subtracted from the total it earns via the party list vote.

In Germany, PR mandates are distributed in 10 territorial districts (*Land*) but parties have the option to pool their Land-level votes at the national level, making the average district magnitude in reality a single 299-member national district rather than a number of state districts with an average of 29.9 members per district (Cox 1997: 287–8). The number of seats changed a number of times over the years (although the number of compensation and SMD seats always were identical to one another) and expanded in each tier after the reunification of East and West Germany. The numbers reported for Germany here reflect the number intended for the 2005 election.

[c] In Japan, there were 200 PR seats in 1996, which was reduced to 180 beginning in 2000. With 11 PR blocs (districts), this gave Japan an average PR district magnitude of 18.18 in 1996.

[d] Partial compensation: Italy used the two-vote mixed-member system in 1994, 1996, and 2001, in which a compensation system known as the *scorporo* partially linked the PR and SMD tiers. If a party won an SMD seat, its PR vote total was reduced by the number of votes (plus one) received by the second-place candidate in the district. The relationship between the two tiers was weak enough and the SMD tier was so relatively large that we usually categorize the system as "unlinked."

[e] In Hungary there are three levels of seat allocation. The SMD and territorial PR tier (the largest components of the system) are not linked; hence we categorize the system as unlinked. However, surplus votes (all votes not used to win a seat in either of the lower tiers) are aggregated in a third national tier, which allocates a minimum of 58 seats (plus any seats not distributed in the territorial PR tier) based on these surplus votes (Benoit 1999: 2–5).

approach based on datasets that included hundreds, or even thousands, of observations. However, given this approach, our cases vary from chapter to chapter, sometimes encompassing roughly 50 elections from more than a dozen countries and other times, when data are less available, including many fewer country observations.

One of the chief advantages of our broad array of country cases is that we compare new and established democracies directly to assess their different experiences with electoral rules. Most comparative work in this area has focused on either new or established democracies and therefore has, as we point out in Chapter 1, assumed away factors that are in fact variables that can be studied systematically. As a consequence, venerable hypotheses such as Duverger's Law, or the argument that proportional representation promotes the election of women, are presumed to apply to all circumstances when, in fact, they may be contingent on particular contexts. Our approach using quantitative measures and district-level analysis provides a useful corrective to such presumptions.

Footnotes to Table 2.1 continued

   This three-level system makes it possible to compute two types of average PR district magnitude. The territorial magnitude (7.60) that we list in the table and also a national-level tier in which district magnitude is 58.

   Hungary's legal threshold was 4% in 1990, but changed to 5% in 1994.

[f] Croatia also has special seats for representation of ethnic minorities, which are not included here.

[g] In 1992 in Croatia, the ratio of SMD to PR seats was 60 to 60 (with an average PR district magnitude of 60), but then changed to 28 SMDs to 80 PR seats in 1995. Croatia has had subsequent elections after 1995 under a strictly PR system. In addition, in 1992 Croatia had a legal threshold in PR of 2%, which it changed to 5% in 1995.

[h] Lithuania changed from a majoritarian to a plurality system within its SMD tier for the 2000 election but changed back to a majoritarian system in 2004.

   In 1996, Lithuania raised the legal threshold in PR from 4% to 5% for individual parties and 7% for coalitions.

[i] Venezuela has several multimember plurality districts. The average district magnitude is 1.2.

[j] Russia changed its electoral system from a mixed-member system to a pure PR system in 2007.

[k] Ukraine held elections under a mixed-member system in 1998 and 2002, after which it changed to a pure PR system.

[l] Albania held elections under a mixed-member system with a two-round majoritarian system in the SMD tier in 1997 and 2001 and a plurality contest in 2005. Electoral system description is based on the 2005 election.

   In addition, Albania used a 4% legal threshold for coalitions of parties in PR.

[m] The information in the table for Bulgaria is based on its 1990 system, under which it held one election, and then changed to pure PR. In 2009, it reintroduced a mixed system with a relatively small SMD tier.

[n] Armenia's system changed the number of SMD and PR seats a number of times, so the ratio between them changed repeatedly as well. The electoral system description in the table is based on the 1999 election.

[o] Dem. Exp/Pty. Inst.: Democratic Experience and Level of Party Institutionalization. Countries are divided into established democracies (Est. Dem.), new democracies (New Dem.), and new democracies with noninstitutionalized party systems (Non-Inst.). See Chapter 3 for a detailed discussion of the coding.

THE CONTAMINATION CRITIQUE AND ITS SHORTCOMINGS

Not all scholars agree with this approach to mixed-member electoral systems. For some analysts, the combination of PR and SMDs in a single system leads each tier to influence or "contaminate" the effects of the other.[6] We completely agree that contamination exists. It would be unrealistic to believe that all actors – but especially political parties – would behave in each tier of balloting as if the other tier did not exist. That being said, much analysis of the contamination effect overstates both its own analytical merits and its critique of the controlled comparison approach. Indeed, we believe that, even recognizing the existence of a contamination effect in mixed-member systems, the controlled comparison approach makes a significant contribution.

The Contamination Critique

In part, some critiques appear to mischaracterize the controlled comparison approach. The principal argument made by "contamination" scholars is that, because the PR and SMD tiers of mixed-member systems are actually used simultaneously in any given election, they cannot be viewed as independent of one another. The presence of each tier is likely to affect behavior in the other; therefore, their effects will not be the same as in "pure" SMD and PR systems. As a result, some scholars – most notably, Federico Ferrara, Erik Herron, and Misa Nishikawa (2005) – raise serious questions about the controlled comparison approach. Ferrara et al. (2005: 4) criticize what they describe as the claims of the controlled comparison approach to use mixed-member systems to "precisely identify how different electoral institutions affect particular outcomes of interest because such studies hold every possible intervening variable constant." The problem with such claims, they argue, is the "faulty" assumptions of the controlled comparison approach, most notably the assumption of independence of the SMD and PR tiers within a single system (Ferrara et al. 2005: 9). Based on this critique, they explain that "The validity of 'controlled comparisons'... hinges on an affirmative answer to... [the] counterfactual question: is the outcome observed in the SMD component of mixed electoral systems the same outcome we would observe under 'pure' SMD?" (Ferrara et al. 2005: 6).

We believe that critiques of this kind make a straw man out of controlled comparison. The controlled comparison approach to the study of mixed-member electoral systems does not claim that the two tiers do not affect each other, and only the most diehard proponent of the controlled comparison approach would suggest that contamination does not exist to some degree. To our knowledge, no study of mixed-member rules has ever claimed to be able to analyze the system to determine *precisely* the impact of each type of electoral

---

[6] See, for example, Clark and Wittrock (2005), Cox and Schoppa (2002), Ferrara et al. (2005), Gschwend et al. (2003), Hainmueller and Kern (2008), Herron and Nishikawa (2001).

rule. Rather, at the most basic level, the "control" in "controlled comparison" is that the approach controls for social context: If we keep social (and temporal) context constant, how do different electoral rules affect politics? In setting up the research design in this way, we are able to dramatically reduce – down to the electoral institutions themselves – the number of factors that appear to affect the political behavior and outcomes under consideration. If the results of such analysis are largely in line with studies that do not similarly control for social context, we can be more confident of the findings. Furthermore, given the debates within political science over the relative impact of societal versus institutional factors in shaping politics, it is valuable to develop research designs that allow the researcher to control for at least one of these sets of factors.

That being said, if the aim of the controlled comparison approach were to determine the precise impact of different sorts of rules – for instance, exactly how many parties emerge in an SMD system as opposed to a PR system – the critique about the validity of controlled comparison hinging on the different components in mixed-member systems being exactly the same as their "pure" counterparts would hold water. However, as we show in nearly every chapter in this book, controlled comparison is not merely about comparing outcomes in the SMD and PR tiers in mixed-member systems. At least as important, our use of controlled comparison is about *explaining* what leads to greater or lesser differences in outcomes under SMD and PR rules when we control for social context. If differences between the two tiers appear in a systematic fashion – even in the face of potential contamination – this controlled comparison approach will have contributed to our understanding of the factors influencing political behavior.

Shortcomings in Analysis of Contamination

Critiques of the controlled comparison approach also face significant problems when it comes to the evidence used to demonstrate the presence of contamination. The most common example cited as evidence of contamination relates to the number of parties: contamination scholars argue that, under mixed-member systems, parties have incentives to run candidates in SMDs even if they have little chance of victory, because even uncompetitive candidates will both attract attention to the party and work on its behalf in the district. In this way, the presence of even an uncompetitive candidate in the winner-take-all SMD will help the party win votes in the PR tier, where voters need to worry less about having to vote strategically. As a result, Duvergerian incentives for parties to exit competition are much weaker in SMDs in mixed-member systems and should lead to more candidates per district than in pure SMD systems (Herron and Nishikawa 2001; Ferrara et al. 2005).

Empirical support for such arguments comes in a number of forms, with two types of evidence probably the most cited. First, contamination scholars offer evidence that, on average, quite a few more candidates run at the district level in SMDs in mixed-member systems than in pure SMD cases. Drawing from a select group of country cases and years, Ferrara et al. (2005: 46) indicate that the average effective number of candidates at the district level in pure SMD systems runs from a low of 1.81 in the U.S. House of Representatives to a high of 2.56 in New Zealand (prior to the advent of its mixed-member system). In contrast, they show a low effective-number-of-candidates score of 2.65 in SMDs in Italy's mixed-member system to a high of 5.98 under Ukraine's. Second, a number of studies of contamination highlight that in mixed-member systems, parties receive larger numbers of PR votes in areas where they run SMD candidates (see, especially, Cox and Schoppa 2002; Ferrara et al. 2005; Hainmueller and Kern 2008; Herron and Nishikawa 2001; Mizusaki and Mori 1998).

Biased Sample. This analysis has significant shortcomings, however. First, empirical studies of contamination tend to be based on evidence from multiple decades of use in pure SMD systems but only between one and four elections per country in the mixed-member system cases. Moreover, the examples drawn from mixed-member systems tend to be from the first couple of elections conducted under the system. Few scholars believe that electoral rules will have their expected effects in the initial election under a new system, as it takes time for political actors to adjust their behavior to the new incentive structures. From the perspective of SMDs affecting the number of parties, voters and elites must first witness the mechanical effect of the rules and then respond strategically (the psychological effect), something that takes at least one election to achieve. And, as we demonstrate in Chapter 4 (see especially Appendix 4A) and Chapter 6, in mixed-member systems strategic defection increases over time and, in turn, the number of candidates in SMDs goes down.

When we look at later elections, SMD results under mixed-member systems tend to be much more in line with those in pure SMD systems (see Appendix 4A). In the second and third elections under the mixed-member system in Italy, the effective number of candidates per district averaged 2.43 (1996) and 2.41 (2001), roughly equal to the number (2.40) in Canada's pure SMD system from 1935 through 1993. In New Zealand, the effective number of candidates dropped steadily over time, so that by its fourth mixed-member election in 2005, it had 2.49 candidates per district, less than its average (2.56) under its pure SMD system (1972–1993). In Japan, the number of candidates dropped dramatically over time as well, down to 2.41 and 2.40 in, respectively, its third (2003) and fourth (2005) elections under the mixed-member system.

Analysis of Japan makes even clearer the comparability of the number of parties in pure SMD systems and SMDs in mixed-member systems. Remember that the logic of contamination is that parties will run candidates to help drum up PR support for the party. According to this logic, the decision by independents (i.e., candidates unaffiliated with any party) to run will have nothing to do with contamination. They have no party for which to try to gain votes. If we drop independents from the analysis of Japan in 2005, the effective number of candidates drops to 2.27. Among the pure SMD cases listed in Ferrara et al.'s analysis, this score is only higher than figures for the U.S.

House of Representatives (1900–1990) and Senate (1914–1990), and 2.27 is equal to the effective number of candidates in pure SMD systems in the United Kingdom (1922–1997). In fact, the 2.40 candidates per district in Japan in 2005 – which includes independents – is equal to or lower than the effective number of candidates in the pure SMD systems in Canada (1935–1993), India (1957–1991), and New Zealand's now-defunct pure SMD system. Even more striking, in 2009, the effective number of candidates (including independents) in Japan dropped further, to an average of 2.26 candidates per district.

Moreover, if we look at the actual raw numbers of candidates – that is, not the vote-weighted "effective" number – Japan does not look much different from pure SMD systems. Japan had, on average, 3.3 actual candidates per SMD in 2005, but this number includes candidates from the Japan Communist Party (JCP), who were present but largely irrelevant in nearly every district in the country. If we exclude the JCP, which, according to party policy until 2007, ran a candidate in nearly every SMD despite its inability to win any, there were on average in each Japanese SMD only 2.42 (2003) and 2.38 (2005) actual candidates.[7] These numbers are less than the average raw number of candidates running in each district in the U.S. House of Representatives' pure SMD system.[8]

In addition, half the examples provided by Ferrara et al. of large numbers of candidates running in SMDs under mixed-member systems come from the initial elections in former Soviet republics. A major problem with such analysis is that the number of parties is unlikely to drop quickly in new democracies, where experience with democratic rules is limited. Moreover, two of the examples provided by Ferrara et al. are Russia and Ukraine, two countries with poorly institutionalized party systems, thereby making a reduction in the number of parties unlikely under any electoral rule.[9]

Ferrara et al. do include later years for the one country – Germany – that has a long history with a mixed-member system, but the years chosen here are problematic as well. Focusing on the 1990–2002 period, Ferrara et al. show an average effective number of candidates score of 2.73 per SMD in Germany's mixed-member system. However, with unification between East and West Germany, 1990 brought in a new period of party fragmentation in Germany, with the introduction of parties from the East (especially the Party of Democratic Socialism [PDS], the successor party to the ruling socialist party in East Germany). As Appendix 4A indicates, there were many fewer candidates in West Germany prior to 1990. By the fourth election under the system in

---

[7] Contamination can hardly be held responsible for the JCP's decision to run a candidate in every district – it had done so even under the previous electoral system that had only a single SNTV tier (Baker and Scheiner 2004). Moreover, after repeatedly failing under the new mixed system, the JCP has decided to scale back its SMD candidacies dramatically.

[8] For example, on average, there were roughly 2.5 actual candidates per district in the U.S. House of Representatives in 2004.

[9] We discuss the importance of party institutionalization in much greater detail especially in Chapters 1, 3, 4, and 6.

1965, the average effective number of parties in SMDs in West Germany was 2.36, and the number pushed even lower over the next two decades.

In short, the contamination literature's biased sample appears to misrepresent the actual difference in the number of parties between mixed-member systems and pure FPTP ones. That is, among established democracies, there is little difference in the number of candidates per district in SMDs under mixed-member systems and in pure SMDs. The one exception is the pure SMD system of the United States, where there are significantly fewer candidates per district than in all the other established democracies discussed here. However, as Grofman et al. (2009) note, the low number of candidates in the United States was unique among long-standing plurality systems. This uniqueness is probably due to the fact that the United States contains its own form of contamination, in that it is the only presidential system among the established democracy examples discussed here. As Cox (1997) points out, the presence of plurality rules directly electing the national president creates incentives for the development of only two national parties that compete throughout the country. With only these two parties likely able to contest elections to the powerful national executive, local political organizations and their supporters have strong incentive to associate with one of the two large, nationally competitive parties; as a result, additional parties are much less likely to flourish, even at the district level. In this way, the particularly small number of candidates in the United States is at least as much a reflection of the FPTP rules that elect the president as those used to elect representatives to the legislature.

Countervailing Evidence

A second problem with the analysis of the effect of contamination on the number of parties is that it highlights one possible causal argument while ignoring another that is at least as likely: research on contamination tends to focus on the idea that additional SMD candidates help deliver extra PR votes for the party, but this argument ignores the fact that the reverse is at least as likely: Given the substantial costs to parties or candidates of running in elections that they are likely to lose, it makes much more sense that candidates are more likely to run in SMDs in areas where the party is already popular. In other words, rather than the presence of a candidate leading to many more PR votes for a party, it is more plausible that a strong base of support (which can be measured by votes in the PR tier) for the party gives candidates greater incentive to run in SMDs for that party.

Indeed, sophisticated quantitative analysis of the Japanese case by Ko Maeda (2008) corrects for the bias inherent in any analysis that fails to take into account this alternative explanation, and finds no evidence of a contamination effect in the Japanese mixed-member system. Maeda's finding raises a substantial problem with the contamination argument: It appears that it is not the existence of separate SMD and PR tiers that is driving more candidates to run in SMDs. Rather, additional candidates are running when their party is more popular, thereby giving them, as candidates, a better chance of winning votes in the SMD race.

Contamination scholars might point out that contamination is likely to be more potent in mixed-member systems other than Japan's, but in our view such a critique does not suggest a serious problem with the controlled comparison approach. More specifically, contamination scholars might argue, correctly, that the lack of "linkage" mechanisms between the SMD and PR tiers in mixed-member systems such as Japan's reduces the level of contamination between the two tiers. In contrast, it might be argued that there would be greater contamination in mixed-member systems that have greater linkage between the two tiers. For example, in Germany and New Zealand, ballots cast in the PR tier determine the total number of seats won by each party and SMD votes merely determine which individual candidates represent each small district.[10] Even when they win large numbers of SMDs under linked systems, parties do not win any more total seats than the number that they are allotted through their vote in PR. Because strategic defection from weaker to stronger parties in the SMD tier will typically have no effect on the total number of seats won by each party, voters in linked systems should have less reason to vote strategically in SMD balloting. In this way, the contamination effect brought on by linkage mechanisms ought to lead to a larger effective number of parties (candidates) in SMD races than would be the case in unlinked mixed-member systems and pure SMD systems. Indeed, Gschwend et al. (2003) and Hainmueller and Kern (2008) offer some evidence of the existence of contamination in Germany.

Such analysis is certainly compelling, but it hardly raises serious concerns about the controlled comparison approach. To begin with, evidence of contamination in linked systems is hardly overwhelming. Hainmueller and Kern's (2008) analysis is restricted to Germany's two largest parties, leaving out the impact of smaller parties whose behavior is presumed to differ most substantially between pure SMD and mixed-member electoral systems. Moreover, Jeffrey Karp (2009) finds little evidence of contamination effects in New Zealand's linked mixed-member system. Given New Zealand's past experience with FPTP that made individual candidates important, along with peculiarities of the New Zealand ballot design that ought to encourage voters to link candidates and their parties, Karp notes that the "limited findings in this context suggest that fears of contamination in other mixed systems might be over-stated" (2009: 49). Indeed, it is striking that, even with reduced incentives for strategic voting, the effective number of parties in SMDs of linked systems is markedly lower than the number of parties in these systems' PR tiers and is comparable to the number of candidates in pure SMD systems. (Again, see Appendix 4A for specifics on the number of parties in mixed-member systems.)

---

[10] We discuss the details of linkage mechanisms later in the chapter, and in Table 2.1 we indicate the presence or absence of linkage mechanisms for each of the mixed-member systems we examine in this book.

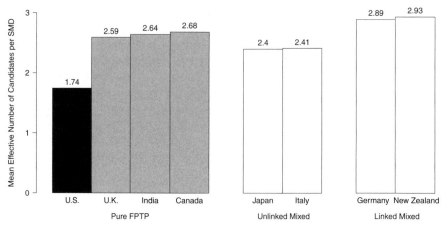

FIGURE 2.2. Comparing the (mean) effective number of candidates in select FPTP and mixed-member systems at the SMD level.

- Source: Matthew Singer's district-level data set of SMD elections
- Data years: U.S. (2002), U.K. (1997), India (1999), Canada (2000), Japan (2005), Italy (2001), Germany (2005), New Zealand (2002)

Ultimately, though, it is important to remember that the controlled comparison approach does not rule out controlling for factors such as linkage between the SMD and PR tiers. In this book, we consistently and explicitly look to measure the effect of tier linkage on the different outcomes we seek to explain. That is, tier linkage is a *variable* that we can – and do – include in our analysis.

More Systematic Analysis of the Difference in the Number of Parties. In addition, more systematic cross-national analysis of the number of candidates running in SMDs under (pure) FPTP and mixed-member systems provides no evidence to support the arguments of contamination scholars.

Figures 2.2 and 2.3 demonstrate the general lack of difference between the number of candidates running under pure FPTP systems and SMDs in mixed-member systems. Figure 2.2 provides the mean effective number of candidates per SMD in recent elections for some of the most well-known FPTP and mixed-member systems. Compared with the pure FPTP countries, the number of candidates per SMD is a bit higher in Germany's and New Zealand's linked mixed systems. However, as we discussed earlier, the higher average numbers of candidates in these linked systems makes great sense, given the weaker incentives that exist under such systems to behave strategically in SMD races. At the same time, Figure 2.2 also shows that the effective number of candidates running in SMDs in Japan and Italy is lower than in most of the FPTP countries in the figure. The exception is the United States, which we already noted was most likely a result of its plurality presidential election system that runs concurrently with congressional elections (along with other rules in the

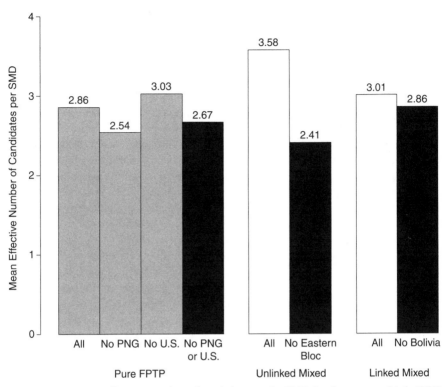

FIGURE 2.3. Mean effective number of candidates at the SMD level across multiple FPTP and mixed-member systems.

- Source: Matthew Singer's district-level data set of SMD elections
- Data:
  - FPTP: Bahamas (2002), Bangladesh (2001), Barbados (2003), Belize (2003), Bermuda (2003), Botswana (1999), Canada (2000), Dominica (2002), Grenada (1999), India (1999), Jamaica (1997), Malawi (1999), Micronesia (2003), Nepal (2008), Papua New Guinea (2002), Solomon Islands (2001), St. Kitts (2000), St. Lucia (2001), St. Vincent (2001), Trinidad and Tobago (2002), U.K. (1997), U.S. (2002), Zambia (2001)
  - Unlinked Mixed: Hungary (1998), Italy (2001), Japan (2005), Lithuania (2000), Thailand (2008), Ukraine (1998)
  - Linked Mixed: Albania (2005), Bolivia (2002), Germany (2005), Lesotho (2008), New Zealand (2002), Scotland (2003), Venezuela (2000), Wales (2007).

United States that privilege the two leading parties). In fact, the argument about the greater constraining effect of pure FPTP systems is further weakened when we see the 2009 Japanese mixed-member system election, which produced an average effective number of candidates per SMD of 2.26, and the 2010 United Kingdom pure FPTP election, which produced an average effective-number-of-candidates score of 2.98 per district.

Figure 2.3, which provides the mean effective number of candidates per district in recent elections in a much wider array of FPTP and mixed systems, allows us to look at the differences in the number of parties much more systematically. On average, FPTP systems have an effective number of candidates per district score of 2.86, and mixed-member systems have a score of 3.36. However, these numbers neither take into account important differences between mixed-member systems nor the effect of outliers in each case. As we see in Figure 2.3, the United States and Papua New Guinea (PNG; a small country with massive levels of social diversity and huge numbers of parties) have a substantial effect on the average of the number of candidates in pure FPTP systems. Removing those two countries from the analysis, we see an average effective number of candidates per district score of 2.67 in pure FPTP systems. As before, we find more candidates per district under linked mixed-member systems, but there is a sizable outlier in this group – Bolivia, whose average score is 4.54. Bolivia's linked mixed-member system, which uses PR balloting to help elect the country's president, creates confusion in terms of its effect on voter and elite incentives. Removing Bolivia from the analysis, we find that linked mixed-member systems have an average score of 2.86, just slightly higher than our adjusted measure for pure FPTP systems. Finally, unlinked mixed-member systems appear to have a very high score (3.58), but, as we discussed earlier, much of this outcome is driven by postcommunist countries whose party systems do not cleanly structure the vote. Excluding such countries from the analysis, we find an average effective-number-of-candidates score of only 2.41 per district – less than the average under pure FPTP rules.

The preceding patterns showing greater similarities than differences between SMD electoral contests within (especially unlinked) mixed-member systems and pure FPTP systems are in line with Singer's (forthcoming) analysis, which provides the most comprehensive cross-national analysis of plurality elections worldwide. Singer concludes that, once one controls for the postcommunist countries, there is no statistically discernible difference between the average district-level number of parties in plurality elections under unlinked mixed-member systems and pure SMD rules.[11]

We replicate Singer's analysis, but (a) restrict the analysis to only pure FPTP systems and mixed-member systems (i.e., those examined in Figure 2.3), and (b) differentiate between linked and unlinked mixed-member systems. (See Appendix 2 and Table 2.2 for the details of the analysis.) In doing so, we find no statistically discernible difference in the effective number of candidates running in pure FPTP systems and SMDs in either linked or unlinked mixed systems. These results undermine the contamination critique that plurality contests within mixed-member systems are systemically different from pure plurality elections and strongly support our emphasis on contextual factors in institutional analyses.

---

[11] Singer's analysis suggests that there may be more parties under linked mixed-member systems, which makes sense for the reasons that we discussed earlier.

Contamination Bias and the Controlled Comparison Approach

Although this analysis finds no strong evidence of contamination, it would be unreasonable to claim that contamination does not exist – but it would be just as unreasonable to suggest that contamination invalidates the controlled comparison approach. The key to using the controlled comparison approach to study mixed-member systems is simply to recognize what type of bias is likely to exist and to be cognizant of the sorts of lessons that can be drawn from the findings that emerge.

Making Bias Useful. Harry Eckstein (1975) and Gary King, Robert Keohane, and Sidney Verba (1994: 209) highlight the usefulness of research designs based on a "least likely" scenario context. That is, it can be useful to test theories in contexts in which they are least likely to hold. If conditions within such a context continue to match the expectations of a given theory – despite having the deck stacked against it – the researcher can have a fair degree of confidence that the theory will apply more generally, especially in contexts that are more favorable.

In this way, the contamination bias that some scholars point to in mixed-member systems works to the advantage of those following the controlled comparison approach. For example, in the case of the number of candidates at the SMD level, we know that parties have at least some incentive in mixed-member systems to run additional candidates (as compared with pure SMD systems). As a result, any findings of fewer parties in SMDs relative to PR – and numbers of candidates that are comparable to pure SMD systems – serve to strengthen the claim of the importance of institutions and their incentives.

Being Aware of the Reasons behind the Analysis. In following the controlled comparison approach to the study of mixed-member electoral systems, it is also important to be clear about what the research aim is. Fundamentally, the contamination literature and our analysis have very different aims. Central to the contamination school is determining whether mixed-member systems are fundamentally the sum of two types of rules or a distinct new type of electoral rule. For our analysis, that question is important only to the extent that it affects our ability to draw conclusions about political behavior from studying the outcomes of mixed-member system elections. Ferrara et al. (2005: 142) argue that "mixed electoral systems are unsuitable for the study of the independent consequences of SMD and PR." However, this point is correct only in reference to the research aim of developing precise point estimates of the impact of SMD and PR electoral rules. At no point in this book is our aim to develop precise point estimates. Fundamentally, social science is about developing theories that then generate testable implications (hypotheses) to try to find support for the theories (or evidence against them). In short, in social science it is usually more important to show patterns that are consistent (or not) with a theoretical story, rather than determining precise point estimates.

We present estimates of the average effect of different types of factors on political outcomes, but these estimates are always for illustrative purposes to help demonstrate a general pattern.

Our principal aim in this book is to use the controlled comparison approach to examine the factors that shape electoral incentives and determine the conditions under which existing electoral system theories do and do not hold. Erik Herron (2002) focuses on contamination to make the argument that in mixed-member systems one should not predict legislators' behavior purely from the tier (SMD or PR) in which they were elected. Rather, he argues, one should focus on the electoral incentives that legislators face. We agree, but also think that this point is neither unique to the issue of contamination effects nor causes problems for the controlled comparison approach. At the heart of Herron's analysis is that we should be conscious, as we are throughout this book, of the political incentives political actors face – whether they are due to a simple electoral rule, combinations of rules, or factors beyond institutions that might affect them. The fact that we find patterns of behavior throughout the book that are consistent with the incentive structures that we highlight – even despite the existence of contamination – offers further support for the approach we pursue.

The Importance of Cross-National and Longitudinal Analysis. In addition to using bias to our advantage, the comparative dimension we offer in this book helps to address further the issue of contamination. As we noted earlier, in this book we compare the results of the PR and SMD tiers to each other within each of our individual mixed-member system countries and also compare the results across countries to assess the impact of different political, social, and demographic contexts on electoral system effects. Vast differences in our findings among different countries – most especially between new (particularly postcommunist) and established democracies – signal the importance of political context rather than institutional explanations such as contamination between the two tiers of the mixed-member electoral system.

If contamination is the main factor driving party proliferation in the SMD tier, for example, we should see such proliferation in all mixed-member systems, not just new democracies, especially those with poorly established parties.[12] Indeed, much of our analysis in this book combines the controlled comparison approach – which demonstrates that electoral rules maintain their expected effects even in mixed-member systems in established democracies – with cross-national analysis – which demonstrates, among other things, that similar rules have very different effects in new (especially postcommunist) democracies. Moreover, by including, at times, comparisons with pure FPTP systems, we are able to demonstrate the extent to which some of our findings are due to contamination in mixed-member systems or are part of a pattern that appears

---

[12] Indeed, larger numbers of candidates in the SMDs in poorly established party systems would be even harder to blame on contamination given that few of those systems use linkage mechanisms between the SMD and PR tiers.

to hold more generally. Finally, our analysis of multiple elections in most of the countries under analysis helps demonstrate the extent to which outcomes in a given country are a general pattern or specific to a particular time. In this way, we are able to examine to what extent outcomes are due to contamination, an oddity of a particular time period, inexperience with new rules, or a result of factors such as a lack of democratic experience.

DEFINING AND CLASSIFYING MIXED-MEMBER ELECTORAL SYSTEMS

Now, having explained how we use controlled comparison in this book, we introduce the details of mixed-member electoral systems.

All mixed electoral systems – as we define them here – share the distinction of providing the electorate votes in simultaneous PR and SMD elections, but four characteristics distinguish mixed systems from one another: linkage/compensatory seats, the SMD electoral formula, the district magnitude and legal threshold of representation in the PR tier, and the ratio of seats in each tier.[13] Table 2.1 presents a description, based on these characteristics, of the 18 mixed systems included in this book. Each of these features is likely to affect numerous political outcomes (such as proportionality and the number of parties), and we therefore include them in our analysis throughout this book. Examining the features differentiating mixed-member systems from one another not only helps us better understand how mixed systems work but also is a necessary part of the explanation when comparing outcomes arising out of the PR and SMD halves of the system.

Linked Tiers

The most important of these characteristics is the extent to which the two tiers are linked together through the use of compensation seats. In unlinked or mixed-member majoritarian (MMM) systems, there is no seat linkage between the single-member district and proportional representation tiers (Shugart and Wattenberg 2001b: 13–17). In unlinked systems such as those in Japan and Russia, the total number of seats each party wins is simply the sum of its totals in each tier. For illustration's sake, we offer the following hypothetical scenario for an unlinked mixed-member system: Imagine that the system has 200 total seats – 100 in PR and 100 SMDs. If a given party – let us say the Free Range Party (FRP) – were to win 30 percent of the PR vote, it would be awarded roughly 30 PR seats. Imagine further that the FRP were to win 50 SMDs. Under this scenario, the FRP would have won 80 seats – 30 in PR and 50 in SMDs – out of the 200 total available.

---

[13] Other scholars have offered similar distinctions among mixed-member electoral systems. For example, Massicotte and Blais (1999: 346) differentiate mixed systems according to three criteria: which electoral formulas are used, how they are combined, and the ratio of seats between tiers. Based on these conditions they come up with five general subtypes within this category of electoral system.

Many find linked or mixed-member proportional (MMP) systems to be somewhat more complicated.[14] In linked systems such as those in Germany and New Zealand, the PR tier is used to compensate for disproportional effects of the SMD tier. In general, in these systems the vote in the list (PR) tier determines the total number of seats a party is awarded. Again, for illustration's sake, we offer the following hypothetical linked system and scenario: Imagine that the system has 200 totals seats, with 100 of these seats determined by SMDs and 100 allocated as "compensation seats" through the PR tier. If the FRP were to win 30 percent of the list vote, it would be awarded roughly 30 percent *of all the seats*. In other words, it would be awarded 60 seats (i.e., 30 percent of 200). Imagine as well that the FRP were to win 40 SMDs. Under this scenario, those 40 individuals would represent their SMDs as members of the FRP. However, remember that the FRP had been allotted 60 total seats based on the PR tier vote, so "compensation" seats would be allocated to the top 20 candidates on the FRP party list (essentially, the PR tier list established by the FRP prior to the election). The remaining 60 SMDs and 80 compensation seats would be allocated to all other parties in the same way, based on their total share of the PR vote and the number of SMDs they won. Obviously, systems with linkage of this kind should lead to substantially more proportional results.

In our cases, Germany and New Zealand maintain the most comprehensive systems of compensation: the PR and SMD tiers hold roughly equal numbers of seats,[15] making it possible to use list tier compensation seats to make up for most disproportionality that might otherwise grow out of the SMD tier. The result is a distribution of seats almost fully controlled by the PR vote. These two systems also have the simplest forms of compensatory seats. A party's SMD seats are simply subtracted from the total number of seats it was allocated through the PR/list-tier votes it won.

However, the German/New Zealand approach is not the only way that countries can arrange the PR and SMD tiers of mixed-member electoral systems so that there is some link between the seats won in each tier. For example, Hungary's system of compensatory seats is extremely complicated. In Hungary, a tertiary tier of compensation seats stands above both the SMD tier and the territorial PR tier, and distributes a minimum of 58 seats to parties based on surplus votes not used to win seats in either the SMD or PR tiers. We classify this system as unlinked (with partial compensation) because the bulk of seats in the system are found in two tiers (local SMDs and territorial PR) that are

---

[14] This system is also called the *additional member system* and some have referred to Germany's as *personalized proportional representation* because parties' share of total seats is determined by the party list vote and SMD seats merely determine the specific individuals to fill half of those seats.

[15] In this sense, one might describe all seats as part of a nationwide set allocated to parties by PR rules, with SMDs helping to determine the individuals who fill half of those seats, and a tier of compensation seats (which we have been referring to as the *PR tier*) that ensure low levels of total disproportionality in the system.

not tied to each other. Parties keep all seats won in the territorial PR and the SMD tier. The small tertiary PR tier is used to compensate for "wasted votes" (votes not used to win seats) but does so for both the SMD and territorial PR tiers. Thus, unlike linked systems in Germany and New Zealand, the PR vote does not ultimately control the total number of seats that parties win in the legislature.

Italy's now-defunct mixed-member system provides an example of an even more indirect and less consequential method of interlocking PR and SMD tiers. In this system, there was no seat linkage between the tiers as there is in Germany or New Zealand. Instead, under the Italian mixed-member system, vote adjustments (*scorporo*) were made for every party of SMD-winning candidates. If a given party's candidate won an SMD seat, the number of votes (plus one) won by the second-place candidate in the district was subtracted from the winning party's vote in the PR tier.[16] In this way, each party in Italy had an "effective vote" in the list tier, equal to the number of list tier votes it received minus the sum of all the second place (plus one) vote totals from each of the SMDs in which its candidates won. This effective vote total was then used to determine the number of seats allocated to each party in the list tier.

In theory, the *scorporo* system could lead to compensation that would even provide an advantage for small parties over large ones, but in practice the system was highly majoritarian, emphasizing the SMD tier and reducing the more proportional elements of the system. It is possible that the system could help small parties substantially: for example, a second-place candidate could receive a large number of votes and the (often large) first-place party therefore might lose the equivalent of more than one PR seat worth of votes, thus disadvantaging the large party in PR more than a system of seat compensation would. However, in Italy, in general the margin of victory by SMD seat winners tended to be fairly large, reducing the impact of the vote adjustments in PR. Moreover, eventually many candidates ran attached to "decoy" party PR lists. These decoy party lists were intended purely to have vote adjustments from the SMD tier made to them (rather than the candidate's "true" party), but not attract the votes of genuine supporters of the candidate and his or her party in PR balloting. In addition, as Table 2.1 indicates and we discuss in greater detail later, the very large number of seats in SMDs relative to PR in Italy made it impossible for the list tier to overwhelm the disproportionality that emerged from the SMD tier. In this way, the linkage between the two tiers was much less powerful than the systems of seat linkage (such as in Germany and New Zealand), and we therefore code Italy as unlinked (with partial compensation).[17]

---

[16] The idea here is to subtract only the total number of votes that would have been required to win the SMD. For example, if an FRP candidate won an SMD where the second place candidate won 10,000 votes, the FRP would have 10,001 subtracted from its list tier vote total.

[17] Our characterization of Hungary's and Italy's mixed-member system as unlinked is in line with other scholars' classifications. Shugart and Wattenberg (2001b: 20–21) code both Hungary

Japan has a different type of linkage between the SMD and PR tiers – but one that does not determine the number of seats. As is common in many mixed-member systems, in Japan a candidate can run as both an SMD candidate and a candidate on the party PR list. However, unlike most other mixed systems, parties in Japan can rank multiple candidates at the same spot on the PR list. It is possible, for example, to place every candidate on the PR list in the top position, and the election results in the SMD tier then determine who gets the PR seats. Candidates who win their SMDs are removed from the PR list. The remaining candidates on the PR list are then placed in rank order according to how well they did in their SMD. The "best losers" from the SMD tier – that is, the candidates who win the largest number of votes as a percentage of the total taken by the winner in their SMD – get the highest rankings on the PR list.[18] However, this provision certainly has no bearing on our categorization of the Japanese case, as it is clearly an unlinked system. The best-loser rule has essentially no impact on the number of seats.[19]

Overhang Seats. It is possible under the linked/MMP system for a party to win more seats through the SMD tier than it is allocated through voting in the list tier. For example, imagine that the FRP wins 30 percent of the list vote, giving it 60 total seats, but then wins 70 SMDs. Depending on the specific system, the rules vary with respect to how to deal with this situation. The most well-known approach to this problem is that of Germany and New Zealand, whose rules would allow the FRP to keep its 10 "overhang" seats.[20] Under these systems, parties other than the FRP would be allocated a total number of seats equal to the number that they earned through list tier voting, and the entire legislature would be expanded to include any overhang seats won (Shugart and Wattenberg 2001b: 23–4). In the preceding example, the legislature would expand to 210 – rather than the predetermined 200 – seats for the duration of

and Italy as a mixed-member-majoritarian system (with partial compensation), which (aside from the "partial compensation") is the same classification as Japan, Russia, Ukraine, and other countries we consider unlinked systems. Ferrara (2004) notes that the PR tier had little impact on the SMD tier in Italy. Massicotte and Blais (1999: 357) state that Hungary's system "is chiefly a superimposition system" (unlinked using our terminology), but it is also partly corrective (linked) due to its tertiary tier.

To be sure, some scholars may disagree with our categorization of Hungary and Italy. For example, Massicotte and Blais (1999: 353–6) count Italy's system as a "corrective" system like Germany's and New Zealand's, in which the results of one tier are dependent on that of the other (similar to our notion of linkage). For this reason, wherever possible we introduce additional analysis with alternative coding schemes that treat Hungary and Italy as linked systems.

[18] For more details, see especially McKean and Scheiner (2000).

[19] In addition, linkage mechanisms typically gear actors toward more "PR-like" behavior (for example, because the system provides for greater proportionality and a reduction in problems related to wasted votes), but in Japan the best-loser rule gives more incentives for PR candidates to behave more like SMD candidates (McKean and Scheiner 2000). The best-loser provision therefore gives the system much more of an SMD "flavor," as do most unlinked systems in general.

[20] In German, these are referred to as *Überhangmandate*.

the legislative term. In recent years, overhang seats have not been unusual in Germany, although they typically have been relatively low in number.

Again, though, the rules surrounding overhang seats vary depending on the system. Bolivia, for example, uses a linked/MMP system, but does not include overhang seats. In Bolivia, the preceding scenario (an FRP winning 30 percent of the PR vote and 70 SMD victories) would lead to the FRP getting to maintain its 70 seats, but the legislature would not expand. Rather, the number of compensation seats would be cut accordingly, and parties other than the FRP would probably receive fewer total seats than their list vote percentage would have merited had the FRP not won the large number of SMDs (Mayorga 2001: 202–3).[21]

Electoral Formula

The electoral formula can be different for each tier of a mixed-member system. The PR tier can translate votes into seats according to a variety of different formulas (see Lijphart 1994; Taagepera and Shugart 1989). Although these differences do influence the proportionality of the PR tier and the system as a whole, the differences are relatively small, they come into play only in the translation of votes into seats (not voter behavior), and they are conditioned greatly by the district magnitude of the PR tier (discussed later).

The electoral formula for the SMD tier is more circumscribed but more consequential. Districts can either employ a plurality (FPTP) system, in which the candidate with the most votes wins the seat, or a majoritarian system (as used in Hungary, Lithuania, and Macedonia), which requires a candidate to win a majority of votes in a district to win election or a second, runoff, election is held. As we discuss in Chapter 3, we expect plurality and two-round majority rules to affect political outcomes differently. In particular, FPTP systems produce markedly greater incentives for strategic defection by voters and elites, and are therefore more likely to constrain the number of parties.

PR District Magnitude and Legal Threshold

Just as in pure PR systems, the district magnitudes and legal thresholds of representation in the PR tier influence how proportional the mixed-member system will be. Many of our country cases elect their PR seat holders in meaningful territorial districts, whereas the others distribute their PR seats in one nationwide district. Many PR systems (including a majority of those we examine here)

---

[21] Shugart and Wattenberg (2001b: 24) note that, when the PR tier is divided into multiple regional districts rather than one nationwide district, overhang seats would have the "disadvantage of increasing a region's share of legislative seats beyond its fixed quota." They therefore do not find it surprising that countries such as Bolivia, which use multiple PR districts, do not use overhang seats, whereas countries such as Germany and New Zealand, which use a system of nationwide compensation, allow for overhang without penalizing smaller parties.

impose some type of minimum legal threshold to attain representation.[22] For example, in Germany a party must win 5 percent of the PR vote to be eligible to win any seats.[23] In many of our quantitative analyses, we include a measure of a country's legal threshold of representation, with the expectation that higher thresholds should produce, for example, greater disproportionality.

SMD/PR Ratio

Finally, mixed-member systems also vary in the number of seats allocated to each tier of the system. Among the countries examined in this book, the most extreme examples of the ratio of SMD to PR seats are Croatia and Italy. The 1995 Croatian electoral system held only 28 SMDs to 80 PR seats, thus creating a principally PR-based system. In contrast, Italy's lower-house mixed-member system allocated 475 seats to SMDs, but only 155 to PR, which therefore gave relatively little weight to the proportional tier of the system. The relative size of each tier works in conjunction with linkage to shape the relative influence of PR and SMD rules on electoral outcomes and voting behavior. The larger the proportion of PR – or, for linked systems, compensation – seats, the more the PR/compensation tier can make up for disproportionality growing out of the SMD tier. The larger the proportion of the total number of seats devoted to the SMD tier, the greater will be the impact of SMDs on overall outcomes in the system.

CONCLUSIONS

We claim that mixed-member electoral systems provide a powerful analytical environment for the study of electoral systems. By combining party-list PR elections and contests between individual candidates in SMDs, these systems place the two major ways countries have organized elections side by side within the same environment. By comparing the relative differences between the PR and SMD tiers of mixed systems across a range of different countries, we can better isolate the effect of electoral rules by testing whether different types of electoral arrangements actually influence behaviors and outcomes as expected when simultaneously applied to the same voters, parties, candidates, and issues in the same election.

---

[22] Some mixed-member systems eliminate the legal threshold for any party that wins a set number of SMDs. In Germany, any party winning three or more SMDs is exempt from the 5 percent PR vote threshold that is usually necessary to be eligible for compensation seats. The same holds in New Zealand for any party that wins even a single SMD. However, to avoid too much complexity, we do not include this additional feature in our analysis.

[23] As Lijphart (1994: 25–30) has shown, legal thresholds and district magnitude work in the same way to constrain party proliferation by setting a vote threshold necessary to gain election: That is, all else being equal, higher district magnitudes require a smaller share of the vote in order to win seats.

We understand and acknowledge that the PR and SMD portions of mixed-member electoral systems do not operate in isolation from one another and that there are contamination effects in which the PR tier influences outcomes in the SMD tier and vice versa. Indeed, our examination of specific features of mixed-member systems such as linked tiers and the ratio of SMD to PR seats is based on the assumption that the extent to which the PR and SMD tiers are intertwined or walled off from each other makes a difference.

However, as we have discussed at length, we strongly disagree with those who argue that the existence of contamination invalidates controlled comparison of PR and SMD contests within mixed systems. Instead, we believe that comparative analyses of the differences (or lack thereof) in the outcomes produced in PR and SMD tiers are telling. The very fact that we find stark differences between outcomes in the PR and SMD portions of mixed-member systems undermines contamination arguments, because contamination should make outcomes in the two halves of these systems more alike. Much more important, our comparative analysis of a broad array of country cases clearly illustrates that the extent and nature of differences between outcomes under PR and SMD rules vary systematically depending on the political context. Outcomes such as the number of parties, strategic defection from weaker to stronger parties, and women's representation are starkly different in PR and SMD tiers in certain countries, whereas the difference between the two tiers is hardly discernible in others. The fact that we find similarities in patterns of outcomes under certain conditions strongly suggests that political context – and not contamination – is driving the variation in electoral system effects that we find.

APPENDIX 2. CROSS-NATIONAL ANALYSIS OF THE NUMBER OF PARTIES AT THE SMD LEVEL: SMDS IN MIXED-MEMBER SYSTEMS DO NOT HAVE MORE CANDIDATES THAN SMDS IN PURE SYSTEMS

As noted in the chapter, Matthew Singer (forthcoming) analyzes the number of candidates at the district level in 53 countries that use SMD elections. Controlling for other factors, including whether the country was a former Eastern bloc nation, Singer finds no statistically discernible difference between the number of candidates who run under pure FPTP and in the SMD tier of unlinked mixed-member systems. His analysis does suggest that the effective number of candidates is greater under linked mixed systems, which is consistent with our discussion of the weaker incentives for voters and elites to defect strategically in SMDs under such rules.

We replicate Singer's analysis with minor changes.[24] (See Table 2.2.) Because we are interested only in the difference between pure SMD and mixed-member

---

[24] In the model whose results we report, we code Hungary and Italy as unlinked systems, but also rerun the model with Hungary and Italy coded as linked systems, and our results do not change markedly (results not shown).

TABLE 2.2. *Multilevel Model of the (Logged) Effective Number of Parties Getting Votes in SMDs in 37 Systems That Use Either Pure FPTP or Mixed-Member Rules*

	Model 1		Model 2	
	Coef.	SE	Coef.	SE
Unlinked mixed systems	0.376	(0.165)*	0.148	(0.161)
Linked mixed systems	0.254	(0.141)	0.182	(0.125)
Former Eastern bloc			0.581	(0.188)*
Became democratic after 1989	0.152	(0.147)	−0.037	(0.143)
Concurrent plur. executive election	−0.009	(0.177)	−0.003	(0.154)
Concurrent maj. executive election	0.398	(0.362)	0.402	(0.316)
Ethnic fragmentation	0.256	(0.233)	0.267	(0.203)
Ln (Population)	0.007	(0.022)	0.020	(0.020)
Non-unitary country	0.077	(0.136)	0.048	(0.119)
Papua New Guinea	1.409	(0.326)*	1.373	(0.285)*
Constant	0.587	(0.146)*	0.557	(0.128)*
N	5,762		5,762	

* $p < 0.05$.
ID Variable: Country (37).
Unit of Analysis: SMD.
Dependent variable: Effective number of candidates at the SMD level (logged).

systems, we drop non-mixed system countries in which some districts have a single seat and other districts have higher district magnitudes. Because the independent variables include both country and subcountry level factors, like Singer we use a multilevel model as suggested by Jones (2008). More specifically, we use the Linear Mixed Model fit by REML provided by the lme4 package in R, with country as the ID variable.

Following Singer, our analysis includes the following variables: *Concurrent Plurality Executive Election*, a dummy variable controlling for concurrent plurality presidential elections, which is expected to constrain the number of district-level legislative candidates; *Concurrent Majority Executive Election*, a dummy variable for concurrent majoritarian presidential elections, which should increase the number of parties; and *Non-Unitary Country*, which controls for the effect of decentralization and is expected to have a positive impact on the number of parties.[25]

Like Singer, we also include five political and social variables that are expected to affect party system fragmentation. *Former Eastern Bloc* is a dichotomous variable for postcommunist states that emerged from under Soviet hegemony following the collapse of communist regimes in the late 1980s and early 1990s. As we argue throughout this book, we expect these countries to have larger numbers of candidates in SMDs owing to weak party institutionalization. *Became Democratic After 1989* is a dummy variable for countries

---

[25] We differ from Singer, who includes two other institutional variables, *double-ballot majority* and *PR/SNTV*, that were no longer applicable in our smaller sample.

that began holding competitive elections after 1989 – new democracies may require some time to reach equilibrium in their party systems following a democratic transition. *Ethnic Fragmentation* is a measure of ethnic hetero-geneity based on ethnic and linguistic diversity developed by Alesina et al. (2003).[26] *Ln(Population)* is the log of the national population. Finally, Papua New Guinea is a known outlier with an extremely large number of candidates per district in plurality elections; thus, we include a control variable, *Papua New Guinea*, to control for its influence.

We separate our key variable of interest, mixed-member systems, into two categories, *Unlinked Mixed Systems* and *Linked Mixed Systems*, to test whether the principal institutional difference within mixed-member systems – linkage between the PR and SMD tiers – has an effect on district-level party proliferation.

Our findings closely match those of Singer (forthcoming), but we find no statistically discernible difference between any kind of mixed-member system and pure FPTP systems. In Model 1, we include all the variables except *Former Eastern Bloc*. When not accounting for the effect of postcommunist states, we find a statistically significant and positive relationship between unlinked mixed systems and the number of parties within plurality districts, but linked systems do not display a similar statistically significant relationship. On its face, this finding would be difficult to explain because one would expect linked rather than unlinked mixed systems to be positively correlated with an increased number of parties, given the greater propensity for the PR tier to determine the final allocation of total seats in the system.

However, Model 2 provides the answer: Once we control for the impact of postcommunist states (*Former Eastern Bloc*), it is clear that there is no sta-tistically significant difference in the number of parties at the district level in plurality contests held in mixed-member systems (whether unlinked or linked) and those held in pure FPTP systems. Instead, the key finding is that our princi-pal variable that measures political context, *Former Eastern Bloc*, is positively correlated with the number of parties and statistically significant. The only other variable with a statistically significant coefficient in the model is *Papua New Guinea*.

---

[26] As we discuss in other chapters, most literature argues that social diversity should not affect the number of parties in restrictive electoral systems such as FPTP. In Chapters 1 and 7, we discuss the issue in greater detail and present evidence linking diversity and the number of parties even under FPTP.

3

How Democratic Experience and Party System Development Condition the Effects of Electoral Rules on Disproportionality and the Number of Parties

Theory, Measurement, and Expectations

Probably the most well-known literature on electoral systems highlights how electoral rules shape the number of parties (see especially Cox 1997; Duverger 1954; Lijphart 1994; Taagepera and Shugart 1989). We, therefore, begin our analysis by exploring how different rules affect the number of parties, but we then turn to how political context – in the form of democratic experience and party institutionalization – conditions the effects of rules.

In this chapter, we lay out the concepts necessary to explore the relationship between electoral rules, context, and the number of parties. First, we discuss the principal expectations about how electoral rules affect disproportionality (i.e., the extent to which parties' seat shares deviate from their share of the vote) and the number of parties. Second, we consider how democratic experience and party system development may condition these effects. Third, we explain how we measure the central variables – especially disproportionality, the effective number of parties, democratic experience, and party institutionalization. Finally, we discuss how specific institutional features of mixed-member systems might also shape the number of parties.

Cutting to the chase, and laying out our most important expectation, we expect restrictive electoral rules (especially FPTP) to be much less likely to constrain the number of parties in new democracies, especially those with poorly developed party systems, than in established democracies.

DUVERGER'S LAW AND THE EXPECTED EFFECTS OF ELECTORAL RULES

In Chapter 1, we laid out the central tenets of the most famous and important hypothesis in the study of electoral systems – Duverger's Law (Cox 1997; Duverger 1954; Riker 1982), which holds that first-past-the-post elections tend to have only two viable parties (or candidates). This district-level outcome is driven by a *mechanical effect* that denies representation to smaller parties because they are unable to attain the plurality of votes necessary to win election. Presumably arising from this mechanical effect is a *psychological effect*: supporters of smaller parties, who want to affect the outcome of elections and not "waste" their votes and/or resources, often defect strategically from their first choice to a candidate or party with better prospects, whereas weak candidates and parties, anticipating such behavior and mindful about wasting scarce resources on a losing race, will choose not to run.

Less well known is Duverger's Hypothesis, which holds that both two-round majority rules and PR rules tend to produce multiparty systems (Duverger 1986: 70). In two-round majority systems, the electoral process formally winnows the number of candidates down: typically, unless one candidate wins a majority of the vote, the top vote-winning candidates (usually the top two, but in some cases it is more) move on to a second round of voting. The top vote-getter in the second round of balloting then wins the seat. In two-round systems, voters can vote for their preferred candidate in the first round and, if the candidate does not make it past that round, voters can then vote for the "lesser of two evils" in the second round. As a result, in the first round of elections there is less incentive to strategically defect – in other words, less reason to cast a ballot or provide resources to a candidate other than one's own top choice in order to affect the outcome of the race – and less reason for parties and candidates to strategically exit the first-round race before it even begins. In this way, the psychological winnowing-down effect that is part of plurality elections (and Duverger's Law) is much weaker in two-round majority contests.[1]

In PR systems, parties typically win seats in proportion to their share of the vote. As a result, the effective threshold to win seats is lower, resulting in more parties capable of gaining legislative representation. Consequently, there is likely to be less strategic defection by voters and elites away from their most preferred party (or candidate) to try to affect the race under PR rules. Moreover, because parties can win seats with relatively small shares of the vote, small parties will be less likely to exit the race strategically under PR rules. Assuming, then, different parties are present to represent multiple different interests in society, in PR a larger number of parties ought to gain votes and seats than would be the case under plurality rules.

Differences in district magnitude (often denoted simply as M), the number of representatives elected from a district, explain much of the difference in the number of parties between SMDs (especially FPTP) and PR (Taagepera and Shugart 1989; Cox 1997).[2] An important mechanism by which electoral systems affect the number of parties is disproportionality – the degree to which

---

[1] In fact, many candidates and parties who are likely to lose may choose to contest the first-round race anyway because they can then, in the second round, trade their support base to one of the leading candidates in exchange for some favor(s).

[2] Cox's (1997) and Reed's (1990) analyses suggest that the number of parties will be capped at the district magnitude plus one. This "$M + 1$ rule" (sometimes called Reed's Rule) regarding district magnitude and the number of district-level parties suggests that all electoral systems affect party systems in basically the same way; the central difference between PR and plurality elections, then, is simply the number of seats.

parties' shares of votes equal their shares of legislative seats. The less a system promotes a close matching of votes and seats, the more disproportional it is, and scholars find that district magnitude is the decisive influence on disproportionality (Taagepera and Shugart 1989). Low magnitudes, especially single-seat districts, usually constrain the number of parties because they produce high disproportionality at the district level – mechanically favoring the top vote winners – and, in turn, inspiring a psychological effect away from contestants who are unlikely to gain representation. If used in conjunction with low legal thresholds of representation (i.e., the minimum vote share legally mandated to win seats), high-magnitude systems are referred to as *permissive* because they permit even small parties to gain seats. Permissive, high-magnitude systems, therefore, should lead to lower levels of disproportionality and greater proliferation of parties (Taagepera and Shugart 1989; Lijphart 1994).[3]

Disproportionality is usually referred to as a mechanical effect of electoral rules; however, in reality, the psychological effect can also shape the level of disproportionality. Rules that make it hard for small parties to win representation – such as FPTP and PR with low district magnitude or a high legal threshold of representation – are considered "restrictive." If, under restrictive rules, small parties continue to contest elections and voters continue to cast ballots for them, disproportionality will be higher than when elites and voters defect strategically to more competitive options. Conversely, if voters and elites respond "appropriately" (i.e., strategically) to the incentives of what are ordinarily highly disproportional systems, disproportionality should actually drop. In this way, the psychological effect of electoral rules can actually reduce the size of the perceptible mechanical effect.

The constraining effect of electoral systems resides most directly at the district level rather than at the national level (Cox 1997; Sartori 1986: 54–55). That is, the core logic of mechanical and psychological effects of electoral rules involves the behavior of political actors within the district in which votes are cast and seats are allocated. Strategic voting under FPTP rules, for example, is usually seen as an effort to win the single seat being contested within the district.

Moreover, even if conditions are favorable for establishing Duvergerian two-candidate races at the district level, we may not see the "projection" of district-level competition to a two-party system at the national level. National projection depends on parties' ability to unite prominent elites across many different districts in single nationwide party organizations. Without projection, the two candidates produced in each SMD may belong to many different parties across the country. Cox cites institutional factors, most notably the direct election of a powerful national executive, as the primary forces behind such nationalization (Cox 1997: 182–193; Cox 1999).[4]

---

[3] For an interesting analysis of how to use district magnitude to balance different electoral aims, see Carey and Hix's (2011) work, which suggests that "low" magnitude PR – especially between three and eight seats – provides a relatively high level of both proportionality and accountability.

[4] For additional insightful analyses of factors that may nationalize party systems, see, among others, Chhibber and Kollman (1998, 2004), who discuss the nationalizing force of central

DUVERGER'S LAW IS FOUNDED ON THE ASSUMPTION
OF WIDESPREAD INFORMATION

Ultimately, the expectation of more strategic defection by voters and elites under plurality rules than under PR leads analysts to predict substantial differences between outcomes under FPTP and PR rules, but this expectation is founded on an assumption that will not always be met. Most notably, Duverger's Law assumes that voters and elites have enough information to distinguish among different candidates' likelihood of success, which in turn makes it possible to shift support strategically from likely losers to viable contestants under FPTP. However, the availability of such information varies, especially across different countries. How does variation in the amount of information affect outcomes under FPTP balloting? What is the effect on the number of parties if voters and elites cannot anticipate likely outcomes?

Cox (1997: 79) argues cogently that underlying Duverger's Law are contextual conditions that provide voters and elites the necessary resources and motivations to defect strategically from their top choice under FPTP rules. Among these conditions, Cox points to the importance of information, highlighting that plurality elections may not reduce the vote for minor parties if the public lacks knowledge about voter preferences and vote intentions. Without such information, there is insufficient sense about which candidates are "out of the running," thus undermining both voters' capacity to defect from weak candidates and candidates' incentive to leave the race.[5] This precondition of sufficient and widespread knowledge necessary for strategic defection at the district level is much less likely to hold during the initial elections in new democracies, especially in cases with little democratic tradition.

There Is Usually Less Reliable Information in New Democracies, so Electoral Rules May Not Have Their Expected Effects

There are many reasons that new democracies may lack the information necessary for widespread strategic behavior by elites and voters. To begin with, voters and elites in new democracies have far less experience playing the game of democratic politics, and therefore usually require time to become sufficiently familiar with the system to be able to act fully strategically. Furthermore, compared with established democracies, new democracies tend to have less well-developed media institutions (Mickiewicz 1997, 2008) and public opinion polling (Oates 2005, 2006). As a result, it is harder to develop reliable estimates of public support for different electoral options – information that is needed to know when to withdraw support from one party or candidate, and to whom to

---

government power, and Hicken and Stoll (2011), who highlight in detail how presidential elections can lead legislative parties to coordinate across districts.

[5] Cox (1997: 79) also highlights three other conditions under which FPTP may not reduce the vote for minor parties: (1) many voters who are not short-term instrumentally rational; (2) widespread certainty regarding likely winners; and (3) the presence of many voters who strongly prefer their first choice and, thus, are nearly indifferent to other choices.

shift support. In addition, established democracies usually provide more stable and certain political environments, whereas in new democracies, the political context is markedly more fluid, with greater party volatility between elections (Mainwaring and Zoco 2007). Such volatility also makes it hard to gain reliable information about likely support patterns in any given election, thus further hindering the ability to behave strategically. As a result of the less reliable bases of electoral information, restrictive electoral rules such as FPTP ought to be less likely to constrain the number of parties in new democracies.

Poorly Developed Party Systems Help Contribute to the Pattern in New Democracies

Although less obvious than the preceding list, the prevalence of weak parties, or what Mainwaring and Scully (1995) call *weak party institutionalization*, also contributes to the informational void found in new democracies and generally reduces the likelihood of strategic defection in electoral contests by voters and elites.[6]

Most directly, strong, well-structured parties transmit information about themselves and their opponents to the public, both through mass appeals and by working through their organizations to mobilize potential supporters. Once such parties exist, the media become more likely to cover the policy positions and likelihood of success of the different party alternatives. Without strong parties to structure the vote, elections lack a fairly simple signal that helps cue voters about the relative competitiveness of different candidates. If parties are not institutionalized, candidates lack the stable constituencies and well-developed social ties that provide cues about the candidates' viability – even when there is widespread and reliable public opinion polling. In turn, voters and elites are less likely to have reliable expectations about the relative competitiveness of the different candidates.

Poorly developed party systems are typically marked by weaker party identification among voters (see, e.g., Ames et al. 2009, Baker et al. 2006), so voting depends on the personal characteristics of candidates and the patronage they distribute. The personal vote can involve deep-seated biases against certain candidates based on factors such as candidates' identity (gender or ethnicity, for example) or something in their record or general personality. Such biases may push voters to stick with a preference that is likely to lose rather than shift to an unacceptable, but more competitive, alternative. Attachments to candidates based on the patronage that they provide may prevent strategic defection because many supporters will be unwilling to shift to a different candidate out of fear of losing a promised reward.

Some strong parties promote strategic behavior by actually advocating it. Larger parties can appeal to supporters of smaller parties on strategic grounds,

---

[6] We discuss party system institutionalization and how we operationalize this concept at length later in this chapter.

urging them not to waste their votes on a "sure loser" or, worse yet, inadvertently create a "spoiler effect," in which divisions within the camp of their most preferred candidate lead to the election of their least-favorite alternative.

Moreover, well-developed parties provide a better basis for rank-ordering preferences than do independents or weak parties. A party system comprising parties with well-established reputations, social constituencies, and "brand name effects" (see Aldrich 1995) provides supporters with a menu of choices that offer clear criteria on which to rank preferences. One can defect from a first choice that is less competitive to a second choice that is acceptable and more competitive only if parties have established identities and reputations capable of providing meaningful and stable information about differences between electoral options. Party systems dominated by independents or marked by extreme volatility that present voters with new choices at every election cycle make such rank ordering much more difficult.

In short, the absence of well-established parties ought to produce different incentives for both voters and elites from what we see in more stable electoral contexts with parties that clearly structure the vote. If strong parties are an essential source of information for elites and voters, then electoral systems should have very different effects when operating within a political environment of weak parties than when they are found within a well-established party system. If, in the absence of strong parties, voters and elites have no strong sense of who might win a district race, they should be less likely to defect from their first preference, as their preferred candidate might, in fact, have a chance to capture the seat. Without strategic defection by voters and elites to consolidate electoral competition, there is apt to be a perception of a wide-open race, which in turn ought to prompt more candidates and parties to throw their hats into the ring (Filippov et al. 1999, Moser 2001a). As a result, even under FPTP rules there is likely to be a proliferation of candidates in new democracies – especially in those with poorly developed party systems.

To some degree, this discussion simply indicates that restrictive electoral rules generally ought to be less likely to constrain the number of parties in new democracies, but it also highlights that the constraining effects of electoral rules should be weakest where party systems are poorly institutionalized.

The Potential for Getting Stuck (in Non-Duvergerian Equilibrium) in New Democracies

In one sense, this discussion is simply a statement that electoral rules are unlikely to have their expected effects in political systems that are not in "equilibrium" – an argument that is hardly new or controversial within the literature.[7] That is, most theories – such as Duverger's Law – of the effects of electoral rules

---

[7] On the other hand, this is a point missed by many voters and politicians in polities that institute new rules and are disappointed when the outcomes do not immediately match the results that are common under equilibrium conditions.

set up expectations for the outcomes that are likely once political actors (such as voters, candidates, and parties) have grown accustomed to a particular system, learned to respond appropriately to the system's incentives, and gained information on the likely behavior of other political actors. Once such learning occurs, voters and elites ought to enter into an equilibrium in which they have little reason to buck the incentives created by the rules, and outcomes will closely match the expectations of most electoral system theories. For example, with time and learning, voters and elites under FPTP rules ought to defect strategically from low-ranking candidates, and the number of viable contestants will winnow down to the small numbers expected by Duverger's Law. With party institutionalization, electoral volatility will, on average, decline, party reputations will emerge, and candidates from large parties will win repeated elections within plurality districts. These patterns should further deter new entrants from entering the race in the first place, and raise skepticism among voters and donors of the viability of any new entrants who do decide to compete.

However, weaker democratic structural roots and party systems may actually mean that some new democracies will take longer to enter into the expected electoral system equilibrium. The lower levels of information in new democracies – especially when the party system is poorly institutionalized – may make it difficult to differentiate between the likely success of any candidate, thus giving many supporters of low-ranking candidates little incentive to defect from their top preference. If weak parties prevail and extreme electoral volatility ensues, a reputation of wide-open contests within districts may take hold and provide a set of incentives that even promote new entrants. As a result of this "non-Duvergerian equilibrium" (Cox 1997), under FPTP rules there may be much less of a shift over time toward the more commonly expected two viable candidates per district. In short, disequilibrium – or, more accurately, a different type of equilibrium – in new democracies can last a long time and may not fade simply with repeated iterations of competitive elections. The pattern of party proliferation may even reinforce itself if the lack of party identification, party structuring, and strategic defection promote a heavily divided vote in SMDs. With multiple viable contestants, SMDs can be won with a small share of the vote, thus reinforcing the perception that anyone can win the race. In turn, additional candidates may enter the race, and supporters of even candidates who are likely to win only a small number of votes will have reason to continue to back their top choice.

Disproportionality and "Projection" in New Democracies. As we discussed earlier, disproportionality is not merely a mechanical effect. Disproportionality will be greater under restrictive rules if the mechanical effect favoring large parties does not induce a psychological effect away from small parties. When information about likely electoral behavior is limited, even under restrictive rules, many parties may continue to contest elections and voters may continue to cast ballots for those parties. If so, many parties may receive substantial numbers of votes but no seats. In this way, restrictive electoral rules in new democracies – especially those with poorly developed party systems – may lead to even higher levels of disproportionality than in established democracies.

In addition, the effect of poorly developed parties can extend even beyond the number of district-level competitors and shape the extent to which district-level outcomes "project" to the national level. On one level, in new democracies, FPTP rules may produce very fragmented district-level contests between many candidates. Failure to constrain the number of candidates in SMDs is also apt to reverberate throughout the country, as the weak party system means that parties may have a hard time coordinating across districts, thus leading to different parties competing in different districts and, therefore, a larger number of parties in the legislature.

Summary of Expectations for New Democracies

In sum, this discussion suggests that it would be a mistake to assume that institutional effects found in established democracies will be replicated in the very different context of new democracies in East Europe, Eurasia, and Latin America. More specifically, compared with those in established democracies, electoral rules in new democracies – especially those with poorly institutionalized party systems – ought to lead to the following:

1. Higher levels of disproportionality
2. Larger numbers of candidates per district under plurality rules
3. A larger gap between the number of parties competing in each district, on average, and the total number competing anywhere across the country (i.e., less projection)

MEASURING DISPROPORTIONALITY AND THE NUMBER OF PARTIES

This book focuses on mixed-member systems as the simultaneous use of PR and SMD electoral rules; our analysis in Chapter 4 will examine disproportionality and the number of parties in 15 countries and 52 elections under mixed-member system rules. (See Table 2.1 for additional details on the countries.) The combination of two types of rules in a single system undoubtedly promotes some "contamination," whereby the presence of one set of rules can affect behavior under the simultaneously coexisting other set of rules. However, as we demonstrate in Chapter 2, this contagion does not critically undermine our controlled comparison approach. We therefore emphasize the autonomous effects of each tier of the mixed-member system: when possible, we calculate the least-squares index of disproportionality and the effective number of parties for each tier of the mixed system, as well as the system as a whole.[8]

---

[8] In linked systems, the PR tier's effective number of parliamentary parties (N_s) and the level of disproportionality are fairly nonsensical, so we do not report values for them. Because of the

The least-squares index of disproportionality (LSq) is a commonly used measure of the degree to which electoral outcomes are proportional: LSq measures how much each party's share of the seats deviates from its share of the vote. As the principal measure of the mechanical effect of electoral rules, disproportionality tends to be highest in plurality/majoritarian SMD systems, which penalize small parties and reward large ones, and lowest in PR systems with large district magnitudes and low legal thresholds of representation. More specifically, the LSq is calculated by squaring the difference in the percentage (e.g., 10 [percent] rather than 0.10) of votes and seats won by each party and then adding them together; this total is divided by 2; and then the square root of this value is taken (see Lijphart 1994: 57–72; Taagepera and Shugart 1989: 77–81, 104–105):

$$LSq = \sqrt{\frac{1}{2}\Sigma(v_i - s_i)^2}$$

For example, if we treat the 2008 U.S. presidential election as a national plurality SMD,[9] the election had an enormously high LSq score of 46.4.[10] The election had two genuine contestants, but of course only one could take the single seat (i.e., win 100 percent of the seats). Similarly, if we consider votes cast in the first round of voting in France's 2002 presidential election as a two-round majority SMD, that election had an even higher LSq score of 59.9. The election had a large number of contestants – 15 different candidates won at least 1 percent of the vote in first-round balloting, with three gaining more than 16 percent, and no candidate reaching 20 percent – but, again, only one candidate could win the single seat up for grabs. In contrast, in the 2009 proportional representation election to the 120-seat Israeli legislature, we see an LSq score of 1.4. Here, the election had a large number of contestants, but nearly all received a share of seats that closely matched their share of the vote.

In measuring the number of parties, electoral system scholars usually do not provide a count of all parties competing (or winning seats) in a given election. Counting all parties (or candidates) suggests that each is just as important in the election as all others, so scholarship often uses the Laakso-Taagepera (1979) effective number of parties (N) score, which provides a measure of party system fractionalization by counting parties weighted by their national shares of votes or seats. The effective number of parties index is calculated by squaring the proportion (e.g., 0.10 rather than 10 [percent]) of the vote or seat shares of each party, adding together the squared shares for each party or candidate, and

use of compensation seats, parties that win a large proportion of the PR vote will receive very few seats in the PR (compensation) tier if they also take a large number of SMDs.

[9] To be sure, the United States uses an electoral college that allocates electors by state. However, in de facto terms, U.S. presidential elections usually function as national plurality elections. Moreover, the elements that make the U.S. presidential electoral system different from standard FPTP rules do not change the basic Duvergerian incentives provided by plurality systems.

[10] All the examples that we compute in this section exclude any party or candidate that receives less than 1 percent of the vote.

then dividing 1 by this sum (see Laakso and Taagepera 1979; Lijphart 1994: 57–72; Taagepera and Shugart 1989: 77–81, 104–105):

$$N_v = 1/\Sigma\left(v_i^2\right) \text{ or } N_s = 1/\Sigma\left(s_i^2\right)$$

N_v provides a measure of the number of *electoral* parties (or candidates) – that is, the number of parties that win votes. N_v can include parties or candidates that win votes, but no legislative seats. In contrast, N_s provides a measure of the number of *legislative* parties – that is, the number of parties that win seats.

The 2009 election in Israel again provides a useful example to indicate the importance of using the effective number of parties measure. Thirty-three parties won more than 500 votes in the 2009 Israeli legislative election, but only twelve won more than 1 percent of the vote, and only two won more than 20 percent of the vote. Despite the large number of parties that contested the race, according to the Laakso-Taagepera measure the effective number of electoral parties (i.e., parties winning votes) score was only 7.4. Twelve parties won seats, but only four won more than 10 percent of all seats, and only two won more than 20 percent. According to the Laakso-Taagepera measure, the effective number of legislative parties (i.e., parties winning seats) score was 6.8.

THE MIXED-MEMBER SYSTEM DATASET THAT WE USE

We calculate disproportionality and the effective number of parties measures for each election in each country for which we could acquire data (a total of 52 country/elections), and list the values at the end of Chapter 4 in Appendix 4A. For each country/election, we measure separately the disproportionality index, the effective number of electoral parties, and the effective number of legislative parties for the SMD tier [LSq (SMD), N_v (SMD), and N_s (SMD)], PR tier [LSq (PR), N_v (PR), and N_s (PR)], and system as a whole [LSq (Overall), N_v (Overall), and N_s (Overall)]. We calculate each of these measures using the number of votes and seats won by each party aggregated across the entire country in a given election.

We should note that in Chapter 4 in our analysis of N_v (SMD) – the effective number of electoral parties (based on vote share) in the SMD tier – we drop Armenia, Russia, and Ukraine. In Armenia, Russia, and Ukraine, independent candidates win a huge share of the SMD vote. In our measure of N_v, we treat all independents as a single residual category, which artificially reduces the effective number of parties measure because independents usually do not behave as a unit. However, this issue is not a problem in our most important analyses, which examine *district-level* outcomes and are thus unaffected by our measurement of independents at the *national* level.

To examine the district-level effect of SMD rules on the number of competitors, we calculate the effective number of SMD candidates per district (N_{cands}, the mean effective number of candidates for all districts in a given country/election). We also use the proportion of votes each party wins in PR balloting within each SMD to calculate the mean SMD-level effective number of PR parties ($N_{parties}$). The calculation of the effective number of candidates per district for the SMD tier – particularly when compared with the effective number of parties per single-member district under PR balloting – provides a good measure of the district-level constraining effect of SMD rules. N_{cands} and $N_{parties}$ are computed as N_v is, except that computations are made for, respectively, all candidates and parties competing within a given district and then taking the average for all SMDs across the country.

Expectations

Within most countries, we expect the mechanical and psychological effects to lead to a relatively small (effective) number of electoral candidates (or parties) under FPTP rules, with larger numbers of parties in PR, which would be consistent with the general pattern in pure FPTP and PR systems: For example, in the 2008 U.S. presidential election, there was an effective number of electoral parties/candidates score of 2.05, markedly lower than the score of 7.4 in the 2009 Israeli legislative election under high-magnitude PR rules. We also expect a substantial difference in the effect of FPTP and PR rules on disproportionality within mixed-member systems. As we showed in our comparison of the 2008 U.S. presidential election and Israel's 2009 legislative election, disproportionality tends to be markedly lower under high-magnitude PR systems.

In the example in which we calculated LSq for a presidential election held under FPTP rules, we calculated disproportionality for a single district, but when there are multiple districts scholars, typically compute the level of disproportionality for the entire country. When we calculate disproportionality across multiple SMDs (which is what we do in Appendix 4A), LSq (SMD) will usually be markedly lower than in a single district. That is, in a single SMD, whoever wins is awarded 100 percent of the district seat, thus introducing significant disproportionality. In contrast, when we calculate disproportionality across numerous districts, the election is no longer entirely winner-take-all. For example, if we aggregate the results of each of the 2008 U.S. SMD House of Representatives elections, LSq (SMD) drops to 4.3. Nevertheless, even this score is higher than the 1.4 witnessed in Israel in 2009.

Aggregate LSq scores for U.S. House SMD races highlight that disproportionality is not just a mechanical effect. The various rules used in the United States to promote a two-party system elicit a strong psychological effect, whereby voters and elites give little attention to parties outside the Republicans and Democrats. As a result, when aggregated across all districts, N_v and N_s both consistently approximate two, thus leading to low LSq (SMD) scores. In the 2000 House election, for example, both parties received roughly 47 percent of the vote nationally (whereas the Libertarian Party won 1.6 percent), with the Democrats taking 49 percent of seats and the Republicans winning 51 percent. The LSq score was 2.97.

DEMOCRATIC EXPERIENCE AND PARTY SYSTEM
INSTITUTIONALIZATION: MEASUREMENT AND EXPECTATIONS

As we discussed earlier, new democracies are apt to lack reliable information about likely electoral outcomes and support patterns, thus cutting into the amount of strategic defection by voters and elites and weakening the constraining effects of restrictive electoral rules. The result is likely to be larger numbers of parties even under FPTP rules and greater disproportionality.

What Is a "New" Democracy?

In our study of mixed-member electoral systems we establish a blunt dividing line separating new and established democracies – the so-called third wave of democratization. Our data are drawn from elections in the 1990s and early 2000s; we define a country as a new democracy if it experienced a democratic transition in 1978 or later (Mainwaring and Zoco 2007). From postcommunist states, our measure of new democracies includes Albania, Armenia, Bulgaria, Croatia, Hungary, Lithuania, Macedonia, Russia, and Ukraine, which experienced the bulk of their democratic transitions in the 1990s. From Latin America, we include Bolivia, which experienced its democratic transition beginning in 1979 and culminating in 1982 (Mayorga 2001: 195; Mainwaring and Zoco 2007: 160). In our data sets, established democracies include Germany, Italy, New Zealand, Scotland, Wales, Japan, and Venezuela, which democratized in 1958 (Mainwaring and Zoco 2007: 160).

What Is a Noninstitutionalized Party System?

In many new democracies, strong parties develop relatively quickly and soon help structure the vote, but such party institutionalization is not universal. Institutionalized parties are those that maintain organizational continuity; develop relatively stable support, ideological consistency, and party legitimacy over time; and hold significant control over nominations (Mainwaring 1999: 27–39).

The countries examined in this book vary in their democratic history and their level of party institutionalization. Many of the countries – including some of the new democracies – have political systems highly structured by parties, but a number of the new democracies – especially among the postcommunist states of the former Soviet Union – suffered from electoral volatility and undeveloped political parties that had very little historical foundation and did not structure the electoral process. Parties in these countries faced difficulty structuring the vote, meaning that they were not the predominant vehicles through which candidates ran for office or attracted votes. In other words, where parties were not well institutionalized, candidates were less likely to run under the heading of a party banner, and significant shares of the vote went to independent candidates – that is, those unaffiliated with any party.

We therefore use the presence of significant independent candidacies as a proxy for a lack of party institutionalization, classifying cases in which independent candidates receive very large shares of the (SMD) vote and seats as noninstitutionalized cases.[11] Of course, a large proportion of independent candidates is only one of several possible indicators of weak political parties (Mainwaring and Scully 1995; Mainwaring 1999). However, as we argue later, we believe this single indicator of a noninstitutionalized party system provides a reliable marker that highlights significant differences in the degree of party development within our broader category of new democracies. In our data set, three countries – Armenia, Russia, and Ukraine – fall into the noninstitutionalized category. There are certainly independent candidacies in established democracies, such as New Zealand and, especially, Japan, but there is a huge gulf between party systems such as those we see in countries such as Armenia, Russia, and Ukraine and those in the more established systems.

Independents win less than 10 percent of the vote in Japan, but in Russia officially nonpartisan candidates took 58 percent of the SMD vote in 1993, 36 percent in 1995, 49 percent in 1999, and 47 percent in 2003. Independents in Russia not only made up a large proportion of candidates competing for office, but they also accounted for the largest proportion of the winners. Fifty-two percent of winners were independents in the 1993 Russian elections, 34 percent in 1995, 46 percent in 1999, and 35 percent in 2003. Ukraine and Armenia had similarly high levels of nonpartisanship in their SMD tiers, with 47 and 42 percent of the SMD vote going to independents in Ukraine in 1998 and 2002, respectively, and 37 percent in Armenia in 1999.

Moreover, even beyond the issue of whether candidates can credibly run and win as independents, the party systems of these three countries are clearly not well developed. Party identification is very weak compared with that in Western democracies, and information in the form of polls tracking the relative strength of individual candidates' support in the SMD tier was late to emerge on a systematic basis (as opposed to polls on party support in PR balloting, which developed more quickly). In addition, our identification of the Russian, Ukrainian, and Armenian party systems during the 1990s as noninstitutionalized coincides with the work of other scholars who have also depicted states of the former Soviet Union as having weaker party systems than their Eastern European counterparts (Evans and Whitefield 1993; Kitschelt 1995).[12]

In other words, in this book we characterize countries as falling into one of three categories: established democracy, new democracy with a relatively institutionalized party system, or new democracy with a noninstitutionalized party system. In reality, democratic experience and party development form a continuum on which countries can range from well-established democracies with highly institutionalized party systems to those with almost no democratic

---

[11] No country in our study required candidates in SMD races to run under a partisan label.

[12] Mainwaring and Zoco's (2007: 160) study of electoral volatility showed that Russia and Ukraine possessed among the highest levels of party system volatility. Armenia was not included in their study.

experience and party systems that provide no stability or cues to help voters and elites make electoral decisions. It is unclear precisely how one would develop such a continuous measure, but it is also not clear that it would even be necessary for our purposes to do so. We do not suggest that each minor shift in democratic experience ought to bring about shifts in the likelihood that electoral rules will have their expected effects, but instead expect significant differences between our three different distinct categories: (1) new democracies with relatively institutionalized party systems (Bolivia, Croatia, Hungary, Lesotho, Lithuania, and Macedonia) ought to have fewer parties at the district level than (2) new democracies with noninstitutionalized party systems (Armenia, Russia, and Ukraine), but significantly more parties in SMDs than (3) established democracies (Germany, Italy, Japan, New Zealand, Scotland, Venezuela, and Wales).

A Note on the Issue of Endogeneity

Some may wonder whether the concept of party institutionalization creates an endogeneity problem for us: some readers might criticize our placement of aspects of the party system on both sides of the equation – that is, party institutionalization as an independent variable and party fragmentation as a dependent variable. Similarly, some critics might suggest that our coding of noninstitutionalized party systems as those in which independent candidates win a large share of the vote means that such systems will have a large number of independent candidates, which, in turn, increases the total number of candidates/parties.

However, we believe that such critiques would be a misreading of our analysis. To argue that parties serve as both cause and effect in our framework incorrectly conflates two distinct elements of a party system – party system institutionalization and party fragmentation. Contexts in which independents receive a larger share of the vote do not necessarily promote large numbers of candidates/parties. Even when a large share of the vote goes to independent candidates, in many cases these votes go to only a small number of very popular candidates. For example, among the established democracies in our dataset, Japan has easily the largest share of the vote going to independent candidates, but the average effective number of candidates per SMD in Japan is among the lowest (and drops down to 2.26 in its fifth election under mixed system rules in 2009). Conversely, FPTP elections with many viable candidates are not always marked by a large vote for independents.

Indeed, rather than conflating weak party institutionalization with party fragmentation, we are asserting that weak parties are one of the primary sources of the lack of information that undermines strategic behavior. In our view, party institutionalization is a useful construct that highlights the important role parties may play in providing electoral information and cues, and thus may make possible – and the lack of strong parties may undermine – strategic behavior and two-candidate competition under plurality rules. In this way, we believe that highlighting the significance of party institutionalization improves on previous notions of the conditions that undermine Duverger's Law: debates over the desirability of particular electoral systems for new democracies center uniformly on issues of party fragmentation and disproportionality, and assume that plurality elections will penalize small parties and constrain the number of parties, even in regions with nascent party systems (see Lijphart 1991; Lardeyret 1991; Reynolds and Carey 2012). When plurality elections do not produce two-candidate contests, scholars often explain the outcome as due to a failure to reach a "stable equilibrium." For example, Clark and Golder (2006: 702) attribute their findings that district magnitude and ethnic heterogeneity do not have their expected effects on party fragmentation in countries that experienced democratic transitions in the 1990s to the fact that party systems may not have reached such an equilibrium. We agree, but argue that variables such as "party system equilibrium," which we conceptualize in part as party system institutionalization, deserve much greater attention as a factor that promotes the acquisition of electoral information.

Finally, and most important, we should highlight that a lack of party institutionalization is simply an extreme version of a different variable – democratic inexperience – that is unlikely to face the same sorts of questions about endogeneity. We argue – and show in Chapters 4 through 6 – that new democracies, in general, experience party fragmentation in plurality elections; and, arguably, most of these new democracies have reasonably well-formed party systems.[13] In essence, we argue that information deficits make it more difficult to differentiate between strong and weak electoral competitors, thus hindering strategic defection by voters and elites and increasing party fragmentation in plurality elections. For the reasons we discussed in this chapter, such information deficits are more prevalent in new democracies than in established ones, and noninstitutionalized party systems simply further exacerbate the information deficit problem.

We Place Each Country into a Single Category for *All* Its Elections

Of course, countries evolve. New democracies become more established and, at some point, they are no longer "new." For example, Hungary's party system solidified around several relatively large and stable parties after its second election, although the fortunes of parties and broader ideological camps continued to fluctuate over time. In addition, noninstitutionalized party systems develop over time. In particular, in Russia, the emergence of a strong "party of power," United Russia, in the early 2000s (Colton and McFaul 2000) meant a greater

---

[13] True, things were "worse" in Russia or Ukraine in the sense that their party systems were so underdeveloped in the 1990s that they experienced extreme candidate fragmentation under FPTP. This is precisely why we consider both party institutionalization and new democracies as causal variables of party fragmentation. However, even in the 2003 Russian election, when a large party – United Russia – emerged and more "partyness" inhabited the system, a Duvergerian equilibrium remained out of reach.

presence for political parties, which in turn reduced the number of candidates at the district level in SMDs (although not to levels close to two-candidate competition).

To be sure, during the end of the period we examine, some new democracies (especially Hungary) had come to resemble established democracies in many ways, but continuing to code them as new democracies does not cause significant problems for our analysis. If anything, maintaining countries within the original categories simply presents a harder test of our claim that electoral rules have different effects in different types of democracies. If new democracies such as Hungary become more like established democracies in later years, then we should be less likely to find a difference between new and established democracies.

In addition, with the important exception of Germany, we examine only the first several elections after a mixed-member system has been introduced. Established democracies were still well established at that point, and new democracies had mostly not yet become fully developed democratically. Given that we do not have a large number of elections for many of these countries (except Germany) and our time period coincides with broad distinctions between these two types of democratic regimes, using this blunt dichotomy of new (third wave) democracies and established democracies is a good proxy for differences between these broad and internally diverse categories of states.

Finally, there is good reason to believe that, even with changes over time, each country fits well into the category into which we originally placed it. Although it is difficult to say precisely when a new democracy should no longer be considered "new" or a noninstitutionalized party system has transformed into an institutionalized one, there are clear indicators, and these indicators suggest the usefulness of our categories. For new democracies, a sustained lower level of party system volatility could be a good indicator of becoming "established." It should be noted that although Hungary had a more stable and developed party system than the other new democracies we examine, its average electoral volatility was significantly greater than the established democracies of Germany, New Zealand, Italy, and Japan (Mainwaring and Zoco 2007: 159). We are therefore comfortable with Hungary's designation as a new democracy throughout the period under investigation. As far as determining when a noninstitutionalized system has become institutionalized, the marginalization of independent candidates would be a telltale sign. In Russia, whereas the emergence of United Russia in 2003 clearly produced an electoral environment more structured by parties, independents remained a central electoral force. In this way, Russia was clearly still a noninstitutionalized system according to our definition.

MIXED-MEMBER SYSTEM RULES: VARIABLES AND EXPECTATIONS

To be sure, our variable measures do not permit us to specify exactly *which* components of new democracies shape the constraining effect of electoral rules, but our core expectations are clear and straightforward to test: we expect to find significant differences between the constraining effects of electoral rules in established democracies and new ones – especially ones such as Armenia, Russia, and Ukraine that have particularly poorly developed party systems.

We expect the greatest differences in outcomes to exist between FPTP and PR rules and between new democracies (especially those with poorly institutionalized party systems) and established ones, but also expect differences in specific mixed system rules to affect the number of parties and system disproportionality. Moreover, even if these mixed-member system factors do not play an overwhelming part in shaping the outcomes that we examine, it is still important, at a minimum, to attempt to control for their effects. As we discussed in Chapter 2, we identify four general categories of mixed-member system institutional characteristics – linkage/compensatory seats, the SMD tier electoral formula, district magnitude and legal threshold of representation in the PR tier, and the ratio of SMD seats to PR seats – that are most likely to be important. (See Chapter 2 and Table 2.1 for significant details on these different rules.)

Of these characteristics, rules governing the relationship between the SMD and PR tiers ought to be most important. Mixed-member systems that use the PR tier to compensate for disproportional effects of the SMD tier – that is, by using vote shares under proportional/party-list voting to determine the total number of seats won by parties overall (in both tiers) – arguably undermine the constraining effect of the SMD half of the system through their mechanical effect on the translation of votes into seats and, in turn, the reduced incentive they give for strategic voting.[14] Obviously, the disproportionality of "unlinked" mixed systems (including mixed-member systems with less direct and weaker forms of compensation such as those used in Italy and Hungary) ought to be greater than that of "linked" systems (such as those in Germany and New Zealand) because the PR tier does not directly counteract the mechanical effects of the SMD tier.[15] In addition, voters in linked mixed-member systems should have less incentive to defect from small parties to large parties at the district level because the SMD vote is largely meaningless for a party's overall share of legislative seats. As a result, we should expect to see a larger effective-number-of-candidates score in SMD races in linked mixed-member systems (Bolivia, Germany, New Zealand, Scotland, Venezuela, and Wales) than in unlinked systems (Armenia, Croatia, Hungary, Italy, Japan, Lithuania, Macedonia, Russia, and Ukraine).

Differences in the SMD electoral formula are also likely to affect electoral outcomes. Different countries do, of course, use different formulas to allocate seats within PR (most notably, d'Hondt and Sainte-Laguë), but the differences

---

[14] More accurately, the PR tier of seats, then, is a "compensation" tier, in which seats are allocated to parties to make up for disproportionality created by the SMD tier.

[15] See Chapter 2 for a full discussion of how we treat systems with partial compensation in Hungary and Italy.

in their impact do not tend to be great. In contrast, the choice of plurality versus two-round majority rules under SMDs has a dramatic effect on electoral outcomes, and we therefore focus on the plurality-majority SMD dichotomy. As we discussed earlier in the chapter, two-round majority rules ought to lead to more parties than FPTP rules. Moreover, disproportionality should be higher in mixed-member systems with majoritarian SMD tiers (as opposed to plurality tiers) because smaller parties are more viable in the first round (and thus more likely to run) but rarely win election to the legislature (see Duverger 1986: 70).

Indeed, we can see such differences in the "pure" U.S. (plurality) and French (two-round majority) cases.[16] As we mentioned earlier, many more candidates compete as viable candidates in French presidential elections. In the U.S. presidential election in 2008, there was an effective-number-of-electoral-candidates score of 2.05, but in the 2002 French presidential election the score was 8.7! With only a single winner in each case, disproportionality was obviously higher in France (59.9) than in the United States (46.4). These differences extend to legislative elections in which our measures of N and LSq are based on nationally aggregated totals for each party. The 2008 U.S. House of Representatives races generated an effective number of electoral parties (N_v) score of 2.2 and an effective number of legislative parties (N_s) score of 1.9 nationally, with an LSq score of 4.3. In contrast, the 2007 elections to the French legislature saw an effective number of electoral parties score of 4.3 and effective number of legislative parties score of 2.5, with an LSq score of 14.8. We should expect similar differences between plurality and two-round majority rules in the SMD tiers of mixed-member systems as well. Among the country cases we look at in Chapter 4, only Hungary, Lithuania (except in 2000, when it used plurality rules), and Macedonia used two-round majority rules in their SMDs, and the rest used plurality rules.

Both lower district magnitudes and higher legal thresholds in the PR tier also should produce greater disproportionality. Six of our 15 country cases elect their PR deputies in meaningful territorial districts – thus, often leading to a lower PR district magnitude – whereas the others distribute their PR seats in one nationwide district. District magnitude and legal thresholds affect the number of parties and disproportionality by modulating the share of the vote needed to win seats. We can see this effect in the pure PR systems in Israel, which uses a 2 percent threshold (with a district magnitude of 120), and Turkey, which uses a 10 percent threshold of representation (with a district magnitude of 550). As we noted earlier, Israel's 2009 legislative elections produced an effective number of parties score of 7.4 for electoral parties (N_v) and 6.8 for legislative

---

[16] In reality, the French legislative electoral system provides an additional complication, which undoubtedly leads to even larger numbers of parties. As in standard two-round majority systems, voting in the first round of balloting in elections to the French parliament determines who will compete in the second round. However, unlike most two-round majority systems, which send only the top two vote winners to the second round runoff, in elections to the French legislature any candidate who receives 12.5 percent of the vote in first-round balloting can compete in the second round runoff.

parties (N_s), with an LSq score of 1.4. In contrast, in 2002, Turkey's legislative elections produced an effective number of parties score of 5.4 for electoral parties (N_v), but only 1.9 for legislative parties (N_s) because only two parties surpassed the 10 percent threshold. Turkey's "proportional" representation system, therefore, had an LSq score of 27! PR thresholds should have a similar effect on outcomes in our mixed-member system countries.

Unfortunately, in our data there is a high correlation between PR district magnitude and PR threshold (the correlation coefficient is 0.56). As the example of Turkey demonstrates, even where district magnitude is substantial, the presence of high PR thresholds can promote high disproportionality. For this reason, in Chapter 4 we include only PR thresholds (and not PR district magnitude) in our analysis. Our country cases range from no threshold in a number of countries to a high of 5 percent in others (see Table 2.1).

Finally, the balance of PR seats to SMD seats in mixed-member systems may also shape disproportionality and the number of parties. For example, Japan's mixed-member system holds 300 SMDs but only 180 PR seats. Larger numbers of seats allocated to the PR tier (especially in linked systems) can compensate for disproportionality created by the SMD tier. In addition, to win the largest possible number of seats, parties and voters ought to place greater emphasis on winning SMDs in systems in which SMD seats make up a larger share of the total. As a result, parties and voters may be more likely to engage in strategic behavior in such systems, and therefore lead to a greater constraining effect than in systems with fewer SMD seats. We calculate the SMD/PR ratio as the number of seats allocated through SMD balloting divided by the number allocated in PR (or, in linked systems, the number of compensation seats).[17]

CONCLUSION

The aim of this chapter was to set up our principal variables and expectations regarding electoral rules, context, electoral system disproportionality, strategic behavior, and the number of parties. Most notably, we expect the effects of electoral rules to vary, so there are very different electoral outcomes in established and new democracies. In Chapter 4, we examine how well actual electoral outcomes match our expectations about the relationship between rules, context, and the number of parties. Then, in Chapters 5 and 6, we dig more deeply and attempt to identify more of the mechanisms that bring about the outcomes that we find in Chapter 4.

---

[17] One might argue that for linked systems we ought to divide by the total number of seats, rather than just the number of compensation seats, because the share of the vote won in PR determines the total number of seats allocated to a party. We reran all our models with this alternative coding scheme and found little difference in the results.

4

How Democratic Experience and Party System Development Condition the Effects of Electoral Rules on Disproportionality and the Number of Parties

What We Actually See

In Chapter 3, we set up a number of variables and expectations regarding disproportionality and the number of parties. In this chapter, we now take advantage of the simultaneous existence of PR and SMD rules in mixed-member systems across a range of established and new democracies to investigate the extent to which these expectations bear out in reality.

We examine four key electoral outcomes: (1) *disproportionality* (LSq), the most common measure of the mechanical effect of electoral rules, (2) *the constraining effect of SMDs on the number of parties*, as measured by the mean effective number of candidates in SMDs (N_{cands}), (3) *the psychological effect*, as measured by the difference – within SMDs – between the effective number of parties winning votes under PR balloting and the effective number of candidates winning votes in SMD balloting ($N_{parties}$ minus N_{cands}), and (4) *the projection of district-level party configurations to the national level*, as measured by the nationally aggregated effective number of parties receiving SMD votes and the effective number of candidates at the district level receiving SMD votes (N_v SMD minus N_{cands}).

In each of these cases, we expect democratic experience and party system development to condition the effects of electoral rules. More specifically, we expect that, compared with established democracies, in new democracies disproportionality will be higher, SMDs will lead to a weaker psychological effect that promotes a larger number of parties, and there will be less matching between the number of parties at the district and national levels. Indeed, in this chapter we find that these expectations bear out.

This chapter demonstrates that in mixed-member systems in well-established democracies, electoral rules usually affect the number of parties and disproportionality in ways that are consistent with most work on electoral systems, but electoral rules have very different effects in new democracies, especially those with noninstitutionalized party systems: Even in mixed-member systems, plurality rules typically lead to significantly fewer parties and higher levels of disproportionality than PR rules. However, there are many more parties and higher levels of disproportionality in new democracies – especially those with poorly institutionalized party systems.

WHY IT IS USEFUL TO STUDY THE NUMBER OF PARTIES IN MIXED-MEMBER SYSTEMS

For over half a century, political science has given great attention to the effect of electoral systems on the number of parties. Many studies have demonstrated how FPTP rules in SMDs tend toward two parties (or two candidates) and PR systems with high district magnitudes tend to have many parties and low disproportionality. However, most studies do not control effectively for other factors, such as divisions within society that might affect the number of parties, so critics could plausibly suggest that a two-party system under FPTP rules within a given country might be due to a lack of social divisions, rather than to the effects of the electoral system.

Mixed-member electoral systems provide a way to help address such critiques. The separate votes cast in the PR and SMD portions of the balloting offer scholars an opportunity to use the controlled comparison approach: mixed systems can represent a social laboratory in which we study the effects of different types of electoral systems in isolation from influences of the social context such as social cleavages, socioeconomic development, and culture. If a given mixed-member system produces a small number of parties under plurality rules but a large number in PR, we can feel confident that in that polity, plurality rules are preventing party proliferation. Moreover, mixed-member systems have been introduced widely since the 1990s, permitting us to compare results across new and established democracies. If outcomes under similar rules vary considerably between new and established democracies, we can infer that something about the context is shaping the different outcomes.

By using a dataset drawn from national- and district-level data from 15 mixed-member electoral systems covering 52 elections, we are able to consider the impact of both electoral rules and democratic history/party system development on the number of parties and disproportionality. Appendix 4A lists the number of parties and disproportionality measures for each of these 52 elections. Six of the country cases – Germany, Italy, Japan, New Zealand, Scotland, and Wales – are consolidated democracies with long experience in competitive elections. One – Venezuela – had a history of stable democratic rule, but in recent years has seen a major implosion of its party system. The remaining countries – Armenia, Bolivia, Croatia, Hungary, Lithuania, Macedonia, Russia, and Ukraine – are states that emerged during the "third wave" of democratization (that has occurred since 1978) after a long period of communist or authoritarian rule. Among these new democracies, three – Armenia, Russia, and Ukraine – maintained noninstitutionalized party systems in the years for which we have data. In addition, these 15 cases provide significant variation in the rules governing their specific mixed-member systems and their levels of party institutionalization (see Chapter 2, Table 2.1).

A number of scholars (e.g., Ferrara et al. 2005) argue that there will be an interaction or "contamination" effect in mixed-member systems, whereby the existence of PR affects results in SMDs and vice versa (see Chapter 2), but, as we explain in Chapter 2, contamination can work to the advantage of our analyses. In certain ways, mixed systems become a "harder" test of the impact of electoral institutions. What would ordinarily seem like an obvious proposition (e.g., SMD rules will lead to less proportionality than PR rules) becomes worthy of testing. If we find that – even despite the contamination effect – electoral outcomes in both the SMD and PR portions of mixed-member systems follow the same tendencies that are predicted for pure SMD and PR systems, it serves to support even more strongly the existence of general electoral system "laws."

Moreover, as we also highlight in Chapter 2, electoral rules often have their predicted effects even when combined in mixed-member systems: contamination effects do not necessarily create entirely new outcomes in mixed systems. We should highlight that we are not saying that, by examining electoral outcomes in SMDs and PR in mixed-member systems, we are estimating the precise impact of such rules in their pure, unmixed forms. Contamination, of course, makes that impossible. Nevertheless, by creating this harder test we learn more about the incentives of electoral systems and how electoral rules generally affect political outcomes, such as the number of parties and disproportionality.

Disproportionality – the "Mechanical" Effect

Disproportionality is typically described as a mechanical effect of electoral rules: when we measure disproportionality, we consider the extent to which an electoral system leads each party's seat share to closely match its share of the vote. However, as we noted earlier, disproportionality is not entirely mechanical, as the psychological effect can also shape it. As we highlight in this section, disproportionality is actually higher in systems – such as new democracies – in which voters and/or elites do not defect from small parties as they "should." In other words, the "psychological" effect of restrictive electoral rules appears to be different in less-established democracies, thus leading to higher levels of disproportionality than we would usually expect.

Of course, disproportionality is, first and foremost, a result of rules, and more restrictive rules do in fact lead to greater disproportionality. Most obviously, there is a significant difference between disproportionality under SMD and PR rules. The mean LSq score for the PR tiers listed in Appendix 4A is 8.61, as compared with 15.37 in the SMD tiers.[1] In fact, in our dataset, SMD LSq is lower than PR LSq only in Russia (1993 and 1995) and Ukraine (1998 and 2002). As we discuss soon, these exceptions are probably due in part to these

---

[1] LSq SMD is 15.49 for the countries/elections for which we were also able to calculate LSq PR scores. For all these figures, to avoid having any country with a particularly large number of elections exert disproportionate weight on the mean in our calculations, we first determine for each country the mean LSq score for all of its elections and then calculate the overall mean by taking the mean for all these country means.

TABLE 4.1. *Relationship between System Characteristics and (1) Disproportionality (LSq) and (2) Effective Number of Candidates at the SMD level (N_{cands})*

	LSq All Countries	LSq No Uninst	N_{cands} (Mean)	Number of Countries
Plurality[2]	14.49	15.80	3.70	13
Majority	18.13	18.13	4.03	3
Unlinked	10.45	10.80	3.83	9
Linked	5.21	5.21	3.35	6
SMD/PR > 1	8.73	8.50	3.42	9
SMD/PR ≤ 1	7.80	7.01	3.97	6
Established Democracies	6.32		3.05	7
New Democracies – with Institutionalized Party Systems	10.37		3.80	5
Noninstitutionalized Party Systems	9.77		4.74	3
Correlation with number of elections (all elections)	−0.41	−0.44	−0.42	
Correlation with number of elections (1st 4 elections)	0.03	−0.08	−0.36	
Correlation between LSq PR and PR Threshold[3]	0.65			

Notes
- Except for the correlations with the number of elections, all figures are calculated by (1) taking the mean score for each election in each country, (2) then taking the mean for all elections for a given country, and (3) finally taking the mean of (2). In other words, each number represents the mean of all of the country means for that category.
- Unless otherwise noted, LSq scores here refer to total disproportionality in the system (LSq Overall). "LSq All Countries" scores refer to the LSq scores for all of the countries in the dataset. "LSq No Uninst" does not include Armenia, Russia, and Ukraine.

two countries' poorly institutionalized party systems, which lead to substantial disproportionality in PR.

At least as important, the LSq SMD scores in Russia and Ukraine are misleadingly low because we lump together independents into one category in our calculations. This large residual category of independents artificially lowers the effective number of parties and disproportionality in the SMD tier by creating the misleading impression of a large and rather successful "party" of independents. For this reason, we drop the noninstitutionalized cases – Armenia, Russia, and Ukraine – from most of our analyses of disproportionality.

Table 4.1 illustrates that other rules also appear to systematically shape disproportionality. Among SMD rules, disproportionality (LSq SMD) is higher

[2] For the Plurality/Majority means for LSq, we refer to disproportionality in the SMD tier (LSq SMD).

[3] To avoid giving a single country disproportionate weight, we use the mean LSq PR measure for each country. Because we cannot calculate LSq PR for linked systems, this constitutes only eight

when there is two-round majority balloting (18.13) than under plurality (14.49). As we noted in Chapter 3, plurality systems provide a stronger incentive for strategic defection away from weak candidacies. Meanwhile, disproportionality in two-round majority contests is calculated based on the deviation between vote shares in the first round – in which many candidates tend to run and win votes – and the final-round capture of the seat, thus leading to very large differences between a party's vote and seat shares. Among PR systems, higher legal thresholds of representation – which prevent many parties that win votes from winning seats – promote greater disproportionality. Table 4.1 indicates the high positive correlation (0.65) between the size of the legal threshold of representation and disproportionality in PR (LSq PR).

Rules specific to mixed-member systems also shape disproportionality. Linkage mechanisms between the SMD and PR tiers, which ensure that electoral outcomes are based to a larger degree on the results of the PR balloting, reduce overall system disproportionality. Mixed-member systems that do not link their tiers have overall system disproportionality scores that are greater than 10, as compared to disproportionality scores of scarcely greater than 5 in linked systems. Mixed-member systems that allocate a larger share of their seats to PR (i.e., the ratio of SMD to PR seats is less than or equal to 1) – which promotes greater proportionality – do, in fact, demonstrate less overall system disproportionality (lower LSq scores) than those with a larger share of SMDs (i.e., the SMD/PR ratio is greater than 1).

The impact of these various rules demonstrates the mechanical impact of institutions on disproportionality, but political context – most notably, democratic experience and party system development – also conditions the effect of rules on disproportionality. As we discussed in Chapter 3, most views about different electoral rules' levels of disproportionality are implicitly based not just on the mechanical effects of electoral rules, but also on the psychological effects that are in response to the mechanical effects. For example, if supporters of small parties strategically defect from their top choice when faced with rules that advantage large parties, there is likely to be less disproportionality. In contrast, if there is no such strategic defection, disproportionality is likely to go way up.

We can see this outcome in Russia's newly democratic system in the 1990s. As we noted earlier, the problem of how to treat independents in calculating disproportionality leads us to unreliable estimates of LSq for SMDs in Russia, so we focus here instead on disproportionality in the PR tier, which used a 5 percent legal threshold of representation. In the poorly institutionalized, low-information party system in Russia in the 1990s, opinion polls regularly recorded more than 40 percent of respondents as undecided. Small parties with little chance of gaining representation often took the risk that they would be the next surprise party to capture undecided votes and be catapulted above the PR thresholds of representation, although few succeeded. For example, in

countries. We find no correlation between PR Threshold and LSq Overall (0.08 for all countries and −0.01 when we drop the noninstitutionalized cases).

1995, only four out of 43 Russian parties crossed the legal threshold, leading to massive disproportionality in PR. LSq in PR was 20.56, the largest score in our dataset.[4]

Table 4.1 offers further evidence of the importance of democratic experience and party institutionalization in conditioning the effects of electoral rules. As the table indicates, disproportionality is markedly higher in countries that had less experience with democracy. Overall disproportionality (LSq Overall) is lower in established democracies (6.32) than in noninstitutionalized party systems (9.77) and new democracies with institutionalized party systems (10.37). If anything, it is likely that our treatment of independents in Armenia, Russia, and Ukraine actually artificially *lowers* the high disproportionality scores in the noninstitutionalized cases, so a more accurate measure would actually indicate an even greater difference between them and the more institutionalized cases.

We parse out the effects of these different institutional and contextual factors by means of multivariable, quantitative analysis, which we illustrate in Figure 4.1 by listing the expected disproportionality scores under a number of different scenarios (see Appendix 4B and Table 4.3 for more details). As we show

---

[4] As explained by Moser (2001a), in Russia the relatively low level of disproportionality in the first postcommunist election of 1993 can be partly attributed to specific features of that election. It was a "snap" election, called in the aftermath of the constitutional crisis sparked by the rebellion of the Congress of People's Deputies in October 1993 against President Yeltsin after he dissolved the Congress. There was little time for parties to form and contest the election held only a few months after the political tumult. The result was that only 13 parties met the requirements to be on the PR ballot. The 1995 election, which was scheduled well in advance and thus allowed all interested political groupings to prepare and organize, witnessed an explosion in the number of parties running in the PR tier. This party proliferation generated greater disproportionality when most of these parties failed to gain representation.

As Moser (2001a) notes, the extreme party proliferation in the PR tier in the 1995 Russian election was an aberration. The reformist camp was marked by a number of party splits within the original coalition that helped bring down the communist system. Moreover, there were many new nationalist and patriotic parties that emerged in the wake of the surprising success of Vladimir Zhirinovsky's ultranationalist Liberal Democratic Party of Russia (LDPR) in 1993 and sought to emulate his success in the PR tier. Indeed, half the votes cast in the PR tier in 1995 went to parties that failed to win the 5 percent of the national vote necessary to secure seats. In part, these processes did not carry over to SMDs to the same extent because party elites often lacked the grassroots organization to effectively field SMD candidates but had the national profile to field a PR party based on the appeal of the party leader. This was precisely the formula Zhirinovsky used in 1993 and subsequent elections. As a result, for example, Zhirinovsky's party (the LDPR) consistently won a significant percentage of the PR votes and seats, but very few SMDs.

Moreover, in Russia, campaign financing encouraged elites to form their own personal PR electoral blocs, even though these blocs had no chance of winning PR seats: The state provided to PR "parties" (called "blocs") free television and radio air time, which these elites used to further their personal campaigns in SMDs. Several "personal" PR parties that served as electoral vehicles for their leaders' successful SMD campaign existed in Russia's 1995 election (Moser 1997: 293; McFaul 1996: 17). Election rules were later changed to curtail this behavior by forcing PR parties and individual candidates that fail to win a certain percent of the vote to pay for the airtime they received during the campaign. Not surprising, with the introduction of new campaign finance rules, disproportionality dropped sharply in PR.

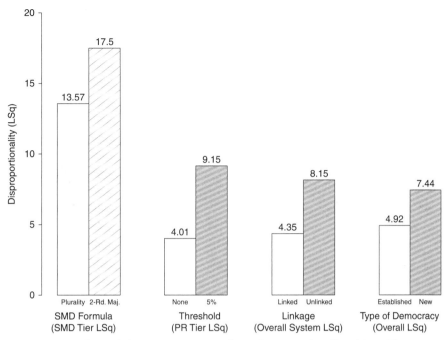

FIGURE 4.1. Rules and democratic context shape disproportionality. *Note:* Figures are expected values drawn from coefficient estimates in Table 4.3, Model 2 (SMD model), Model 4 (PR model), and Model 5 (LSq Overall) – see Appendix 4B. Except for the PR Threshold expected value (which sets the Russia 1995 dummy variable at 0), the expected values are based on calculations that hold other variables at their means.

We do not include an estimate for noninstitutionalized party systems because our aggregation of independents into a single "party" artificially lowers the LSq SMD and LSq Overall scores. When not including Noninstitutionalized Democracies, the difference between plurality and two-round majority SMD rules is statistically discernible only at the 0.173 level. All other differences shown here are statistically discernible at the 0.1 level.

in Figure 4.1, disproportionality in the SMD tier of mixed-member systems is roughly four points higher when a two-round majority formula system is used than when plurality rules are (although the difference is not statistically discernible, probably because of the very small number of cases in our dataset that actually use two-round majority rules).[5] Also, as the figure shows, in the PR tier, each additional percentage point on the legal threshold of representation adds at least one point onto the disproportionality score (even controlling for the aberrational 1995 Russia election). As a result, we can expect PR systems

---

[5] For reasons explained earlier, we do not include the three noninstitutionalized countries in the SMD tier analysis. In addition, we wanted to control for democratic experience (i.e., whether the country is a new or established democracy) in the SMD tier analysis, but do not do so because of concerns over collinearity; the correlation between two-round majority rules and whether a country is an institutionalized new democracy is 0.75.

with a five percent legal threshold to have scores on average at least five points higher than systems with no threshold.

We control for more factors in our analysis of the disproportionality of the whole mixed-member system (LSq Overall), and find the influence of both institutional and contextual factors (see Figure 4.1). We find a strong relationship between the use of tier linkage and overall system disproportionality: even controlling for other factors, unlinked systems have disproportionality scores that we can expect to be, on average, about four points higher than those of linked systems.[6] Most interesting, though, rules are hardly the only factor shaping disproportionality in our mixed systems. Even controlling for rules, new democracies have disproportionality scores that we can expect to be roughly 2.5 points higher, on average, than in established democracies.[7]

District-Level Constraining Effects on the Number of Candidates

Given the presence of substantial disproportionality, SMDs should constrain the number of parties. However, as we show in this section, this constraining effect is conditioned by context – namely, democratic experience and the level of party institutionalization in a country.

As we discussed earlier, electoral rules work first and foremost at the district level; to study them properly, we need to examine district-level outcomes. For this reason, in considering the number of parties under SMD rules, we focus on votes cast at the single-member *district* level. Again, for each country/election, we calculate N_{cands}, the effective number of candidates in each SMD, based on the share of votes won by each candidate under SMD balloting. (More specifically, we take the mean value of N_{cands} across all districts within a given country in a given election.)

Over time, the district-level effective number of candidates (N_{cands}) pushes toward two (especially in the established democracies – see Appendix 4A), as expected by Duverger's Law. For example, in some years, the average effective number of candidates in Germany dropped particularly close to two, especially prior to the reintroduction of East Germany in 1990. In Japan in 2009 (which is not included in our dataset), the mean effective number of candidates in all SMDs dropped all the way down to 2.26.

However, we also see cases of extreme candidate proliferation (N_{cands} of more than 5) in Hungary (first two elections), Lithuania (all elections after

---

[6] However, this result is based on coding Hungary and Italy as unlinked systems. If we code them as linked systems, the impact of tier linkage becomes no longer statistically discernible.

[7] We also find that, even controlling for other factors, overall system disproportionality is, in fact, higher in systems that allocate larger shares of seats to SMDs than to PR. In addition, consistent with the idea that the psychological effect also shapes disproportionality, we find tentative evidence that disproportionality drops over time, presumably as political actors gain experience and information. (See Table 4.3.) On average, and all else equal, LSq Overall can be expected to drop by about one point from the first to the third election under the mixed system.

1992), and one election each in the early years of the noninstitutionalized Russian (1995) and Ukrainian (1998) cases. As noninstitutionalized party systems, the high effective number of candidates figures cannot be too surprising in Russia and Ukraine, especially in early elections under the new mixed-member system. In addition, Hungary and Lithuania (1996 and 2004) had institutional reasons for candidate proliferation in their use of two-round majoritarian rather than plurality systems. Nevertheless, the number of candidates decreased over time in Hungary, as voters and elites grew more accustomed to the system. In addition to using two-round majority rules (except in 2000), Lithuania also probably experienced unusually high party system fragmentation in its SMD tier, owing to repeatedly changing its SMD rules. In 2000, Lithuania changed from a two-round majority system to plurality contests, only to change back to its old majoritarian system at the next election in 2004. Moreover, changes to the rules in the PR tier in 1996 – specifically raising the legal threshold from 4 to 5 percent for individual parties and to 7 percent for pre-election coalitions – prompted parties to form larger, consolidated party lists to contest PR elections, but then also run candidates under individual party labels in the SMD tier, thus leading to further proliferation of SMD parties and candidacies (Krupavicius 1997).

We can also be more systematic in our discussion of the factors that shape the effective number of candidates. Table 4.1 indicates that, on average, the effective number of candidates is lower in systems with a high SMD/PR ratio, with plurality rules in the SMD tier, and when larger numbers of elections have been held under the system.[8] Perhaps most striking, established democracies (N_{cands} of 3.05) have, on average, fewer candidates than do new democracies with institutionalized party systems (N_{cands} of 3.80), and new democracies with institutionalized party systems have lower effective number of candidates scores than countries with noninstitutionalized party systems (N_{cands} of 4.74).

Contrary to expectations, unlinked systems, on average, have higher effective number of candidates scores than linked systems do, but this result is almost certainly due to the fact that all the noninstitutionalized party systems in the dataset also use no linkage mechanism. Table 4.2 divides our country cases into three different groupings: established democracies, new democracies with institutionalized party systems, and noninstitutionalized party systems. Table 4.2 demonstrates that within each category of democratization/party institutionalization, the average effective number of candidates is always lower in unlinked systems (although there are no linked noninstitutionalized cases and only one linked new democracy in the whole set).

---

[8] Because Lithuania changed its SMD electoral formula from majority to plurality in 2000, we code Lithuania 2000 as a first election. And, because it then changed the rule back to two-round majority in 2004, we code that election as a first election as well. However, if instead we code those elections as the third and fourth elections in Lithuania, most results do not change markedly, although the number of election variables become no longer statistically significant at the 0.1 level.

TABLE 4.2. *Mean Effective Number of District Candidates (N_{cands}) – Broken Down by Rules and Party System Context (number of country cases in parentheses)*

	Unlinked	Linked
Established Democracies	2.63 (2)	3.22 (5)
New Democracies – Institutionalized Party Systems	3.75 (4)	4.00 (1)
Noninstitutionalized Party Systems	4.74 (3)	– (0)
	Plurality	**Majority**
Established Democracies	3.05 (7)	– (0)
New Democracies – Institutionalized Party Systems	4.03 (3)	4.16 (3)
Noninstitutionalized Party Systems	4.74 (3)	– (0)
	SMD/PR > 1	**SMD/PR <= 1**
Established Democracies	2.92 (5)	3.39 (2)
New Democracies – Institutionalized Party Systems	3.98 (3)	3.53 (2)
Noninstitutionalized Party Systems	4.21 (1)	5.00 (2)

This interactive effect of unlinked systems and party institutionalization provides a clear example of how both institutional rules and political context ought to be considered when examining the impact of electoral systems on party systems. Indeed, there are marked differences in the impact of electoral rules, depending on the development of the country's party system (Table 4.2). Only three of our country cases use two-round majority SMD rules; all three are new democracies with institutionalized party systems. However, those three cases have, on average, a higher effective number of candidates than in the three new democracies with institutionalized party systems that use plurality rules in their SMDs.

We see a similar interaction between context and the SMD/PR ratio. Contrary to expectation, in new democracies with institutionalized party systems, lower SMD/PR ratios (in the Croatian and Hungarian cases) are associated with a smaller effective number of parties than higher ratios (perhaps in part because of their lack of seat linkage between the SMD and PR tiers). On the other hand, for both established democracies and noninstitutionalized party systems, high SMD/PR ratios have, on average, the expected lower effective number of candidates scores per SMD. Moreover, as Table 4.2 shows, for each electoral institution the number of parties increases with each shift in party system context – in other words, as we move from established democracies to new democracies with institutionalized party systems and from the latter category to noninstitutionalized party systems.

We conduct multivariable analysis, which allows us to see that, in particular, democratic experience/party institutionalization and the country's experience with the electoral system affect the number of candidates at the district level (see Table 4.4 and Appendix 4B for more detail). Based on this analysis, as

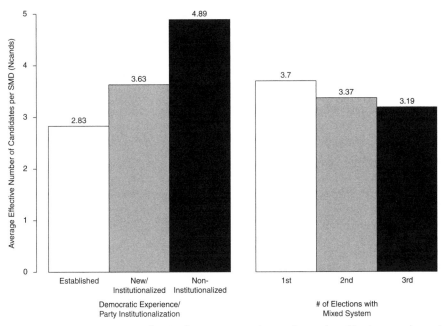

FIGURE 4.2. Democratic and mixed-system experience shape the effective number of candidates at the SMD level.[9]

Figure 4.2 demonstrates, we can expect to see the largest number of candidates in countries with noninstitutionalized party systems. Holding other factors constant, we can expect noninstitutionalized party systems to have effective number of candidates scores (N_{cands}) that are roughly two points higher than they are in established democracies (4.89 to 2.83). Furthermore, we can expect even new democracies with better institutionalized party systems to see a greater proliferation of candidates, with an effective number of candidates score (3.63) that is, on average, nearly one point higher than in established democracies.

Looking at Figure 4.2, the reader may wonder why the average effective number of candidates under SMD rules is so high (2.83) in established democracies. The reason is that these figures are based on the expected values, whereas all other factors are set to their mean values. However, if we consider a scenario in which an established democracy is in its fifth election under the mixed-member system, has no linkage between the PR and SMD tiers, and uses plurality rules in the SMD, the expected effective number of candidates is 2.39, which is lower than the average even for pure FPTP systems.

It clearly takes time for the constraining effects of SMDs to kick in. Figure 4.2 indicates that with each election, even controlling for other factors, the

---

[9] Figures are expected values drawn from coefficient estimates in Table 4.4, Model 6 (Appendix 4B). The expected values are based on calculations that hold other variables at their means. Differences shown here are statistically discernible at the 0.1 level.

effective number of candidates drops, especially between the first (when the expected N_{cands} is 3.7) and second elections (when the expected N_{cands} is 3.37). This latter finding coincides with other work that shows that strategic voting increases with democratic experience (Tavits and Annus 2006).

Surprisingly, and contrary to what was suggested by the summary statistics listed in Tables 4.1 and 4.2, our multivariable analysis uncovers no evidence of any impact on the effective number of candidates of rules such as tier linkage, plurality rule in SMDs, and the ratio of SMD to PR seats. It is likely that, in part, we were unable to uncover a relationship between electoral institutions and the number of candidates because of high correlations between the party system variables and electoral rules. For example, in our dataset, two-round majority rules are used only in new democracies with institutionalized party systems and noninstitutionalized party systems only have unlinked tiers. Unfortunately, given the small number of country cases, we cannot use interaction terms to investigate this possible explanation.

It is also likely that, in part, we find no evidence of the impact of mixed-member system rules on the district-level number of parties because other factors – such as party institutionalization – are critical to determining differences in the number of parties across different mixed systems and, for example, linkage mechanisms are not. Instead, perhaps such rules are important in helping to determine the number of candidates under SMD balloting relative to the baseline – the number of parties in PR – within any given country. We consider this possibility more in the next section.

At the same time, we do not want the weaker evidence of the effect of rules to obscure the more striking point: the analysis here shows clearly that, more potent than any electoral system rule, democratic experience and party system institutionalization play a major role in shaping the number of parties. The constraining effects of plurality rules are unlikely to be felt fully until a country has substantial democratic experience and institutionalizes its party system.

The Psychological Effect: The Difference between the Number of Parties under PR and SMD Rules

The controlled comparison approach to studying mixed-member systems is especially useful in helping to investigate the psychological effect of electoral rules. As we noted earlier, a difficulty with comparing electoral outcomes under different rules is that we usually cannot tell whether differences in outcomes are due to differences in rules or due to differences in the various countries' societies (or other factors that might shape the number of parties). However, when we compare the number of parties under SMD and PR rules within a single country, we actually control for society and other potentially important variables. In this way, when we see a difference in the number of parties across the SMD and PR tiers within a single country, we can have greater confidence that it is due to the differences in the electoral rules. Of course, there may be a contamination effect in mixed-member systems, but if outcomes in the SMD and PR tiers of mixed systems still follow the same general pattern seen in pure systems, it strongly suggests that the incentives set up by each of the two tiers separately still generally hold.

Moreover, and most important, our concern here is not merely whether there is a difference between the number of parties under PR and SMD rules, but rather what factors lead to variation in the magnitude of these differences. By looking at a variety of mixed-member systems, we can examine reasons for the systematic variation between countries.

As we discussed earlier, the constraining effect of SMDs is at the district level; we therefore focus on votes cast at the SMD level for candidates competing in SMD balloting and parties under PR. More specifically, for each country/election, we compare the difference between the effective number of parties in each SMD based on PR-party balloting in the district ($N_{parties}$) and the effective number of candidates in each SMD based on SMD-candidate balloting in the district (N_{cands}). In these calculations, large, positive values indicate that the effective number of parties score is much higher under PR balloting than for candidates in SMD balloting.

Figure 4.3 illustrates the mean value of N_{cands} and $N_{parties}$ for all the elections and countries for which data were available for both variables in Appendix 4A. As expected – and despite a possible contamination effect that may have led to a higher effective number of candidates under SMD balloting – the mean value of N_{cands} is markedly lower (a difference of 0.71) than the mean value of $N_{parties}$. Moreover, this figure is based, in very large part, on the large number of elections using the mixed-member system in Germany. If we calculate the mean N_{cands} and $N_{parties}$ for each country and then take the mean of those country means (for all countries/elections for which we could compute $N_{parties}$), the average effective number of candidates score is 3.55, compared with a score of 4.48 for the effective number of PR parties per district.

Based on our earlier discussion, we should expect political context to shape the psychological effect. There should be fewer candidates competing in SMDs (N_{cands}) than parties in PR ($N_{parties}$) in any given country/election. However, the stronger constraining effect under restrictive rules in countries whose parties structure the vote should make this difference greater in established democracies than in newly democratizing countries.

Indeed, Figure 4.4, which is based on quantitative analysis that simultaneously controls for a variety of different factors, illustrates that the psychological effect does indeed appear to be markedly stronger in established democracies (see Appendix 4B and Table 4.5 for detailed discussion). The gap between the effective number of parties under PR and the effective number of candidates in SMD balloting is considerably greater in established democracies than in new democracies. As Figure 4.4 illustrates, all else being equal, we can expect a tiny difference (−0.23) between the effective number of PR and SMD parties in new democracies. In fact, the difference is not statistically distinguishable from zero.

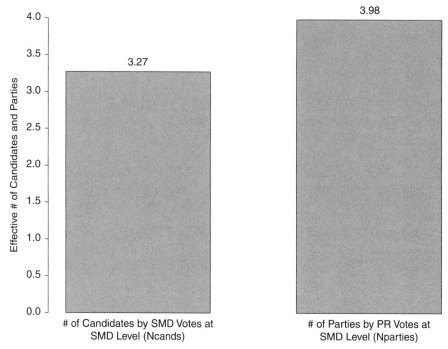

FIGURE 4.3. The average effective number of parties in SMDs and PR (SMD level).[10]

In contrast, on average, and all else being equal, we can expect the $N_{parties}$ score to be 1.26 greater than the N_{cands} score in established democracies. In other words, relative to PR, SMDs constrain the number of parties more in established democracies than in new ones. Interestingly, there is no statistically discernible difference between the two types of new democracies (institutionalized and noninstitutionalized) in our data. This lack of a difference appears to be simply due to the fact that noninstitutionalized party systems not only have larger numbers of parties contesting SMD races, but larger numbers competing in PR as well – thereby creating a difference between $N_{parties}$ and N_{cands} that is not statistically discernible from that in the institutionalized new democracies.

In our discussion in the previous section of the apparent lack of a relationship between mixed-member system linkage mechanisms and the effective number of candidates in SMDs (N_{cands}), we suggested that perhaps such rules are important in helping to determine the number of candidates under SMD balloting relative to the baseline – the number of parties in PR – within any given country (i.e., $N_{parties}$ minus N_{cands}). Indeed, Figure 4.4 illustrates that the psychological effect appears to be different under different linkage mechanisms.

---

[10] These figures represent the mean of all 41 countries/elections in which both N_{cands} and $N_{parties}$ could be computed.

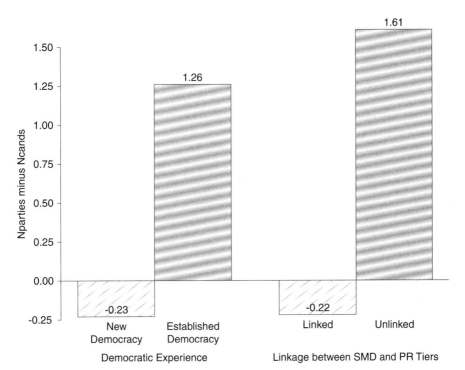

FIGURE 4.4. Democratic experience and tier linkage shape the psychological effect (the effective number of PR parties [$N_{parties}$] minus the effective number of SMD candidates [N_{cands}]).[11]

Under linked rules, the difference between $N_{parties}$ and N_{cands} is not statistically distinguishable from zero. In contrast, on average, and all else being equal, in unlinked systems $N_{parties}$ is 1.61 greater than N_{cands}, thus suggesting that linkage rules shape the psychological effect of SMDs in mixed systems.[12]

---

[11] Figures are expected values drawn from coefficient estimates in Table 4.5, Model 6 (Appendix 4B). In calculating expected values, all variables are set at their means (except for the country dummy variables, which are set at 0). Other information: There is no statistically discernible difference between the impact of noninstitutionalized and institutionalized new democracies on $N_{parties} - N_{cands}$, but there is a statistically significant difference (p < 0.1 level) in the effect on $N_{parties} - N_{cands}$ between New and Established Democracies and between Linked and Unlinked Systems. The difference between $N_{parties}$ and N_{cands} is not statistically discernible from zero for New Democracies and for Linked systems.

[12] We also include other variables in our analysis. Two in particular stand out. First, because the number of parties in PR is likely to be affected by the legal threshold of representation, we also include in our analysis a measure of the legal threshold. In addition, similar to our analysis in the previous section, we control for the number of elections using the mixed-member system in each country. Also, for reasons that we outline in Appendix 4B, we include controls for the 1995 election in Russia, and elections in general in Lithuania and Bolivia. Including the SMD/PR ratio and plurality rules in the analysis introduces collinearity problems, so we leave these variables out of the analysis.

District Projection to the National Level

Finally, we look at the degree to which district-level effects "project" to the national level by comparing the effective number of candidates produced in each district (N_{cands}) to the nationally aggregated effective number of parties produced by the SMD tier (N_v SMD). As we discuss at length in other chapters, the effects of electoral rules work most directly at the district level, and unless a party system is fully nationalized – with all parties competing across the country – the number of parties at the district level is unlikely to match the number of parties aggregated across the country. As we argue in Chapter 3, we should expect significant projection in established democracies with a long history of well-developed national parties. However, we should expect much less projection from the district to the national level in new democracies with less democratic experience and, consequently, less opportunity to nationalize the party system.

Indeed, these are precisely the patterns we see in our data. Because of the problem we noted earlier relating to the measurement of independents in the noninstitutionalized cases, we look only at the institutionalized party systems in our dataset. The average scores for N_v SMD and N_{cands} for established democracies are 3.09 and 2.74, respectively – a difference of only 0.35. The difference is much greater in new democracies where the mean N_v SMD and N_{cands} scores are 5.67 and 4.26, respectively, for a gap of 1.41.[13]

Figure 4.5 illustrates the results of more systematic, multivariable analysis that provides further evidence of the importance of democratic and electoral experience in shaping projection (see Appendix 4B and Table 4.6 for more details). As shown in Figure 4.5, holding other factors constant, we can expect, on average, the gap between the nationally aggregated effective number of parties (N_v SMD) and the district-level effective number of candidates (N_{cands}) to be only 0.27 in established democracies, but 1.66 in new democracies. Figure 4.5 also indicates how projection appears to increase over time, presumably as parties become nationalized across more of the country: all else being equal, we can expect the nationally aggregated effective number of parties (N_v SMD) to be, on average, 1.16 points more than the average for the effective number of candidates at the district level (N_{cands}). However, on average, we can expect the

---

Interestingly, we find no significant effect of the number of elections or the legal threshold of representation. Most likely, we find no discernible change over time because time affects the number of parties under SMDs and PR. The lack of an effect of PR threshold may be due to the fact that especially in new democracies many parties chose to contest elections irrespective of the size of the PR threshold.

[13] These figures are the mean for all countries/elections. If we compute the means by first taking the mean for each country (across all elections) and then take the mean of each of the country means, the difference is 0.54 for established democracies (N_v SMD is 3.59 and N_{cands} is 3.05) and 1.39 for new democracies (N_v SMD is 5.19 and N_{cands} is 3.80). Each of these differences is statistically discernible from zero.

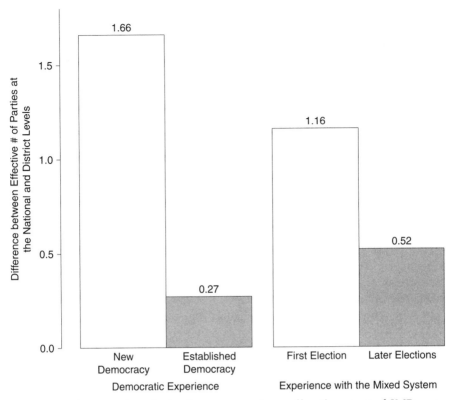

FIGURE 4.5. Democratic and mixed-system experience affect the extent of SMD party projection from the district to the national level (N_v SMD minus N_{cands}).[14]

difference to be only 0.52 points in later elections. In short, district "bipartism" is much more likely to project to a similarly small number of parties across the country in established democracies, especially after the initial elections under a new mixed-member system. In contrast, there is far less projection in new democracies.[15]

---

[14] Figures are expected values drawn from regression estimates in Table 4.6, Model 1 (Appendix 4B). All other differences shown here are statistically discernible at the 0.1 level. We drop noninstitutionalized party systems from this analysis because our aggregation of independents into a single "party" inaccurately lowers the measure of the effective number of parties at the national-level (N_v SMD) score. In calculating expected values, all variables are set at their means.

[15] Hungary stands out among our new democracies for its lack of difference between N_{cands} and N_v (SMD). Hungary arguably has the most well-developed party system among postcommunist states. The lack of difference between N_v (SMD) and N_{cands} is likely due to the fact that early on large, national parties dominated the Hungarian party system and thus projected the outcomes within districts to the national level. In our quantitative analysis, we find no evidence

THE POTENTIALLY EXACERBATING FORCE OF PRESIDENTIALISM

One potential criticism of this analysis is that it does not control for presidentialism, which some might argue is the primary cause of the proliferation of parties in our noninstitutionalized cases – that is, because our noninstitutionalized cases also have strong presidencies, perhaps voters in those systems do not see legislative elections as important, and therefore feel less of a need to cast a strategic ballot for inherently less important legislative elections.[16] This argument is compelling; unfortunately, the high correlation between presidentialism (particularly presidents with substantial powers) and both new democracies and noninstitutionalized party systems makes it impossible for us to investigate systematically in our quantitative analysis.

However, this counterargument does not undermine our own explanation about the effects of a lack of democratic experience or party institutionalization. It is certainly possible that voters see less need to cast ballots strategically in legislative elections when presidents are strong. However, elites ought to come together to create legislative parties and/or coalitions of legislative parties that can work with a powerful president, and therefore gain the rewards of cooperating with him, or become capable of putting up a strong candidate to win presidential elections. The fact that such coordination did not occur in the examples we examine highlights the important role played by democratic inexperience and poor party institutionalization in making it more difficult for elites to work together.

That being said, we do not wish to dismiss the importance of presidentialism. In particular, presidentialism may exacerbate the problem of weak party institutionalization. As Clark and Wittrock (2005), Filippov, Ordeshook, and Shvetsova (1999), and Hicken and Stoll (2008) indicate, presidential systems – especially those with very strong presidential powers – can lead elites to have difficulty consolidating parties. In addition, Samuels and Shugart (2010) indicate that presidential systems can lead to internal divisions within parties, which also can lead to greater difficulty institutionalizing these parties.

---

of a difference in projection between plurality and two-round majority rules. This lack of a difference may be because both types of rules permit the same amount of projection or because of the Hungarian exception, which uses majority SMD rules but has substantial projection anyway. (It may also be because of the high correlation [0.75] between institutionalized new democracies and two-round majority rules.)

[16] Thanks to Royce Carroll for raising this cogent point. A similar but distinct criticism might use Golder's (2006) analysis – in particular, the finding that presidential systems with many candidates (as can be the case in developing democracies) lead to larger numbers of legislative parties – to argue that larger numbers of legislative parties in noninstitutionalized systems grow out of a proliferation of presidential candidates. However, the principal problem with this latter criticism is that the number of candidates actually dropped to a relatively small number – and certainly smaller than the average number of legislative candidates competing in SMDs – in early presidential elections in noninstitutionalized systems such as Armenia, Russia, and Ukraine (Moser 2001a: Chapter 6).

CONCLUSIONS

In this chapter, we examine how electoral rules affect party systems in different political contexts. Our analysis indicates that electoral rules under mixed-member systems retain their expected effects on disproportionality and the number of parties, provided that the political context is conducive to strategic defection.

The findings of this chapter can be grouped into four major conclusions. First, our findings highlight the degree to which PR and SMD electoral systems work as expected, even when they are combined in a mixed-member system under many political circumstances. Our controlled comparison approach, which compares the number of parties under PR and SMD rules, does not reject the potential existence of so-called contamination between the two tiers of a mixed system, but our analysis lends credence to the position that, to a great extent, mixed-member systems maintain the independent effects of PR and SMD tiers. Most notably, we find fewer parties and higher disproportionality under SMD rules than in PR.

Second, and most important, our findings in this chapter reinforce one of the central themes of the book – the importance of political context, in particular the role of democratic experience and party institutionalization, in conditioning the impact of political institutions. Traditionally, most work on the effect of electoral rules on strategic behavior and the number of parties assumes the presence of established party systems with high levels of information about likely electoral support and outcomes, but our analysis shows that the effects of electoral rules vary with the level of democratic and party system development. The most striking differences we found in the number of parties and disproportionality among our mixed-member systems were the result of variation in the degree of party institutionalization and democratic experience, rather than institutional variation. Outcomes in postcommunist states that lacked democratic experience and well-developed parties consistently ran counter to the patterns found in countries with more institutionalized parties, and experienced a proliferation of candidates in their plurality tiers. Most notably, the fact that SMD contests in countries with more established democracies and party systems constrained the number of district-level electoral competitors to a much greater degree than was the case under either PR rules or less-developed democracies or party systems suggests that contagion from the combination of PR and SMD rules was not the primary cause for the fragmentation experienced in postcommunist states such as Russia and Ukraine. We can probably generalize from these findings to "pure" (i.e., not mixed-member) electoral systems because there is every reason to expect pure SMD systems as well to produce similarly fragmented electoral competition in a context of inchoate parties. Indeed, recent work by Wahman (ND) on pure plurality systems in Africa shows a similar pattern, thus offering more evidence that states with weakly institutionalized party systems experience a proliferation of candidates at the district level.

Third, time and learning seem to have a systematic effect on the impact of electoral rules. In many of our analyses, there was a significant difference between how electoral systems affected the number of parties in the first election versus subsequent elections. This change over time highlights how political learning can influence the extent to which electoral systems shape outcomes.

However, despite clear evidence of learning and change over time, on average new democracies still have not "caught up" with established democracies in terms of the constraining effects of restrictive electoral systems. Despite a number of years under their mixed-member systems, new democracies such as Russia still remained a greater distance away from equilibrium Duvergerian outcomes. It appears more difficult for many new democracies to reach that equilibrium and its associated outcomes than it is for established democracies. Future scholarship will do well to consider with greater precision the issue of the evolution over time of electoral system effects in mixed-member systems, particularly with respect to how such learning and change over time may differ between established and developing democracies.

Fourth, whereas many have assumed that mixed system-specific rules – most notably, the choice to use or not use linkage mechanisms – play an important role in shaping behavior in mixed-member systems, this chapter demonstrates the effect of such rules. In particular, we find that linkage arrangements shape the psychological effect of SMDs in mixed systems. On average, unlinked mixed-member systems – in which incentives for strategic behavior are stronger – witness a larger gap between the number of parties under PR and SMD rules, thus suggesting a greater constraining effect of SMDs under such rules.

The results we present in this chapter are consistent with the most basic implications of the framework that we outlined in Chapters 1 and 3. The impact of electoral rules can be seen most clearly in our analysis of the "psychological effect" – that is, the difference between the district-level number of SMD and PR parties. The fact that the magnitude of the psychological effect – or, more precisely, the difference between the number of parties under PR and SMD rules – appears to grow with greater democratic experience and party institutionalization suggests strongly that political context conditions the impact of electoral rules.

However, the data analysis in this chapter does not address a key aspect of this relationship: it does not demonstrate the mechanisms underlying the outcomes that we find. That is, the analysis does not show *why* we see the variation that we do in the number of parties. Duverger's Law holds that plurality rules constrain the number of parties because of strategic defection by voters and elites, and we argue that such strategic defection is less likely to occur in new democracies, especially those with poorly institutionalized party systems. In Chapters 5 and 6, we address this mechanism more directly by examining the interactive effect of party system development and the strategic incentives created by SMD rules on voter and elite behavior.

APPENDIX 4A. EFFECTIVE NUMBER OF PARTIES AND DISPROPORTIONALITY FOR EACH COUNTRY/ELECTION

Country/ Election	N_v Overall	N_s Overall	N_v PR	N_s PR	N_v SMD	N_s SMD	N_cands SMD (SMD votes)	N_parties SMD (PR votes)	LSq Overall	LSq PR	LSq SMD
Armenia 1999	5.56	3.85	4.61	3.13	4.00	3.03	4.21	UN	10.56	8.45	11.72
Bolivia 1997	6.17	5.36	5.93	n/a	6.38	5.63	4.65	4.42	4.11	n/a	6.64
Bolivia 2002	6.28	4.96	5.82	n/a	6.58	4.41	4.55	4.29	5.68	n/a	13.81
Bolivia 2005	3.94	2.30	4.69	n/a	3.34	3.83	2.79	UN	13.14	n/a	6.10
Croatia 1995	3.63	2.52	3.78	2.90	3.39	1.70	2.67	UN	10.43	6.43	23.62
Germany 1953	3.13	2.75	3.09	n/a	3.17	1.83	2.79	3.11	6.39	n/a	22.63
Germany 1957	2.70	2.39	2.71	n/a	2.69	1.53	2.55	2.64	5.85	n/a	23.33
Germany 1961	2.78	2.51	2.81	n/a	2.76	1.87	2.63	2.67	4.63	n/a	15.32
Germany 1965	2.51	2.38	2.56	n/a	2.46	1.89	2.36	2.46	2.80	n/a	11.26
Germany 1969	2.45	2.24	2.49	n/a	2.41	2.00	2.30	2.39	4.22	n/a	7.10
Germany 1972	2.31	2.34	2.39	n/a	2.24	1.90	2.14	2.29	1.55	n/a	10.55
Germany 1976	2.33	2.31	2.36	n/a	2.30	1.99	2.21	2.27	0.84	n/a	6.07
Germany 1980	2.48	2.44	2.54	n/a	2.41	2.00	2.31	2.44	1.77	n/a	7.37
Germany 1983	2.42	2.51	2.55	n/a	2.28	1.66	2.21	2.47	1.85	n/a	17.47
Germany 1987	2.72	2.80	2.87	n/a	2.57	1.77	2.48	2.76	2.23	n/a	16.46
Germany 1990	3.14	2.65	3.36	n/a	2.92	1.69	2.79	2.98	5.88	n/a	20.29
Germany 1994	2.97	2.91	3.15	n/a	2.80	1.81	2.61	2.91	2.69	n/a	17.56
Germany 1998	2.99	2.45	3.27	n/a	2.72	1.87	2.70	3.13	5.60	n/a	15.70
Germany 2002	3.01	2.85	3.21	n/a	2.83	1.99	2.69	3.03	3.69	n/a	12.44
Germany 2005	3.40	3.44	3.75	n/a	3.06	2.05	2.88	3.52	3.34	n/a	12.07
Hungary 1990	7.00	3.79	6.71	4.31	6.00	2.03	5.97	UN	13.74	9.34	31.88
Hungary 1994	5.75	2.90	5.49	3.73	5.60	1.35	5.64	UN	16.21	8.53	40.89
Hungary 1998	4.76	4.17	4.35	3.13	5.00	3.57	4.84	UN	9.12	14.00	20.56
Hungary 2002	2.92	2.06	2.77	2.12	2.97	2.02	2.86	UN	8.96	10.77	12.06

(continued)

APPENDIX 4A *(continued)*

Country/Election	N_v Overall	N_s Overall	N_v PR	N_s PR	N_v SMD	N_s SMD	N_{cands} SMD (SMD votes)	$N_{parties}$ SMD (PR votes)	LSq Overall	LSq PR	LSq SMD
Hungary 2006	2.70	2.10	2.70	2.17	2.69	2.01	2.64	UN	9.49	6.89	13.31
Italy 1994	2.97	2.19	7.54	n/a	2.89	1.91	3.04	5.88	11.61	n/a	16.39
Italy 1996	2.66	2.39	7.15	n/a	2.66	2.29	2.43	5.80	5.13	n/a	8.35
Italy 2001	2.56	2.10	5.94	n/a	2.45	1.98	2.41	5.67	12.30	n/a	14.06
Japan 1996	4.10	2.94	4.28	3.84	3.86	2.36	2.95	4.01	10.80	3.19	15.95
Japan 2000	4.58	3.18	5.16	4.72	3.82	2.39	2.77	4.79	11.50	2.36	15.60
Japan 2003	3.23	2.59	3.42	3.03	2.92	2.27	2.41	3.34	5.73	4.05	10.55
Japan 2005	3.20	2.26	3.72	3.15	2.69	1.76	2.40	3.64	15.56	4.65	22.58
Lithuania 1992	4.36	2.99	3.83	2.86	6.03	3.21	3.50	UN	8.89	7.02	13.38
Lithuania 1996	7.87	3.40	7.94	3.16	7.75	3.21	5.59	5.34	15.76	16.34	20.37
Lithuania 2000	7.06	4.21	5.57	3.43	10.77	6.84	5.80	5.13	10.79	10.64	11.61
Lithuania 2004	5.11	5.41	5.78	4.82	8.52	5.99	5.17	5.23	5.11	4.40	7.82
Macedonia 1998	4.15	2.76	5.04	4.00	4.42	2.58	2.94	3.60	12.13	5.65	16.78
New Zealand 1996	4.25	3.76	4.39	n/a	4.10	2.62	3.27	4.04	3.42	n/a	13.19
New Zealand 1999	3.79	3.45	3.93	n/a	3.65	2.07	3.01	3.71	3.20	n/a	15.52
New Zealand 2002	3.74	3.82	4.16	n/a	3.31	1.93	2.85	3.95	4.25	n/a	15.43
New Zealand 2005	3.04	2.98	3.06	n/a	3.02	2.45	2.49	2.78	1.75	n/a	6.45
Russia 1993	7.14	8.16	7.58	6.40	3.23	2.55	4.72	UN	4.60	4.94	4.27
Russia 1995	10.00	5.71	10.68	3.32	6.10	5.03	5.91	9.00	14.14	20.56	11.09
Russia 1999	7.94	7.63	6.76	5.65	4.26	3.31	4.64	5.26	5.87	6.84	6.85
Russia 2003	5.10	3.38	4.72	2.82	3.42	3.09	3.52	4.80	14.96	12.54	19.72

Scotland 1999	3.96	3.34	4.34	n/a	3.60	1.77	3.09	3.95	5.64	n/a	29.65
Scotland 2003	4.96	4.23	5.64	n/a	4.32	2.24	3.47	4.86	5.50	n/a	23.88
Ukraine 1998	7.14	5.88	9.01	4.95	3.85	3.33	5.98	6.34	5.30	10.68	4.34
Ukraine 2002	6.72	5.42	5.82	4.67	4.20	3.40	4.62	5.24	12.42	17.48	11.96
Venezuela 1998	5.88	5.88	7.69	n/a	5.26	4.55	4.27	UN	2.57	n/a	4.59
Wales 1999	3.37	3.03	3.80	n/a	3.73	2.04	3.21	3.21	7.71	n/a	24.13
Wales 2003	3.98	3.00	4.18	n/a	3.74	1.95	3.07	3.77	9.87	n/a	28.75
Means	**4.29**	**3.44**	**4.64**	**3.74**	**3.93**	**2.63**	**3.42**	**3.98**	**7.33**	**8.90**	**15.18**

Notes:

Except for N_{cands} and $N_{parties}$, we calculate each measure using the number of votes and/or seats won by each party aggregated across the entire country in a given election.

N = The effective number of parties, calculated by squaring the *proportion* of the vote (v) or seat (s) won by each party, adding the squared proportions together, then dividing 1 by this total:

- $N_v = 1/\Sigma(v_i^2)$ – i.e., the effective number of parties competing in elections/winning votes, e.g., N_v PR = the effective number of parties based on votes cast in the PR tier
- $N_s = 1/\Sigma(s_i^2)$ – i.e., the effective number of parties winning seats
- N_v Overall: Vote shares for each party are determined by (a) summing each party's vote share in both PR and SMDs and then (b) dividing that number by 2.

N_{cands} SMD = We calculate N_v based on *SMD* balloting for each single-member district. N_{cands} is the mean of all of those N_v scores for each country/election.
$N_{parties}$ SMD = We calculate N_v based on *PR* balloting for each single-member district. $N_{parties}$ is the mean of all of those N_v scores for each country/election.
LSq = The least-squared index of disproportionality, calculated by squaring the difference in the percentage of votes and seats won by each party and then adding them together; this total is divided by 2, and then the square root of this value is taken:

$$LSq = \sqrt{\tfrac{1}{2}\Sigma(v_i - s_i)^2}$$

- e.g., LSq SMD = disproportionality based on votes and seats won in the SMD tier

n/a = Not applicable. In linked systems, the PR tier's effective number of parliamentary parties (N_s) and the level of disproportionality are fairly nonsensical. Because of the use of compensation seats, parties that won a large proportion of the PR vote will win very few seats in the PR tier if they also won a large number of SMDs.
UN = Unavailable: the data for the variable were not available to the authors at the time of writing.

APPENDIX 4B. MULTIVARIABLE ANALYSES

We use the data listed in Appendix 4A to conduct multivariable quantitative (least squares) analyses of the effect of rules and democratic experience/party institutionalization on a variety of different outcomes. Our measurement of the independent variables is the same across all our analyses. Furthermore, the unit of analysis in each model is the same: the country/election. Because the results within each country case are unlikely to be independent, we correct the standard errors by "clustering" (using Stata's "cluster" command) by country.[17] We also run additional models (not shown) using Cook's D measures to search for and drop outliers, which does not lead to major changes in the results.

Disproportionality (LSq)

All our analyses of disproportionality (presented in Table 4.3) use the log of the LSq measure as the dependent variable. These analyses are intended not to present a set of fully specified models, but rather to show the rough relationship between key independent variables and the dependent variable under consideration. As we note in the chapter, the large number of independent candidates in our noninstitutionalized cases causes problems for our measures of LSq SMD and LSq Overall. We therefore run our models both with and without the noninstitutionalized cases.

The dependent variable in the first model is LSq SMD, disproportionality in the SMD tier. Our independent variable is *Plurality*, a dichotomous variable coded 1 for countries that elect SMD candidates according to FPTP rules and 0 for countries that use a two-round majority formula. Model 1 demonstrates the expected negative relationship between plurality rules and level of disproportionality in the SMD tier – LSq is lower under plurality rules than in two-round majority SMDs. However, when we drop the noninstitutionalized cases (Model 2), the coefficient on Plurality is significant only at the 0.173 level.[18] This lack of statistical significance may be due to the small number of elections (nine) and countries (three) in our dataset that used two-round majority rules.

Our second set of models examines the effect of PR thresholds on LSq in the PR tier.[19] We code *PR Threshold* as equal to the percentage of the PR vote legally mandated in order to win PR seats. As expected, PR Threshold has a positive and statistically significant coefficient: Higher thresholds lead to greater disproportionality. This relationship holds whether we do (Model 4)

---

[17] We also rerun all of our models with an approach that does not cluster by country, but rather corrects for heteroskedasticity between the cases (Stata's "hc3" command). The results of these models are similar to those that we get by clustering by country.

[18] We do not include institutionalized new democracies as a dummy variable because of the variable's −0.75 correlation with Plurality.

[19] As we explain in Chapter 3, LSq measures are nonsensical in the PR tiers of linked mixed-member systems, and so we only include here the 22 country/election cases for which we calculated LSq PR.

TABLE 4.3. *Impact of Electoral Rules and Democratic Context on Disproportionality (LSq)*

	(1) SMD Tier	(2) SMD Tier No Uninst.	(3) PR Tier	(4) PR Tier	(5) Whole Syst. No Uninst.	(6) Whole System
Plurality	−0.326[+] (0.175)	−0.254 (0.175)				
PR Threshold			0.176*** (0.032)	0.165** (0.035)		
Russia 1995				0.810*** (0.092)		
Institutionalized New Democracy					0.414* (0.153)	0.457* (0.155)
Noninstitutionalized						0.214 (0.162)
Unlinked					0.628** (0.159)	0.636** (0.162)
SMD/PR Ratio (log)					0.347[+] (0.175)	0.387[+] (0.184)
Election Number (log)					−0.157[+] (0.072)	−0.108 (0.090)
Constant	2.862*** (0.155)	2.862*** (0.157)	1.385*** (0.152)	1.390*** (0.159)	1.447*** (0.135)	1.375*** (0.144)
Observations	52	45	22	22	45	52
Clusters	15	12	8	8	12	15
R^2	0.056	0.043	0.427	0.519	0.575	0.551

- Dependent variable: LSq logged.
- Unit of analysis: Country/Election.
- Least squares models with standard errors corrected by clustering by country.
- Standard errors in parentheses; [+] $p < 0.1$; * $p < 0.05$; ** $p < 0.01$; *** $p < 0.001$.

or do not (Model 3) control for the aberrational 1995 election in Russia, in which LSq PR was particularly high.

Our third set of models examines the impact of a number of different variables on the overall level of disproportionality (LSq Overall). Our independent variables are (1) *Institutionalized New Democracy*, coded 1 for institutionalized new democracies and 0 otherwise; (2) *Noninstitutionalized*, coded 1 for the noninstitutionalized cases and 0 otherwise; (3) *Unlinked*, coded 1 for unlinked systems, and 0 for linked systems; (4) *SMD/PR Ratio (log)*,[20] the logged ratio of the number of SMD seats to the number of PR seats; and

---

[20] Throughout our different analyses in this appendix, the results do not change markedly if for linked systems we measure the number of PR seats as the total number of seats – including those allocated in SMDs – in the country (as might be appropriate given that linked systems provide parties a share of *all* the seats that matches their share of the PR vote).

(5) *Election Number (log)*, which is the log of the number of elections conducted under mixed-member system rules in the country.

The results in Table 4.3 are largely as expected. Most important, Institutionalized New Democracy has a positive and statistically significant coefficient, indicating that overall system disproportionality is higher in new democracies than in established democracies. Because of the problems we noted earlier with our measure of independents, we run one version of the analysis without the noninstitutionalized party systems (Model 5) and one with them that includes a Noninstitutionalized dummy variable (Model 6). The Noninstitutionalized dummy variable has a positive, but nonsignificant, coefficient. More important, though, there is little difference in the results with or without them.

Moving to the rules, themselves, Unlinked has a positive and significant coefficient – unlinked systems are more disproportional than linked ones. SMD/PR Ratio (log) has a positive and significant coefficient – systems with a smaller share of PR seats have high disproportionality. Election Number (log) has a negative coefficient in both Models 5 and 6 – that is, disproportionality is lower in later elections – but it is significant only when we drop the noninstitutionalized cases (Model 5).

The Effective Number of Candidates in SMDs (N_{cands})

In Table 4.4, we present results for models in which the dependent variable is the log of the mean N_{cands} – the effective number of candidates at the SMD level – for each country/election. We categorize each country by the level of democratic experience/party institutionalization and create a dichotomous variable for each. For most of our analyses, we measure a country's experience with its mixed-member system with a dichotomous variable, *1st Election*, coded 1 in the first election and 0 in other years. However, we also use the log of the number of elections under the mixed-member system (Model 6).

As with disproportionality, we use the independent variables Unlinked, SMD/PR Ratio (log), and Plurality, but the results for the democratic experience and number of elections variables remain roughly the same no matter which, if any, of these electoral institution variables we include in the model. In all the models in Table 4.4, Unlinked and Plurality have coefficients in the expected negative direction. SMD/PR Ratio (log) usually has a tiny positive coefficient. However, none of the three variables ever has a statistically significant coefficient in the models in Table 4.4.

We run a series of models (see Table 4.4). Model 1 includes all elections in our dataset and uses Established Democracy as the base type of democracy. Most important, in Model 1, the coefficients on both Institutionalized New Democracy and Noninstitutionalized are positive and statistically significant, indicating, all else being equal, that established democracies have lower N_{cands} scores, with the seemingly largest difference between established democracies and noninstitutionalized party systems. To make it easier to view the difference between institutionalized and noninstitutionalized new democracies,

TABLE 4.4. *What Shapes the Effective Number of Candidates at the SMD Level (N_{cands})?*

	(1) All Cases	(2) All Cases	(3) Drop Lithuania	(4) Drop Lithuania	(5) 1st 4 Elections	(6) Election Number	(7) Drop Outliers	(8) H & I Linked
Institutionalized New Democracy	0.335** (0.107)	-0.270 (0.160)	-0.403** (0.119)	0.243* (0.110)	0.274* (0.126)	0.249+ (0.127)	0.423*** (0.068)	0.327** (0.104)
Noninstitutionalized	0.605*** (0.111)			0.645*** (0.097)	0.557*** (0.123)	0.549*** (0.119)	0.605*** (0.107)	0.599*** (0.100)
Established Democracy		-0.605*** (0.111)	-0.645*** (0.097)					
1st Election	0.133* (0.047)	0.133* (0.047)	0.138* (0.050)	0.138* (0.050)	0.088+ (0.048)		0.132* (0.054)	0.140* (0.049)
Election Number (log)						-0.135* (0.057)		
Unlinked	-0.070 (0.102)	-0.070 (0.102)	-0.120 (0.087)	-0.120 (0.087)	-0.093 (0.107)	-0.099 (0.104)	-0.070 (0.080)	-0.061 (0.093)
SMD/PR Ratio (log)	0.019 (0.144)	0.019 (0.144)	0.027 (0.123)	0.027 (0.123)	-0.045 (0.156)	-0.050 (0.153)	0.019 (0.145)	-0.003 (0.118)
Plurality	-0.119 (0.156)	-0.119 (0.156)	-0.209 (0.169)	-0.209 (0.169)	-0.189 (0.179)	-0.161 (0.171)	-0.150 (0.107)	-0.085 (0.099)
Constant	1.099*** (0.171)	1.704*** (0.252)	1.842*** (0.231)	1.197*** (0.187)	1.256*** (0.200)	1.356*** (0.217)	1.130*** (0.108)	1.061*** (0.111)
Observations	52	52	48	48	40	52	46	52
Clusters	15	15	14	14	15	15	13	15
R^2	0.586	0.586	0.596	0.596	0.564	0.644	0.727	0.586

- Dependent variable: N_{cands} (mean effective number of candidates, SMD level), logged.
- Unit of analysis: Country/Election.
- Least squares models with standard errors corrected by clustering by country.
- Standard errors in parentheses; $+$ $p < 0.1$; $*$ $p < 0.05$; $**$ $p < 0.01$; $***$ $p < 0.001$.

115

we run Model 2, which uses Noninstitutionalized as the base category. Here the coefficient on Institutionalized New Democracies is negative – suggesting that institutionalized new democracies have more of a constraining effect than noninstitutionalized ones – but the coefficient is not statistically significant.

However, institutional and contextual factors make Lithuania an unusual case that experienced especially high fragmentation in the SMD tier. The regular fluctuations between two-round majority and plurality elections within the SMD tier likely undermined strategic voting in SMDs. Moreover, rules that promoted the formation of coalitions in the PR tier (raising the legal threshold to 5 percent for parties and 7 percent for coalitions) further complicated strategic behavior in the SMD tier by prompting parties to run as members of larger coalitions in the PR tier but field their own candidates in SMD contests (Krupavicius 1997).

We believe that the lack of a discernible difference in Model 2 between noninstitutionalized and institutionalized new democracies is a result of the anomalous Lithuanian case; dropping Lithuania from the analysis gives us results more in line with our expectations. Models 3 and 4 replicate Models 2 and 1, respectively, but with Lithuania no longer in the analysis. In these models, we still find a significant difference between the number of candidates in established democracies and both noninstitutionalized and institutionalized party systems in new democracies (Model 4), but also a significant difference between institutionalized and noninstitutionalized new democracies (Model 3). In Model 4, the positive sign on the coefficients for Institutionalized New Democracy and Noninstitutionalized indicates that established democracies have a lower N_{cands} score than do new democracies. In Model 3, the negative sign on Institutionalized New Democracy indicates that N_{cands} is lower in such countries than in the Noninstitutionalized type.[21]

Under all of these specifications the coefficient on 1st Election is in the expected positive direction and statistically significant: N_{cands} is higher in the first election under a new mixed-member system. In Model 5, to ensure that the results are not biased by Germany's long history with its mixed-member system, we rerun Model 1 with only the first four elections in each country. The results largely stay the same. In Model 6, we rerun Model 1 but replace 1st Election with Election Number (log), which has a negative and statistically significant coefficient, indicating that with each election – especially the initial ones under the mixed system – N_{cands} drops.

In Model 7, we use Cook's D measures to search for and drop outliers, with no major changes in the results. Finally, to be certain that our coding of

---

[21] We run alternative models in which we include Lithuania in the analysis as a dichotomous dummy variable. The results do not change markedly from the results in which we drop it altogether. We believe that the appropriate specification with the dummy variable would include interactions between the dummy variable and the institutional variables, so we opt to report the simpler model that drops Lithuania altogether.

Hungary and Italy as unlinked systems is not dramatically altering our results, in Model 8 we rerun Model 1 but now code those two countries as linked. The results do not change markedly.

THE PSYCHOLOGICAL EFFECT ($N_{PARTIES} - N_{CANDS}$)

In results that we report in Table 4.5, the dependent variable is $N_{parties} - N_{cands}$. We use independent variables that are similar to those in the previous Appendix 4B analyses. We do not include SMD/PR Ratio and Plurality because doing so introduces substantial collinearity, most notably because of our smaller number of country cases (as we do not have $N_{parties}$ measures for all countries).

In our base model (Model 1), which includes no controls for outlier countries, only Institutionalized New Democracy and Unlinked have statistically significant coefficients, but there are some important outliers and we include a dichotomous dummy variable for each in the remainder of the models. First, as we discussed earlier, there was an explosion of parties competing under PR in Russia in 1995, leading to a massive gap between the number of parties under SMDs and PR that year – even though the country also had a whopping N_{cands} score of 5.91. In addition, there are two clear outlier countries in the dataset in which $N_{parties}$ is smaller than N_{cands}: Bolivia (1997 and 2002) and Lithuania (1996 and 2000). We have already discussed Lithuania. In Bolivia, the PR vote helps elect the national president, thus increasing the incentives for strategic defection among voters and elites in PR balloting and presumably reducing the effective number of parties relative to the number in the SMD tier. In Lithuania, party proliferation in the SMD tier was likely inflated by the continual fluctuation of the rules governing this tier.

In Model 2, which is identical to Model 1 but now includes the country controls, the coefficients on Institutionalized New Democracy and Noninstitutionalized are in the expected negative direction and statistically significant – in other words, the psychological effect of SMDs, which constrains the number of parties in SMDs relative to PR, is weaker in new democracies than in established ones.

The coefficient on Unlinked is in the expected positive direction and statistically significant: Unlinked systems lead to more strategic defection in SMDs. Interestingly, the coefficients on 1st Election and PR Threshold are both roughly zero, suggesting that neither has much impact on the difference between the number of parties under SMDs and PR.

As robustness checks, we run a series of alternative specifications of our models. To ensure that later elections held under the system in Germany did not bias the results, we run Model 3, which only includes the first four elections for each country. The results scarcely change from Model 2. To ensure that our lack of a finding of the effect of time was not due to our blunt, dichotomous 1st Election variable, we replace 1st Election with Election Number (log) (Model 4), with little change in the results.

TABLE 4.5. *What Shapes the Psychological Effect ($N_{parties} - N_{cands}$)?*

	(1) All Cases	(2) Country Controls	(3) 1st 4 Els.	(4) # of Els.	(5) H & I Linked	(6) New vs. Old Dem.	(7) $N_{parties}$ (log) − N_{cands} (log)
Institutionalized New Democracy	−1.454+ (0.669)	−1.347+ (0.670)	−1.220+ (0.655)	−1.412* (0.598)	−0.646*** (0.135)		
Noninstitutionalized	−0.654 (0.874)	−1.544+ (0.789)	−1.640+ (0.779)	−1.619+ (0.742)	−0.201 (0.527)		
New Democracy						−1.496+ (0.720)	−0.419* (0.161)
Unlinked	1.391+ (0.717)	1.841* (0.783)	1.716* (0.764)	1.797* (0.705)	0.236 (0.523)	1.828* (0.759)	0.466* (0.168)
1st Election	−0.136 (0.151)	0.004 (0.107)	−0.093 (0.105)		−0.008 (0.181)	0.015 (0.115)	−0.014 (0.026)
Election Number (log)				−0.175 (0.135)			
PR Threshold	−0.016 (0.097)	0.058 (0.126)	0.091 (0.133)	0.090 (0.126)	−0.087 (0.107)	0.053 (0.110)	0.009 (0.024)
Russia 1995		2.342*** (0.174)	2.301*** (0.154)	2.307*** (0.230)	2.411*** (0.237)	2.314*** (0.191)	0.238*** (0.051)
Lithuania		−1.234+ (0.617)	−1.433+ (0.662)	−1.358+ (0.613)	−0.515 (0.565)	−1.073*** (0.232)	−0.225** (0.057)
Bolivia		0.765 (0.689)	0.491 (0.715)	0.682 (0.620)	−0.412 (0.389)	0.905 (0.798)	0.253 (0.180)
Constant	0.559 (0.428)	0.162 (0.593)	0.258 (0.580)	0.275 (0.518)	1.079+ (0.494)	0.180 (0.534)	0.092 (0.113)
Observations	41	41	30	41	41	41	41
Clusters	11	11	11	11	11	11	11
R^2	0.512	0.726	0.735	0.741	0.342	0.725	0.722

- Dependent variable: $N_{parties}$ minus N_{cands} – i.e., the mean effective number of parties receiving votes under PR balloting in each SMD minus the mean effective number of candidates receiving votes under SMD balloting in each SMD (determined for each country/election).
- Unit of analysis: Country/Election.
- Least squares models with standard errors corrected by clustering by country.
- Standard-errors in parentheses; $^+ p < 0.1$; $^* p < 0.05$; $^{**} p < 0.01$; $^{***} p < 0.001$.

TABLE 4.6. *What Shapes Projection of the Number of Parties from the District to the National Level (N_v SMD − N_{cands})?*

	(1) 1st vs. Later Elections	(2) Election Number	(3) Plurality Rules Only	(4) N_v (log) − N_{cands} (log)
Institutionalized New Democracy	1.387[+] (0.632)	1.325[+] (0.694)	1.425[+] (0.753)	0.187** (0.059)
1st Election	0.647[+] (0.328)			0.119* (0.051)
Election Number (log)		−0.372[+] (0.172)	−0.258* (0.099)	
Plurality	0.807 (0.659)	0.814 (0.692)		0.119 (0.109)
Constant	−0.582 (0.686)	−0.006 (0.700)	0.667** (0.183)	−0.033 (0.114)
Observations	45	45	36	45
Clusters	12	12	10	12
R^2	0.395	0.406	0.486	0.366

- Dependent variable: N_v minus N_{cands} – i.e., the effective number of parties in SMD voting aggregated to the national level minus the mean effective number of candidates receiving votes under SMD balloting in each SMD (determined for each country/election).
- Unit of analysis: Country/Election.
- Least-squares models with standard errors corrected by clustering by country.
- Standard errors in parentheses; [+] $p < 0.1$; * $p < 0.05$; ** $p < 0.01$; *** $p < 0.001$.

In Model 5, which matches Model 2 except that Hungary and Italy are now coded as linked systems, the results change markedly – most notably, with the coefficient on Noninstitutionalized becoming nonsignificant. However, we are skeptical about this model. First, we believe that it is correct to code Hungary and Italy as unlinked. Second, in Model 5, we see a massive drop in the size of the R^2, suggesting a much worse fit in explaining variation. At least as important, among the countries/elections that we examine in this analysis of the psychological effect, the correlation between this alternative measure of Unlinked and Noninstitutionalized party systems is 0.55, suggesting that collinearity may be causing problems with the estimates.

Given the lack of statistically significant difference between the two types of new democracies, we rerun Model 2, but now create a single, aggregated New Democracy variable (Model 6). This model provides results that are similar to those in Model 2, and now we see a statistically significant and negative coefficient on New Democracy, indicating that the difference between $N_{parties}$ and N_{cands} is, as expected, much greater in established democracies. Finally, we rerun Model 2 but now operationalize the dependent variable as the log of $N_{parties}$ minus the log of N_{cands} (Model 7), with little change in the results.

Dropping the country dummy variables leads to no major change in the results for Models 6 and 7 (results not shown).

Projection from the Single-Member District Level to the National Level (N_v SMD – N_{cands})

In the results that we report in Table 4.6, the dependent variable is the nationally aggregated effective number of parties in the SMD tier (N_v SMD) minus the mean SMD-level number of parties (N_{cands}) for each country/election. Positive coefficients therefore suggest less matching of N_v SMD and N_{cands} – that is, less projection. For reasons we discussed earlier, we drop the noninstitutionalized party systems from the analysis.

We run four models. In Model 1, our independent variables are Institutionalized New Democracy, 1st Election, and Plurality. In Models 2 and 3, we replace 1st Election with Election Number (log). We were concerned about the high collinearity between Plurality and Institutionalized New Democracy, so in Model 3 we drop Plurality. In Model 4, we change the dependent variable to the log of Nv SMD minus the log of N_{cands}.

The results are largely as expected and consistent across analyses. The coefficient on Institutionalized New Democracy is positive and statistically significant, indicating greater projection in established democracies. The coefficient on 1st Election is positive and statistically significant, and the coefficient on Election Number (log) is negative and significant, indicating greater projection as countries have greater experience with a mixed-member system. Plurality has a nonsignificant coefficient.

5

Political Context, Electoral Rules, and Their Effects on Strategic and Personal Voting

In Chapter 4, we began to consider the conditionality of electoral system effects through an analysis of the number of parties in mixed-member systems. We saw that FPTP rules produce their expected effects in established democracies, most notably by constraining the number of parties. At the same time, we saw a very different result under FPTP rules in new democracies, which tended to produce many more parties. We argued that these different outcomes were due to far greater strategic defection in established democracies by candidates and their supporters who faced little chance of success in SMDs, but this argument was merely conjecture; we did not demonstrate the behavior that underlay the different results. To get at these mechanisms, we need to delve more deeply into whether voters and elites in different contexts do, in fact, behave in this way. We need to address the question: Is there, in fact, more strategic defection in established democracies than in new ones? In Chapters 5 and 6, we address this issue of strategic defection under different contexts.

In this chapter, we study votes cast under mixed-member systems to learn more about the factors that shape voting behavior. Our principal aim is to explore the conditions under which voters will be likely to cast *strategic* ballots, whereby they withdraw support from their preferred candidate in order to affect the race, but our strongest findings in this chapter relate to the personal vote. In the study of mixed-member electoral systems, work on strategic voting is particularly well established. Ticket splitting in which a greater number of votes are cast for large parties in the SMD tier than in the PR tier (and a smaller number of votes are cast for minor parties in SMDs) has been put forward as evidence that voters react strategically to restrictive electoral rules – such as FPTP – that tend to deny representation to minor parties.[1] On this topic, the literature gives substantial attention to strategic voting, but does not account

---

[1] See Bawn (1999), Cox (1997), Fisher (1973), and Roberts (1988) on Germany's mixed system and Reed (1999) on Japan's.

sufficiently for another factor that can drive ticket splitting: the personal vote – additional SMD votes cast for a candidate due to the candidate's personal appeal to voters.

In this chapter, we provide a classic form of the controlled comparison approach in which we examine ticket splitting in a number of different mixed-member electoral systems – Germany, Japan, Lithuania, New Zealand, Russia, Scotland, Ukraine, and Wales. However, prior to analyzing the actual difference between parties' share of SMD and PR votes, we indicate the shortcomings inherent in any analysis of such ticket splitting that does not take into account the presence of the personal vote. We then introduce analysis of the difference in votes cast under SMD and PR rules that is sensitive to the potential presence of both strategic and personal voting. This analysis indicates that, in a number of the countries under investigation, the personal vote plays a significant role in the overall base of support of SMD candidates and, hence, explains much of the difference in SMD and PR support in mixed-member systems.

At the same time, this chapter's analysis is also consistent with the central argument of this book: political context appears to condition the impact of electoral rules on political outcomes. Most notably, this chapter suggests that strategic defection plays a more significant part in voting behavior under SMDs in established democracies than in new ones. Moreover, voters' and politicians' experience with rules is also important to their ability to defect strategically under SMDs. This chapter suggests that personal voting appears to be especially prevalent in the initial elections under a mixed system. Over time, there is often a shift toward greater strategic defection under SMDs, but we are more likely to be able to perceive this shift in established democracies than in new ones with poorly established party systems.

RESEARCH ON STRATEGIC VOTING IN MIXED-MEMBER SYSTEMS

Mixed-member electoral systems provide a unique opportunity to examine the extent of strategic voting through a controlled comparison of voting patterns under different electoral rules. Naturally, examining survey data is often the best approach to studying such strategic voting. However, such data are not always readily available. Moreover, even when they are available, they may not provide ideal measures because they merely measure how respondents *claim* that they will behave, rather than measuring their actual behavior. For this reason, a number of analyses – most notably Kathleen Bawn (1999) and Steven Reed (1999) on ticket splitting in, respectively, Germany and Japan – provide a creative, nonsurvey data approach to studying such strategic defection in SMDs by comparing district-level PR and SMD vote totals under mixed-member system rules. These analyses cogently assert that the ballots that voters cast in the PR tier represent "sincere" votes, as most voters can feel assured that PR rules will permit their preferred party to win PR tier representation and therefore can worry less about wasting their votes on a party that will go unrepresented.[2] In contrast, voters who sincerely prefer a weak candidate in SMD races have incentive to shift their votes strategically to a different candidate in the district race to avoid wasting their votes on a likely loser. By examining systematically the differences between PR and SMD votes cast at the same time under mixed-member system rules, these analyses make cogent claims about when voters will move away from their sincere preference (for whom they cast a PR ballot) in SMD races.

Taking advantage of the opportunity provided by the two votes in mixed-member systems, Bawn and Reed each present compelling evidence of voters' strategic defection under FPTP rules. Most noteworthy, they each present multivariable analyses in which the dependent variable is equal to the SMD vote percentage of a given candidate minus the PR vote percentage won by the candidate's party (with votes aggregated within each SMD). Bawn and Reed each find that the closer the race in which candidates are involved, the larger the gap between the number of SMD votes cast for them and the number of PR ballots cast for their parties. In short, their results suggest that ticket splitting is most prevalent when voters' SMD ballots are most likely to "count." In other words, Bawn's and Reed's analyses suggest that voters strategically move away from their preferred party's candidate to a more competitive one to affect the outcome of the SMD race.

But the Personal Vote May Affect the Results

However, strategic defection is hardly the only condition under which voters may cast a ballot for a candidate from a party that they do not prefer most. Indeed, the personal vote is likely to often lead to such behavior, and the personal vote could just as easily generate statistical outcomes of the kind that scholars usually attribute to strategic defection in mixed systems.

In many cases, voters will vote for a candidate primarily for personal reasons (Cain, Ferejohn, and Fiorina 1987; Carey and Shugart 1995). The candidate may be well known, be personally likable, provide favors, or demonstrate a proven capacity to serve the district and its constituents, and all these factors may be more important to voters than what the candidate's party represents. For example, even voters who do not support an incumbent politician's party may support the incumbent candidate for these reasons.

Scholars studying ticket splitting in mixed-member systems have noted the importance of candidate popularity. For example, Bawn argues that candidates may win more votes in the SMD race than their parties do under PR because of different types of personal votes cast for them.[3] However, most mixed-member

---

[2] Naturally, this assumption proves more unwieldy as the PR threshold of representation increases: when thresholds are high, voters may vote for a party other than their most preferred even under PR rules.

[3] See also the analysis of Karp et al. (2002), which points out the significant impact of candidates' personal popularity on split-ticket voting in New Zealand's mixed-member system.

system analyses that focus on the difference between candidates' SMD vote and the PR vote of the candidates' parties do not control for the personal vote and, as a result, there is reason to rethink the meaning of their results.

As we explain in greater detail in the next section, in many cases it is not clear what we should make of a finding that candidates involved in a close district race receive more votes in their SMD race than their party does in PR. For many candidates, such an outcome is totally consistent with a significant personal vote, and not just strategic voting: for example, a large number of personal votes cast for a second-place candidate may lead the candidate to (1) be in a closer race with the front-runner and (2) receive a markedly larger number of SMD votes than his or her party receives PR ballots. This indicates a potential flaw in Bawn's analysis. Nevertheless, as our findings suggest, the fact that Germany is a particularly party-oriented system – see Conradt (2001) – may counteract this problem, as there simply may be much less personal voting there.

This makes cross-national comparison essential, as the long-standing German system may be a unique case among mixed-member systems and generalizations based on the German experience may be inapplicable to other cases. Reed's analysis of ticket splitting in Japan in 1996 includes a variable to take into account the potential impact of the personal vote (1999: 263). However, in general, proxy measures of the personal vote are difficult to find, particularly so in analysis that examines a variety of country cases. In part, including incumbency as an independent variable – as Bawn does – helps capture the personal vote because incumbents ought to receive more personal votes than other types of candidates. However, many other factors, which are not easily quantified, are likely to promote a personal vote, so it is clear that adjustments need to be made to the standard models of strategic voting in mixed systems.

DISENTANGLING THE PERSONAL VOTE FROM STRATEGIC VOTING

In many cases, such as the example offered earlier regarding second-place candidates in Bawn's analysis, it is difficult to decipher whether ticket splitting is driven by personal votes or strategic defection, but for certain candidates – in particular, those in first place – the results make it easier to distinguish between them.

We follow Bawn's cue and measure competitiveness of the SMD race as the difference between the vote percentages won by the first- and second-place candidates in a district. This variable, which we call *Margin*, is also what Bawn uses to examine whether voters cast strategic ballots in SMDs. According to most theories of strategic voting, candidates will be more likely to receive additional SMD votes when they are in close races, but fewer voters will shift their support strategically in races that are not close. In other words, if there is *strategic defection*, the SMD–PR vote gap should decline as Margin increases (i.e., the race becomes less competitive). In other words, there should be a negative relationship between Margin and the SMD–PR vote gap.

However, if there is substantial *personal voting*, we should see a positive relationship between Margin and the SMD–PR vote gap: first-place candidates may have a larger SMD–PR vote gap when they are not in a close race – that is, if they win by a very large margin. The logic here is that, because of these candidates' considerable individual popularity, they both dominate the competition (win by a large margin) and receive many more SMD votes than their parties obtain in PR.

To put it another way, it makes little sense to think that voters who consider strategically defecting from their first choice will, all else being equal, become more inclined to cast additional SMD votes for the winner when the race is not close. Rather, for the first-place candidate, a positive correlation between the margin of victory and the SMD–PR vote gap would suggest that the candidate was getting many personal votes, which also led the candidate to win by a larger margin.[4] At the same time, a negative correlation between the margin of victory and the SMD–PR vote gap indicates very clearly the presence of strategic voting. That is, the personal vote is most likely present to some degree in nearly any electoral system and would create a bias in favor of a positive correlation between Margin and the SMD–PR vote gap for the top candidate. Therefore, a negative correlation would indicate that so many additional votes were being cast for the top candidate in close races – in short, strategic votes – that they counteracted the effect of the personal vote's positive correlation bias.

In the previous section, we noted the difficulty of disentangling the personal vote and strategic defection from one another for candidates in second place, but we can certainly use votes for third (and worse) place candidates in much the same way that we do for first place – only we expect the correlations to work in the opposite direction. That is, if there is substantial strategic defection by voters in SMDs, we will see voters shifting their votes away from poorly ranked SMD candidates when there is a close race between first and second place in the SMD. To put it differently, if there is substantial strategic defection in SMDs, the correlation between Margin and the SMD–PR vote gap for third (and worse) place candidates will be positive: SMD races between first and second place that are not close will lead to third (and worse) place candidates retaining more of the SMD support from voters who prefer their party, so they will hold a larger share of SMD votes relative to their party's votes in PR.

DATA AND EXPECTATIONS FOR WHEN WE WILL FIND STRATEGIC DEFECTION IN SMDS

Based on these insights, we reexamine ticket splitting under mixed-member system rules in an effort to highlight the conditions under which strategic defection is particularly likely in SMDs.

---

[4] A positive correlation between the two does not necessarily rule out the possibility of strategic voting. Indeed, without strategic voting, the positive correlation between margin of victory and the SMD–PR vote gap may have been larger. However, in this sort of analysis, the positive correlation between the two variables makes it impossible to know whether strategic voting is taking place.

To consider the impact of these different features on personal voting and strategic defection, we look at the following cases: Germany (1998 and 1953),[5] New Zealand (1999 and 2002), Japan (2000, 2003, and 2005), Lithuania (2000),[6] Russia (1995, 1999, and 2003), Scotland (2003), Ukraine (2002), and Wales (2003). We examine each election in each country separately (i.e., we run a separate model for each country/election). We examine only cases for which we could control for a variety of potential variables, especially whether any given candidate was an incumbent. For this reason – with the exception of Germany in 1953, which we include to offer a base of comparison for the other cases – we look only at elections after the initial one that used the mixed-member system.

We focus on the relationship between (a) the competitiveness of the SMD race and (b) the difference between candidates' share of the SMD vote and their party's share of the PR vote. Based on the relationship between these variables, we can make inferences about the extent of strategic defection and personal voting in SMDs in each country.

Our Major Expectations

What factors ought to shape strategic and personal voting in our different cases?

As we discussed earlier – especially in Chapters 1, 3, and 4 – we should be less likely to find evidence of strategic defection by voters away from their top choice in SMDs in new democracies (especially in those with poorly institutionalized party systems). The lower levels of information about likely outcomes in new democracies can make it more difficult to differentiate between the chances of success for many different candidates. Indeed, when parties do not structure the vote, there may be a particularly strong sense that any of a large number of candidates could win the SMD race. As a result, voters should be less likely to withdraw support from their top choice.

Second, we expect to find greater evidence of strategic defection after the initial elections under mixed system rules, especially in established democracies. As we discussed earlier, in the first elections under a new electoral system, there may be uncertainty over both the rules and likely support for different parties under the rules, which may in turn promote behavior – even in established

---

[5] The most recent election we include in our analysis for Germany is 1998 because we do not have complete data on incumbency for later years. The first year West Germany used the mixed-member system in its current form was 1953. We were slightly limited in our datasets for Germany. For Germany 1953, we had data only on the top 11 parties at the national level and for Germany 1998 we had data only on the top five parties. However, other parties received extremely small shares of the vote. For the remaining country/election cases, we examine the SMD–PR vote gap for all candidates.

[6] We analyze Lithuania only in 2000 because in other years the country used two-round majority rules in the SMD tier, which reduced the incentive for strategic defection in the first round of SMD balloting.

democracies – that is similar to what we described in new democracies more generally. Presumably, over time, voters and elites gain information on likely support patterns and become generally better able to distinguish between different candidates and their likelihood of success. As a result, we should expect to find greater evidence of strategic defection away from more poorly ranked candidates in later elections. However, for the reasons that we discussed in the previous paragraph, we still expect to find less evidence of strategic defection in new democracies, even after they have had some experience with the system.

What factors are likely to affect the amount of personal voting? Clearly, in many countries in both the established and newly democratic worlds, voters often cast ballots for a candidate primarily for personal reasons (Cain, Ferejohn, and Fiorina 1987; Carey and Shugart 1995). The candidate may have high name recognition, possess attractive personal qualities, or demonstrate a proven capacity to serve the district and service the district's constituents. All these factors may be more important to a voter than the party label of the candidate and what that label represents. New democracies and weak party systems may be especially likely to promote a personal vote: in the absence of widespread, concrete party preferences, many voters are left with no partisan cues on how to cast their vote and must instead rely on patronage, incumbency, and the personal characteristics of candidates.

Rules governing mixed-member systems may also affect this tendency toward more or less personal voting. As Carey and Shugart (1995) most thoroughly and systematically argue with respect to non–mixed-member systems, the type of electoral system used has a major impact on the degree to which politics is generally more party-oriented or personalistic. Indeed, there are important features of mixed-member systems as well that ought to shape politics in this way. As we argue throughout the book, the most important distinguishing feature of a mixed-member electoral system is whether the two tiers are linked together through a system of compensatory seats, in which seats or votes won by a party in the SMD tier are subtracted from its total determined by the PR tier. For example, in Germany, New Zealand, Scotland, and Wales, SMD winners take the first set of seats won by their party and the remaining seats (the total determined by the PR tier minus the total won by the parties' candidates in SMDs) are allotted to candidates on the parties' PR lists (see Chapter 2).

We expect that parties in unlinked systems will have a particularly strong incentive to focus on taking SMDs because each district seat they win will be added onto the national party seat total. Insofar as more personalistic campaigning will be likely to increase the number of SMD votes a candidate receives, parties will have incentive to encourage their SMD candidates to behave more personalistically. For this reason, in unlinked mixed systems, parties may have a stronger incentive to nominate candidates with more individual popular appeal and thus increase the number of personal votes.[7] In contrast, in

---

[7] Such personalistic behavior may not be as prevalent in countries with strong, cohesive parties that may suppress the differences among copartisans for the sake of party unity. Nonetheless,

systems with linked tiers, parties will have far less incentive to encourage their candidates to behave personalistically. In linked systems, winning SMDs will not usually increase the total number of seats the party will be allotted, unless candidates' individual behavior manages to increase support for the party as a whole (not always a likely proposition). Indeed, too much individualism on the part of candidates may hurt the party by introducing an image of party incoherence.[8]

Finally, prior electoral system experience is likely to affect behavior under the new mixed-member system, especially in Japan. In Japan the now-defunct single nontransferable vote (SNTV) system, which governed Japan's lower house until electoral reform in 1994, played an important part in exacerbating the highly personalistic nature of the Japanese political system. Clearly there were many incentives created by the new Japanese mixed-member system for personalistic politics (see, e.g., McKean and Scheiner 2000), not the least of which being the lack of linkage between the two tiers, but path dependence from SNTV also made continued personal voting likely.[9]

Variation in the Countries and Expectations for Each

The countries in our data set vary in terms of the factors that ought to play an important role in shaping the personal vote. Germany, New Zealand, Scotland, and Wales offer strong linkage mechanisms between the PR and SMD tiers, whereas Japan, Lithuania, Russia, and Ukraine offer no such compensatory linkage. Germany, New Zealand, Japan, Scotland, and Wales are consolidated democracies, whereas democracy is new to Lithuania, Russia, and Ukraine, with particularly poorly established party systems in Russia and Ukraine.

---

we would expect more personalistic campaigning and voting in unlinked systems that reward such behavior.

[8] The linkage between the two tiers may also affect the likelihood of strategic defection. Mixed-member systems such as Germany's, which use the PR tier to compensate for disproportional effects of the SMD tier, may partly undermine the constraining effect of the SMD portion of the system. Arguably, voters in linked mixed-member systems have no incentive to defect from small parties to large parties since the SMD vote has virtually no effect on the final distribution of legislative seats. For this reason, Jesse (1988) argues that evidence of defection from small parties to larger ones in Germany reflects a misunderstanding of the incentives of the system.

[9] Unfortunately, in some country cases it is difficult to determine the "experience" that will be carried over from the old system to the new one. For example, under its previously used pure FPTP system and parliamentary form of government, New Zealand promoted programmatic party government, which emphasized party over the individual candidate, but voter disaffection in the 1980s led to dealignment, a weakening of the links between voters and parties (Denemark 2001). On one hand, then, New Zealand's prior experience reinforced the incentives created by its linked mixed-member system institutions and promoted party-oriented politics under the new system. On the other hand, the weakened ties between voters and parties that developed toward the end of the SMD experience (combined with the SMD institution, which "socialized" voters in the electoral experience of casting their ballots for individual candidates) might also have carried over into the new system and therefore promoted more personalistic politics.

Finally, Germany has had its mixed-member system for decades, but the system is relatively new in the other cases.

Based on the earlier discussion, we expect the personal vote to be the least prominent in Germany because of its significant democratic and mixed system experience and its linked tiers. Therefore, in our analysis of ticket splitting in Germany, there is good reason to expect that the personal vote will not be so great as to mask the presence of strategic defection in SMDs. In contrast, we expect the personal vote to be more prevalent in cases that have no linkage mechanisms (Japan, Lithuania, Russia, and Ukraine), a lack of democratic consolidation (Lithuania, Russia, and Ukraine), and a history of more personalistic behavior/voting (Japan).

It is more difficult for us to say whether we should expect to find substantial strategic defection in New Zealand, Scotland, and Wales. The use of linked tiers in all three would presumably reduce the emphasis on personal voting. However, New Zealand's pre–mixed-member system experience could have pushed the country toward either party-oriented or personalistic politics (see footnote 9). The new mixed-member systems in Scotland and Wales were implemented as part of a move in the 1990s to devolve power somewhat within the United Kingdom to the various subunits, and, in the process created the Scottish Parliament and the National Assembly for Wales (ESRC 2003: 4). However, in both countries, there was a general sense on the part of voters as time went on that it was the central Westminster government – and not their own Scottish or Welsh assembly – that was the real powerholder (Boon and Curtice 2003; ESRC 2003: 4; Glendinning and Scully 2003). Voters who felt this way – and there were many – also probably believed that their votes for the Scottish or Welsh assembly were unlikely to make a real policy difference within the larger and more important U.K. government. Such voters may have seen less benefit from shifting support away from their most preferred option in their own national assembly, even under more restrictive FPTP rules. Moreover, in both Scotland and Wales, surveys indicate that voters had very little sense of the differences between the parties (Boon and Curtice 2003: 4; Glendinning and Scully 2003: 6, 18). Lacking such information, voters probably faced relative difficulty shifting their votes strategically to affect the outcome of the race.

HOW WE DO THE ANALYSIS

To draw inferences about when voters cast personal or strategic votes, we examine the relationship between the competitiveness of the race – the margin between the top two candidates – and the SMD–PR vote gap for each candidate running in the elections in our dataset.

More specifically, we seek to explain reasons for the difference in each party's share of SMD and PR votes (aggregated at the SMD level). Positive SMD–PR vote gaps indicate a candidate receiving more SMD votes than her party receives PR votes in a given district and a negative vote gap indicates the opposite. We do not include (1) any party with PR votes but no candidate running in the SMD and (2) any candidate who has no party receiving PR votes. As in earlier work, we assume that PR votes represent voters' true party preferences and examine the extent to which voters split their tickets. Unlike previous work, however, we focus on two types of "rational" ticket splitting: personal voting (increased SMD support for a candidate due to personal popularity) and strategic defection (increased support for a candidate to affect the outcome of the SMD race).[10]

We control for a number of variables – most notably, whether the SMD candidate was an incumbent – that ought to affect the SMD–PR vote gap, but our principal focus is on the relationship between the margin of victory and the SMD–PR vote gap. (See Appendix 5 for a full discussion and reporting of the models we use and the coding for all variables.) As Bawn did, we calculate our measure of district competitiveness, *Margin*, by subtracting the vote share won by the second-place candidate from the vote share won by the SMD winner. However, we do not expect all candidates to be affected in the same way by strategic defection. The logic underlying Duverger's Law involves voters casting strategic votes for one of the likely top two candidates. According to a similar logic, we expect that as the race gets closer (Margin declines), voters will be more likely to seek to influence the final outcome and, therefore, will be more inclined to cast SMD ballots for one of the top two candidates rather than for candidates likely to finish third or worse.

For the reasons we discussed earlier, we examine separately the relationship between the margin of victory and the SMD–PR vote gap for first-place candidates, second-place candidates, and those in third or worse. First, for first-place candidates, a negative relationship between Margin and the SMD–PR vote gap indicates substantial strategic defection – in other words, these candidates win more SMD votes (relative to their parties' share of PR votes) when the race is close (Margin is low) because voters shift their votes from their preferred choice to the first-place candidate to affect the outcome of the race. In contrast,

---

[10] A third type of rational ticket splitting is also possible: threshold-beating voting. When there is a legal threshold of representation in the PR tier, large parties may have incentive to try to shift some of their PR support to a small party that is a potential coalition partner to help the small party overcome the threshold. Many supporters of the large parties would be encouraged to split their tickets to give SMD votes to the large-party candidate and PR votes to the smaller potential coalition partner. Scenarios of this kind do, in fact, emerge in particular elections in countries such as Germany. In many cases, it is certainly possible that voters are casting a strategic vote in the PR-list tier, especially to help certain parties reach a PR threshold. It is difficult to conceive of a systematic way of controlling for such behavior, but more important, there is no reason to think that such behavior would bias our results to create an illusion of strategic voting for candidates in SMDs when in fact there was none. That is, studies such as those cited here, and our own in this chapter, also examine the correlation between closeness of the SMD race and the degree to which PR and SMD votes match one another. As Cox (1997: 82) notes, "there is no reason to think that strategic *list* votes should be cast differentially in constituencies that are close in terms of the candidate votes." Therefore, the possible existence of strategic defection in the PR tier of a mixed-member system should not undermine this analysis of strategic ticket splitting in such systems.

a positive relationship indicates a heavy personal vote – the candidate receives more SMD votes (relative to the party's share in PR) when he or she has a large margin of victory. In other words, the substantial number of personal votes the first-place candidates receive helps them win many more votes than both their party in PR and the second-place candidates in the SMD races.

Second, we examine second-place candidates separately but only as a control: as we explained earlier, a negative relationship between the margin of victory and the SMD–PR vote gap could be consistent with *both* substantial personal voting and strategic defection by SMD voters. For this reason, we give little attention to the relationship between Margin and the SMD–PR vote gap for second-place candidates. Third, for candidates finishing in third place or worse, the logic is the reverse of that for first-place candidates: A positive correlation between the margin of victory and the SMD–PR vote gap would be a clear indication of strategic defection away from the candidate – in other words, the poorly ranked candidate wins more SMD votes (relative to the party's share of PR votes) when the race is not close (Margin is high) because voters do not feel that shifting their votes to a stronger candidate would ultimately affect the outcome of the (not close) race.

WHERE DO WE SEE THE PERSONAL VOTE AND WHERE DO WE SEE STRATEGIC VOTING?

Based on the quantitative analysis drawn out in Appendix 5, Figure 5.1 illustrates graphically the relationships between the margin of victory and the SMD–PR vote gap for first- and third- (or worse) place candidates. Each pair of bars represents a pattern of personal or strategic voting for each of our countries/elections. The left-hand bar for each country/election represents the relationship between the margin of victory and the SMD–PR vote gap for first-place candidates. The right-hand bar represents the relationship for third- (or worse) place candidates.[11] Large amounts of strategic voting would lead to a correlation between the margin of victory and the SMD–PR vote gap that is negative for first-place candidates and positive for third- (and worse) ranking candidates, so – to place both bars on the same strategic-personal vote scale – for candidates in third (and worse) place in Figure 5.1 we reverse the sign on the estimated relationship between margin of victory and the SMD–PR vote gap. In this way, all bars with a negative value in Figure 5.1 indicate strategic defection by voters and all bars with a positive value indicate a strong personal vote.

At the same time, we should caution the reader to focus on the direction of the bars, but not to make too much of their magnitude (i.e., height). Because these bars are, in effect, and all else being equal, the difference between all the personal and strategic votes, it is difficult to know what exactly a given bar's height means. For example, a short, positive figure might indicate a small

[11] Gray-shaded bars indicate estimates that are not statistically significant at the 0.1 level.

132

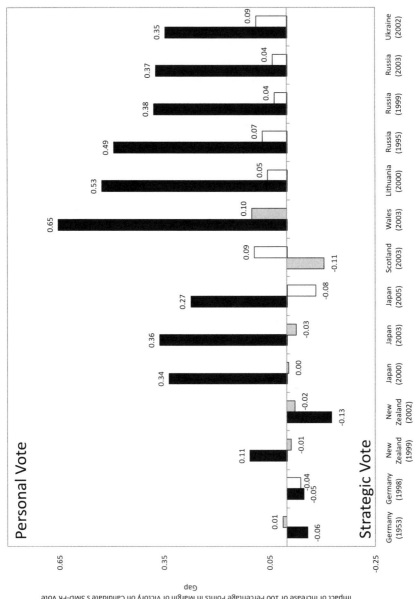

FIGURE 5.1 (See caption on facing page)

but observable amount of personal voting or it might mean large amounts of strategic voting combined with even larger amounts of personal voting. For this reason, we simply interpret bars in the positive direction to be a clear indication of personal voting and those in the negative direction to be a clear indication of strategic defection by voters away from uncompetitive candidates to more competitive ones in the SMD.

Most important, Figure 5.1 provides evidence of strategic defection by voters in SMDs in a number of established democratic cases, but shows nothing but a personal vote in the new democracies (Lithuania, Russia, and Ukraine). In each of the new democracies, larger margins of victory are associated with larger (positive) SMD–PR vote gaps for first-place candidates and larger (negative) vote gaps for low-ranked candidates. To put it differently, in the new democracies, first-place candidates receive *fewer* SMD votes (relative to their party in PR) when locked in a close race in the SMD, exactly the opposite outcome from what would happen if voters were choosing to shift their votes strategically when their vote most mattered (close races). For example, in Lithuania, every additional percentage point difference in the margin of victory is correlated with a 0.53 percentage point increase in first-place candidates' SMD–PR vote gap. This finding coincides with our expectations regarding the relative lack of strategic defection in SMDs in new democracies. Most likely, the results for Lithuania, Russia, and Ukraine are due to (1) more SMD votes going to candidates based on their personal characteristics, especially as a result of the poorly defined labels of the parties, and (2) less strategic defection, because it is more difficult for voters in such systems to distinguish among different candidates' likelihood of success.

In contrast, the established democracies demonstrate a number of different patterns, but provide examples of strategic defection, especially as countries gain experience with their mixed-member systems. The figure for Germany in 1998 offers strong evidence of strategic defection by voters there. The fact

---

FIGURE 5.1. Evidence of personal and strategic voting – relationship between SMD margin of victory (1st place vote – 2nd place vote) and the SMD–PR vote gap. *Notes:*

- Positive values indicate evidence of personal voting. Negative values indicate evidence of strategic voting (away from uncompetitive candidates to more competitive ones). Drawn from coefficients in Tables 5.1, 5.2, and 5.3.
- Bars (black) on the left of each country pair indicate the impact of margin of victory on the SMD–PR vote gap for first-place candidates.
- Bars (white) on the right of each country pair indicate the impact of margin of victory on the SMD–PR vote gap for candidates in third place or worse. To place measures for both first- and third-place (or worse) candidates on the same scale, we multiply the estimate associated with the third-place (or worse) candidates by −1.
- Gray bars (both left and right) indicate estimates that are not statistically significant.

that there is personal voting in any system creates a bias toward a positive relationship between margin of victory and the SMD–PR vote gap. The fact that in Germany in 1998 the relationship is negative strongly suggests that many voters in districts with close races shifted their SMD votes strategically from weak candidates to competitive ones. Voting behavior with respect to poorly ranked (third-place or worse) candidates offers additional evidence that strategic defection in SMDs drove significant amounts of ticket splitting in Germany in 1998: as Figure 5.1 shows, candidates in third (or worse) place tended to have fewer SMD votes (relative to their party's share under PR) when the top two candidates in the district were involved in a close race (Margin was low).

At first, New Zealand demonstrated a strong pattern of personal voting: for New Zealand in 1999 – the second election under the new mixed-member system rules – there was a positive correlation between margin of victory and the SMD–PR vote gap among first-place candidates – that is, first-place candidates received more SMD votes (relative to their party in PR) when winning their SMD race by a wide margin. The results here strongly suggest the impact of partisan dealignment during the 1980s and 1990s and voters' experience under the previous SMD institution, whereby all ballots were cast for individual candidates. Both these factors probably contributed to greater personal voting for individual candidates in the initial elections under New Zealand's mixed-member system. This finding is consistent with Karp et al.'s (2002: 17) conclusion that the strength of New Zealand voters' attachment to particular candidates – and not to specific parties (see also Denemark 2001) – had a significant impact on the likelihood of ticket splitting.

However, over time, strategic voting became more readily apparent in New Zealand. Unlike 1999, in the 2002 New Zealand election there is clear evidence of strategic defection in the form of a negative relationship between the margin of victory and first-place candidates' SMD–PR vote gap. In other words, the closer the race (Margin is low), the larger the number of SMD votes each first-place candidate won (relative to the party's share under PR). This result suggests all the more strongly the importance of experience with a system. New Zealand had used an FPTP system prior to the introduction of its mixed-member rules in 1996, but redistricting occurred in the SMDs when the new rules were instituted, with the number of districts reduced from more than 90 to roughly 60. When combined with the dealignment of the party system, these institutional changes may have created greater uncertainty about likely behavior under the new system. Presumably, over time, as information about the new rules and behavior under them increased, along with greater certainty about the shape of the party system, voters and elites were better able to act strategically, leading to the change in results between 1999 and 2002.

A similar shift occurred in Japan. In all three elections listed in Figure 5.1, we see strong evidence of a personal vote – a strongly positive relationship between margin of victory and the SMD–PR vote gap – for first-place candidates. First-place candidates received more SMD votes (relative to their parties in PR) when they were not in a close district race. Interestingly, though, in the fourth election under the mixed system in 2005, we also find strong evidence of strategic voting away from bottom candidates. This makes sense in the Japanese context: Japan's history of personalistic electoral rules, along with the new mixed-member system rules that prioritized victory in SMDs, provided incentive for personalistic behavior and voting. But over time the system became increasingly focused on two parties (and two candidates per district – see Chapter 4). In 2005, splits away from the ruling Liberal Democratic Party made district-level electoral competition especially fierce, as, for example, the party ran strong challenges in a number of districts against longtime dominant incumbents who had just been expelled from the party. As a result, competition was cast much more in two-candidate terms in many districts. Voters who had personal reasons for supporting first- and second-place candidates most likely continued to do so. But supporters of uncompetitive candidates now had clearer targets to whom to strategically shift their votes.

In large part, the figures for New Zealand and Japan indicate the importance for strategic voting of simply gaining experience with an electoral system. In New Zealand's third election and Japan's fourth election under the new rules, we see a shift toward more perceivable strategic defection. As we discussed earlier, it was difficult to predict the likely form of voting behavior in Scotland and Wales. Ultimately, Figure 5.1 shows that behavior in both cases definitely fit the personal vote mode, but there is tentative (and nonsignificant) evidence of strategic defection in Scotland. However, this analysis is only of the second election under the new systems in Scotland and Wales; future elections may show greater evidence of strategic defection.

Perhaps, then, the strong finding of strategic voting in SMDs in Germany in 1998 is just a result of the country's long history with its mixed-member system rules, dating back to 1953. To consider this possibility, we also examine the relationship between the margin of victory and the SMD–PR vote gap for candidates in West Germany's first election under the two-vote mixed-member system rules in 1953. However, as Figure 5.1 illustrates, even in 1953 there is evidence of strategic voting: in West Germany in 1953, for first-place candidates there was a strong negative relationship between the margin of victory and the SMD–PR vote gap – that is, first-place candidates won more SMD votes (relative to their party in PR) when contesting a close race.[12] To speculate, the immediate move toward strategic voting in Germany is a result of previous electoral experience: in 1949, voters had cast ballots (in a one-vote mixed-member system) for candidates in SMDs (Scarrow 2001: 56), with less dramatic redistricting and partisan dealignment between 1949 and 1953 than occurred when New Zealand reformed its rules.

However, experience with electoral rules can go only so far in explaining the balance of personal and strategic voting – taken as a whole, the analysis here appears to suggest that strategic defection will simply be less apparent in new

---

[12] However, as we explain in Appendix 5, because we do not have information on features such as candidate incumbency for Germany in 1953, we cannot run models as fully specified as we do for the other cases examined here.

democracies, especially those with poorly institutionalized party systems. Figure 5.1 shows strong evidence of strategic defection by voters in Germany as far back as 1953, in New Zealand's third election in 2002, and Japan's fourth election in 2005. However, Figure 5.1 also shows that in Russia in 2003, the country's fourth election under the mixed-member system rules, the personal vote still dominated politics. In short, the most notable feature of Figure 5.1 is the overwhelming evidence of personal voting in the new democracies, with no evidence of movement toward strategic defection by voters in such countries even when they gained greater experience with democratic rule and mixed-member electoral systems.

Using Margin of Victory in the Previous Election to Explain Current Behavior

There is a potential problem with the approach that we have followed. In essence, we are using "time t" variables to predict personal and strategic voting in an election that is also in time t. That is, in regular English: we claim that voters should be more likely to cast strategic votes when in a close race, but our measure of the closeness of the race is based on the actual outcome of the election. In other words, we are implying that voters use (a) the outcome of the election to predict (b) how they are going to vote. This behavior is of course impossible because, in reality, (b) occurs before (a).

Ultimately, however, this issue is not terribly problematic, for two reasons. First, much of the analysis here focuses on the personal vote. When we find that an increase in the margin of victory is associated with an increase in the SMD–PR vote gap, we are not suggesting that voters are using the closeness of the race to determine how to vote. Rather, the correlation between the two indicates that the margin of victory and SMD–PR vote gaps were both greater because voters were casting personal votes. In these cases, it actually makes greater sense to examine margin of victory and the SMD–PR vote gap in the same election.

Second, in most elections, especially in established democracies, there is widespread knowledge of likely vote outcomes. It is unusual to have an electoral romp when a close race was expected or to have a close race when one candidate was considered overwhelmingly dominant (Cox 1988). In this way, outcomes might be considered a proxy for what observers thought in advance was going to happen.

Nevertheless, this last point is merely an assumption on our part; therefore, we now also examine the extent to which voters really are using past information to drive their strategic behavior. If the information in Figure 5.1 accurately depicts voters' strategic behavior, we should see similar patterns in a figure that uses the margin of victory in the previous election (time $t - 1$) to predict voters' decision to vote strategically in the current election (time t). For all the cases in which we could match electoral districts in consecutive elections, we rerun our models, now replacing the margin of victory in the district in the current election with that in the previous one. (See Appendix 5 for the detailed results of the models.)

We expect results to be largely the same as those illustrated in Figure 5.1. Most of all, as before, we do not expect to see evidence of strategic defection in the new democracies. On top of the other impediments to strategic defection in new democracies, elections tend to be so volatile and uncertain in Russia and Ukraine that it would be difficult for voters to use past results as a reliable predictor of future behavior.[13] Indeed, if anything, in new democracies we expect to see no relationship between the margin of victory in the previous election and the SMD–PR vote gap in the current one.

Figure 5.2 illustrates the impact of the margin of victory in the previous election on candidates' SMD–PR vote gap in the current one. Again, most striking, the figure demonstrates no sign of strategic defection in the new democracies. For Russia in 2003, we find no statistically discernible relationship between the margin of victory (in the previous election) and the SMD–PR vote gap. Interestingly, there is a relationship between them in Ukraine, but it continues to point to the importance of the personal vote in shaping differences in SMD–PR vote gap for candidates.

On the other hand, as in the previous figure, Figure 5.2 provides evidence of strategic defection by voters in SMDs in Germany and a shift over time to substantial evidence of strategic defection by voters in SMDs in New Zealand in 2002. The figure demonstrates no evidence of strategic defection by SMD voters in Japan. However, the lack of evidence of strategic defection in Japan should not be surprising: In Figure 5.1, there were no solid signs of strategic defection by Japanese SMD voters until 2005. However, in 2005 the split in the ruling party just prior to the election led to a shift in the competitive context that made past results much less of a guide for the new election.[14]

CONCLUSIONS

The analysis in this chapter demonstrates the clear impact of the personal vote in mixed-member electoral systems in an array of countries and highlights how the personal vote complicates our ability to recognize when there is strategic

---

[13] We do not include Lithuania in this analysis because the 2000 election was the only one it held using plurality rules – as opposed to two-round majority – in the SMD tier. The results of the two-round majority rule SMD elections in 1996 were undoubtedly a poor guide to likely outcomes under the FPTP rules in 2000.

[14] We also reran the models using margin of victory in the previous election in Scotland and Wales. For the most part, there was no statistically discernible relationship between the margin of victory in the previous election and the SMD–PR vote gap (results not shown). We speculate that this is due to electoral volatility in the form of shifts in voting behavior between the 1999 and 2003 elections in both cases. (See, for example, the increasing effective numbers of candidates in Scotland between the two elections.)

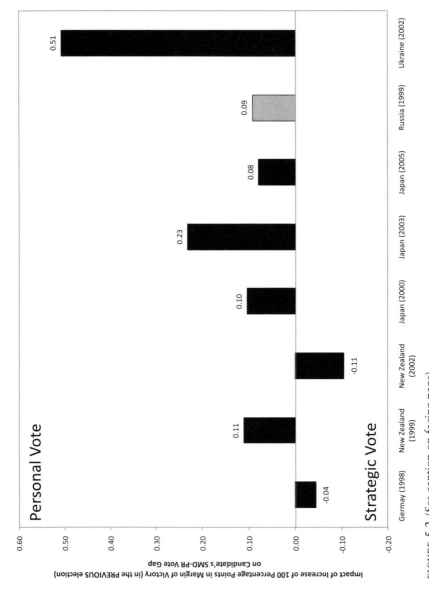

FIGURE 5.2 (See caption on facing page)

138

defection by voters in the SMD tier of mixed systems. Much of what is taken as evidence of strategic voting in mixed-member systems in previous studies may in fact be due to candidates' personal electoral support.

This chapter suggests that political context – especially a country's experience with democracy and the development of its party system – conditions the effect of electoral rules. FPTP rules are supposed to promote strategic defection by voters, but we find evidence of strategic defection by voters in SMDs only in established democracies – especially after voters and elites have had time to get used to the workings of the electoral system. We find evidence of strategic defection by SMD voters in Germany, New Zealand, and Japan, but absolutely none in Lithuania, Russia, and Ukraine. Moreover, in the first elections under their mixed-member systems, we find strong evidence of the personal vote in New Zealand and Japan, but then see strong signs of strategic defection by SMD voters in later elections in those two countries. That being said, experience with an electoral system is hardly enough to promote strategic behavior. Even in its fourth election under its mixed-member system, Russia continued to demonstrate strong signs of personal voting and no signs in the analysis here of strategic defection by its SMD voters.

The analysis in this chapter also suggests the importance of a polity's previous experience with electoral rules. The strongly personalistic voting patterns in Japan make particularly good sense given the country's long history (up until 1994) with the SNTV system that has been called the most personalistic electoral system in use (Carey and Shugart 1995). The patterns connoting strategic behavior even in Germany's first election under the new system in 1953 are probably, in part, a result of the country's immediately prior experience with a districting system similar to the SMD tier under the mixed-member system.

This chapter also highlights the limits of analysis that focuses solely on the effects of institutions. Institutions clearly do matter – Germany's linked

---

FIGURE 5.2. Evidence of personal and strategic voting – relationship between SMD margin of victory (1st place vote – 2nd place vote) in the *previous* election and the SMD–PR vote gap.
Notes:

- Positive values indicate evidence of personal voting. Negative values indicate evidence of strategic voting. Drawn from coefficients in Table 5.4.
- Except for Germany (1998), each bar indicates the impact of margin of victory on the SMD–PR vote gap for first-place candidates. The coefficient on this variable was in the expected direction but nonsignificant for Germany, but (unlike all the other country cases) the relationship between margin of victory and SMD–PR vote gap was positive and statistically significant for third-place (and worse) candidates in Germany. To illustrate that strategic voting clearly was present, we use the third-place Margin measure for Germany (and reverse the sign on the figure to match the direction of the scale correctly here).
- Gray bar (Russia) indicates statistically nonsignificant (0.1 level) estimate.

system no doubt has strongly influenced what we have described as its low levels of personal voting. However, substantially more appreciable personal voting in New Zealand's, Scotland's, and Wales' first mixed-member system elections indicates that current institutions are not a sufficient explanation for political behavior. Clearly, New Zealand's personal voting was due to other factors – most likely, society-based factors such as voter anger and party dealignment (Denemark 2001), and the shift from different districting patterns. Moreover, the widespread prevalence of the personal vote in Lithuania, Russia, and Ukraine is certainly, in very large part, a result not of their electoral institutions but, rather, of the still developing nature of their democracies and party systems.

One interesting aspect of the findings is the exceptionalism of the German case, which serves to support Bawn's (1999) evidence of strategic ticket splitting in Germany. The personal vote – as we have been discussing it for the other countries – was not readily apparent in our analysis of Germany, a country noted for its heavy emphasis on party-based political behavior. Thus, although there is relatively little ticket splitting in Germany compared with other mixed-member systems (Karp et al. 2002), our analysis suggests that strategic calculations were at the heart of such voting in Germany. However, this point is striking in that it indicates that, despite the presence of linked tiers that eliminate the importance of SMDs in determining the total number of seats a party wins, voters in Germany appear to care about avoiding a wasted vote, even if that vote is simply to determine the individual who will represent their district. That is, if their top choice appears unlikely to win the district race, they seek a part in determining the final outcome within the district, and therefore are willing to shift their SMD votes strategically away from their top choice to affect the selection of that representative – even if the election of that representative has little effect on the total number of seats their preferred party ultimately wins.

In this way, it is not quite correct to say that the personal vote did not play an important part in Germany. Indeed, it is noteworthy that it is Germany – a system in which district races typically do not have a large effect on overall seat shares – where strategic defection by SMD voters is especially discernible. In many ways, this pattern suggests that German strategic voting in SMDs is in fact a particular type of personalistic voting. That is, it seems that voters' strategic moves are not pursued to benefit their party in the legislature, but rather to elect an individual of whom they particularly approve in their district. It is interesting – albeit unfortunate – that, using our approach of comparing SMD and PR results, it is impossible to determine whether voters' "strategic" moves are done in the hopes of increasing party seat shares or simply to help elect a preferred individual candidate.[15]

---

[15] It would, of course, represent a misunderstanding of the workings of the system if voters in the linked-tier systems in Germany and New Zealand were using their SMD votes to try to increase the seat shares of their preferred parties (unless it was done with full recognition of the possibility of gaining overhang seats – see Chapter 2).

Some readers may be frustrated by the analysis here at this point: just because there is heavy personal voting – which, according to our analysis, overrides our ability to perceive strategic defection by SMD voters – this does not mean that strategic voting does not occur. We share this concern. To address the issue of the conditionality of electoral system effects, it is important that we be able to recognize strategic behavior more clearly when it emerges in the countries and elections that we study. For this reason, in Chapter 6 we turn to a new approach to examine strategic defection by SMD voters and elites in mixed-member systems.

APPENDIX 5. OLS MODELS OF THE SMD–PR VOTE GAP IN MIXED-MEMBER SYSTEMS

To address the issues in Chapter 5 more systematically, we run a series of ordinary least squares (OLS) models. Our dependent variable is – at the district level – each party's share of the SMD vote minus its share of the PR vote. Positive SMD–PR vote gaps indicate a candidate receiving more SMD votes than his or her party receives PR votes in a given district, and a negative vote gap indicates the opposite. We do not include (1) any party with PR votes but no candidate running in the SMD and (2) any candidate who has no party receiving PR votes.

Our analysis is similar to that in Moser and Scheiner (2005), but with a few differences: First, in this new analysis we consider a wider variety of country and year cases. Second, we eliminate here the mean-centering (Hamilton 1998) approach used in the earlier analysis. Third, we correct what were a very small number of minor errors in a few of the datasets. In addition, as we explain shortly, in contrast to the earlier analysis, which treated only actual independents as making up an independent vote, we create a control variable that treats any candidate who does not have a party running in the district in the PR tier as contributing to the independent vote.

Independent Variables

We examine three sets of factors that shape the direction and magnitude of parties' SMD–PR vote gaps: (1) factors relating to the margin of victory, (2) factors relating to candidate identity, and (3) general controls.

Margin of Victory. Similar to previous analyses, we examine the impact on the SMD–PR vote gap of the closeness of the SMD race. As Bawn did, we calculate our measure of the closeness of the SMD race (*Margin*) by subtracting the vote percentage won by the second-place candidate from the vote percentage won by the first-place candidate.[16]

---

[16] As Reed did, we also ran models with Margin based on the gap between any candidate (no matter what place) and first place. However, overall, the substantive meaning of the results scarcely changed (results not shown).

We expect that as the race gets closer (Margin declines), voters will be more likely to seek to influence the final outcome and therefore will be more inclined to cast SMD ballots for one of the top two candidates rather than for candidates likely to finish third or worse. For the reasons discussed in the text of Chapter 5, we introduce interaction terms with Margin, and are therefore able to differentiate between the correlation between Margin and the SMD–PR vote gap for candidates who place in different positions in the race: 1st*Margin, 2nd*Margin, and Bottom*Margin.

Candidate Identity. Incumbency is the most obvious factor relating to candidate identity. As Bawn did, we include a variable indicating whether the party runs an incumbent in the SMD, and a separate variable indicating whether the party faces an incumbent of another party in the district. Incumbents have a substantial advantage over other candidates because of voters' greater familiarity with them and the candidates' proven record of service for the district (Cain, Ferejohn, and Fiorina 1987). Moreover, even when they support a specific party on the PR ballot, voters may be less likely to support the party's SMD candidate if a candidate from a different party holds the SMD seat. Therefore, we expect the coefficient on *Incumbent* to have a positive sign – that is, incumbents should receive more SMD votes than their party wins PR votes. In contrast, the coefficient on *Incumbent Opponent* ought to be negative because candidates facing an incumbent should find that many supporters of their party in the PR race support the incumbent in the SMD.

In addition, in many districts, more than one type of incumbent is present. That is, within a given SMD there may be at least one candidate who enters the election as the sitting incumbent from the PR list of one of the parties. Although we do not expect candidates holding a PR seat to have the same drawing power as candidates holding the SMD seat, all else being equal, PR incumbents ought to have greater individual support than other candidates and we thus expect *PR Incumbent* to have a positive sign.

In the Japanese case, former seat holders – who do not hold office at the time of the election – also have an incumbent-like personal vote advantage, so we add for the Japan model *Returnee* to represent such candidates. In Russia (1999), a small number of candidates were running in districts other than the ones in which they were actually SMD incumbents. We code them as *Other SMD Incumbents*.

Control Variables. We also include two additional control variables. First, in some cases, votes for an SMD candidate are due neither to voters' sincere first preference for the candidate's party nor to strategic defection. Rather, in many cases, a voter's preferred party simply runs no candidates in the SMD. To control for the variety of cases such as this one, we include a variable, $SMD_{cands}/PR_{parties}$, the ratio of SMD candidates to parties running in the district in PR balloting. In a world with no ticket splitting, districts where all parties ran candidates (and no independents appeared) would see no SMD–PR vote gaps at all. Holding the number of PR parties constant, as the number of SMD candidates drops, additional votes become available to be divided among the SMD candidates still running and SMD–PR vote gaps increase. Therefore, we expect a negative sign on $SMD_{cands}/PR_{parties}$ – more SMD candidates should lead to lower values in the SMD–PR vote gap.

Second, following Reed's (1999) cue, when possible we include *Independent SMD Vote*, a measure of the proportion of the SMD vote won by candidates who do not have a party running in the district in the PR tier. As the share of the SMD vote won by independents increases, the number of votes available to other SMD candidates will usually decline, thereby reducing their likely SMD–PR vote gaps.[17] As with the $SMD_{cands}/PR_{parties}$ variable, we expect the proportion of Independent SMD Vote to be inversely related to SMD–PR vote gaps; thus, we expect a negative sign on this variable's coefficient.

In addition, in the case of Lithuania, we add a third control, which we call *Alliance*. In the case of Lithuania's Brazauskas Social Democratic Coalition, four parties formed a single PR list but nominated candidates in the SMD tier under separate party labels (but coordinated nominations to avoid contesting the same SMD seat). As a result, the coalition consistently experienced huge negative SMD–PR vote gaps: many voters who backed the coalition had their own preferred party within the coalition, and therefore did not always support the coalition's SMD candidates if they were from a different party. For this reason, we include the variable *Alliance*, a dummy variable coded 1 for candidates/parties in an alliance/coalition and 0 for all others, to control for these extra-large negative SMD–PR vote gaps. We expect a large negative coefficient on Alliance in the Lithuania model.

Results

Table 5.1 lists the results for Germany and New Zealand; Table 5.2 lists the results for Japan, Scotland, and Wales; and Table 5.3 lists the results for Lithuania, Russia, and Ukraine. The results for the controls are typically in the expected direction and often significant. Most important, we find evidence of strategic defection by voters under SMDs in many of the established democracies – especially in later elections under the mixed-member system – but no evidence of strategic defection by voters in SMDs in the new democracies.

For Germany, the negative and significant coefficient on 1st*Margin and the positive and significant coefficient for Bottom*Margin strongly suggest that there was substantial strategic defection. The results for both New Zealand and Japan shift over time from only demonstrating the presence of a personal vote to greater evidence of strategic defection by SMD voters. In 1999 in New Zealand and all three elections in Japan, the coefficient on 1st*Margin is positive and statistically significant, indicating the presence of personal voting in both countries. However, in New Zealand in 2002, the coefficient on 1st*Margin becomes negative and significant, clearly an indication of strategic defection by SMD voters. In 2005, the last Japanese election in our dataset, we

---

[17] In our samples, $SMD_{cands}/PR_{parties}$ is not correlated with Independent SMD Vote.

TABLE 5.1. *Correlates of the Gap between Parties' Share of SMD and PR Votes (Germany and New Zealand)*

	(1) Germany 1998	(2) New Zealand 1999	(3) New Zealand 2002	(4) Germany 1953
1st*Margin	−0.0466***	0.105*	−0.127**	−0.0573*
	(3.72)	(2.21)	(2.91)	(2.43)
2nd*Margin	−0.0536***	−0.182***	−0.00555	−0.0311
	(4.28)	(3.87)	(0.13)	(1.32)
Bottom*Margin	0.0384***	0.0116	0.0222	−0.0122
	(5.29)	(0.7)	(1.21)	(1.03)
1st Place	0.0586***	−0.0026	0.0272	0.0324***
	(24.27)	(0.2)	(1.47)	(4.45)
2nd Place	0.0552***	0.0332**	0.0272+	0.00864
	(21.59)	(2.64)	(1.9)	(1.19)
Candidate Identity				
SMD Incumbent	0.0104***	0.0842***	0.0981***	
	(4.85)	(7.7)	(5.64)	
Incumbent Opponent	−0.00249+	−0.0101*	−0.0127	
	(1.72)	(2.03)	(1.51)	
PR Incumbent			0.0145	
			(1.34)	
Controls				
SMD$_{cands}$/PR$_{parties}$	0.00743	0.00613	0.00579	
	(1.11)	(0.41)	(0.21)	
Independent SMD Vote		−0.00275	−0.00745	
		(0.08)	(0.08)	
Constant	−0.0307***	−0.00978	−0.014	0.0227***
	(4.57)	(0.60)	(0.48)	(6.96)
N	1555	678	593	1449
R-Sq	0.58	0.276	0.218	0.024
Adj-R-Sq	0.578	0.266	0.205	0.02

OLS models with *t* statistics in parentheses.
All models are for candidates/parties at the SMD level.
$^+p < 0.1$; $^* p < 0.05$; $^{**} p < 0.01$; $^{***} p < 0.001$.

can see a positive and significant sign on the coefficient on Bottom*Margin, also an indication of strategic defection.

The remaining cases all show strong signs of personal voting. In Scotland, there is tentative evidence of strategic defection, as the coefficient on 1st*Margin is negative, although it is statistically significant only at the 0.117 level. At the same time, the coefficient on Bottom*Margin for Scotland is negative and statistically significant, indicating the presence of a personal vote. With the exception of the Bottom*Margin variable for Wales – which is in

TABLE 5.2. *Correlates of the Gap between Parties' Share of SMD and PR Votes (Japan, Scotland, and Wales)*

	(5) Japan 2000	(6) Japan 2003	(7) Japan 2005	(8) Scotland 2003	(9) Wales 2003
1st*Margin	0.335***	0.362***	0.273***	−0.106	0.652***
	(16.21)	(16.51)	(11.13)	(1.57)	(6.58)
2nd*Margin	−0.125***	−0.0815***	−0.195***	−0.128+	−0.327**
	(6.00)	(3.66)	(7.98)	(1.96)	(3.26)
Bottom*Margin	0.00417	0.026	0.0813***	−0.0927**	−0.0999
	(0.25)	(1.24)	(3.77)	(2.74)	(1.59)
1st Place	0.0876***	0.0508***	0.0740***	0.0374*	−0.136***
	(13.67)	(7.00)	(11.52)	(2.08)	(4.09)
2nd Place	0.0898***	0.0465***	0.0813***	0.0095	0.0233
	(14.45)	(6.87)	(12.77)	(0.60)	(0.77)
Candidate Identity					
SMD Incumbent	0.0323***	0.0256***	0.0453***	−0.00305	0.0735**
	(5.10)	(3.83)	(5.76)	(0.19)	(2.70)
Incumbent Opponent	−0.00836+	−0.0107*	−0.00803	−0.0128	−0.0192
	(1.81)	(2.10)	(1.14)	(1.37)	(1.07)
PR Incumbent	0.0101+	0.0175**	0.0204***	−0.00866	0.0204
	(1.75)	(2.83)	(4.25)	(0.81)	(0.75)
Returnee	0.0131+	0.0215**	0.0267***		
	(1.82)	(2.66)	(3.80)		
Controls					
SMD$_{cands}$/PR$_{parties}$	−0.131***	−0.133***	−0.126***	−0.173***	0.00364
	(10.80)	(10.71)	(10.35)	(15.27)	(0.07)
Independent SMD Vote	−0.00181	−0.00092	−0.00165	−0.103**	−0.00656
	(1.57)	(0.71)	(1.41)	(2.70)	(0.12)
Constant	0.0875***	0.0985***	0.0674***	0.210***	0.0175
	(9.23)	(8.48)	(6.36)	(12.93)	(0.27)
N	1101	916	916	363	200
R-Sq	0.738	0.647	0.735	0.74	0.408
Adj-R-Sq	0.736	0.643	0.732	0.732	0.377

OLS models with *t* statistics in parentheses.
All models are for candidates/parties at the SMD level.
$^+ p < 0.1$; $^* p < 0.05$; $^{**} p < 0.01$; $^{***} p < 0.001$.

the direction indicating personal voting, but the coefficient reaches significance only at the 0.113 level – the coefficients on 1st*Margin and Bottom*Margin for Wales, Lithuania, Russia, and Ukraine are all in the directions indicating personal voting and are statistically significant.[18]

We should also briefly discuss the impact of incumbency on the SMD–PR vote gap. For the most part, we simply use the variable as a control, but it also

[18] We should note that in nearly every case, the coefficient on 2nd*Margin is negative and significant, but as we pointed out earlier, this result is consistent with both personal and strategic voting.

TABLE 5.3. *Correlates of the Gap between Parties' Share of SMD and PR Votes (Lithuania, Russia, and Ukraine)*

	(10) Lithuania 2000	(11) Russia 1995	(12) Russia 1999	(13) Russia 2003	(14) Ukraine 2002
1st*Margin	0.527***	0.493***	0.378***	0.373***	0.346***
	(8.64)	(10.82)	(8.84)	(10.17)	(5.26)
2nd*Margin	−0.328***	−0.101*	−0.151***	−0.0563	−0.219*
	(5.67)	(2.16)	(3.58)	(1.38)	(2.33)
Bottom*Margin	−0.0546*	−0.0692***	−0.0356+	−0.0407+	−0.0880**
	(2.32)	(3.78)	(1.78)	(1.85)	(2.62)
1st Place	−0.0153	0.0372***	0.0163	0.0425**	0.298***
	(1.63)	(4.07)	(1.43)	(2.85)	(9.73)
2nd Place	0.0229*	0.0412***	0.0536***	0.0449**	0.173***
	(2.46)	(4.43)	(4.77)	(2.74)	(4.44)
Candidate Identity					
SMD Incumbent	0.0358***	0.0492***	0.0290**	0.0896***	0.0412
	(4.20)	(7.21)	(2.99)	(7.78)	(1.07)
Incumbent Opponent	−0.00582*	−0.00298	0.0000301	−0.00792	0.00478
	(2.08)	(0.94)	(0.01)	(1.18)	(0.39)
PR Incumbent	0.00575	−0.00333	−0.00873	0.0341*	−0.0289
	(0.47)	(0.49)	(0.90)	(2.25)	(0.74)
Other SMD Incumbent			0.0815+		
			(1.87)		
Controls					
SMD$_{cands}$/PR$_{parties}$	−0.00442	−0.110***	−0.113***	−0.117***	−0.0697***
	(0.28)	(6.92)	(6.49)	(4.25)	(15.30)
Independent SMD Vote	−0.119***	−0.0638***	−0.0237*	−0.0305*	−0.00871
	(4.71)	(7.54)	(2.33)	(2.10)	(0.39)
Alliance	−0.179***				
	(26.06)				
Constant	0.0286	0.0722***	0.0736***	0.0494**	0.0292+
	(1.49)	(9.33)	(6.69)	(3.09)	(1.77)
N	573	1460	1052	848	443
R-Sq	0.618	0.434	0.28	0.504	0.692
Adj-R-Sq	0.61	0.43	0.272	0.498	0.685

OLS models with t statistics in parentheses.
All models are for candidates/parties at the SMD level.
$^+ p < 0.1$; $^* p < 0.05$; $^{**} p < 0.01$; $^{***} p < 0.001$.

offers a partial proxy for the personal vote – at least insofar as incumbency represents the personal vote. The results for the SMD Incumbent variable are fairly consistent. In every case except for Scotland, the coefficient on the variable is positive, and, except for Scotland and Ukraine, it is statistically significant. Of the remaining countries, the coefficient on the variable is largest in New Zealand in 2002 and smallest in Germany: in substantive terms, in New Zealand 2002, all else being equal, incumbents tend to have a 9.8 percentage

TABLE 5.4. Correlates of the Gap between Parties' Share of SMD and PR Votes Based on Margin of Victory in the Previous Election

	(15) Germany 1998	(16) New Zealand 1999	(17) New Zealand 2002	(18) Japan 2000	(19) Japan 2003	(20) Japan 2005	(21) Russia 1999	(22) Ukraine 2002
1st*Margin	-0.0024	0.111*	-0.105+	0.104***	0.232***	0.0791***	0.0926	0.507**
	(0.21)	(2.18)	(1.91)	(4.28)	(9.95)	(4.11)	(1.38)	(3.09)
2nd*Margin	-0.121***	-0.0271	0.0258	-0.0193	-0.0629**	-0.0685***	-0.0914	0.0731
	(10.48)	(0.52)	(0.47	(0.80)	(2.68)	(3.58)	(1.33)	(0.55)
Bottom*Margin	0.0442***	-0.0106	0.0181	-0.0164	-0.012	-0.00612	-0.00474	-0.00348
	(6.40)	(0.60)	(0.82)	(0.86)	(0.58)	(0.37)	(0.17)	(0.07)
1st Place	0.0560***	-0.00011	0.0197	0.111***	0.0558***	0.0786***	0.0726***	0.365***
	(23.66)	(0.01)	(0.94)	(16.08)	(6.86)	(11.93)	(5.54)	(11.75)
2nd Place	0.0674***	-0.0165	0.0203	0.0611***	0.0353***	0.0484***	0.0434***	0.109**
	(27.24)	(1.26)	(1.37)	(9.52)	(4.68)	(7.67)	(3.37)	(2.94)
Candidate Identity								
SMD Incumbent	0.00697***	0.0852***	0.0982***	0.0509***	0.0345***	0.0564***	0.0259*	0.0593
	(3.38)	(7.72)	(5.22)	(7.32)	(4.68)	(6.53)	(2.55)	(1.50)
Incumbent Opponent	-0.00159	-0.0101	-0.0119	-0.0153**	-0.0121*	-0.0112	-0.0000276	0.00215
	(1.12)	(1.87)	(1.33)	(2.97)	(2.12)	(1.46)	(0.01)	(0.16)
PR Incumbent				0.0150*	0.0185**	0.0238***	-0.00946	-0.0226
				(2.34)	(2.74)	(4.46)	(0.94)	(0.55)
Returnee				0.0177*	0.0271**	0.0281***		
				(2.19)	(3.06)	(3.64)		
Other SMD Incumbent							0.0863+	
							(1.90)	
Controls								
SMD_cands/PR_parties	0.00624	0.00628	0.00874	-0.148***	-0.160***	-0.123***	-0.116***	-0.0679***
	(0.95)	(0.42)	(0.26)	(11.17)	(11.32)	(9.22)	(6.56)	(14.13)
Independent SMD Vote		-0.00072	-0.0229	-0.00137	0.000365	-0.00138	-0.0327*	-0.0297
		(0.01)	(0.16)	(1.06)	(0.26)	(1.06)	(3.11)	(1.26)
Constant	-0.0313***	-0.00494	-0.0166	0.104***	0.122***	0.0805***	0.0745***	0.0176
	(4.71)	(0.29)	(0.47)	(10.43)	(9.53)	(7.00)	(6.98)	(1.09)
N	1555	598	536	1101	900	900	1052	426
R-squared	0.603	0.306	0.239	0.674	0.588	0.689	0.215	0.665
Adj-R-Sq	0.603	0.295	0.225	0.671	0.583	0.685	0.207	0.657

OLS models with *t* statistics in parentheses.
All models are for candidates/parties at the SMD level.
+ *p* < 0.1; * *p* < 0.05; ** *p* < 0.01; *** *p* < 0.001.

point larger SMD–PR vote gap than nonincumbents, whereas in Germany incumbents' vote gap is merely one percentage point.

The very large positive coefficient on SMD Incumbent in New Zealand is surprising because of the substantial linkage mechanism between the two tiers, but strongly suggests the impact of voters' experience under the previous SMD institution, in which all ballots were cast for individual candidates. This finding coincides with Karp et al.'s conclusion that the strength of New Zealand voters' attachment to particular candidates had a significant impact on the likelihood of ticket splitting (2002: 17).

The small size of the coefficient on SMD Incumbent in the German model makes sense, and suggests why strategic voting – as demonstrated by the negative coefficient on 1st*Margin and the positive coefficient on Bottom*Margin – would be detected in the German case, but not in the others. As discussed earlier, because Germany maintains strong linkage mechanisms, has a party system that has been consolidated for decades, and has substantial experience with its mixed-member system, the German system is founded first and foremost on party-line voting. The personal vote is less potent than in the other countries examined here; therefore, its presence did not outweigh that of strategic voting.

Analysis Using Margin from $t - 1$ Elections

Finally, we rerun our models in all of the country/election cases for which we had sufficient data to be able to replace the Margin variable with an identical variable that is based on the results of the previous election in the district. As shown in Table 5.4, replacing Margin for election t with Margin for election $t - 1$ does not have a major impact on the results of the models. On one hand, the results with respect to Bottom*Margin are far weaker than in the time t models. Using the $t - 1$ measure of Margin, the coefficient on Bottom*Margin is statistically significant only for the German case. However, on the other hand, the coefficients on 1st*Margin for the $t - 1$ measure do not change markedly from the results for the time t measure. The direction of the coefficients on 1st*Margin is the same as in the time t model, and remain significant in every case except for Germany and Russia.

6

How Democratic Experience and Party System Development Condition the Effect of Electoral Rules on Strategic Defection

In Chapter 4, we showed that there is significant variation in the number of parties under different electoral rules and political contexts, but we did not demonstrate the mechanisms – such as strategic defection by voters and elites – that underpin the different results we found. In Chapter 5, we began to show how rules and context shape strategic defection by voters under SMD rules, but the existence of a "personal" vote often obscured our view of much of the strategic voting that probably did occur. In this chapter, we introduce a different approach, which we use to highlight more directly how political context – most notably, democratic experience and party system development – conditions the impact of SMD rules on strategic defection in mixed-member electoral systems.

Specifically, we use Cox's (e.g., 1997) "SF ratio" measure (usually the vote total of the third-place contestant [the "Second loser"] divided by the vote total of the second-place contestant [the "First loser']) to help draw inferences about strategic defection under particular electoral rules. As we do throughout this book, we use mixed-member systems to gain analytical leverage on electoral system effects. In this chapter we examine patterns of strategic defection in mixed-member systems in 41 elections in 11 different countries, considering how SF ratio patterns within a given country differ between the SMD and PR tiers of mixed-member systems. We show how SF ratio patterns in SMDs – unlike those in PR – often highlight the presence of strategic behavior, presumably because many voters and elites, when facing a competitive district race, transfer their support from candidates/parties who are unlikely to win to one of the top two contestants.

Most important, we show that strategic defection is more common in established democracies than in new democracies with poorly institutionalized party systems. Many voters and elites in institutionalized party systems clearly respond to the strategic imperatives of plurality rules, strategically supporting a "lesser of two evils" when the top two candidates face a competitive race. However, we find no evidence that voters and elites do so in new democracies, especially those with less well-developed party systems, in which voters and elites often cannot distinguish sufficiently between many candidates' likelihood of victory and therefore have little incentive to strategically withdraw their support from their preferred alternative.

ELECTORAL RULES AND STRATEGIC DEFECTION

Scholars typically view strategic behavior as fundamental to elections in established democracies. We define *strategic voting* as casting ballots for alternatives other than one's first preference to improve the expected outcome of the election. Electoral rules affect behavior through the strategic imperatives that their mechanical effects impose on voters and elites. Most notably, restrictive rules such as first-past-the-post give supporters of weak candidates/parties – usually those in third place and worse – an incentive to defect to more competitive alternatives. Work by scholars such as Duverger (1954) highlights how strategic defection of this kind by voters and elites leads to two candidates per district under plurality rules.

Of course, it is somewhat odd to suggest that voters who support a competitive party or candidate who is also their top preference are somehow not strategic, so in many ways it makes more sense to reframe the literature's argument in terms of "preference revelation": compared to more permissive rules, plurality rules give voters less incentive to reveal their true preferences. Under permissive PR systems, even small parties can gain representation, so scholars typically argue that most voters – even those who back a small party – have good reason to cast a vote for their most preferred party, thus revealing their true party preference.[1] In our discussion, we mostly use the term *strategic voting* – or, often, *strategic defection* – as shorthand to describe this phenomenon, but in the next subsection we will briefly return to the idea of preference revelation.

Insightful analysis demonstrates that strategic voting occurs in all types of electoral systems (see, e.g., Abramson et al. 2010; Cox 1997; Tavits and Annus 2006), but most scholarship usually focuses on plurality systems. Indeed, evidence of strategic voting under plurality rules in established democracies is abundant and persuasive (see, e.g., Barnes et al. 1962; Fisher 1973; Bawn 1993, 1999; Niemi et al. 1992; Cox 1997; Alvarez and Nagler 2000; Alvarez et al. 2006). Scholars highlight that various individual and contextual factors – education, socioeconomic status, degree of party identification, and constituency effects (e.g., competitiveness of the race) – influence the propensity of voters to behave strategically (Spafford 1972; Johnston and Pattie 1991; Niemi et al.

---

[1] Again, we thank Bill Clark and Ken Kollman for the excellent suggestion that we reframe our discussion of electoral rules incentives for "strategic voting" as incentives for "preference revelation."

1992). Moreover, as Gary Cox (1997) and William Riker (1982) argue convincingly, strategic behavior is hardly limited to voters: much strategic behavior is by elites who choose not to waste resources supporting uncompetitive, low-ranking options, and who choose not to run as candidates for small parties that are likely to lose.

As we highlight in Chapters 3 through 5, mixed-member electoral systems can be useful in helping to demonstrate how different electoral rules affect the likelihood of strategic defection. Past analysis of ticket splitting under mixed systems offers suggestive evidence of the existence of greater strategic defection under SMD rules, as the top candidates tend to win many more votes in SMDs than their parties do in PR (see Bawn 1999; Cox 1997; Fisher 1973; Moser and Scheiner 2000; Roberts 1988; Reed 1999). Most studies assume that votes cast in PR balloting usually represent voters' true preferences, and that many of the "extra" SMD votes going to the top candidates in SMDs under mixed-member systems are strategic ballots cast by voters who want to affect the race.

However, two problems emerge as we attempt to draw lessons from many past analyses about the reasons for split-ticket voting in mixed-member systems. First, the approach commonly used to demonstrate strategic voting in mixed systems is not wholly reliable because it is often difficult to differentiate between strategic and personal voting (see Chapter 5). Second, most studies of strategic voting focus on established democracies, but what happens when we extend the analysis to new democracies?

How Democratic Experience and Party Institutionalization Might Condition the Effect of Electoral Rules on Strategic Defection

The literature on the effects of electoral rules emphasizes how voters and elites acting under plurality rules have a sharply reduced incentive to reveal their true preferences in the electoral process, but, as we argue throughout this book, democratic experience and the level of party system development condition the power of plurality rules to push voters and elites away from acting in accord with their true preferences.

As we discuss in Chapters 1 and 3, strategic voting requires information on candidates' electoral viability. Duverger's Law – the idea that there will be two parties or candidates per SMD – is founded in large part on strategic defection away from candidates outside of the top two. Achieving Duvergerian two-party outcomes requires "reasonably accurate and publicly available information on candidate standing" (Cox 1997: 79). Voters and elites will be able to move from uncompetitive to competitive options only if they are aware of likely levels of support for different candidates and parties.

As we have discussed throughout this book (and especially in Chapters 1 and 3), democratic experience and well-established parties are critical to producing information about likely electoral outcomes. Lack of democratic experience and less-developed media institutions and public opinion polling (and, in some cases, more restricted press freedoms) reduce the amount of information citizens have about electoral politics. In addition, in well-developed party systems, candidates' party affiliations give voters one of their best clues about the potential electoral fortunes of the different candidates. Without such cues, it is more cumbersome for voters to determine who is and is not competitive, thus making it difficult to know when to withdraw support from one's preferred choice and to what candidate it would be effective to transfer support (Filippov et al. 1999). The transitory nature of party organizations in unstable new democracies promotes great volatility between electoral periods and provides little opportunity for voters to cultivate lasting preferences for one party or another (see, e.g., Ames et al. 2009; Baker et al. 2006). In the absence of widespread, concrete party preferences, many voters are left with no partisan cues on how to cast their votes and must instead rely on patronage, incumbency, and the personal characteristics of candidates.

For these reasons, in newly democratic systems (especially those with poorly institutionalized parties), voters and elites may be more likely to reveal their true preferences within the electoral process – that is, vote for their first preference – even in elections contested under restrictive rules. If there is less reliable information about likely vote distributions, candidates ought to have less reason to exit strategically from the race (and additional candidates and parties may, in turn, actually decide to enter the race), and voters and elites will have less reason to withdraw their support from their preferred candidate, as any candidate might, in theory, win (Filippov et al. 1999). Under such conditions, larger numbers of candidates may win substantial shares of the vote. As a result, the vote percentage needed to win the race may become quite low, thus introducing a vicious circle by reinforcing this perception that anyone can in fact win.

In fact, some evidence suggests that voters in new democracies strategically defect from their top choice far less than voters in established democracies. Raymond Duch and Harvey Palmer (2002) use survey data to show that almost 13.6 percent of Hungarian voters behaved strategically when faced with a "wasted-vote situation" – that is, when their most preferred option was likely to go unrepresented. However, these estimates of Hungarian voters acting strategically pale in comparison to the roughly 50 percent of (uncompetitive) third-party supporters who defect to major party candidates in British elections, according to estimates by R. Michael Alvarez, Frederick Boehmke, and Jonathan Nagler (2006).

SF RATIOS AS AN APPROACH TO STUDYING STRATEGIC DEFECTION IN SMDS

In this chapter, we introduce systematic analysis of strategic electoral behavior in 11 countries and 41 elections that use mixed-member system rules to build on earlier work (such as Duch and Palmer's) on the strategic vote in new democracies. Our dataset and approach allow us to draw conclusions about the effects of both context and rules in shaping strategic defection. We examine electoral results in five new democracies (including three postcommunist states) and six consolidated democracies. Our cases of postcommunist democracies (especially Russia and Ukraine) have party systems that are much less developed than that of Hungary (Kitschelt 1995; Evans and Whitefield 1993), and therefore should be even less likely to promote strategic behavior.[2] Because of the problems we discussed in Chapter 5 with previous approaches to analyzing the difference in votes between the SMD and PR tiers in mixed-member systems, we take a different tack to studying strategic defection. We use Cox's (1997) SF ratio measure (which, as we explained earlier, is the ratio of the vote won by the "Second loser" – third place – to that of the "First loser" – second place) to examine strategic defection in an array of mixed systems. Because we can compare SF ratios in the PR and SMD tiers of mixed-member systems, they provide us a unique opportunity to view strategic defection under plurality rules.

SF ratios can indicate strategic behavior – or, perhaps more accurately, strategic defection – in the following way: in plurality contests, voters and elites should strategically withdraw their support from weak competitors and instead back one of the two leading contestants. Under this common scenario, little support will go to candidates who finish in third place (i.e., the "second loser") or worse, and the second-place candidate (i.e., the "first loser"), therefore, will have many more votes than the third-place candidate in the district. As a result, the SF ratio – that is, the third-place vote divided by the second-place vote – will be roughly zero. In this way, an SF ratio of roughly zero in a competitive SMD is an indication that the district has entered into a stable "Duvergerian equilibrium" (see Cox 1997), consistent with expected behavior and outcomes under plurality rules.

In contrast, though, in cases in which voters and elites are unwilling or unable to pull their support away from third (and lower ranked) candidates, SF ratios will tend to be higher – or, to put it differently, the difference between second place and third place will be smaller. On one hand, in SMDs where there is widespread, accurate information about likely outcomes, few competitive districts ought to maintain midrange (i.e., roughly 0.5) SF ratios for very long: At first there may be a lack of reliable information about likely outcomes, which makes midrange SF ratios possible in early elections under a new electoral system. However, over time, voters and elites ought to withdraw support from third-place candidates who lag well behind second place, and competitive districts ought to tend toward the Duvergerian equilibrium (SF ratios of roughly 0). We highlight that this outcome is an equilibrium in competitive districts because there is less incentive for voters and elites to defect in similarly strategic ways in noncompetitive districts, where a shift in support is unlikely to change the outcome of the race.

---

[2] We do not include Hungary because we could not obtain PR vote totals at the SMD level.

However, as Cox (1997) notes, even in competitive plurality districts it is possible to enter into an equilibrium in which voters and elites do not move away from the third-place candidate. That is, at times there may be little perceptible difference in the likely success of the top two "losers" in a race (i.e., second and third place in an SMD). In this scenario, supporters of both the second- and third-place candidates have incentive to continue to back their preferred candidate and there will be little defection away from either candidate. An SF ratio of roughly 1 is consistent with this "non-Duvergerian equilibrium" – a state that is likely to remain stable until reliable information emerges that one of the two leading "loser" candidates (i.e., second and third place) is more viable than another.

The histograms in Figure 6.1 offer two contrasting SF ratio patterns under mixed-member system rules: a pattern consistent with strategic defection away from low-ranking candidates in Germany's well-established democracy and a pattern that demonstrates no such defection in the newly democratic, poorly institutionalized Russian party system. The top left-hand figure represents the distribution of SF ratios in German SMDs in 2005, the country's 15th election under the electoral system, and is consistent with the common expectation of a Duvergerian equilibrium. The tall bar to the left within the figure indicates that in the bulk of districts, very few votes went to third-place candidates relative to the number won by second-place candidates. To be sure, this result is partly due to the fact that two parties are overwhelmingly stronger than all others in Germany, but this explanation is hardly sufficient. The top right-hand figure indicates that in PR balloting (aggregated at the SMD level), in most districts voters appear to prefer the second-place party by a wide margin over the third-place party, but not to the extent that they do under SMD balloting. In short, the tall bar near zero that we see in the SMD figure does not appear to be purely a result of an overwhelming preference for the two top parties over all the others.

However, we see little evidence of the same sort of strategic defection (or Duvergerian equilibrium) in Russia. In SMDs in Russia in 1999, the largest number of districts had SF ratios that approached 1 – that is, to the right-hand side of the figure. In other words, Figure 6.1 suggests that a significant share of Russian SMDs in 1999 were in a state of non-Duvergerian equilibrium, in which there was little perceivable difference in the number of votes won by the second- and third-place candidates in the district.[3] This pattern stands in contrast not only to the pattern in Germany, but also to the pattern in PR voting in Russia. Whereas the modal pattern under SMD balloting in Russia had the third- and second-place candidates winning roughly identical shares of the vote, the pattern in PR is much flatter, with significantly bigger differences

---

[3] These SF ratio patterns do not allow us to say that there was no strategic defection in SMDs in Russia – just that there is much less evidence of strategic defection away from third-place candidates.

between the second- and third-place party votes. The differences between the SMD and PR SF ratio patterns suggest that voters and elites were attempting to back a viable contender in the SMD race, but that it was difficult for them to decipher which candidates were in fact the most viable.[4]

Moreover, the patterns over time differ markedly for the German and Russian cases. Germany moved swiftly from no clear pattern in its SMD SF ratio distributions in its first (two-vote) mixed-member system election in 1953 (see Appendix 6A1), to modes near zero in the elections that immediately followed (figure not shown). In other words, most German SMDs quickly entered into a state of Duvergerian equilibrium, where they remain to the present. In contrast, the most common SF ratio was roughly 1 in SMDs in Russia in 1993 (results not shown) and 1995 (see Appendix 6A2), as well as in 1999 (see Figure 6.1). In short, it appears that large numbers of Russian SMDs were locked in a non-Duvergerian equilibrium, in which voters and elites could not decipher which top "loser" was the most viable challenger, and, therefore, had no incentive to defect from one to the other in order to affect the outcome of the race.[5]

How Can We Use SF Ratios in Mixed-Member Systems to Study Strategic Defection?

Using SF ratios to understand strategic behavior is not without potential problems,[6] but we can set up analysis of SF ratios in mixed-member systems in a way that allows us to identify the presence of strategic behavior.

Our analysis focuses on the SF ratio in SMD candidate races as the dependent variable, and uses both the SF ratio in the PR tier at the SMD level and the level of competitiveness in the SMD race as explanatory variables. By including the SF ratio in PR balloting (within the same district as the SF ratio for SMD voting) as a control, our other explanatory variables help us to identify and explain divergence between SF ratio patterns under PR and SMD rules. Most notably, by examining the correlation between the closeness of district SMD races and the SF ratio in the district, we can draw inferences about whether SF ratio patterns are, in part, a result of voters' and elites' responses to the strategic incentives created by the district race.

---

[4] As noted in Chapters 1 and 3, the PR vote in Russia arguably provided more information in the form of voter surveys that showed the relative support for PR parties and thus indicated that some of these parties were unlikely to overcome the 5 percent legal threshold; but similar information was usually not available for local SMD races between candidates (see also Moser 1999).

[5] As Appendix 6A2 indicates, in 2003, the fourth election under Russia's mixed system, the pattern shifted so that fewer districts held SF ratios of roughly 1. As we discuss later, we attribute this shift to the increasing levels of party institutionalization that occurred with the development of President Putin's United Russia party.

[6] See the online appendix for discussion of these potential shortcomings.

Germany

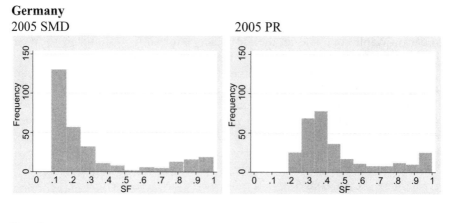

Russia

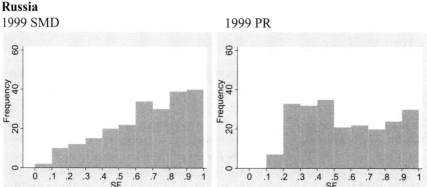

FIGURE 6.1. District-level SF ratio patterns suggest greater strategic defection in SMDs in Germany than in Russia. Bars indicate the number of districts maintaining a particular SF ratio (e.g., between 0.9 and 1.0).

When we examine SF ratios in mixed-member systems, we are able to conduct intracountry comparisons across the two tiers within the system. Work on ticket splitting in mixed-member systems typically assumes that most PR ballots cast are in line with voters' true preferences (see Bawn 1999; Cox 1997; Reed 1999). For this reason, when we compare SF ratio patterns in the SMD and PR tiers of mixed-member systems, we have an aggregate estimate of voters' true preferences (in the form of their vote in the PR tier) and the extent to which voters deviate from these preferences under SMD rules. If, independent of the SF ratio patterns in the PR tier, SF ratios tend toward zero in SMD races (especially if they do so increasingly over time or in more competitive races), we then have reason to suspect that strategic defection is the reason why.

In many ways, the best test of whether voters and elites are responding to the strategic imperatives of SMD rules is if they shift their behavior when in districts that face a close race – that is, when a person's vote will be more likely to have an impact on the final outcome. The closer the race, the more likely voters and elites should be to defect strategically from their preferred options and instead support a more competitive candidate. We therefore include in our analysis a measure of the closeness in the SMD race of the votes won by the top two candidates. We should expect to see that the closer the race, the more the SF ratio will tend toward zero.

But Democratic Experience and Party Institutionalization Should Condition the Effect of Electoral Rules on Strategic Defection and SF Ratio Patterns

As suggested by our earlier discussion, we expect to see lower SF ratios under SMD rules in districts with close races in established democracies with institutionalized party systems, but a different outcome in SMDs in new democracies with poorly institutionalized party systems. In the latter context, the uncertainty over likely electoral outcomes makes it more difficult to know who is and who is not in the running in the district race. No matter how competitive the race is, if voters and elites cannot judge the likely effect of shifting their support from one candidate to another, they will be unlikely to defect strategically from their most preferred candidate.

There may even be reason to expect that in new democracies close races might lead to *higher* SF ratios: as we discussed earlier, if – as is common in new democracies, especially with poorly institutionalized party systems – there is significant uncertainty over the likely results of the race, there may be a greater sense that *anyone* could win the race. As a result, candidates and parties ought to be less likely to exit the race and additional candidates may choose to run. With larger numbers of candidates contesting the race, the share of the vote taken by the winner would be likely to go down, thus encouraging even more candidates to contest the race, as only a small share of the vote would be needed to win. At the same time, with a large number of candidates, the share of the second-place candidate's vote would also go down. Moreover, because of the uncertainty over the likely outcome, voters and elites would be unlikely to defect strategically away from lower-ranked candidates. Therefore, third-place candidates would be likely to receive a decent share of votes that, when combined with a smaller share of the vote won by the second-place candidate, would lead to a higher SF ratio (i.e., larger number of third-place to second-place votes). In this way, close races in poorly institutionalized party systems might go hand in hand with high SF ratios. Meanwhile, in districts where one candidate dominates the SMD competition, voters and elites are likely to be aware of the candidate's strength. In such cases, fewer candidates ought to challenge the strong frontrunner, and, with fewer additional candidates, the second-place candidate may be more likely to win a larger share of the vote, thus making it possible to create a greater difference between the share of the vote won by the second- and third-place candidates. In turn, we might then see a lower SF ratio in SMD races in which there is a large margin of victory – precisely the opposite pattern from what we would expect for established democracies.

Other Factors That May Shape the SF Ratios

We also expect that, over time, strategic defection ought to increase and SF ratios ought to decline. Voters and elites in the first elections under any new system are apt to lack sufficient information about candidates' likely success to be able to defect wholly strategically, so many will be likely to continue to support their genuine first preference, even under plurality rules. However, with repeated electoral experience, voters and elites ought to be more capable of behaving strategically and drive the system toward Duvergerian equilibrium, thus pushing SF ratios in the SMD balloting toward zero.[7]

In addition, variation in mixed-member system rules may lead to variation in the amount of strategic behavior. Specifically, as we argue in particular in Chapter 3, voters and elites in mixed-member systems that link their tiers may not wish to cast a ballot for a party other than their top choice simply to win an SMD seat that does not even add to their preferred party's total. In contrast, in unlinked systems, by increasing the share of the total seats that a given party will win, individual SMD outcomes appear to "matter" more. Therefore, with greater incentives for strategic behavior we should expect, all else being equal, lower SF ratios in SMDs in unlinked systems.

EXAMINING SF RATIO PATTERNS ACROSS
11 MIXED-MEMBER SYSTEMS

We examine SF ratios in single-member districts for each election in each country in our dataset. With 41 elections in 11 countries, the dataset includes more than 8,500 observations. The country cases in this chapter vary widely in their level of democratic experience, the institutionalization of their party systems, their prior electoral system history, and the rules that govern their mixed-member systems. From advanced industrial democracies we examine Germany (15 elections in our dataset, 1953–2005), which has used its mixed-member system for decades, as well as Italy (3 elections, 1994–2001), Japan (4 elections, 1996–2005), and New Zealand (4 elections, 1996–2005), which introduced their mixed-member systems in the 1990s. We also include elections to the Scottish Parliament and the Welsh National Assembly (2 elections each, 1999–2003), which introduced their mixed-member systems in 1999. From new democracies, we have Bolivia (2 elections in our dataset, 1997–2002); postcommunist Lithuania (3 elections, 1996–2004), Macedonia (1 election,

---

[7] Indeed, such behavior would be consistent with what Tavits and Annus (2006) find in postcommunist states: strategic voting in PR elections (in the form of defections from parties unlikely to overcome the legal threshold for representation) increases with democratic experience.

1998), and Russia (3 elections, 1995–2003), which introduced their mixed-member systems in the early 1990s; and Ukraine (2 elections in the dataset, 1998–2002), which introduced its mixed-member system in the late 1990s. In 1992, 1996, and 2004, Lithuania used a two-round majority system in its SMDs, as did Macedonia in 1998. For the two-round majority cases, we measure the SF ratio as the ratio of votes of fourth place (the second loser in the first round of two-round majority balloting) to third place (the first loser).

General SF Ratio Patterns

In Appendix 6A, we present SF ratios for the first and most recent election in each country for which we have SMD and PR vote figures broken down at the SMD level. For each country/year case, the left-hand figure is a histogram representing the distribution of SF ratios (i.e., how many districts have SF ratios between 0 and 0.1, how many are between 0.1 and 0.2, and so on) for SMD races. The right-hand figure is a histogram for PR races. For both, the SF ratio is the third-place vote divided by the second-place vote (whether party in PR or candidate in SMD voting) at the SMD level.[8] What place a party finishes in a PR race within SMD boundaries is, of course, meaningless in terms of winning seats within the district, but this is the very point: by looking at the results of both SMD and PR voting, we can compare how outcomes correspond with the differing incentives offered by SMD and PR races. In a number of countries (see Appendix 6A1), the SF ratios largely meet the expectation that, even as ratios in SMD races tend toward zero, those in PR contests do not. Assuming that votes in PR races approximate voters' true preferences, this pattern is suggestive of strategic behavior: most likely, the difference between the two tiers is due to strategic behavior in SMDs, whereby many voters and elites shift their support away from their preferred candidate/party to one who is more likely to be competitive.

Differences between Established and New Democracies

Our principal interest is in the differences between established and new democracies, especially those with poorly institutionalized party systems: indeed, SF ratios in established democracies tend toward zero after the first election under the new mixed-member system,[9] and in new democracies they do not (see Appendix 6A) – thus suggesting greater strategic defection in established democracies. The pattern of high SF ratios is evident in all of the new democracies. In every figure in Appendix 6A2 (the SF ratio patterns for new democracies), relatively few districts have SF ratio patterns in the SMD tier that approach zero, and in fact the most common pattern is of SF ratios that push

---

[8] Again, for two-round majority systems, the ratio is of the fourth-place to the third-place vote.
[9] See the online appendix for discussion of the exceptions among the established democracies.

toward 1. The cases of Russia and Ukraine help highlight the reasons for these patterns. In the initial mixed-member system elections in both Russia and Ukraine, information on likely political outcomes was limited. Among other factors in Russia and Ukraine, the free press was not well developed and there was limited democratic experience and district-level polling, so voters knew relatively little about the people and groups contesting legislative elections. In addition, as we detail in Chapters 1 and 3, in both Russia and Ukraine parties did not structure the vote; indeed, a huge proportion of the SMD vote in both countries went to independent candidates who had no party affiliation. In such a context, in a large number of districts it was difficult to determine which candidates were competitive and which were not. In other words, it appears that voters and elites did not have sufficient information to defect strategically from their first choice even if they wanted to.

Moreover, the fact that candidates could win an SMD in Russia and Ukraine with a small share of the vote made victory appear possible for even a weak candidate, thus further encouraging more candidates to run, and voters and elites not to abandon their preferred candidate. The average margin of victory was roughly the same across both the new and established democracies in our dataset: 16 percent in established democracies and 17 percent in new democracies (and among new democracies, 19 percent in the poorly institutionalized Russian and Ukrainian cases). However, the large number of candidates coming forward in Russia and Ukraine led winners and second-place candidates to take a smaller share of the vote: in our established democracies, the average vote shares won by the first- and second-place finishers were, respectively, 50 and 34 percent. In contrast, in our new democracies, they were, on average, 38 and 21 percent (and 39 and 20 percent for Russia and Ukraine). As a result, any candidate with decent name recognition or a significant voting constituency could win a district race – and even those with neither might consider themselves to be potential challengers, as only a small percentage of the vote was required to win.

In this context of second-place candidates who win a small share of the vote, and voters and elites who had little incentive to withdraw their support from their preferred candidates, SF ratios were very high – often approaching 1. Because there was little strategic defection away from them, third-place (and lower) candidates received a substantial number of votes, especially compared with the relatively small number that second-place candidates received. Moreover, in this context, the problem for voters and elites was not merely gaining sufficient information to differentiate between second and third place. Rather, in some cases such as Russia and Ukraine, it was difficult to distinguish between probabilities of victory for *any* of challengers. The ratios between the votes won by lower-ranked candidates (e.g., fourth/third-place and fifth/fourth-place) also tended toward 1 (figures not shown).

These patterns suggest that a general lack of information about likely electoral outcomes led SMD competition in many new democracies into a state of non-Duvergerian equilibrium, which made it unlikely that the number of candidates per district would winnow down toward two, as both predicted by Duverger's Law and typically occurred in established democracies.

Closeness of the Race Shapes the SF Ratios Differently in Established and New Democracies

As we discussed earlier, there ought to be more strategic defection in close races under SMD rules. We highlight the impact of the closeness of the race in greater detail later when we discuss our multivariate, quantitative analysis of the factors shaping SF ratios, but we offer one example here. Figure 6.2 presents the SF ratio patterns for Japanese SMDs for the three elections in Japan from 2000 through 2005.[10] Figure 6.2(a) indicates that SF ratios tend toward zero when the single-member district race is close (i.e., the difference between first and second place is five percentage points or less). In contrast, Figure 6.2(b) indicates that the SF ratio is higher when the district race is not close (i.e., first and second place are separated by more than 35 percentage points).

However, close SMD races are less likely to lead to a drop in SF ratios in new democracies. On one hand, lower levels of information may make voters and elites more uncertain about potential electoral outcomes, and therefore make them less likely to respond to the competitive context in the district. On the other hand, as we noted earlier, in new democracies and poorly institutionalized party systems, bigger margins of victory may be associated with less hope for victory by lower-ranked candidates and, thus, less desire to enter into the race in the first place. When a dominant candidate is present, fewer additional candidates may choose to run. As a result, voters and elites may face less difficulty distinguishing between the viability of the lower-ranked candidates and therefore may be better able to defect strategically from very weak candidates, thus potentially driving the SF ratio down. In contrast, contests with no dominant candidate might promote greater uncertainty about likely outcomes, and, thus, inspire more candidates to enter. With more candidates, the share of the vote won by the second-place candidate would be likely to be relatively small, and with greater uncertainty about likely outcomes, there would probably be less strategic defection from lower-ranked candidates. As a result, the ratio of third-place to second-place candidate votes would be likely to be high. In this way, in poorly institutionalized cases, SF ratios might be higher in close races.

Examples from Russia

For example, in the 1995 Russian elections in District #99 (Leningrad Oblast), 16 candidates contested a seat in an atmosphere of low information. In a

---

[10] We do not include the first election under the mixed-member system (1996) in which the lack of experience with the system overwhelmingly pushed the SF ratio pattern much further away from zero.

(a) SMDs where the difference between first and second place is less than .05

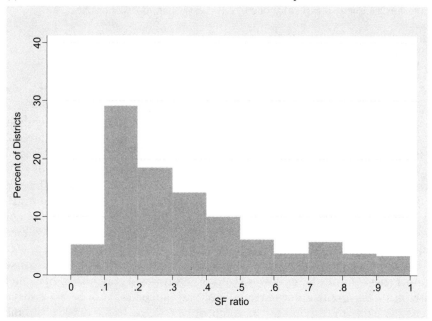

(b) SMDs where the difference between first and second place is greater than .35

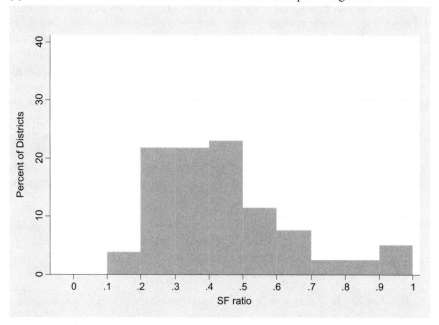

FIGURE 6.2. SF ratios patterns in (post-1996) Japan suggest that there is greater strategic defection in close races.

very competitive race, the winner received a vote share of only 10.4 percent, followed by the second-place candidate with 8.4 percent of the vote. As we might expect in such a situation, in which voters and elites cannot differentiate between competitive and noncompetitive candidates, there was very little drop-off in the vote for third (7.9%), fourth (7.4%), or even fifth place (7.2%). In contrast, in the 2003 Russian election, when United Russia had begun to emerge as a major political force in Russia, this same district had only seven candidates and the winner received 32 percent of the vote, compared with 25 percent for second place. In this less competitive atmosphere, there was a substantial drop-off in the vote share won by the third-place candidate (11%).

Russia's SF ratios in its early elections showcase how a lack of party institutionalization can result in a non-Duvergerian equilibrium that undermines strategic defection from lower-ranked candidates to more competitive ones, but increased party development in Russia from 1993 to 2003 also shows how changes within the party system can affect the strategic environment facing voters and elites and result in different patterns of SF ratios. Although independent candidates remained a major force in Russia throughout this period, parties became an increasingly prevalent and important part of SMD races. Indeed, the percentage of SMD seats going to major parties (those winning PR seats) in Russia steadily increased over time: 31.5 percent in 1993, 37 percent in 1995, 44 percent in 1999, and 54 percent in 2003. Moreover, by the 2003 election, United Russia had emerged as a major national electoral force capable of winning seats in many districts across the country. Candidates from United Russia won 97 SMD races (nearly 45% of all valid SMD elections) whereas, the Communist Party, the largest SMD party in the previous two elections, won only 62 seats (28% of all SMD seats) in 1995 and 46 seats (21% of all SMD seats) in 1999.[11] The emergence of a single large party capable of winning many SMDs promoted a less competitive electoral environment, especially because United Russia was a so-called "party of power" (Colton and McFaul 2000), which had the resources and power of the state behind it.[12]

By the 2003 election, the emergence of United Russia as a large, nationwide party changed the strategic environment in many districts; thus, new entrants could no longer reasonably assume to have a decent chance at victory. In

---

[11] In each of these elections, there were fewer than 225 seats filled on election day because several district elections were deemed invalid for one reason or another. According to Russian election law, SMD races would be declared null and void if (1) there are extensive violations of electoral law, (2) there is less than 25 percent voter turnout in the district, or (3) the winner receives fewer votes than the "against all" option given to Russian voters in SMDs. Invalid SMDs would be filled later through by-elections.

[12] The emergence of a successful "party of power" in United Russia was very detrimental to competitive elections and democratic development in general. Elections were less free and fair and various forms of electoral manipulation increased dramatically after the party's formation during the 2000s under President Vladimir Putin (Myagkov, Ordeshook, and Shakin 2009).

short, the existence of a party (United Russia) that was likely to win many votes and thus secure victory with larger vote shares deterred smaller parties and independents from throwing their hats into the ring. For example, where United Russia won seats, wide-open races (in which the winner captured no more than 25 percent of the vote) were uncommon: only 6 percent of United Russia winners won with 25 percent or less of the vote, whereas 22 percent of victorious independents and 9 percent of winning candidates from other parties won in such wide-open races. Conversely, United Russia's electoral successes tended to restrict electoral competition: 57 percent of United Russia winners won with a large vote share (40 percent or more of the vote), whereas independents won with at least 40 percent of the vote only 42 percent of the time (and winners from other parties did so 51 percent of the time).

As a consequence of these developments within the party system, Russia moved out of the non-Duvergerian equilibrium seen in 1995 and 1999, in which SF ratios approximated 1 because virtually any candidate had a reasonable chance to win the district seat, to a transitional pattern of middling SF ratios. Of course, the party system did not become completely institutionalized, as demonstrated by the continued prevalence of independents through the 2003 election, so it did not yet establish the type of institutionalized party system that promotes strategic defection from nonviable candidates to the top two contestants in SMD contests that are found in established democracies. Candidate proliferation dropped significantly in Russia's 2003 election (from an average effective number of candidates of 4.64 to 3.52) but did not yet approach a two-candidate configuration (see Appendix 4A).

It is quite likely that further party institutionalization would have pushed Russian voters and elites toward greater strategic defection and greater consolidation of the party system under its SMDs. Unfortunately, coinciding with the rise of United Russia was a decline in democratic practices in Russia (and, moreover, the country switched to a pure PR electoral system, thus making it impossible for scholars to continue to study defection under SMD rules).

MORE SYSTEMATIC ANALYSIS

We should be careful not to read too much into the SF ratio patterns by themselves: the SF ratio patterns in West Germany in 1953 offer no evidence of strategic defection, but the multivariate analysis in Chapter 5 strongly suggests that strategic defection was common that year. By using statistical analysis that controls for all the different factors we have discussed, we can see much more clearly what leads to higher or lower SF ratios and, by extension, the extent to which particular patterns are the likely result of strategic defection.

Indeed, our quantitative, multivariable analysis offers strong evidence that the different factors we have discussed play an important part in shaping the extent of strategic defection. (See Appendix 6B for more detail on the quantitative analysis.)

Using Behavior in PR as a Baseline

As a control – and as part of the general controlled comparison approach – we include in the analysis *SFPR*, which is the ratio of the PR vote won by the party with the third-largest list vote total to the PR vote won by the party with the second-largest total (both measured at the SMD level).[13] At the most basic level of course, particular SF ratios emerge in SMDs, not because of large-scale strategic behavior, but because a given proportion of voters simply prefers the second-place candidate's party over the party of the third-place candidate. As we discussed earlier, studies of ticket splitting in mixed-member electoral systems tend to assume that most ballots cast in PR are sincere votes, so we use SFPR as a proxy measure for what the SF ratio would look like with sincere voting. If there is only straight ticket voting, the SF ratio (in the SMD tier) and SFPR will correlate perfectly, so including SFPR, in effect, allows us to use the other variables to explain much of the divergence from straight ticket voting.

Indeed, many voters are likely to vote for the same party across both tiers, so there should be a positive correlation between the two ratios: higher ratios in PR should be associated with higher SF ratios in SMD balloting, and this is precisely what we see. Figure 6.3 demonstrates that when the ratio of the vote for third-place to that of second-place parties in PR is zero, all else being equal, the SF ratio in the SMD tier will be 0.11, and when there is no difference in the second- and third-place PR votes (SF ratio of 1), the SF ratio in the SMD tier will be 0.72.

Differences in Strategic Defection between Established and New Democracies

With that control included, the most important point to draw from Figure 6.3 is the very different SF ratio patterns in new and established democracies – in particular, there appears to be markedly more strategic defection in established democracies than in new ones. All else being equal, SF ratios in new democracies are, on average, quite a bit higher than in established democracies – 0.57, compared with 0.33 in established democracies – suggesting that there is more strategic defection in established democracies.

Closeness of the Race Shapes the SF Ratios Differently in Established and New Democracies

This point about differences in strategic defection is made more convincingly when we look at the relationship between SF ratios and the closeness of the race. In established democracies, the closer the race, the lower the SF ratio: in races in which the winner completely dominates, taking just short of 100 percent

---

[13] Again, we use vote totals from the fourth- and third-place contestants for the two-round majority SMD systems.

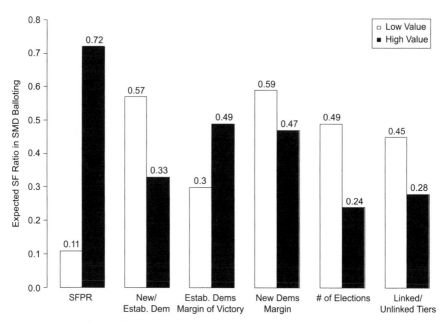

FIGURE 6.3. Relationship between each major variable and the SF ratios in SMD balloting.[14]

of the vote, all else being equal, we can expect an SF ratio of 0.49. However, when the race becomes too close to call (i.e., no difference in the vote between first and second place), Figure 6.3 indicates that the SF ratio will drop sharply, all the way down to 0.3. Strategic defection – away from the third-place candidate to the top two candidates – in close races best explains this pattern. A very different pattern exists in new democracies, however, where SF ratios appear to be *higher* when races are close – 0.59 in close races, but 0.47 in ones in which the winner dominates completely.

These differing results make sense: because information is less readily available in new democracies with less institutionalized party systems, uncertainty should be higher in such systems, thus making it more difficult for voters to recognize who is in and out of the running. Moreover, competitive races may introduce greater uncertainty, along with a stronger belief that *anyone* could win once there is a competitive race. Voters and elites therefore may actually be *less* likely to defect from their most preferred options in competitive races.[15]

[14] The expected values are based on coefficient estimates from Model 2 in Table 6.1 and by taking the lowest and highest values for the variable in question, while holding all other variables at their means. The effect of each variable is statistically discernible from zero (at the 0.1 level of significance).

[15] The main analysis we discuss in the text of this chapter does not take into account how past results shape the current one, but in separate analysis reported in Appendix 6B we include the SF ratio in the previous election as an explanatory variable. In this new analysis, we no longer

Increasing Strategic Defection over Time

Strategic defection also appears less common in the first elections under mixed-member system rules, since voters and elites may not yet sufficiently understand the rules and be able to predict likely outcomes, but, over time, such defection should increase even in new democracies.[16] As time passes, more information about the workings of the system emerges, voters gain greater information on specific parties and candidates, and voters simply become more experienced with the functioning of democracy (Tavits and Annus 2006). We see this pattern in Figure 6.3: all else being equal, we can expect an SF ratio of 0.49 in the first election (the low value for "# of elections") under a mixed-member system, but the ratio declines with each election, leading to an expected value of 0.24 in the 15th election.

Effect of Mixed-Member System Tier Linkage

As we noted earlier, mixed-member system rules governing the linkage between the SMD and PR tiers also ought to affect strategic behavior. Arguably, voters in linked mixed-member systems have less incentive to defect from their most preferred candidate to try to affect the outcome of the district race because the SMD vote has virtually no effect on the final distribution of legislative seats. In contrast, unlinked mixed-member systems, such as that of Japan, should be more likely to witness strategic voting. Admittedly, we offered this idea with less than thorough confidence, given that we saw strong evidence in Chapter 5 of strategic defection in linked systems such as those in Germany and New Zealand. However, Figure 6.3 offers tentative evidence that SF ratios are, in fact, higher in linked systems (0.45 to 0.28 in unlinked systems), suggesting that there is more strategic defection, all else being equal, in unlinked systems.

Democratic Experience Shapes the Effect of Electoral Rules on Strategic Defection

Returning to the main point in this book, what does this suggest about the differences in the likelihood of strategic behavior in new and established democracies? Figure 6.4 draws out the concepts here more fully by comparing the expected SF ratios in SMDs separately in the new and established democracies in our dataset. More specifically, Figure 6.4 provides an estimate of the SF

---

find a statistically discernible effect of the margin of victory in new democracies, but the effect of the margin of victory in established democracies variable remains statistically significant (albeit smaller).

[16] We run an additional model not reported in Appendix 6B in which we interact the number of elections with whether the country is a new or established democracy. If anything, SF ratios drop slightly faster in new democracies, most likely because they are at a higher point to begin with.

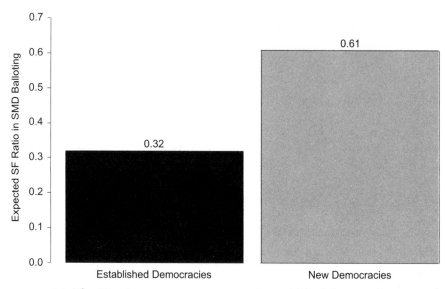

FIGURE 6.4. The SF ratios we can expect to see in established democracies are much lower than those in new democracies.[17]

ratios that we can, on average, expect for new and established democracies, based on our quantitative analysis and the mean values of the characteristics that we include in that analysis (such as the mean level of electoral competition) in each kind of democracy. As Figure 6.4 shows, based on this analysis, we can expect the average SF ratio to be roughly 0.3 in established democracies but greater than 0.6 in new democracies, most likely as a result of markedly greater strategic defection in countries with a longer history of democracy and better established party systems.

Finally, as we noted in Chapter 5, the analysis here could be criticized for using the outcome of any given election to predict whether voters and elites would behave strategically in that same election. That is, it might be suggested that we are claiming that strategic voting is a result of voters knowing in advance how the election is going to turn out. However, as we pointed out in Chapter 5, in reality in most elections – especially in established democracies – there is widespread knowledge of roughly how elections are likely to turn out, which makes actual outcomes a reasonable proxy for expectations before votes are actually counted (Cox 1988).

[17] To calculate both sets of expected values, we use the coefficients from Model 2 in Table 6.1. In calculating the expected values for both categories, we use the mean number of elections for all kinds of democracies. In calculating the expected values for the New Democracies category, we use the mean values of the variables (except for number of elections) from the new democracies in our dataset. We use the means of the established democracies in our dataset to determine the expected values for the Established Democracies category.

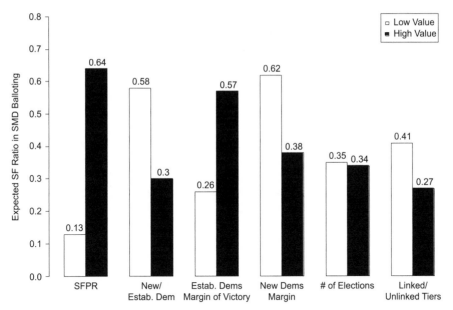

FIGURE 6.5. Relationship between each major variable and the SF ratios in SMD balloting, based on margin of victory in the *previous* election.[19]

Nevertheless, as we have argued throughout this book, information about likely outcomes is much less widespread in new democracies. Moreover, in general, we would do well to attempt to use other measures of the likely closeness of the race to see if the results are robust. For this reason, we rerun the principal model we discussed in this chapter (Model 2 in Table 6.1), but replace our measure of the closeness of the race (the margin of victory in the current election) with the margin of victory in the SMD in the previous election (see Appendix 6B).[18] We expect results to be largely the same as those illustrated in Figure 6.3. Most of all, we do not expect to see evidence of strategic defection in the new democracies. On top of the other impediments to strategic voting in new democracies, elections tend to be more volatile in new democracies, making it harder to use past results as a reliable predictor of future behavior.

Based on this new model (Model 5 in Table 6.1), Figure 6.5 illustrates the relationship between the different variables we have discussed and SF

[18] In this new model, we also include the SF ratio from the previous election as an explanatory variable.

[19] The expected values are based on coefficient estimates from Model 5 in Table 6.1 and by taking the lowest and highest values for the variable in question, while holding all other variables at their means. With the exception of the number of elections, the effect of each variable is statistically discernible from zero (at the 0.1 level of significance).

ratios in SMD races. Ultimately, each variable we consider in Figure 6.3 has a similar effect in Figure 6.5.[20] However, the relationship between the closeness of the race and the SF ratio is even more dramatic in Figure 6.5. In established democracies, SF ratios tend to be low in districts that had a close race in the previous election, and high in districts in which the previous election was uncompetitive – and the difference between the impact of close and uncompetitive elections appears even greater when we use the previous election to measure competitiveness. In contrast, in new democracies, a close race in the previous election is even more likely to lead to a *higher* SF ratio than the already very high bar suggested in Figure 6.3. In other words, Figure 6.5 shows even more strongly that close races tend to elicit strategic behavior in established democracies, but appear to inspire even less strategic defection in new democracies.

CONCLUSIONS

In this chapter, we find that SMD rules appear to have their expected effect of significant strategic defection from candidates ranked third and worse in established democracies, but little evidence of such behavior in new democracies with poorly institutionalized party systems. We find consistent differences between SF ratio patterns under PR and SMD rules. Moreover, we find that, in close races in established democracies, SF ratios under SMD rules were particularly likely to approach zero, a clear sign of strategic behavior by voters and elites. However, in new democracies, SF ratios tend to move away from zero under SMD rules, and, if anything, the SF ratios appeared *higher* in close races, suggesting a general lack of strategic defection.

Our findings in Chapters 4 through 6 fit together into a narrative that showcases the significant impact that political context can have on electoral system effects. Our analysis of established democracies offers support for the general Duvergerian view of plurality elections: when provided with a political context conducive to strategic behavior, voters and elites try to affect SMD races by defecting away from low-ranking candidates and instead support one of the top two competitors, thus winnowing down the number of parties. This dynamic is particularly strong when highly competitive elections make strategic defection more effective. In short, voters' and elites' strategic defections – of which we found evidence in Chapters 5 and 6 – push down the number of parties, which leads to the relatively Duvergerian two-party outcomes under FPTP rules in established democracies that we saw in Chapter 4.

---

[20] Because we use the results of the previous election to calculate a few of our variables, we have to drop the first election under the mixed system for each country from the analysis. The greatest effect of the number of elections was between the first and second election. Not surprising, therefore, in the new model there is no longer a statistically discernible relationship between the number of elections and SF ratios.

However, in political contexts with less democratic experience and less well-developed parties, a very different dynamic takes hold. With limited information about the distribution of public opinion or without well-developed parties to provide cues about candidates' and parties' electoral chances, it becomes more difficult for voters and elites to know who is in and out of the running for the district seat. Given the uncertainty in this context about likely outcomes, there is little point for many voters and elites to remove their support from their most preferred candidates, so there is little strategic defection.

Ordinarily, it is expected that voters and elites under plurality rules will gradually come to coordinate around two principal candidates, but with great uncertainty in the early years of a new democracy and a new electoral system, there will be little of the strategic defection that is necessary for such coordination. The problem is even greater where parties do not structure the vote and, hence, are unable to inject information and cues that might promote greater strategic defection, as well as constrain additional candidates from running. Instead, the significant uncertainty over likely outcomes creates the impression that anyone can win, which, in turn, gives additional candidates reason to run in the race. With larger numbers of viable candidates, the electorate becomes even more divided and victory becomes possible with even a small share of the vote. This pattern, then, further reinforces the sense that anyone can indeed win; therefore, voters and elites have strong incentive to continue to support their preferred candidate, who could very well take the seat.

In this way, in new democracies, especially those with poorly institutionalized party systems with low levels of information about likely outcomes, it is totally rational – and, in a sense, "strategic" – for countless voters and elites to continue to support their preferred candidate even under restrictive rules. If their top choice has a reasonable shot at victory, it would be irrational to support a different candidate. In such contexts, many voters and elites *ought* to eschew strategic defection from their top choice even under plurality rules.

At the same time, without greater strategic defection, not only will more candidates run in each SMD in the initial mixed-member system elections in countries such as Russia, but serious movement toward Duvergerian two-party outcomes occurs only slowly. As we highlighted in Chapter 4, the average effective number of candidates per SMD in Russia was 4.72 in 1993, 5.91 in 1995, and 4.64 in 1999. Only after a major party, United Russia, emerged to dominate SMD elections and begin to change the strategic environment in 2003 did the effective number of candidates per SMD in Russia drop significantly, to 3.52.

Skeptics might argue that the problem with this analysis is that electoral rules have their expected outcomes only under equilibrium conditions and that, especially in the early years of a new electoral system, we should not expect electoral rules to have their expected effects. This point is wholly correct. However, what is striking about the analysis in this chapter is that it appeared that many of the new democracies we examined probably were in a state of equilibrium under SMD rules – but it was a *non-Duvergerian equilibrium*. Because of the lack of information, voters and elites were unable to differentiate between the likelihood of different candidates' success. When, as we saw in a number of new democracies, candidates in second, third, fourth, and even fifth place all polled roughly equal shares of the vote – thus leading to SF ratios of roughly 1 – they found themselves in an equilibrium from which they could not readily extricate themselves, as few actors had a real incentive to change behavior. It was unlikely that such an equilibrium would be disrupted without greater information – probably by means of a more thoroughly structured party system – that would allow voters and elites to distinguish between the likelihood of different candidates winning. Indeed, as we discussed earlier, it took a substantial change in the party system in Russia – a greater prevalence of major parties and the emergence of a strong national "party of power" in United Russia – to change the strategic environment enough to disrupt the non-Duvergerian equilibrium found in earlier Russian elections such as the one in 1995. Such developments provided clearer signals to voters and elites regarding who would most likely be competitive in district races and, thus, who might be out of the running. As a consequence, patterns of SF ratios changed and candidate proliferation declined (although Russia did not yet approximate two-candidate competition).

Along these lines, it is possible, of course, that we simply do not have enough elections in our analysis. It took three elections before the SF ratio pattern in Japan finally leaned more solidly toward zero. Indeed, in 2003 we did see some shift away from SF ratios around 1 in Russia, and in Chapter 4 we saw a shift over time toward fewer parties in numerous countries' SMDs, even in new democracies. However, these developments do not approximate the degree of strategic behavior and subsequent reduction in the number of parties found in established democracies after similar amounts of experience with the new electoral system.

Given the overwhelming evidence of an unmistakable pattern that distinguishes new democracies from established ones, there are reasons for pessimism about the possibility of voters and elites being able to gain sufficient information and defect more strategically under restrictive rules in new democracies in the near future without major changes in the contours of their party systems. Time and democratic experience alone are unlikely to change the underlying dynamic that has undermined strategic behavior in new democracies such as those in Russia and Ukraine.

APPENDIX 6A1. HISTOGRAMS OF SF RATIOS (FIRST AND MOST RECENT ELECTION FOR WHICH WE HAVE DATA): ESTABLISHED DEMOCRACIES[21]

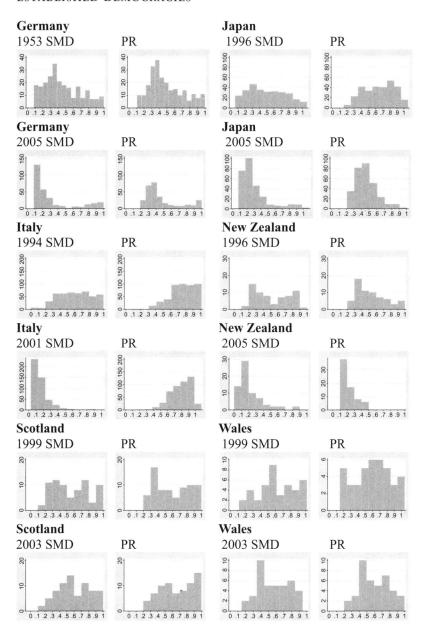

[21] We include in Appendices 6A1 and 6A2 only those countries that we have data for both the PR and SMD tiers for two elections.

APPENDIX 6A2. HISTOGRAMS OF SF-RATIOS FOR NEW
DEMOCRACIES[22]

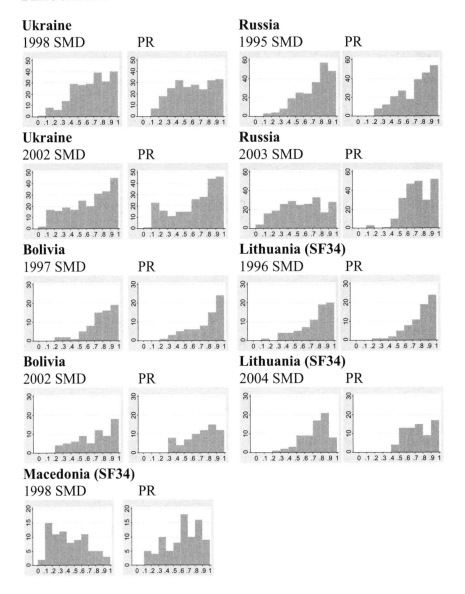

[22] We were unable to acquire PR results at the SMD level for 1993 in Russia, so we begin with 1995 in this appendix. We were unable to acquire district-level data for the 1992 Lithuanian election, so we begin with 1996. Lithuania (except for 2000) and Macedonia both used two-round majority rules in their SMDs, so, for them, the SF-ratio is the ratio of votes for fourth and third place, rather than third and second place.

APPENDIX 6B. MULTIVARIATE ANALYSIS OF SF RATIOS IN MIXED SYSTEMS[23]

The unit of analysis is the district level in each election in each country in our sample. For the bulk of our models, our dependent variable is the SF ratio in the SMD. We use a logit transformation of the SF ratio to make it unbounded.[24] Because the independent variables include both national and subnational level factors, we use a multilevel model as suggested by Jones (2008). More specifically, we use the Linear Mixed Model fit by REML provided by the lme4 package in R. Because of similarities between the results within a given country, we expect the error term to be correlated with the observations within each country case. We therefore use country as the ID variable, thereby adjusting the standard errors accordingly. Our dataset includes more than 8,500 observations, drawn from 41 elections in 11 countries.

Explanatory Variables

We expect negative coefficients on variables that should lead to greater strategic defection and positive coefficients on variables that make strategic defection less likely. Our analysis includes the following independent variables: *SFPR* is the ratio of the PR vote won by the party with the third-largest PR vote total to the PR vote won by the party with the second-largest PR vote total (both measured at the SMD level).[25] We code *Established Democracy* as 1 for established democracies and 0 for the new democracies. *Margin of Victory* is the difference between the proportions of the vote won by the first- and second-place candidates in the district. We create an interaction term, *Margin*Established Democracy*, between Margin of Victory and Established Democracy. *Election Number (log)* is the log of the number of elections held in the country under the mixed-member electoral system in the election under consideration (e.g., Election Number in the first election is 1). We expect the coefficient to be negative, as strategic defection ought to increase and the SF ratio ought to go down with each election under the system. We log the variable because we expect it

---

[23] An earlier version of the analysis in this chapter was presented in Moser and Scheiner (2009), but the current analysis is different from the previous one in a number of ways. The data here include a number of additional countries and elections and we also changed the models somewhat. In addition, in this chapter we run a series of models with different specifications. Finally, Moser and Scheiner (2009) use a standard random effects model, but here we utilize the linear mixed model (although there are no marked differences in the results between them here).

[24] We also run two additional models in which the dependent variable is the SF-ratio for each district broken down into one of three SF ratio categories: 0–0.25, 0.25–0.75, and 0.75–1.0. The substantive results do not change markedly, so, to conserve space in the book, we place the results of this additional analysis in the online appendix.

[25] The SF ratio for two-round majority systems is the fourth-place vote divided by the third place vote.

to have a particularly large impact in the first elections. *Unlinked* is coded 1 for unlinked systems and 0 for linked mixed-member systems.[26]

Results

In Model 1, we follow the logic we laid out in Chapters 1 and 3, and place our countries into one of three categories. We code Germany, Italy, New Zealand, Japan, Scotland and Wales as "Established Democracies"; we code Russia and Ukraine as "Noninstitutionalized Party Systems"; and we code Bolivia, Lithuania, and Macedonia as "New Democracies/Institutionalized Party Systems." In Model 1, therefore, we include two 0–1 dummy variables, *Established Democracy* and *New Dem/Inst. Party System*, that we also interact with Margin of Victory. As Model 1 in Table 6.1 indicates, although we see significant coefficients in the expected direction on the established democracy variables, we do not with the New Dem/Inst. Party System variables: The coefficients for both New Dem/Inst. Party System variables are negative and nonsignificant. In short, we find no evidence that there is a difference in the level of strategic defection in institutionalized and noninstitutionalized party systems in new democracies.

The other results in Model 1 are as expected; therefore, in Model 2 we create a single dichotomous country classification: countries are either established democracies (the same group as mentioned earlier) or not; in the model, we include both the Established Democracy dummy variable and the interaction between it and Margin of Victory. In the results of this model, our expectations bear out, most notably with respect to strategic defection and the difference between new and established democracies. The coefficient on Established Democracy is negative (and statistically significant), indicating that, all else being equal, SF ratios are lower in established democracies. Most important, the coefficient on Margin*Established Democracy is positive and statistically significant. When combined with the coefficients on Margin of Victory and Established Democracy, it is clear that greater competitiveness in established democracies leads to lower SF ratios. This is strong evidence of strategic defection by voters and elites in SMDs. In contrast, the uninteracted Margin of Victory variable has a negative (and significant) coefficient, indicating that closer races lead to *higher* SF ratios in new democracies. This result suggests that there is much less strategic defection in these countries. The results for other variables are largely as expected. The coefficient on SFPR is positive and statistically significant. Election Number (log) is negative and statistically significant, indicating that SF ratios go down over time. The coefficient on Unlinked is negative (and significant at the 0.1 level), suggesting that unlinked systems have more strategic voting.[27]

---

[26] As we explain in Chapter 2, we code Italy as unlinked.

[27] We were somewhat concerned that the lack of a difference between institutionalized and noninstitutionalized party systems in new democracies was a result of the unique type of politics in the

TABLE 6.1. *Multilevel Model of Correlates of the SF Ratio*

	(1) 3 Types of Democracy	(2) Estab. vs. New	(3) Don't restart Lith elections	(4) Lagged DV	(5) Lagged DV and Margin	(6) Italy Linked
Election Number (log)	−0.400	−0.400	−0.398	−0.042	−0.028	−0.400
	(0.021)***	(0.021)***	(0.021)***	(0.037)	(0.036)	(0.021)***
SFPR	2.976	2.974	2.969	2.356	2.432	2.973
	(0.064)***	(0.064)***	(0.064)***	(0.085)***	(0.084)***	(0.064)***
Margin of Victory	−0.478	−0.491	−0.483	−0.223	−1.011	−0.492
	(0.183)**	(0.181)**	(0.182)**	(0.273)	(0.347)**	(0.182)**
Est. Democracy	−1.664	−1.224	−1.274	−1.300	−1.573	−1.103
	(0.430)***	(0.342)***	(0.374)**	(0.360)***	(0.366)***	(0.472)*
Margin*Est. Dem.	1.289	1.303	1.297	0.639	2.344	1.304
	(0.213)***	(0.211)***	(0.211)***	(0.302)*	(0.368)***	(0.211)***
Unlinked	−0.827	−0.708	−0.678	−0.650	−0.636	−0.334
	(0.324)*	(0.340)*	(0.373)+	(0.337)+	(0.343)+	(0.470)
SF ratio $t-1$				0.266	0.250	
				(0.013)***	(0.013)***	
New Dem/Inst. Party System	−0.598					
	(0.437)					
Margin*New Dem/Inst. Party System	−0.343					
	(0.394)					
Constant	0.170	−0.309	−0.267	−0.309	−0.254	−0.611
	(0.459)	(0.356)	(0.389)	(0.365)	(0.371)	(0.466)
N	8603	8603	8603	4875	4875	8603
Countries	11	11	11	9	9	11

Standard errors in parentheses:
$+ p < 0.1$; $* p < 0.05$; $** p < 0.01$; $*** p < 0.001$.
ID variable: Country (11).
Unit of analysis: Single-member district.
Dependent variable: Logit transformation of the district SF ratio (2nd loser vote divided by 1st loser vote).

177

As robustness tests, we rerun our models, but alter the coding of the variables in Model 2 and/or add new variables. We were concerned that our results were being driven in part by our decision to restart the number of elections under the mixed system in Lithuania both when the SMD tier shifted to plurality in 2000, and then back to two-round majority in 2004. Therefore, in Model 3, we code 2000 as Lithuania's third under the mixed system, and 2004 as the country's fourth election. The results of the model are little different from those in Model 2.

We also run Model 4, which replicates Model 2 but with a control for autocorrelation. We include as an independent variable *SF ratio t − 1*, which was the SF ratio (with the logit transformation) in the district in the previous election. The lagged dependent variable (*SF ratio t − 1*) has a strongly positive and significant relationship with the SF ratio in the current election, but the results for the other variables do not change markedly. The coefficients on the margin of victory variables are smaller, but they continue to indicate the same patterns as in Model 2. We see no evidence of strategic defection in new democracies (Margin of Victory is now nonsignificant), but see quite a bit in established democracies. Election Number (log) now has a nonsignificant coefficient. We expect the greatest difference in strategic behavior to be between the first two elections, so we attribute this nonsignificance to the elimination of the first election from the analysis.

To differentiate between elections in which the leading candidate won with a large share of the vote and those in which the winner gained substantially less than 50 percent of the vote, in Moser and Scheiner (2009) we included the variable *50 − Winner*, which is the absolute value of 50 minus the winning candidate's percentage of the vote. We argued that, in races in which the winner had a relatively small share of the vote, voters would be less willing to defect from their first preference. However, we decided to drop this variable from our principal analysis because of concerns over collinearity. There is a −0.52 correlation between 50 − Winner and Established Democracy.[28]

---

three cases of institutionalized party systems in new democracies that we have in our dataset: in Bolivia, the PR vote helps determine the outcome of the presidential race, making it likely that there will be less sincere voting in PR there. Lithuania and Macedonia both used two-round majority systems in their SMDs (although Lithuania switched to plurality for its 2000 election), which may lead to a very different electoral calculus from that in plurality systems. To make sure that these cases did not bias the other results in some way, we reran Model 2 but with dichotomous dummy variables for Bolivia and two-round majority systems. The results here do not change markedly from those in Model 2 (results not shown).

[28] We ran a model with this variable for illustrative purposes (results not shown). In the model, the coefficient on 50 − Winner is positive and statistically significant, indicating that the further the winner's vote total gets from 50 percent, the higher the SF ratio. All the variables from Model 2 remain significant, but the margin variables switch signs. Margin of Victory now has a positive coefficient and Margin of Victory*Established Democracy now has a negative coefficient, strongly suggesting collinearity.

It may be inappropriate to use time t information on the closeness of the race to predict voters' strategic behavior in the election at time t. To address this concern, in Model 5, we measure closeness of the race by using the Margin of Victory in the district in the previous election. We also use this measure to create a new interaction term between Margin of Victory (previous election) and Established Democracy. In addition, we include SF ratio $t - 1$ in the model. The substantive meaning of the results for Model 5 does not differ markedly from those in Model 2: we still see little evidence of strategic defection in new democracies and still find substantial strategic defection in established democracies.

In Model 6, we rerun Model 2, but with Italy coded as a linked system. Changing the coding leads to the coefficient on Unlinked becoming nonsignificant (although still in the negative direction), giving us less confidence that there is, in fact, more strategic defection in unlinked systems; however, the coefficients and standard errors on the others variables in the model scarcely change.

7

Social Diversity, Electoral Rules, and the Number of Parties

Thus far, this book has focused on the interactive effect on political outcomes of electoral rules and the level of democratic and party system development. In this chapter, we shift our focus to how electoral rules interact with a different category of political context, *social diversity*, to affect the party system.

A long line of research has argued that the number of parties in a country is the product of an interactive process between the number of social cleavages and the electoral system, whereby social heterogeneity has little effect on the number of parties under "restrictive" rules such as first-past-the-post (Duverger 1954; Ordeshook and Shvetsova 1994; Amorim Neto and Cox 1997; Clark and Golder 2006; Singer and Stephenson 2009). Many scholars posit that as the number of distinct groups in society increases, so will the number of parties, but that this relationship will exist only under "permissive" electoral rules (such as PR with high district magnitude and little or no legal threshold of representation). The incentives of the electoral system under restrictive rules drive voters, groups, and elites to withdraw their support from candidates who are unlikely to be competitive, and instead line up only behind those truly "in the running" – thereby leading to a small number of parties (or candidates), irrespective of the number of distinct groups in society.

In this chapter, we reexamine these relationships. We analyze district (and subdistrict) level data from five mixed-member electoral systems – Japan, New Zealand, Russia, Ukraine, and Wales – which permits us to compare the relationship between social (usually ethnic) heterogeneity and the number of parties under different electoral rules within the very same geographic regions at the same time. To address most properly the link between social diversity, electoral rules, and party fragmentation, it is necessary to examine the relationships at the district level; to our knowledge, the analysis in this chapter is the first to do so in comparing SMD and PR rules.

Our district-level analyses indicate a very different relationship between social diversity, electoral rules, and party fragmentation than is usually posited.

First, and consistent with the novel analysis of Stoll (ND), we find that, rather than having simply a positive and linear relationship with party fragmentation, in heterogeneous societies social diversity tends to have a curvilinear effect: increasing social diversity leads to increases in the number of parties up to a certain threshold, after which diversity is associated with a decline in party system fragmentation.

Second, and most important, the analysis in this chapter suggests that most expectations about the modifying impact that electoral systems have on the relationship between ethnic diversity and party system fragmentation is exaggerated. We find that the effect of ethnic diversity is very similar under both single-seat (plurality) and multiseat (proportional) rules. Social diversity leads to nearly equal shifts in the number of parties under both PR and SMDs (although, controlling for diversity, there is usually less overall party fragmentation in SMD elections, especially in established democracies).

In this way, this chapter highlights another area in which context conditions outcomes under electoral rules. Interestingly, in contrast with earlier work, we find no evidence that there is an interaction between rules and social diversity in shaping the number of parties. Instead, we find that context – in the form of both social diversity and the level of democratic development – conditions the outcomes we see under multiple electoral rules. That is, in the established democratic contexts we examine, when there is little social diversity, plurality rules tend to have the outcome – smaller numbers of parties – that approximates what scholars expect from restrictive rules. However, as social diversity increases, we see shifts in the number of parties even under FPTP systems.

SOCIAL AND ETHNIC DIVERSITY, ELECTORAL SYSTEMS, AND THE NUMBER OF PARTIES

Most commonly, the relationship between ethnic diversity, electoral systems, and party fragmentation is depicted in the following way: Social heterogeneity, for which ethnic diversity is a primary source, provides the raw material for the number of parties found in a country. Electoral rules provide a filter that allows or prevents such forces from being manifest as political parties. Consequently, societies with more ethnic groups should have larger numbers of political parties as long as electoral systems are permissive enough to allow such groups to form their own parties.

Dating back to Duverger, scholars have contended that the number of political parties comprising a country's party system is, first and foremost, a product of the number of social divisions within society.[1] William Clark and Matt Golder, in re-articulating the sociological dimension of Duverger's

---

[1] Duverger (1954) argued that political parties were the reflection of social cleavages or "spiritual families" consisting of groups of individuals with like interests determined by monumental social forces such as industrialization.

(a) Under Permissive Electoral Rules

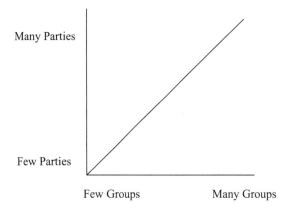

(b) Under FPTP Rules

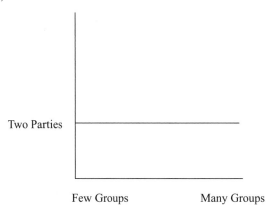

FIGURE 7.1. The most common view of the relationship between social diversity and party fragmentation.

arguments, explain, "Duverger's theory... implies that the number of parties should be an increasing function of the number of politically salient spiritual families in a polity" (2006: 682): As long as there are multiple distinct social groups, there should be multiple parties. In this way, the literature on party systems suggests that there is a positive and linear relationship between the number of social groups and the number of parties (see, e.g., Clark and Golder 2006; Singer and Stephenson 2009). We illustrate this relationship in Figure 7.1(a).

As Clark and Golder note, the literature on party systems tends (mistakenly, in their view) to divide into competing sociological and institutional schools. The sociological school highlights the importance of social cleavages, such as class or ethnic divisions. Seymour Martin Lipset and Stein Rokkan's (1967) seminal work exemplifies the sociological school's emphasis on social cleavages as the critical factor determining various characteristics of the party system, including the number of parties within a country. The institutional school emphasizes the effect of electoral systems in allowing or limiting the formation of parties around social divisions. Pioneering works by Douglas Rae (1967) and Arend Lijphart (1994), among others, represent the institutional school's focus on the influence of electoral systems and other institutions on the number of parties.

Currently, the most widely accepted explanation for the number of parties in a country represents a combination of these two approaches: scholars such as Clark and Golder argue cogently that, all else being equal, (a) ethnic diversity promotes party proliferation by producing discrete electoral constituencies that will support different political parties, but (b) the electoral system serves as a filter for these social cleavages. Electoral systems with higher district magnitudes, and thus lower electoral thresholds, allow more social cleavages to be represented by distinct parties, as illustrated in Figure 7.1(a). Electoral systems with lower district magnitudes restrict those opportunities because of their bias against smaller parties (Cox 1997: 206; Clark and Golder 2006: 681–682; Singer and Stephenson 2009: 486). Most notably, as we discuss in Chapters 3 through 6, FPTP systems create incentives for weak parties and candidates to exit the race and for voters to cast ballots strategically only for one of the two competitive candidates. As a result, irrespective of the level of social diversity, in FPTP systems there ought to be no more than two candidates per district, as illustrated in Figure 7.1(b).

Work on this interactive effect has evolved exactly as science should, with each study building with greater precision and rigor on the previous one. Most notably, Peter Ordeshook and Olga Shvetsova's (1994) and Octavio Amorim Neto and Gary Cox's (1997) seminal cross-national analyses demonstrate an interaction between diversity and electoral rules. More recently, Clark and Golder's (2006) insightful work highlights how restrictive SMD rules ought to act as a brake on the impact of diversity, and offers quantitative analysis that more cogently demonstrates the interaction. Building on Clark and Golder's analysis, Matthew Singer and Laura Stephenson's (2009) important contribution introduces district-level data on electoral rules and the number of parties, thus providing even more convincing empirical support that has solidified this interactive model as the leading explanation of the number of parties within the political science literature.[2]

---

[2] Powell also highlights the importance of both social diversity and electoral rules in shaping the number of parties, most notably pointing to Duverger's argument that social diversity is the most decisive factor but that restrictive electoral rules can put a brake on diversity's influence (Powell 1982: 82–83).

In short, significant analysis suggests that there is a positive, linear relationship between social cleavages and party systems – increasing diversity leads to more parties – and that the relationship largely disappears under FPTP rules.

NO EFFECT OF DIVERSITY UNDER FPTP? WHAT IF NOT ALL GROUPS WILL VOTE STRATEGICALLY?

The argument that diversity will have a different effect under restrictive rules (such as FPTP) than in permissive ones (such as PR with a large number of seats per district and a low legal threshold of representation) is based on the assumption that voters and elites will all respond to the incentives of electoral rules. That is, the mechanical effect of restrictive electoral arrangements, especially FPTP systems, ensures that only parties/candidates with a large share of the vote win seats. As a result, most scholars argue that these rules inspire a psychological effect, whereby voters and elites strategically withdraw their support from likely losers and instead back candidates who are likely to be competitive. Indeed, the most common assumption of work on the interaction between electoral rules and diversity is that minority (often ethnic) groups constitute voting blocs that prefer their own (usually non-majority) parties, but will support these parties only if the electoral system rewards them with representation. If all groups strategically defect from their first preference if that party is unlikely to win representation and, in turn, support a more viable alternative, then the correlation between social diversity and party system fragmentation will be weak or nonexistent under plurality electoral systems.

However, what if not all supporters of likely losers defect strategically to more competitive alternatives? If so, social diversity might shape the number of parties/candidates even under restrictive rules such as FPTP. Even if a majority of voters casts ballots for one of the top two candidates, if (a) not all small parties exit the race and (b) a relatively large proportion of voters continue to support their top preference irrespective of the chances of success, we are likely to see a relationship between social diversity and the number of parties under FPTP.

Most work views Duvergerian strategic defection as the norm, but, as we note elsewhere in this book, Cox (1997: 79) highlights four conditions under which FPTP rules may not eliminate significant levels of support for small parties (or weak candidates): voters who are not concerned with affecting who wins in the current election (i.e., not "short-term instrumentally rational"); a lack of public information about voter preferences and vote intentions (and, hence, insufficient sense about which candidates are "out of the running"); widespread certainty regarding likely winners; and the presence of many voters who strongly prefer their first choice and, thus, are nearly indifferent to other choices. Voters falling into any of these categories will be less likely to shift their ballots strategically away from their top preference. The presence of large numbers of such voters, therefore, ought to lead to larger numbers of parties under FPTP rules than Duverger's Law would predict. As illustrated by our discussion throughout this book, we certainly believe that these conditions are important in shaping electoral behavior and outcomes under FPTP rules.

Although not clarifying the relative importance of Cox's conditions in the process, scholarly analysis has found that, in fact, only a subset of voters actually casts ballots strategically (see Cox 1997: 83–4). In analysis of strategic voting in the United Kingdom, even the highest estimates suggest that in competitive districts – that is, where a strategic ballot would be most rational – only about half of all supporters of likely uncompetitive candidates actually defect from their top choice to try to affect the outcome of the race (Alvarez et al. 2006). Indeed, the presence of so many voters who do not strategically shift their ballots from weak candidates even under plurality rules would undermine the expected interactive relationship between electoral systems and social diversity on the number of parties. If so, we would expect social diversity to affect party fragmentation, even under restrictive rules such as FPTP.

Of course, restrictive rules still ought to constrain the number of parties. Even if many voters see little difference between parties other than their top choice, we know that many voters still do shift their ballots strategically from weak candidates to strong ones, especially under plurality rules (see, e.g., Cox 1997, Alvarez et al. 2006, and our own Chapters 5 and 6) – even if not all voters choose to do it. Moreover, certainly in many cases elites who would otherwise promote or run as minority or minor-party candidates may choose to exit races strategically when they are certain to lose.

In sum, there is reason to believe that there may be a relationship between social diversity and party fragmentation even in FPTP elections, but there still ought to be greater party fragmentation under permissive rules. In this way, as we illustrate in Figure 7.2(a), if in a given polity there is a relationship between diversity and the number of parties under permissive rules, then a relationship is likely to hold under FPTP rules as well – although with fewer parties under the more restrictive rules.

POTENTIAL SHORTCOMINGS WITH WORK ON THE INTERACTIVE EFFECT OF DIVERSITY AND RULES ON PARTY FRAGMENTATION

However, the notion that social diversity would shape the number of parties under FPTP runs counter to most cross-national quantitative work that indicates that diversity affects party fragmentation under permissive rules, but not under restrictive ones. We believe that two issues may be responsible for the lack of evidence that diversity affects party fragmentation under restrictive rules. First, social diversity may not have a linear (or even monotonically increasing) effect on party fragmentation, and, therefore, analyses founded on the assumption of a linear relationship may miss when there is in fact a (nonlinear) relationship. Second, the direct effects of both social diversity and electoral rules are at the district level, but most analyses of their relationship with the number of parties are based on nationally aggregated data.

(a) Linear model

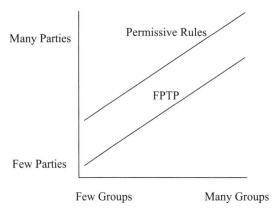

(b) Curvilinear Model

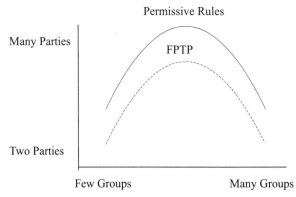

FIGURE 7.2. If social diversity affects the number of parties even under FPTP.

Challenges to the Linear Perspective: Increasing Diversity May Not Always Lead to More Parties

Recent analyses (especially Madrid 2005a; Stoll ND) challenge the assumption that social diversity has a linear relationship with the number of parties. There are a number of conditions under which the relationship between social diversity and the number of parties might be nonlinear – especially upside-down U-shaped. In particular, this curvilinear pattern would be apt to occur when there is not a one-to-one matching of social groups to parties.

Such a pattern might emerge in numerous ways, but Heather Stoll (ND) offers a particularly compelling example: as one moves from relatively homogeneous environments to contexts with greater diversity, there ought to be an uptick in the number of parties because each group would be large enough to play a meaningful governing role – if not as a majority party, perhaps as the head of a minority government or part of a coalition. However, further increases in diversity – when there are larger numbers of (especially small) groups – actually reduce the likelihood that any of the groups will play a meaningful governing role. Under these circumstances, political entrepreneurs have an incentive to create parties (or promote candidates) that can reach beyond a single group, which in turn leads to a consolidation of the party system around a smaller number of parties. Each of the curves in Figure 7.2(b) approximates the pattern representing this curvilinear (upside-down U-shaped) relationship.

The focus of this chapter is not on the form of the relationship between diversity and the number of parties, but on whether there is an interaction between social context (in the form of social heterogeneity) and electoral rules in shaping party fragmentation. However, it is important for us to address briefly the functional form of the relationship between diversity and party fragmentation: if diversity affects party fragmentation in a curvilinear fashion but we look only to see whether the pattern is linear, we may entirely miss the fact that a relationship exists at all.

Ultimately, our preceding discussion about curvilinearity is speculative because we do not have the necessary data to test the mechanisms;[3] however, for our purposes in this chapter, *why* such a relationship might exist is not as important as the fact that it often *does*. Looking at nationally aggregated data for a substantial number of countries, Stoll provides compelling evidence of the nonlinear relationship between social diversity and the number of parties. In addition, Moser's (2001c) district-level analysis of the relationship between ethnic diversity and the number of parties in postcommunist countries demonstrates the upside-down U-shape that we illustrate in Figure 7.2(b).

How does the discussion here relate to electoral rules? Our discussion in the previous section suggested that the shape of the relationship between social diversity and the number of parties may be similar under both permissive and restrictive rules (albeit with more parties under permissive rules). If so, and if the relationship is in an upside-down U-shaped pattern, then we may find similar U-shaped relationships between social heterogeneity and party fragmentation under both permissive and restrictive rules, as illustrated in Figure 7.2(b).

We Can Understand the Impact of Diversity Better If We Use District-Level Data

Most studies of the impact of ethnic diversity and electoral systems on party systems are limited by their use of nationally aggregated measures.[4]

---

[3] In the online appendix, we speculate on a number of conditions that might lead to a curvilinear pattern.

[4] Singer and Stephenson (2009) are noteworthy for their use of district-level measures of the number of parties and Hicken and Stoll (2011) use a measure of the number of parties that is the mean for all districts in each country, but even these studies use a nationally aggregated measure of social diversity.

Stoll (2004: 57) suggests the greatest problem with using such measures when she asks, "why should aggregate (national) groups be the ones that matter, particularly when we are studying the strategic incentives provided by electoral systems at the district level?" That is, as we highlight in Chapters 1 through 3, the direct effect of electoral systems is at the district level and theories that seek to explain the effective number of elective parties rely first on a district level logic (see Duverger 1954; Cox 1997; Singer and Stephenson 2009). For example, Duverger's Law is founded on the logic that voters and elites within a district seek to affect the outcome of that district's race (Cox 1997).

Social diversity at the national level may be wildly different from diversity in any given district, and the number of parties in any given district may be very different from what we see once votes from all districts are aggregated (see Riker 1986; Cox 1997). Even when a group is in the minority across most of the country, it may be able to win seats in a few SMDs where it actually makes up a majority. A study based purely on nationally aggregated data would miss the fact that this national minority is quite large in some districts, and such a study might misinterpret the reasons that a party representing a national minority group might win votes under restrictive rules. Moreover, the nationally aggregated number of parties is the sum of the votes for parties across all districts in the country. However, as we noted in Chapter 2, without particular factors to link parties across different districts,[5] a Duvergerian (two-candidate) outcome in each district could lead to hundreds of different parties winning votes and seats if different parties win a seat in each district.

For this reason, Mark Jones (2004a: 75) concludes, "Thus any analysis of legislative elections must either be conducted at the district level or else make several, usually unrealistic, assumptions regarding the distribution of the vote and influence of electoral laws in aggregate at the national level." At a minimum, to understand the effects of social diversity and rules on party fragmentation, any study using national aggregated measures must assume that the level of diversity in each district will match the measure for the entire country, and the number of parties within each district will project very closely to the nationally aggregated number receiving votes across the entire country.

To be sure, there have been analyses that examine both diversity and the number of parties at the district level, usually by studying national presidential elections (see, for example, Dickson and Scheve 2010; Golder 2006; Jones 2004a; Stoll ND), thereby treating the entire country as one single-member district. Taken as a whole, this work suggests that both diversity and rules (as well as an interaction between the two) affect the number of presidential

---

[5] Most notably, presidential elections – particularly those concurrent with legislative elections – and central governmental power affect the degree of coordination of the different districts across the country. See Chhibber and Kollman (1998, 2004), Cox (1997), Golder (2006), Hicken and Stoll (2011), and Shugart and Carey (1992). See Chapters 3 and 4 for additional discussion of "projection" from the district to national level.

candidates. Moreover, Dickson and Scheve (2010) and Stoll (ND) each find that social diversity has a nonlinear relationship with party fragmentation.

Nevertheless, the national winner-take-all stakes of a presidential election may be so much greater than the stakes of a legislative election as to make the two less comparable. More important, presidential elections typically vary only between FPTP and two-round majority rules, and therefore do not permit a more direct comparison of the different interactions between diversity and different types of electoral rules, such as large district magnitude PR and SMD rules, in shaping the number of parties.

The most prominent district-level work on diversity and the number of parties in legislative elections is by Jones (1997) and Raul Madrid (2005a). Jones (1997) provides a district-level analysis of U.S. House of Representatives elections in Louisiana and shows a clear, positive relationship between racial heterogeneity and the effective number of candidates under two-round majority SMD rules. Madrid (2005a) examines electoral results at various subnational levels under different electoral rules in Bolivia, Ecuador, Guatemala, and Peru and finds a relationship (which is often curvilinear) between diversity (which he measures as the size of the indigenous population) and the number of parties. However, although both Jones and Madrid find that social diversity clearly is strongly correlated with the number of parties, neither study offers a direct analysis of the interaction between diversity and rules.

The relative lack of work analyzing diversity and party fragmentation at the district level leads us to some uncertainty about the true relationship between the two variables: in fact, the curvilinear relationship between the size of the minority group and party system fragmentation found by Madrid (2005a) may be driven by his subnational-level analysis, whereas the positive, linear relationship found in cross-national analyses by Ordeshook and Shvetsova (1994), Amorim Neto and Cox (1997), Clark and Golder (2006), and Singer and Stephenson (2009) may be driven by their national-level measures of ethnic diversity. For this reason, Amorim Neto and Cox (1997: 168) note at the end of their seminal article that "it may be fruitful in further investigations of the interaction (or lack thereof) between social and electoral structure, to use constituency-level electoral returns and constituency-level indicators of social diversity." That being said, as Jones (1997: 350–1) points out, many countries do not maintain reliable data on diversity, and measures may not be comparable across cases.

However, because the logic underlying Duverger's Law and the interaction between electoral rules and social diversity are founded on a district-level dynamic, it is important to use district-level data to understand them. For this reason, in this chapter, we use data disaggregated to the district (and sometimes subdistrict) level to study the interaction between ethnic diversity, electoral systems, and the number of parties in five countries: Japan, New Zealand, Russia, Ukraine, and Wales.

In addition to allowing the most direct analysis of the link between diversity, electoral rules, and the number of parties, this approach has a number of advantages. Our intracountry analysis does not permit us to examine factors, such as presidential elections, historical legacies, and party institutionalization, that vary cross-nationally, but the approach permits us to control for all these factors and focus solely on the impact of diversity and electoral rules. In addition, this approach allows us to focus for each country on the specific types of diversity that are most important within that context. Moreover, as Jones (1997: 350–1) notes, accumulating information on diversity and minority group size at the subnational level reduces the likelihood of nonrandom measurement error, as these data tend to be more consistent within individual countries than across different countries. Finally, the use of data disaggregated to the district or subdistrict level provides methodological advantages, such as a larger number of observations and a greater range of variance on key variables related to electoral outcomes and the number and size of groups.

SOCIAL DIVERSITY, ELECTORAL RULES, AND THE NUMBER OF PARTIES IN FIVE MIXED SYSTEMS

We analyze the relationship between district-level ethnic diversity and district-level party fragmentation under five mixed-member electoral systems: Japan (2005), New Zealand (2002), Russia (1995), Ukraine (2002), and Wales (2003). We examine what impact, if any, variation in social diversity across subnational districts has on the number of political parties under multimember PR electoral rules and plurality rules operating simultaneously in the same country.

We chose mixed-member systems for which we could obtain subnational-level data on both social diversity and electoral results. In New Zealand, Wales, and Japan, our measures are calculated for each SMD. In Russia and Ukraine, census data were not available at the electoral district level, but we were able to collect election data for *raions*, the administrative districts (roughly equivalent to a U.S. county) in each country that coincided with the census data. Raions do not cross electoral district boundaries, and SMDs tend to be composed of multiple raions. In Russia's ethnic federal system, regions named after non-Russian ethnic groups are designated "ethnic homelands" of the titular minority and thus contain the majority of Russia's non-Russian population (see Harris 1993; Gorenburg 2003; Moser 2008). Because of missing data and other constraints, we limited the analysis of raions in Russia's 1995 election to 397 raions in 17 out of the 32 ethnic regions that existed within the Russian Federation in 1995. In Ukraine we have electoral and ethnic data for all raions in the country.

These cases represent a range of political, electoral, and demographic contexts from a variety of geopolitical regions. Japan, New Zealand, and Wales are consolidated democracies, whereas Russia's and Ukraine's democracies were still developing in the period we examine. Japan, Russia, and Ukraine use unlinked mixed-member systems, whereas New Zealand and Wales are examples of linked systems. All five systems use an FPTP rule in the SMD tier.

The most common approach in the literature uses ethnic fractionalization to measure social diversity.[6] We create a similar measure for New Zealand (2002), Russia (1995), and Ukraine (2002). For Wales (2003), our measure of diversity is founded on language, with English and Welsh speakers constituting the two principal groups. For each of these four country cases, we measure diversity as the effective number of ethnic/language groups (ENEG).[7] We also analyze Japan (2005), which has little ethnic heterogeneity. However, Japan has significant variation in the levels of urbanization across the country, with urban areas marked by greater diversity than the countryside. We therefore follow Cox (1997) in using level of urbanization as a measure of social diversity in Japan.[8]

EXPECTATIONS

The literature on the interactive effect of diversity and electoral rules typically seeks to explain – that is, use as its dependent variable – the effective number of electoral parties (ENEP or parties/candidates winning votes). Following this literature, for each district/raion, we calculate the effective number of electoral parties under PR balloting and the effective number of electoral candidates in SMD balloting.[9]

If, as is commonly expected, greater diversity leads consistently to more parties, the number of groups (ENEG) and number of parties (ENEP) should be positively correlated with one another. However, as we also discussed, it is possible that increases in the number of parties will go hand in hand with ethnic diversity only up to a point, and then start to decline with additional diversity

---

[6] For insightful exceptions, see Stoll (2008, ND).

[7] We calculate the effective number of ethnic groups by squaring the proportion of the population for each ethnic group, and then dividing 1 by the sum of these squares:

$$\text{ENEG} = 1/\Sigma \ (\text{Group Proportion}_i{}^2).$$

This is analogous to our effective number of parties index (ENEP). See Chapter 3 and Laakso and Taagepera (1979), Lijphart (1994: 57–72), and Taagepera and Shugart (1989: 77–81, 104–105).

We use two separate measures of ethnic diversity in New Zealand, where Maori voters cast ballots for elections in the SMD in which they live or for elections in special Maori districts. Many Maori voters place themselves on the special Maori rolls and so do not affect the number of parties in the geographical district in which they live. To make a claim that ethnic divisions have an impact on the party system, perhaps we should include in our measure only Maori voters who actually cast ballots in the geographic district competition. Therefore, in the analyses listed in Figure 7.3 and Table 7.1, our measure of ethnic diversity subtracts out the number of Maori choosing to vote on the Maori rolls. (In addition, we subtract all New Zealanders who list themselves as "other" or "unknown.") We also rerun the analysis using all Maori residing in each district. However, the correlation between the two measures is 0.99 and the results using the two different measures scarcely differ from each other. Thanks to Mark Jones and Rob Salmond for suggesting the alternative measure.

[8] As Cox does, we measure urbanization in Japan according to population density. Districts with larger numbers of people per square kilometer are considered more urban.

[9] See Chapter 3 for greater detail on the measurement of the effective number of parties.

(i.e., upside-down U-shape). If so, we should expect large values of ENEG to be negatively correlated with ENEP. To investigate this possibility, we introduce a second measure, *ENEG2*, which is calculated by squaring ENEG. If the curvilinear upside-down U-shape relationship exists, we will simultaneously see (1) a positive relationship between ENEG and ENEP, and (2) a negative relationship between ENEG2 and ENEP.

If electoral rules independently affect the number of parties, ENEP should be lower under SMD rules than in PR (even controlling for social diversity). Scholars most commonly argue that the constraining effect of FPTP rules disrupts the connection between ethnic diversity and party fragmentation. On the other hand, our earlier discussion highlighted evidence that only a subset of voters actually cast strategic ballots, and, if so, ethnic diversity would shape the number of parties under both PR and SMDs. At the same time, we know from much literature that an additional subset of voters (as well as many elites) does behave strategically, so, even if many voters do not, it is likely that there will be fewer parties under SMD rules independent of social diversity.

SOCIAL DIVERSITY HAS A RELATIONSHIP WITH PARTY
FRAGMENTATION – EVEN UNDER FPTP

In Figure 7.3, we illustrate the district (or raion) level relationship between social diversity, electoral rules, and the number of parties for each (SMD or PR) tier within each country. For each illustration, the horizontal axis represents the effective number of groups (ENEG) and the vertical axis represents the effective number of parties (ENEP). These illustrations demonstrate, first, that the relationship between diversity and the number of parties often appears to be curvilinear (upside-down U-shaped). More important, the illustrations indicate that, although there tend to be fewer parties under SMD rules, the effect of diversity is no different under restrictive rules than it is under permissive rules – contrary to most work on the topic, social diversity affects the number of parties, even under FPTP rules.

Curvilinear Relationship between Diversity and the Number of Parties

The illustrations show that the relationship between social diversity and the number of parties is not always uniformly positive. For all the illustrations, as social diversity increases from its lowest levels, there is also, on average, an increase in the number of parties. However, for New Zealand, Russia, and Ukraine, at the highest levels of social diversity, there is also a sharp drop in party fragmentation. Our quantitative analysis considers these relationships more systematically: as demonstrated by the second equation listed in the illustrations for New Zealand, Russia, and Ukraine, there is a positive, linear relationship between ethnic diversity and the number of parties if we do not include the most diverse districts. For example, under SMD balloting in New Zealand, if we exclude the ten most diverse districts in the country, each increase

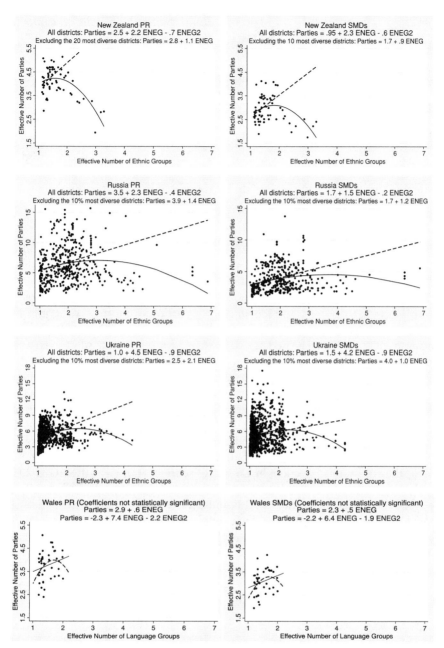

FIGURE 7.3. Diversity and the number of parties (district and subdistrict level).
Notes:

- For ease of illustration, all variables shown in Figure 7.3 are left in their unlogged form, and the coefficients are based on models that include only the variables shown.
- All coefficients listed in the illustrations in Figure 7.3 are statistically significant, except for Wales. For Wales, the coefficients in the separate PR and SMD models reported in Figure 7.3 are not statistically significant. However, when including both SMD and PR tiers in a single model, ENEG's coefficient is statistically significant (see Table 7.1).

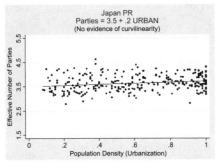
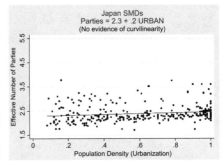

FIGURE 7.3 (continued)

of 1.0 in the ENEG score is associated with an increase of 0.9 in the ENEP score. For the New Zealand, Russia, and Ukraine illustrations, we use a dashed line to represent this linear relationship.[10]

However, although the dashed line nicely demonstrates the average relationship between diversity and the number of parties for most districts, it is, of course, a poor representation of the most diverse districts that have many fewer parties in each country. The first equation we list for New Zealand, Russia, and Ukraine indicates the relationship between ENEG and ENEG2, on one side, and ENEP, on the other, and suggests that there is, in fact, a curvilinear relationship between social diversity and party fragmentation. For example, under PR balloting in New Zealand, each increase of 1.0 in the ENEG score is associated with an increase of 2.2 in ENEP, but also, simultaneously, each increase of 1.0 in the ENEG2 score is associated with a *decline* of 0.7 in ENEP. More specifically, we would expect that in PR balloting in a district with an ENEG score of 1.0, there would on average be an ENEP score of 4.0; when ENEG is 2.0, we can expect an average increase in ENEP up to 4.1; but when ENEG is 3.0, we can expect that on average ENEP will decline all the way down to 2.8.[11] Indeed, the solid lines (curves) based on these equations for New Zealand, Russia, and Ukraine indicate a curvilinear upside-down U-shape, and – from a visual perspective – match the scatter plots quite well.[12]

[10] In our somewhat more detailed analysis in Appendix 7, we log ENEP and ENEG (and ENEG2), with little change in the basic findings. However, for ease of explanation and illustration, the figures (including coefficients) that we present in Figure 7.3 are based on simple models involving only unlogged values of ENEP and ENEG (and ENEG2) – although we use population density instead of ENEG for Japan. The fitted lines and equations shown in the figure are based on the coefficients derived from these simple OLS models – and include no additional variables – that we ran separately for each tier (SMD or PR) for each of the countries.

[11] For example, when ENEG is 2.0 (and, therefore, ENEG2 is 4.0), we compute the expected ENEP (4.1) as follows from the coefficients listed in the New Zealand PR illustration in Figure 7.3: ENEP = 2.5 + (2.2 * 2.0) − (0.7 * 4.0).

[12] In Appendix 7, we list two sets of results for each country: Table 7.1(a) lists the coefficients for the "linear" models (i.e., no ENEG2 in the model) and Table 7.1(b) lists the coefficients for the "curvilinear" model (i.e., includes ENEG2). For every country except for Japan, the adjusted R-squared is higher for the curvilinear model – i.e., the curvilinear model explains more of the variance in the data than the linear model.

The curvilinear pattern does not hold as clearly for Wales and Japan. Within Figure 7.3's illustration for Wales, neither the linear nor the curvilinear pattern is present to a statistically discernible degree, but in models that we discuss in Appendix 7 (in which we include PR and SMD balloting in a single model, log ENEG and ENEP, and control for electoral system type), we find a positive and statistically significant effect of ENEG on the number of parties – that is, a linear effect: more groups leads to more parties. For this reason, we use a solid line to represent the linear relationship between diversity and party fragmentation in the Wales illustrations. Furthermore, although not significant at conventional levels, the coefficients on ENEG (positive relationship with ENEP) and ENEG2 (negative relationship) are in the expected direction, and we use a dashed curve to represent the curvilinear relationship between diversity and party fragmentation. Most likely, it is more difficult to discern a curvilinear pattern in Wales – in other words, the pattern is not statistically significant – for two reasons. First, there are very few observations in Wales, as there are only 40 districts. Second, there is relatively little variation in diversity in Wales: there are no districts in Wales with an ENEG score of greater than 2.

In Figure 7.3's Japan illustrations, the relationship between the level of urbanization and the number of parties in districts in Japan is uniformly positive. Why is the relationship not curvilinear in Japan? One possible explanation is that urbanization is not as good a measure of diversity as our measures of groups in the other countries, but an equally plausible explanation is that there simply is little fundamental diversity across Japan. Indeed, the positive relationship between urbanization and the number of parties in Japan is not overwhelmingly strong – there are not markedly more parties in urban districts relative to rural ones. Compared with rural districts, Japan's most urban districts have, on average, only about 0.1 to 0.2 more parties.

Different Numbers of Parties under Different Electoral Rules

To illustrate differences in outcomes under different electoral rules, we present two figures for each country, one for SMD balloting and one for the PR vote (within the same districts/raions). Similar to what we saw in Chapter 4, on average there are more parties in each district under PR balloting than under FPTP balloting, even when we control for social diversity. With one exception, the distribution in Figure 7.3 is higher – that is, there are more parties – in each country's PR illustration than in SMDs. In each equation in Figure 7.3, the first number listed (the intercept in the regression equation) is the expected effective number of parties while holding social diversity constant. For example, comparing the first number (2.5) in the New Zealand PR figure with the first number (0.95) in the New Zealand SMD figure, we see that, controlling for social diversity, on average there were roughly 1.55 (i.e., 2.5 minus 0.95) more parties in a district under PR balloting than in FPTP in New Zealand.[13]

---

[13] The positive and statistically significant sign on the PR variable for every country except Ukraine in Appendix 7 indicates that, even controlling for social diversity, on average there is a

However, this difference between PR and SMD rules does not hold in Ukraine. In line with our analysis in Chapters 3 through 6, Ukraine's lack of democratic experience – and, presumably, its poorly developed party system – probably made strategic defection less likely even under SMD balloting.[14]

There Is Little Evidence of Interaction between Diversity and Rules

Most striking, Figure 7.3 demonstrates little difference across electoral rules in the relationship between diversity and the number of parties. Contrary to most expectations, the coefficients attached to the diversity variables are nearly identical in the SMD and PR illustrations for each country. Indeed, each curve/line based on these coefficients looks very much like the one next to it in the PR–SMD pairs. In other words, although there are differences in the number of parties under different rules, social diversity appears to have roughly the same relationship with party fragmentation under both FPTP and PR rules.

In fact, in the analysis that we discuss in Appendix 7, we ran models of the interaction between diversity and rules in shaping the number of parties, and the pattern still holds: for all five countries, social diversity has a statistically significant relationship with the number of parties, and – except for Ukraine – there is no evidence that the relationship is mediated by electoral rules. Moreover, in the case of Ukraine, diversity does appear to be related to the number of parties under SMD rules as well as PR, but the curve has a sharper slope (both up and down) under PR.

Summary of Findings

Most work on electoral rules suggests that plurality rules condition the impact of social diversity, leading to (at most) two candidates per district irrespective of the level of diversity; however, based on the illustrations in Figure 7.3, it appears that this Duvergerian two-candidate outcome holds in SMDs only under certain social conditions, most notably when in socially homogeneous populations. Outside Ukraine, the most homogeneous districts in Figure 7.3 always have an average effective number of candidates score that is lower than 3.0 in SMD balloting. Outside Ukraine, we see the most candidates, on average, in New Zealand and Wales, which maintain linked mixed-member systems that may do less than unlinked rules to constrain the number of parties.[15] Meanwhile

---

statistically discernible difference between the number of parties in the SMD and PR tiers, with more parties under PR than FPTP.

[14] In this way, the significantly smaller number of parties in the SMDs compared with PR in the newly democratic Russian system is surprising, but is probably because the data are from the aberrational 1995 election in which an extraordinary number of parties – even greater than the 5.91 ENEP score in Russia's SMDs that year – appeared in PR balloting (see the Chapter 4 appendices).

[15] See Chapters 2 and 3 for a discussion of how linked rules can lead to larger numbers of candidates under SMD. Also, as we explain in the online Appendix to Chapter 6, there are a number of other reasons for less strategic defection in Wales.

the most homogeneous districts in the unlinked Japanese and Russian systems' SMDs have, on average, effective number of candidates scores that are under 2.5.[16] Indeed, the small numbers of candidates across *all* types of districts under FPTP rules in Japan should not be surprising, given how homogeneous Japanese society is.

In short, it appears that electoral rules and social diversity have an "additive" effect on the number of parties, but not an interactive one: electoral rules appear to affect the number of parties independent of social diversity. Furthermore, social diversity appears to shape the effective number of parties, irrespective of electoral rules.

THESE FINDINGS ARE NOT UNIQUE TO MIXED-MEMBER ELECTORAL SYSTEMS

To what extent might our focus on mixed-member electoral systems be responsible for these findings, which appear to fly in the face of significant work that shows no effect of social diversity under FPTP rules? The simultaneous existence of a PR tier within a given mixed system might lead voters and other political actors to behave differently from how they would in a "pure" SMD system. Does social diversity affect the number of parties differently in pure SMDs than in the SMDs of mixed-member systems?

Comparing the impact of diversity on the number of parties in New Zealand prior to and after electoral reform provides a straightforward approach to address this question. New Zealand used a pure FPTP system prior to the introduction of its linked mixed-member system in 1996. If this chapter's finding that ethnicity has no greater impact in PR than in SMDs is a result of our focus on mixed-member systems, then we should find a difference between the effect of diversity prior to reform and afterward in New Zealand's SMDs. That is, if contamination due to mixed-member system rules is creating different strategic incentives, ethnic diversity should shape the number of parties in SMDs under the mixed-member system but not under the pre-reform, pure SMD system. On the other hand, if our findings represent more of a universal rule, ethnic diversity should affect the number of parties in New Zealand in similar ways under both the pure SMD system and SMDs in the mixed-member system.

New Zealand is a particularly useful case here because it is a linked mixed-member system. As we showed in Chapter 4, strategic incentives in the FPTP component of linked mixed-member systems tend to be weaker than under FPTP rules under unlinked mixed systems. In this way, if we find that the relationship between social diversity and party fragmentation is similar under both pure FPTP systems and FPTP in a linked mixed-member system, we probably would see the same pattern under FPTP in unlinked systems as well.

Figure 7.4 demonstrates the relationship between ethnic diversity and the number of parties in each single-member district in all elections in

---

[16] Taagepera (2007: 103) argues that an effective number of parties score between 1.5 and 2.5 in FPTP systems is essentially consistent with Duverger's logic.

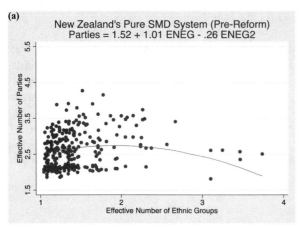

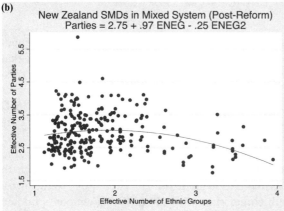

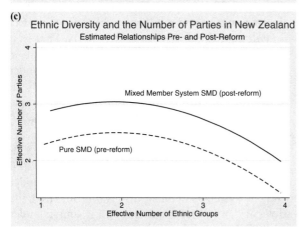

FIGURE 7.4. Effect of ethnic diversity on party fragmentation in New Zealand – pre- and post-reform (1987–2005).

Notes: For ease of illustration, all variables in this figure are left in their unlogged form, and the coefficients (all statistically significant) are based on models that include only the variables shown. The curves in Figure 7.4 (c) are drawn based on a model identical to Model 3 in Table 7.2, except that the variables are left in their unlogged form. As shown in Table 7.2 in Appendix 7, there is little change in the results when logging the variables.

New Zealand between 1987 and 2005 (three before reform and four after).[17] Figure 7.4(a) represents the pre-reform, pure SMD system. In this figure, each dot represents the number of parties and number of groups in a given SMD in New Zealand in a given election (1987–1993) under the country's pre-reform electoral system. In Figure 7.4(b), each dot represents the number of parties and number of groups in a given district in a given election under FPTP balloting in the mixed-member system period (1996–2005). Figure 7.4(c) compares the average effect of diversity on the number of parties both before and after reform in New Zealand's SMDs.[18] We present the quantitative analysis in greater detail in Appendix 7 and Table 7.2.

Figure 7.4 shows that the effect of ethnic diversity on party fragmentation that we saw even in SMDs earlier in this chapter does not appear to be simply a result of the mixed-member electoral system. The principal difference between pre-reform (Figure 7.4(a)) and post-reform SMDs (Figure 7.4(b)) in New Zealand is that the distribution in the post-reform system is higher – on average, there are more parties in the mixed-member system. In other words, there is some contamination effect in the mixed-member system. However, most important, Figure 7.4 shows that (1) diversity affected the number of parties even under a pure FPTP system, (2) the relationship between diversity and the number of parties was curvilinear, and (3) there was little difference in the effect of diversity between New Zealand's pure FPTP system and its FPTP rules under its linked mixed-member system. Contamination does not appear to affect the impact of diversity on the number of parties in SMD balloting in New Zealand: the two curves in Figure 7.4(c) are nearly identical to one another, except that the post-reform curve is higher. Both are curvilinear and, in both, increases in social diversity have roughly the same effect on the number of parties.

WHY ARE OUR RESULTS SO DIFFERENT FROM WHAT HAS COME BEFORE?

Our findings in this chapter are important because they run counter to nearly all prior theoretical and empirical work on the interaction between electoral

---

[17] We do not have data for all years on the number of voters in each district who placed themselves on the Maori rolls. For this reason, in Figure 7.4 and Table 7.2 in Appendix 7, our measure of heterogeneity includes all Maori residing in each district. However, as we noted earlier, the correlation between our two measures for 2002 is very high and there is scarcely any difference in the results from our different analyses of that year, irrespective of which measure of diversity that we use. We therefore feel confident with our more "brute force" measure here.

[18] We estimated the fitted lines from the coefficients from simple OLS models we ran for each period. The pre-reform model includes ENEG, ENEG2, and a dichotomous dummy variable representing the aberrant 1993 election. The post-reform model includes ENEG, ENEG2, and a variable representing the number of years since reform. (In calculating the expected values, we set the year as the mean year in the post-reform period.) The first number in each "Parties = . . . " equation in Figures 7.5 (a) and (b) represents the coefficient for the intercept. The numbers accompanying the ENEG and ENEG2 variables represent the coefficients for those variables. The results for these simple models match up closely with the more complete interactive models we discuss in Appendix 7 and report in Table 7.2.

rules and social diversity. Very careful cross-national scholarship by Amorim Neto and Cox (1997), Clark and Golder (2006), Ordeshook and Shvetsova (1994), and Singer and Stephenson (2009) offers convincing evidence that social diversity affects the number of parties under permissive electoral rules (such as many PR rules), but not under restrictive ones (such as FPTP). However, our results suggest a very different relationship between social diversity, rules, and the number of parties, and that the basic contour of this relationship is the same under SMD and PR rules. Why do we find a relationship between social diversity and the number of parties when previous work finds none?

Unlike other studies on this issue, we directly compare SMD and PR electoral contests within the same country using data at the district level (or within raions), so perhaps the use of subnational data on ethnic diversity produces different outcomes from studies that use national-level data on ethnic diversity. If so, because the effects of rules work more directly at the district level, we believe that our district-level analysis provides insights into this question that analysis of nationally aggregated data cannot. Indeed, in work with Caitlin Milazzo (Moser, Scheiner, and Milazzo ND), we analyze the relationship between district-level diversity and the number of parties in a number of FPTP systems, and still find the same curvilinear relationship.

However, the most likely reason for the difference between previous findings and ours is that we specifically explore the possibility of curvilinearity in the relationship between diversity and the number of parties. Quantitative work may be unable to recognize a correlation between variables if it does not test for the correct functional form of the relationship. If the effect of diversity on the number of parties is curvilinear, analysis that considers only the possibility of a linear pattern may miss the existence of any relationship at all. Among analyses of the interaction between diversity and electoral rules in shaping party fragmentation, we believe that this chapter is the first to consider the possibility of a curvilinear pattern representing the relationship between diversity and the number of parties.[19] Moser, Scheiner, and Milazzo (ND) replicate Clark and Golder's (2006) analysis, but – like the analysis in this chapter – also consider the possibility that diversity has a curvilinear relationship with the number of parties. In reanalysis of Clark and Golder's large, cross-national dataset, Moser, Scheiner, and Milazzo (ND) find (1) evidence of a curvilinear (upside-down U-shaped) relationship, and (2) that this relationship holds under both permissive and restrictive rules – on average, there is no difference between the impact of diversity under SMDs and more permissive systems.

CONCLUSION

In this chapter, we reexamine how social heterogeneity and electoral systems interact to influence the number of parties and provide the first analysis of their

---

[19] Of course, Madrid (2005a) and Stoll (2008, ND) consider curvilinearity under permissive electoral rules.

relationship that we know of that uses district (and subdistrict) level measures. Analyzing these new data, we find that, contrary to the most widely accepted view, social diversity shapes party fragmentation even under restrictive electoral rules such as FPTP.

The most common view in political science is that the larger the number of distinct groups in society, the larger the number of political parties that will receive support in elections, but that this relationship holds only in "permissive" electoral systems. The view that FPTP constrains the impact of social diversity is founded on the assumption that under restrictive rules, most voters who prefer weak candidates or parties shift their ballots strategically to more competitive options. However, survey research indicates that even under FPTP many voters continue to cast ballots for their sincere first preference, even when we would expect them to shift their vote strategically to a more competitive alternative (Alvarez et al. 2006; Cox 1997: 83–4). If, in fact, social heterogeneity helps determine the number of parties – as is commonly demonstrated – and, even under restrictive rules, large numbers of voters sincerely continue to cast ballots for their uncompetitive top choices, then there is good reason to expect social diversity to shape the number of contestants even under FPTP rules.[20]

Our analysis indicates, first, that social diversity frequently has a curvilinear (upside-down U-shaped) relationship with party fragmentation: districts with larger numbers of social groups tend to also have greater party fragmentation, but only up to a point, after which increases in social heterogeneity tend to be associated with a drop in the number of parties.

What is more important – and is a major break from nearly all recent work on the subject – our analysis suggests that electoral rules and social diversity each independently shapes the number of parties. We find no compelling evidence of an interaction between them,[21] and, in contrast to the dominant view on electoral systems, we find that social diversity shapes the number of parties under restrictive FPTP rules as well as under permissive PR.

This analysis suggests another area in which context conditions electoral system outcomes, although in a different way from the other chapters in this book. In other chapters, we demonstrate interactive relationships between rules and national contexts that differ across countries. Contextual factors such as democratic experience and the level of party institutionalization actually alter the incentives that exist for different sorts of behavior under particular electoral rules. In this chapter, we find that political contexts that may vary across

---

[20] This point is partly consistent with Taagepera's (2007: 112) that, although the mechanical effect of electoral rules is highly consistent, strategic behavior arising out of FPTP's psychological effect may not occur in many cases. Nevertheless, there is still significant evidence that some voters do cast strategic ballots, and, as shown in Chapter 3 and in Figure 7.3, there are consistently fewer contestants under FPTP than in PR systems, which suggests the importance of the psychological effect in shaping the number of parties.

[21] This finding is consistent with the analysis of Jones (2004a), who finds that electoral (i.e., plurality versus two-round majority) rules better explain the number of candidates in presidential elections than an interaction between diversity and rules.

districts within countries can also condition the likelihood of FPTP systems having their expected Duvergerian (two-candidate) outcome. Homogeneous districts are more likely to approach two-candidate competition under plurality rules in established democracies, but increasing social diversity leads to shifts in the number of candidates, often away from the Duvergerian outcome that we typically expect under FPTP.

Future Work Ought to Do More to Understand the Mechanisms

To be sure, our analysis does not yet address the mechanisms that channel social heterogeneity into the party system. Future work should seek out new data sources that make it possible to understand *why* we see the patterns that we do.

In many ways, this chapter's analysis is just a first cut at understanding the relationship between social heterogeneity and party fragmentation. Critics might argue that the number of ethnic (or language) groups is an overly blunt measure of diversity. Not only are there other types of diversity (see Stoll 2008, ND), but ethnic diversity is also not necessarily equal to the important social cleavages that really divide a polity, either socially or politically. Certainly, there is something to this point, but we believe that our measures are the logical next step in trying to understand the relationship between diversity, rules, and party fragmentation. First, the measures used here are already commonly used to study the interaction between social diversity and electoral rules. Second, obtaining any data on social diversity is difficult, and this chapter has been unique in its district-level measures. To our knowledge, no "better" district-level dataset exists. Third, the proof of the usefulness of our measures is in the strength of our results. We use our measures as a proxy for general social diversity. Societies with many ethnic (or language) groups will generally be more diverse than those with few, and it is striking that our results are so strong with these measures. Unless there is specific bias for which we have not accounted, there is reason to think that our results would hold even more strongly if scholars were to develop a more "perfect" measure of diversity.

Nevertheless, future work should take steps to expand the variety of measures of social heterogeneity, especially adding in measures of class or income diversity. Recall that Stoll's (ND) explanation for why diversity might have a curvilinear (upside-down U-shape) relationship with party fragmentation was founded on the idea that when there are many small social groups, political entrepreneurs may develop parties that can attract support from multiple different groups. It seems unlikely that these political entrepreneurs attract the multiple groups by means of ethnic appeals, but perhaps they do so through class appeals. For example, some ethnic minorities may, on average, have lower incomes, and parties might use class appeals to reach out to such an array of groups.[22]

---

[22] Madrid (2008) demonstrates this dynamic in his concept of "ethnopopulism" in Latin America.

In addition, future work would do well to consider more specifically who is behaving strategically. It is likely that members of district-level majority groups, on average, strategically shift their ballots more frequently under restrictive rules than minority groups do,[23] but it would be helpful for future work to examine whether this speculation bears out in reality.

Furthermore, we cannot say for sure whether this "strategic behavior" is strategic defection by voters or strategic exit by parties and candidates. Without knowing specifically which parties run in both PR and SMDs, we cannot be certain about which different groups' parties and candidates choose to exit races under the more restrictive rules (SMDs). However, when parties exist specifically to represent ethnic (especially minority) groups – who perhaps receive an expressive benefit from the party's presence or simply prefer their party by a huge margin over all others – it seems less likely that candidates of such parties will drop out of the race merely because they have little chance of winning. Future work might examine which parties actually do and which do not run candidates in areas of social diversity.

At least as important, what explains when elites and voters will choose to behave strategically or sincerely? Cox (1997: 79) suggests that there may be less strategic voting when voters are not short-term instrumentally rational, when there is great certainty about who is likely to win, when it is unclear who is uncompetitive (and who is actually competitive), and when voters strongly prefer their top choice over all other alternatives. To what extent do these factors ultimately explain the patterns we see in this chapter? In addition, perhaps voters take cues not just from the district-level strength of their parties, but also from the parties' national or regional strength (Chandra 2009); our own analysis may also be limited because we do not control for parties' strength within government. Ecological inference (EI) analysis (King 1997) of how different types of groups distribute their votes to different candidates and parties – and strategically withhold them – at the district level may allow scholars to understand better these questions.

In the end, though, the most effective approach to addressing the questions we raise here would be analysis of survey data; we echo Chandra's (2009) call for the discipline to collect data on ethnic groups and their voting behavior.

APPENDIX 7. QUANTITATIVE ANALYSIS OF SOCIAL DIVERSITY, ELECTORAL RULES, AND THE NUMBER OF PARTIES

Our dependent variable is the log of the effective number of electoral parties, as determined by the number of votes won by each party/candidate. We run separate ordinary least squares models for each country, with the unit of analysis being the SMD (Japan, New Zealand, and Wales) or the raion (Russia and Ukraine). Each model includes each district/raion twice, once for SMD balloting and once for PR balloting. We include *PR*, a dichotomous

---

[23] See the online appendix for speculations on this point.

TABLE 7.1. *Diversity, Electoral Rules, and the Number of Parties*

	NZ	Russia	Ukraine	Wales	Japan
(a) Linear Models					
PR	0.336***	0.529***	0.00391	0.207***	0.423***
	(10.79)	(14.85)	(0.19)	(5.29)	(44.83)
Diversity	−0.236***	0.276***	0.333***	0.277*	0.0751***
(ENEG)	(−4.07)	(5.96)	(9.68)	(2.29)	(4.69)
Constant	1.158***	1.026***	1.469***	0.999***	0.818***
	(33.59)	(26.64)	(84.40)	(18.57)	(68.06)
Adj-R-Sq	0.516	0.243	0.042	0.283	0.772
N	124	792	2072	80	600
(b) Curvilinear Models					
PR	0.336***	0.529***	0.00391	0.207***	0.423***
	(12.60)	(15.37)	(0.20)	(5.31)	(44.81)
Diversity	1.037***	1.143***	1.323***	1.296	0.0200
(ENEG)	(5.28)	(9.29)	(14.01)	(1.61)	(0.23)
Diversity2	−1.070***	−0.624***	−1.005***	−1.205	0.0461
(ENEG2)	(−6.71)	(−7.56)	(−11.20)	(−1.28)	(0.66)
Constant	0.876***	0.820***	1.351***	0.817***	0.830***
	(17.05)	(17.77)	(67.98)	(5.38)	(37.14)
Adj-R-Sq	0.645	0.293	0.097	0.289	0.772
N	124	792	2072	80	600

t statistics in parentheses.

$^+ p < 0.1$; $^* p < 0.05$; $^{**} p < 0.01$; $^{***} p < 0.001$.

Notes:

OLS models

Unit of analysis: SMD for New Zealand, Wales, and Japan; raion (administrative unit, which is smaller than an SMD) for Russia and Ukraine.

Dependent variable: effective number of parties (logged).

Diversity is measured as the log of the effective number of *ethnic* groups (ENEG) for New Zealand, Russia, and Ukraine, the log of the effective number of *language* groups for Wales, and densely inhabited districts (DID, a measure of population density or urbanization) for Japan.

Diversity2 = Diversity squared.

dummy variable coded 1 for PR balloting and 0 for SMD. Indeed, as we see in Table 7.1, PR has a positive coefficient in every model and is statistically significant in every case except Ukraine: controlling for diversity, there are more parties under PR rules than under SMD balloting.

Our core independent variable is *Diversity*. For all the countries in our dataset except Japan, we measure diversity by means of the log of the effective number of "ethnic" groups (*ENEG*). For New Zealand, Russia, and Ukraine, this is ethnic diversity; for Wales, it is language group diversity. For Japan, we use the level of urbanization (i.e., population density – unlogged, although there is little difference in the core results when we log) as a proxy for Diversity (see Cox 1997). To test for curvilinearity, we include a second measure, *Diversity2*, the square of Diversity.[24]

Table 7.1 offers two types of models: (a) models that consider only a linear relationship and (b) those that also test for curvilinearity. In Table 7.1(a), the coefficient on Diversity is significant for every country, suggesting that there is a relationship between social diversity and the number of parties. For four of the countries, the coefficient is positive, but for New Zealand the coefficient is negative, undoubtedly because of the small number of parties at high levels of diversity (see Figure 7.3). Table 7.1(b) lists the results for the "curvilinear models." In every case except Japan, the coefficients are in the expected directions – positive for Diversity and negative for Diversity2. Japan's coefficients are both positive but approximately zero. The coefficients for Wales are in the expected direction, but nonsignificant at the 0.1 level.[25] For the other three countries, the coefficients on Diversity (positive) and Diversity2 (negative) are statistically significant and in the expected directions. Except for the models for Japan, the adjusted R-squared is always higher for the Table 7.1(b) models, indicating that the curvilinear pattern explains a greater share of the variance in the data than the linear pattern.

To examine whether diversity has a different impact on the number of parties under different electoral rules, we run additional models in which we also interact PR with Diversity (*PR*Diversity*) and Diversity2 (*PR*Diversity2*). Except for the Ukrainian case, we find no evidence of an interaction between diversity and rules:[26] There is no major change in the coefficients or statistical significance associated with Diversity and Diversity2 for the five country cases. New Zealand, Russia, and Ukraine still have coefficients on Diversity (positive) and Diversity2 (negative) that indicate that there is a curvilinear relationship, and Wales and Japan continue to have positive coefficients on Diversity. For the Ukraine models, PR*Diversity has a positive and significant coefficient, and PR*Diversity2 has a negative and significant coefficient, thus suggesting that the effect of diversity on the number of parties is even stronger in PR. However, the interaction terms are wholly nonsignificant for the other four country cases – diversity appears to have the same effect on the number of parties under both SMD and PR rules.

---

[24] In a preliminary set of models, we had also included for Japan, New Zealand, and Wales a dichotomous dummy variable to indicate the presence/absence of an incumbent in the district under SMD balloting. We expected votes to concentrate on the incumbent and bring down ENEP. Surprisingly, the variable is never statistically significant. Therefore, for the sake of consistency across our countries, we do not include it in any of the models that we report.

[25] For Wales, the *p*-values on the coefficients are 0.112 (Diversity) and 0.205 (Diversity2).

[26] We do not include these results in our tables here, but for the specific coefficient estimates, see the results in the online appendix.

TABLE 7.2: *New Zealand Pre- and Post-Reform in SMDs*

	Pre-Reform SMD	Post-Reform SMD	Pre- and Post-Reform SMDs
Diversity	0.333***	0.577***	0.333**
(ENEG)	(3.44)	(3.55)	(3.04)
Diversity2	−0.318***	−0.500***	−0.318**
(ENEG2)	(−3.56)	(−4.35)	(−3.15)
New System			0.345***
			(6.21)
New System*Diversity			0.243
(New*ENEG)			(1.34)
New System*Diversity2			−0.182
(New*ENEG2)			(−1.27)
Since Reform		−0.0838***	−0.0838***
		(−8.73)	(−9.76)
Election 1993	0.273***		0.273***
	(15.73)		(13.90)
Constant	0.801***	1.146***	0.801***
	(39.97)	(20.16)	(35.32)
Adj-R-squared	0.509	0.296	0.449
N	281	245	526

t statistics in parentheses.
$^{+}$ $p < 0.1$; * $p < 0.05$; ** $p < 0.01$; *** $p < 0.001$.
Notes:
- OLS models
- Unit of analysis: SMD
- Dependent variable: effective number of parties (logged)
- Diversity: effective number of ethnic groups (logged)
- New System: coded 1 for SMDs in mixed-member system; 0 for pre-reform period

New Zealand Pre-/Post-Reform Comparison

To address the possibility that our results are due to "contamination" in the mixed-member systems, we compare the relationship between diversity and the number of parties in New Zealand's mixed-member system SMDs to their relationship under the pure FPTP system that existed in New Zealand prior to 1996. We examine ethnicity and the number of parties in all SMD district elections in New Zealand between 1987 and 2005 (three before reform and four after).

Our analysis here is the same as in Table 7.1(b), but we now add the following variables to the analysis: *New System* is a dichotomous dummy variable coded 1 for the post-reform system. We expect the coefficient on New System to be positive, as contamination from the PR tier to the SMD tier ought to lead to more parties than under the pure SMD system. Our most important variables are two interaction terms, *New System*Diversity* and *New System*Diversity2*.

We also include two control variables. First, we use *Since Reform*, a count variable that indicates the number of elections held since reform. For example, 2005 (the fourth election under the new system) is coded 4. Greater experience with the new system should lead to fewer parties/candidates. We also include *Election 1993*, a dichotomous dummy variable coded 1 for the 1993 election and coded 0 in all other years. The election of 1993 was an odd one, part of the transition away from the old system, and there was an explosion of additional parties in that year.

As shown in Table 7.2, all variables except for *New System*Diversity* and *New System*Diversity2* are statistically significant. The nonsignificant coefficients on the interaction terms suggest that diversity does not affect party fragmentation differently under the new system than it did under the pre-reform, pure-FPTP system. Contamination does not appear to be shaping the impact of social diversity on the number of parties.

8

How Political Context Shapes the Effect of Electoral Rules on Women's Representation

In this chapter, we turn our attention away from strategic defection by voters and elites and the number of parties under plurality rules to focus on the types of people who win office in democratic elections. More specifically, we explore how political context conditions the impact of electoral rules on the election of women to legislative office.

The election of women to public office is inherently important. Intuitively, female representation offers symbolic benefits for gender equality (see Phillips 1995), and there is evidence that female legislators behave differently from their male counterparts (Mansbridge 1999; Bratton and Ray 2002). It is therefore noteworthy that electoral systems are important in shaping the degree to which women win elected office. Significant research indicates that larger shares of women gain office under closed-list proportional representation rules than in single-member districts, but this finding is more consistent in consolidated democracies than in new ones.

The literature implicitly highlights two features of PR that especially help women's representation. First, the closed-list party vote in many PR systems would appear to help women over the more candidate-centered balloting under SMDs: compared with the process by which candidates are nominated for SMD races, national party leaders appear more inclined to nominate women, so closed party lists and centralized party nomination processes are seen as more conducive to women's representation (Norris 1993; Valdini 2005, 2006). Moreover, some voters may not wish to vote for a woman under SMD rules when they cast their ballots for individual candidates, but see no problem with casting a ballot for a list that includes women under PR where they vote for a party. Second, the higher district magnitudes of PR systems also appear to offer women a better shot at election than single-member districts (especially FPTP) by lowering the effective threshold (i.e., the share of the vote) necessary for election.

In this chapter, we reexamine these institutional explanations for women's representation. Most studies of women's representation use data aggregated at the country level, testing whether the electoral system and various highly aggregated societal and political measures are correlated with the overall proportion of women elected to the national legislature. We first follow this same general strategy, using a data set of 49 mixed-member elections in 18 countries to examine the difference in the proportion of seats going to women in the PR and SMD tiers – thus holding constant within each country case other factors that may affect women's representation. We can then examine how certain features of these countries – such as their status as a new, established, or postcommunist democracy; specific electoral rules; and party system fragmentation – affect the gap in women's representation between PR and SMD tiers.

Similar to our conclusions about other electoral system effects, we find a distinct difference between new (particularly postcommunist) and established democracies in the impact of PR and SMD rules on women's representation. In established democracies, women tend to win a much larger share of closed-list PR than SMD seats, but in postcommunist countries, on average, there is relatively little difference between the share of seats held by women under (closed-list) PR and SMD rules.

To understand better the reasons behind these differences, we use a unique data set of more than 9,000 legislative deputies elected in 27 mixed-member system elections held in 10 countries to examine what features of a political system increase the likelihood of women holding office.[1] This analysis helps explain why, in postcommunist states, PR does not provide the advantages for female election over the SMD tier that it does in established democracies.

This analysis highlights conditions under which PR provides women a greater chance at gaining legislative office than SMDs. First, closed-list PR (presumably with centralized nomination procedures) helps promote women only if there is not significant resistance within society to the idea of women as political leaders. Not surprisingly, women are simply less likely to hold office in countries where women are generally viewed as less capable political leaders, so women are less likely, on average, to hold national legislative office under *any* electoral rule in countries such as Japan and the postcommunist world. Second, the advantage women gain from the high district magnitude (i.e., large number of seats per district) component of PR rules over SMDs holds only when SMD rules constrain the number of candidates running for office in a single-member district. Put differently, the number of parties shapes the likelihood of women holding legislative office under SMD rules: when many candidates run in an SMD, women are much more likely to win office. In this way, party proliferation in postcommunist systems (see Chapter 4) has helped increase female representation in the SMD tier, while having little effect – at least that is discernible in our analysis – on the election of women in PR.

The implication is that institutions have a markedly greater effect on women's representation in established democracies than in new ones where

---

[1] This analysis diverges somewhat from our controlled comparison approach, but reinforces and further specifies the reasons behind our findings of PR-SMD differences within countries.

there are large numbers of candidates competing even in single-member districts: in established democracies, PR is more likely to help women gain office and SMDs are less likely to promote women's representation. In contrast, in new democracies with many viable competitors in SMDs, there is little difference in the likelihood of women getting elected under PR and SMD rules.

In this sense, our argument is a contextual one: even when closed-list PR rules are in place, there will be less female representation if there is societal resistance to the idea of women as political leaders. This does not mean that ambitious female candidates will derive no benefit from closed-list PR rules when there is little societal push for women's representation. However, it does suggest that PR will not necessarily aid women's representation under such conditions. Moreover, the discussion in this chapter brings us full circle back to our earlier argument in the book about the importance of democratic experience and party institutionalization in conditioning the impact of electoral rules. In this chapter, we find that when there is candidate proliferation under SMD rules – as is the case in poorly institutionalized, postcommunist polities – female candidates competing in single-member districts have a greater shot at holding office.

ELECTORAL SYSTEMS AND WOMEN'S REPRESENTATION

Literally dozens of cross-national analyses, regional comparisons, and individual case studies of the determinants of female representation show a strong link between the type of electoral system and the proportion of women elected to the legislature, particularly in Western democracies. On average, advanced democracies employing closed party-list proportional representation have more than double the proportion of female legislators of countries using single-member district elections – 20 percent under PR to 9 percent in SMDs (Rule 1994: 18). Moreover, women's representation grows at a dramatically higher rate in countries with PR elections than in countries that use SMDs (Matland and Studlar 1996: 709). Studies of countries using both PR and SMD elections (e.g., different rules for upper and lower houses of parliament or mixed-member electoral systems) typically show a similarly large difference in women's representation between the two types of electoral rules (Rule 1987; Moser 2001b; Matland and Montgomery 2003; Kostadinova 2007).

Cross-national studies of women's representation also examine other factors expected to influence women's representation in legislatures, including various measures of the socioeconomic status of women, women's participation in the labor force, culture, the strength of the women's movement, the timing of women's suffrage, the ideological composition of the party system and/or ruling coalition, the size and nature of the welfare state, and other electoral rules such as gender quotas and internal party nomination procedures.[2] In spite of notable and important exceptions highlighted later in this chapter, the

---

[2] These studies are too numerous to produce an exhaustive list here, but include Iversen and Rosenbluth 2008; Rule 1987, 1994; Norris 1985, 1987, 2004; Matland 1998; Kenworthy and

consensus is that closed-list PR is a statistically and substantively significant factor that promotes women's representation even after controlling for other potential causes, and this argument receives particular attention because it is perhaps the only factor over which politicians, and hence voters, have direct control (Salmond 2006: 176).

Why Should PR Promote the Election of Women?

Scholars suggest that a range of interrelated features of closed-list PR – in which voters cast ballots for party lists – increase the likelihood of women holding office. Closed party-list elections mute cultural biases against women by forcing voters to vote for parties rather than individuals. The candidate-centered elections associated with SMD systems potentially allow gender to be a much more influential factor in the voting decision, usually to the detriment of female candidates (Norris 1987: 130).[3] In part, the problem for women in SMDs, therefore, is a prejudice against female candidates in portions of the general voting population (Valdini 2005, 2006).

Other analyses focus on party behavior under closed-list PR. Some argue that parties respond better to pressures for increased women's representation if nomination decisions are centralized, as is common under closed-list PR. In SMD elections, nominations are often under the control of local party organs or decided in primaries, and therefore focus on more parochial concerns or incentives and not the representation of women (Norris 1993: 314–315). Moreover, parties under closed-list PR may run women on their lists to balance their ticket to appeal to a broader electorate, a phenomenon that is probably less common when a single candidate is the center of competition in any one district (Matland and Studlar 1996: 709).[4]

The higher district magnitude in PR systems undoubtedly plays a part in the expectation that women will do better under PR. High district magnitude reduces the vote threshold necessary to gain representation, so even small parties and small constituencies can win seats. In contrast, under plurality rules, with the classic Duvergerian outcome of two principal candidates per district, the winning candidate must take a very large share of the vote. If female candidates face cultural biases against their candidacies among large portions of the electorate, they become a risk for parties needing to achieve a plurality to win the seat. Moreover, even without such biases, typically the strongest candidates in SMDs hold substantial career experience – such as local government positions that promote political or financial connections – that

Malami 1999; Inglehart and Norris 2003; Reynolds 1999; Paxton and Kunovich 2003; Salmond 2006; Rosenbluth, Salmond and Thies 2006; Krook 2010.

[3] However, there is evidence that, if they get their party's nomination, female candidates in the United States perform as well as their male counterparts (Darcy, Welch, and Clark 1994: 175).

[4] That being said, as one of the Cambridge University Press reviewers pointed out to us, in some cases parties under SMDs do try to balance gender and minority group nominations across different districts.

help them win a large number of votes. Fewer women than men have such backgrounds, and childbirth and childrearing interrupt the careers of many women who would otherwise develop significant political and financial networks (Iverson and Rosenbluth 2010).

These differences in average career experience are more apt to be a disadvantage for women when there is only a single district representative. SMD representatives must focus on the needs of the locality, thus raising the importance of close relationships with an array of different key groups in the district and offering greater advantage to more senior politicians who have had the opportunity to develop such relationships. In addition, in SMDs politicians gain advantage from developing a personal following, and gaining seniority creates greater opportunities to develop such a following. It should not be surprising, therefore, to see that relatively few women hold office under any electoral system, including SMDs, in which seniority is a particularly valuable asset for political candidates (Iversen and Rosenbluth 2008).

Moreover, high rates of incumbency and incumbency reelection under SMDs tend to freeze gender inequalities in place. Incumbency advantage is more easily overcome in party-list PR systems, which experience greater turnover (Schwindt-Bayer 2005; Matland and Studlar 1996: 709; Norris 1993: 314–315).

However, increasing district magnitude too much may actually hinder women's representation. Richard Matland (1993) and others emphasize the role of party magnitude – the number of representatives elected by each party within an electoral district – as a decisive factor influencing women's representation. Parties with higher party magnitudes go deeper into their party lists, where more women may be present. Consequently, higher legal thresholds and lower district magnitudes actually help women get elected by increasing the number of seats won by each party that exceeds the threshold in the PR tier. Larger parties gaining more seats under PR are able to create longer lists of candidates who are likely to win seats; women lower on these lists, therefore, have a better chance of winning office. In this way, the positive impact of party magnitude on women's representation complicates the effect of district magnitude. On one hand, district magnitude that is too low, especially a district magnitude of 1, is expected to harm prospects for the election of women for the reasons we mentioned earlier. On the other hand, high district magnitude may cause excessive party system fragmentation, which can undermine women's representation by keeping parties small and thus unable to reach the lower positions on their party lists that are more apt to be comprised of female candidates.

Matland and Dudley Studlar (1996) integrate many of these elements into a contagion model to explain the higher representation of women under PR. The relatively high district magnitude of most PR systems allows for the representation of smaller parties, some of which are more committed to the promotion of women. Larger parties then emulate these smaller, women-friendly parties because centralized control over nominations makes it easier to do so, and the proportionality of PR systems puts pressure on larger parties to respond to even small shifts in the share of votes for competing parties (Matland and Studlar 1996: 712–713).

To be sure, scholars see political factors even outside closed-list PR rules as important in shaping women's representation, but many of these factors are often linked with PR electoral systems. First, gender quotas – which guarantee women seats or nominations that increase the likelihood of winning seats – are more commonly used with closed-list PR than with SMDs, and increase substantially the number of women elected in countries around the world (Davidson-Schmich 2006; Krook 2009; Kunovich and Paxton 2005; Schmidt and Saunder 2004; Meier 2004; Jones 1996, 2004b), in part by reducing the necessity for women's representation of high party magnitude (Jones 2009).

Second, electoral system effects are realized through and mitigated by political parties, complicating any simple equation between a particular electoral system and the promotion of women's representation. However, electoral rules do shape the electoral fortunes of different types of parties. For example, closed-list PR tends to promote the fortunes of left-leaning parties and coalitions (Iversen and Soskice 2006), which tend to elect more women, whereas the existence of strong right-wing parties tends to be negatively correlated with the proportion of women elected to parliament (Rule 1987; Norris 1985). In addition, women's parties, although rare, represent another way that electoral systems can promote particular types of parties that are more likely to represent women. For example, Women of Russia, which accounted for 36 percent of the women elected to the Russian State Duma in 1993, owed its existence to the closed-list PR tier. A strictly SMD electoral system would have virtually shut the party out of the legislature because it did not have the large cadre of competitive local candidates capable of winning seats in SMDs.

Differences between "Western" and Non-Western Democracies

However, there is limited evidence at best that the link between PR and female representation holds in all kinds of democracies. One study (Kenworthy and Malami 1999) finds no difference between developed and developing countries in the effect of electoral systems on women's representation. Additional studies contend that the effect of closed-list PR on the election of women extends to new democracies in Africa and Eastern Europe, but then present findings that suggest that the impact of PR may be less dramatic in these regions (see, e.g., Lindberg 2004; Yoon 2004; Matland and Montgomery 2003; Kostadinova 2007). A number of analyses suggest that there are significant differences between established and developing democracies. Matland (1998) finds that PR does not have the same impact on women's representation in less developed countries and suggests that countries must reach a threshold of economic and political development for electoral systems to have their expected effect on the election of women. Studies by Oakes and Almquist (1993) and Inglehart and Norris (2003), which include countries outside the established democracies of the West, do not find any statistically significant relationship between PR and women's representation. In addition, Moser (2001a, 2001b) shows that postcommunist states employing mixed-member electoral systems tend not to produce the same systematic benefits for women's representation in the PR tier as in established democracies.

RECONSIDERING THE IMPACT OF ELECTORAL RULES ON WOMEN'S REPRESENTATION

Despite its important substantive contributions, the literature that extends the analysis of women's representation to new democracies offers few theoretical reasons that the relationship between electoral systems and women's representation might differ between new and established democracies. We seek to develop a logic that could explain these potential differences, and argue that two principal factors promote the difference in women's representation between many established and new democracies. Put differently, we suggest two ways in which political context conditions the effects of electoral rules. First, social norms that downgrade the status of women in many new democracies remove the incentive many parties have to promote women in PR. Second, in many new democracies significant party proliferation in SMDs gives women a greater shot at winning candidate-focused elections.

Not All Parties Perceive an Advantage to Nominating Women

Central to analysis of women's representation under different electoral rules is the assumption that parties have an incentive to put forward a balanced PR-list ticket that can appeal to a wide audience.

However, in some cases, social or cultural norms may be indifferent to, or even run against, promoting women. Pressure for gender balancing may be less prevalent in new democracies because of lower socioeconomic development and weaker civil societies. Lower socioeconomic development may leave historically marginalized groups, such as women, with few resources to influence politics. Weaker civil societies may result in a less active women's movement, thus removing an advocate for female representation, and constraining the contagion of female representation under PR (Matland and Studlar 1996).

In other words, social norms are likely to affect the election of women under any electoral rule: if on average, the public does not support women in public office, women will be less likely to hold office under any electoral rule.

The Importance of Party Fragmentation

The winner-take-all aspect of SMDs is undoubtedly a major part of the disadvantage that women are perceived to have in SMDs. Gender balancing is not as important in SMD elections because they are composed of isolated district contests and parties are probably not judged by their full slate of nominations to the extent that they are in closed-list PR: under winner-take-all rules, the incentive is to run a candidate who can attract a large vote share. In part, the problem for women in SMDs, therefore, is a prejudice against female candidates in the general voting population. In part, it is also that success under winner-take-all often requires qualities, such as career experience and political or financial connections, that help to generate the large number of votes needed to win a seat, and women are generally less likely to have such backgrounds.

However, when many viable candidates are running in SMDs – as is common in many new democracies – the vote threshold necessary for victory is lowered, and the disadvantages faced by many female candidates may be less onerous. In other words, party fragmentation under SMDs may encourage women to run for office – and increase their odds of victory. In contrast, party fragmentation may hinder the election of women in PR by lowering the average party magnitude. That is, women are more likely to gain election if a few large parties elect many representatives per PR district than if many parties elect a small number of representatives (Matland 1993; Matland and Taylor 1997; Reynolds 1999).

The Effect of Electoral Rules on Women's Representation Should Be Different in Postcommunist and Established Democracies

In this way, the disparity between women's representation under PR and SMD electoral rules should vary depending on social norms with respect to the position of women in society and the level of party fragmentation. Variation in these factors should be particularly great between established and new – especially postcommunist – democracies. As a result, in established democracies, female candidates should have a greater advantage in closed-list PR races (relative to SMDs), but in new democracies there should be less disparity between women's representation under different rules. Figure 8.1 summarizes this argument regarding electoral systems and women's representation in postcommunist states.

First, greater workforce gender equality in postcommunist countries eliminates a major issue for mobilizing women, making a strong women's movement less likely. In general, women's organizations in postcommunist states have not yet been able to pressure parties to address issues that are important to them or to integrate them as formal or informal corporate members (Sperling 1999; Matland and Montgomery 2003). As a result, there is less pressure on parties to promote women through their party lists. Consequently, the argument that greater party control over nominations under PR will have a positive impact on women's nomination is undermined because parties face fewer pressures to nominate women and thus have less incentive to do so. Conversely, if parties are not considered a vehicle for women's nomination, then the absence of party control over nominations in SMD races in weakly institutionalized party

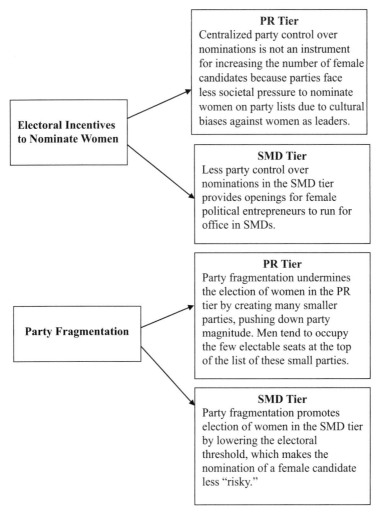

FIGURE 8.1. Factors hypothesized to affect women's representation under PR and SMD rules in postcommunist states.

systems could provide openings for entrepreneurial female politicians to run as independents.

Second, the high levels of party fragmentation in postcommunist democracies (see Chapter 4) should reduce the likelihood of women winning PR seats, but also increase their chances of winning SMDs, thus eliminating much of the disparity between women's representation under the two rules. With so many parties winning seats in PR – but few winning very many seats – most seats can only go to candidates from the top (usually male-dominated) spots on their party lists. In contrast, party fragmentation under SMDs should increase the likelihood of women winning even plurality races.

WHEN ARE WOMEN MORE LIKELY TO GET ELECTED UNDER
DIFFERENT TYPES OF ELECTORAL RULES?

To what extent do these arguments describe reality? Using two unique data sets, we can examine the conditions under which women come to hold legislative office.

Differences in the Proportion of Seats Women Win in PR and SMD Balloting

We begin with a dataset on women's representation in 49 elections held in 18 mixed-member systems from 1990 to 2007 (see Table 8.1). All the countries use closed-list rules in the PR tier, and all except Hungary, Lithuania (except for 2000), and Macedonia use plurality rules in the SMD tier. There is significant variation in the PR–SMD gender gap ("% of Women in PR tier minus % of Women in SMD tier" in Table 8.1), with countries such as Germany electing a much larger share of women under PR, and other countries – such as many postcommunist states and Scotland and Wales – witnessing negligible differences between the two tiers, or even greater proportions of women elected under SMD rules.

The table shows that, on average, both established and new democracies have greater female representation in the PR tier than the SMD tier. Averaging all the elections, 14.2 percent of SMD office holders are women, compared with 19.4 percent of PR office holders. However, we should note that the summary averages for established democracies found in Table 8.1 do not provide the full picture. The gap in women's representation between the PR and SMD tiers in established democracies is affected by two major outliers: in Scotland (1999) and Wales (1999) and, in de facto terms, after then as well, the Labour Party used a gender quota system known as "twinning" to alternate female and male candidates in safe seats in the SMD tier of the mixed-member systems. It was this move that most likely led to a larger share of women under SMDs in elections to these two parliaments (Krook and Squires 2006), which, in turn, substantially reduced the PR–SMD gap in women's representation in established democracies generally. As Figure 8.2 shows, if we exclude Scotland and Wales from the calculations, PR rules in the established democracies produce 10.2 percentage points more women than the SMD tier. This difference is more than twice as large as the PR–SMD gender gap in new democracies, suggesting that PR provides greater benefits for women's representation in established democracies than in postcommunist ones.[5]

---

[5] One might argue that, in relative terms, there is not much difference here between new and established democracies; that is, in both cases the proportion of seats held by women in PR is roughly twice that in SMDs. However, as we show later, once we control for certain key factors, there are significant differences between, in particular, postcommunist and established democracies in the likelihood of women getting elected under different rules.

TABLE 8.1. *Women's Representation in PR and SMD Tiers in 49 Elections in 18 Mixed-Member Systems*

Country and Election Year	% of Women Elected: PR tier	% of Women Elected: SMD tier	% of Women in PR Tier minus % of Women in SMD Tier
New Democracies			
Albania 2005	7.50	7.14	0.36
Armenia 1995	24.24	2.65	21.59
Armenia 1999	5.36	1.39	3.97
Armenia 2003	8.00	1.89	6.11
Armenia 2007	12.22	0.00	12.22
Bolivia 1997	17.74	1.47	16.27
Bolivia 2002	27.42	10.29	17.13
Bolivia 2005	28.33	7.25	21.08
Bulgaria 1990	12.50	5.83	6.67
Croatia 1992	3.33	5.00	-1.67
Croatia 1995	8.75	0.00	8.75
Hungary 1990	10.53	3.41	7.12
Hungary 1994	13.33	8.52	4.81
Hungary 1998	9.52	6.86	2.67
Hungary 2002	10.48	7.47	3.01
Hungary 2006	11.90	6.86	5.04
Lesotho 2007	10.00	16.25	−6.25
Lithuania 1992	7.14	7.04	0.10
Lithuania 1996	18.84	14.93	3.91
Lithuania 2000	12.86	7.25	5.61
Lithuania 2004	22.86	16.90	5.96
Macedonia 1998	11.43	5.88	5.55
Russia 1993	14.98	11.66	3.32
Russia 1995	6.67	13.78	−7.11
Russia 1999	5.80	8.29	−2.49
Russia 2003	10.86	8.44	2.42
Ukraine 1998	7.05	6.01	1.04
Ukraine 2002	7.08	3.72	3.36
New Dem. Average	**12.38**	**7.00**	**5.38**

(continued)

We conduct multivariable analysis of the PR–SMD gender gap in the countries/elections listed in Table 8.1. We discuss the analysis in detail in Appendix 8 (especially Table 8.2), and in Figure 8.3 we illustrate the average effect, while controlling for other variables, of each of the important factors that we examine. Based on our quantitative analysis – and illustrated by the bar on the left of the figure – we should expect that in an "average" country (i.e., all variables

TABLE 8.1 *(continued)*

Country and Election Year	% of Women Elected: PR tier	% of Women Elected: SMD tier	% of Women in PR Tier minus % of Women in SMD Tier
Established Democracies			
Germany 1994	37.29	13.19	24.10
Germany 1998	39.25	23.78	15.47
Germany 2002	39.75	26.00	13.75
Germany 2005	40.62	22.56	18.06
Italy 1996	17.95	8.73	9.22
Italy 2001	19.25	8.47	10.78
Japan 1996	8.00	2.33	5.67
Japan 2000	12.22	4.33	7.89
Japan 2003	11.11	4.70	6.41
Japan 2005	13.89	6.71	7.18
New Zealand 1996	45.45	16.92	28.53
New Zealand 1999	36.54	31.37	5.17
New Zealand 2002	27.45	26.09	1.36
New Zealand 2005	44.23	23.19	21.04
Scotland 1999	33.93	41.10	−7.17
Scotland 2003	35.71	43.84	−8.13
Scotland 2007	28.57	35.62	−7.05
Venezuela 1993	7.22	4.95	2.27
Wales 1999	30.00	47.50	−17.50
Wales 2003	40.00	55.00	−15.00
Wales 2007	35.00	52.50	−17.50
Est. Dem. Average	**28.73**	**23.76**	**4.98**

are equal to their mean value) the share of PR seats won by women will be 5.08 percentage points higher than the share of SMDs won by women.

Most striking, even controlling for a variety of factors, the PR–SMD gender gap is much lower in postcommunist countries than in established democracies. Figure 8.3 illustrates that, all else being equal, we can expect an average PR–SMD gap of 8.69 percentage points in established democracies, but almost no difference (1.47 percentage points) in postcommunist countries. The figure also shows that the presence of larger numbers of parties – the effective number of parties (N_s Overall), calculated by a weighted measure of the parties' shares of the total seats – reduces the proportion of women elected in PR relative to SMDs: when there are few (N_s Overall is 2.1) parties, we can expect many more (7.41 percentage points) women to get elected in PR than in SMDs. But when there are many (8.16) parties, we can expect more women (1.74 percentage points) to be elected in SMDs than in PR.

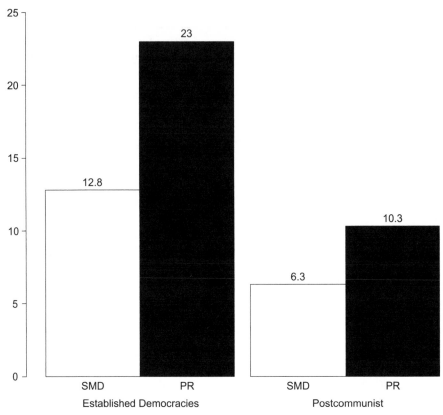

FIGURE 8.2. Average percentage of seats won by women.
Notes:

- Figure drawn from numbers in Table 8.1 – excludes Scotland and Wales
- Calculations:
  1) For each country, we determine (separately for PR and SMD rules) the mean share of seats held by women across all elections.
  2) For each category (e.g., established democracies), we then determine the mean of all country means.

Figure 8.3 also illustrates the average effect of the legal threshold of representation and quotas.[6] Consistent with the literature, we find that PR thresholds

---

[6] Although not listed in Figure 8.3, in the analysis in Appendix 8 we also include country dummy variables for (1) the Bolivia and Lesotho outliers, (2) the presence of "women's parties" – i.e., Armenia 1995 and Russia 1993, which had parties devoted to the election of women, and (3) whether countries linked their tiers. The analysis highlights that even controlling for other variables, Bolivia had a large positive PR–SMD gender gap, Lesotho had large negative gap, countries with strong women's parties were associated with a large positive gap, and there is no statistically discernible effect of tier linkage.

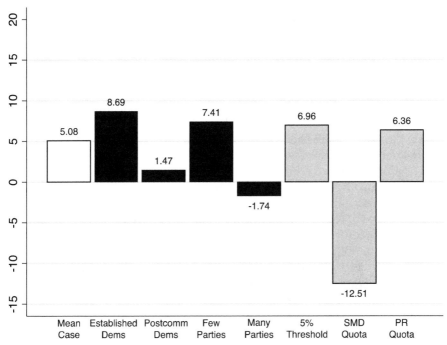

FIGURE 8.3. Expected difference in share of seats held by women (PR seat percentage minus SMD seat percentage), country-level analysis.

Notes:

- Drawn from estimates in Table 8.3. In estimating expected values, other variables are set at their means, except:
  - Lesotho and Bolivia are set at 0
  - Postcommunist is set at 0.5 (except when calculating the effect of Established and Postcommunist Democracies)
  - The colors of the bars have no meaning; all variables are statistically significant at the 0.05 level, except for PR Quota, which is statistically significant at the 0.1 level (see Table 8.3).
- Numbers of parties:
  - "Few Parties" is the estimate of the PR–SMD gap when the effective number of parties (N) score is 2.1.
  - "Many Parties" is the estimate of the PR–SMD gap when N is 8.16.

lead to an increase in the proportion of seats women win in PR relative to SMDs, presumably by increasing party magnitude (and, thus, how far down parties go on their PR lists). Not surprising, gender quotas used in the PR tier lead women to win a larger share of seats in PR, and gender quotas used in the SMD tier (found only in Scotland and Wales) lead women to win a larger share in SMDs.

Analysis of the Gender of Individual Legislators

Nevertheless, this analysis does not explain what it is about postcommunist democracies that leads to fewer women getting elected, and how the number of parties affects the election of women. Moreover, the country-level analysis does not get at the mechanisms directly – that is, the percentage of women holding office in a particular country is really the accumulation of many individual women. What shapes the likelihood that a woman holds legislative office? And what shapes her likelihood of holding, specifically, a PR seat or an SMD seat?

To address these mechanisms more directly, we draw from an original dataset of roughly 9,000 legislators who won office in 27 elections held in 10 different countries from 1992 to 2007. The data set includes legislators from Germany (1998, 2002, 2005), Hungary (2002, 2006), Italy (1996, 2001), Japan (2000, 2003, 2005), Lithuania (1992, 1996, 2000, 2004), New Zealand (1999, 2002, 2005), Russia (1993, 1995, 1999, 2003), Scotland (1999, 2003), Ukraine (1998, 2002), and Wales (1999, 2003). Using this dataset, we run a series of multivariable, quantitative models that estimate when it is more likely that a given legislator will be female,[7] and demonstrate that public attitudes toward women as political leaders and party fragmentation affect women's representation.

Strength of Societal Demand for Female Representatives and General Differences Between Established and Postcommunist Countries. Not all societies are the same when it comes to supporting the election of women to higher office. We can see this in the results of a World Values Survey (WVS) question, which asked respondents whether they agreed with the statement, "Men make better political leaders than women do" (World Values Survey 2009). There is substantial variation in responses to this question among the countries in our data. For example, as Table 8.2 shows, few (only 16.2 percent of all respondents) agreed with the statement in New Zealand, but many (83.2 percent) agreed with the statement (i.e., expressed a view that men were better leaders) in Armenia. Put differently, respondents in Armenia appear more resistant to the election of women to public office than those in countries such as New Zealand. The table also shows that support for women as political leaders is hardly universal across established democracies: in Japan, for example, large numbers of respondents agreed that men were better political leaders.

Moreover, as Figure 8.4 illustrates, countries with a bias toward male leaders do in fact elect a smaller percentage of women to national legislative office under both PR and SMD rules. The relationship is not linear; rather, there are

---

[7] Appendix 8 and Table 8.4 provide the details of the analysis. We are not investigating what makes it more likely that a woman will be elected, which would require data on all candidates. However, certainly the number of women in office is suggestive of their ability to win elections. See the online appendix for additional discussion of this issue.

TABLE 8.2. *Percentage of Respondents Who Agree with the Statement,*
"Men Make Better Political Leaders than Women Do"

Country (Year)	"Men Are Better Leaders"
Countries where few people agree with the statement	
New Zealand (2004)	16.2
Germany (2006)	18.8
Italy (2005)	19.2
Scotland (2006)	19.7
Wales (2006)	19.7
Countries where many people agree with the statement	
Venezuela (2000)	40.0
Macedonia (2001)	40.9
Japan (2005)	43.9
Bulgaria (2006)	47.9
Albania (2002)	51.4
Hungary (1998)	52.5
Croatia (1996)	54.2
Ukraine (2006)	54.8
Lithuania (1997)	55.9
Russia (2006)	61.6
Armenia (1997)	83.2

Source: World Values Survey (2009)
• Percentages represent the sum of those who "strongly agree" and "agree."

two groupings: countries where only about 15 to 20 percent of the population expressed agreement with the notion that men are better political leaders tend to have higher rates of women holding office, whereas few women hold legislative office in countries whose populations express more of a bias toward male leaders. However, within each grouping, there is variation. For example, despite large numbers of respondents who agreed that "men make better leaders,"

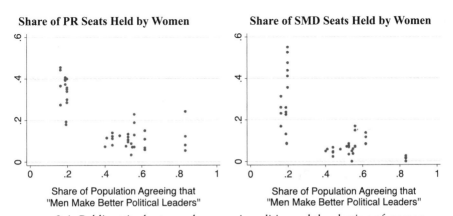

FIGURE 8.4. Public attitudes toward women in politics and the election of women.

we can see three elections – one in Armenia (1995) and two in Lithuania (1996 and 2004) – in which women received roughly 20 percent of all PR seats, which is somewhat higher than the other "male leader bias" countries. Furthermore, in the countries in which attitudes favored men less, women's representation in PR varied from just under 20 percent all the way up to nearly 50 percent. Therefore, to avoid confusing our analysis with these blips within each grouping, we categorize countries as either having a male leader bias (i.e., countries where at least 40 percent of respondents agreed with the statement that men make better leaders) or not (i.e., countries in which less than 40 percent agreed with the statement).[8]

Drawing from our multivariate analysis of individual legislators (Appendix 8, Table 8.4), Figure 8.5 demonstrates, not surprisingly, that legislators are more likely to be male in countries in which many people prefer male leaders. Controlling for other factors, in countries with a public bias toward male leaders, there is only a 10 percent chance that any given SMD legislator will be female, as compared with 18 percent in countries without a strong male bias. Similarly, in male leader bias countries, there is, all else being equal, a 12 percent chance of any given legislator being female under PR rules, in contrast to a 20 percent chance in countries with much less bias.

We cannot say whether the differences between countries are due to differences in their culture, political economy (e.g., women's place in the labor force or need for home-based child care), and/or some other factor.[9] However, whatever the reason, it appears that different underlying patterns of support for women in political leadership positions do affect the likelihood that women will hold national legislative office.

Impact of the Number of Parties. Figure 8.6 suggests a major reason for the greater success of women in SMDs relative to PR in many postcommunist countries: party fragmentation increases the likelihood of women being elected in SMDs, while having no discernible effect on women's representation in PR. In PR balloting, when N_v – the effective number of electoral parties score (based on votes) – is 2.12 (the 5th percentile for all legislators in the data set), there is, all else being equal, a 15 percent chance that a given PR legislator will be a

---

[8] In short, it is a dichotomous variable, "*Men are better leaders,*" coded 1 for the countries with greater than 39 percent agreement with the statement and 0 for all other countries, and it has a statistically significant (and negative) effect on the likelihood of legislators being female. If we use the continuous measure of the variable, which simply lists the share of the population that agrees with the statement, its coefficient is in the expected negative direction – more agreement with the statement is correlated with low probabilities of legislators being women – but is significant only at the 0.13 level. Most likely, the lack of significance is due to the substantial variation in women's representation among the "male leader bias" countries.

[9] For work on the potential link between political economy and women's representation, see Iverson and Rosenbluth (2010), Iverson and Rosenbluth (2008), and Rosenbluth, Salmond, and Thies (2006).

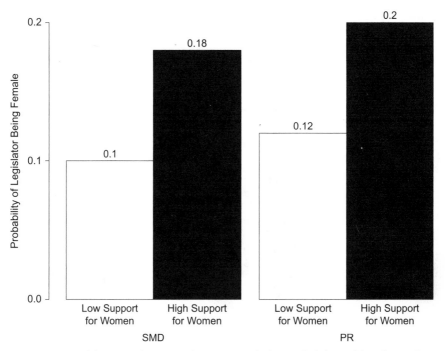

FIGURE 8.5. Public attitudes toward women and the probability of legislators being female.

Notes:

- Level of societal support refers to average responses within countries to the WVS question about whether "Men are better leaders."
- In generating predicted probabilities for Figures 8.5–8.8, we use the coefficient estimates from Model 2 in Table 8.4, the values for the PR Threshold and the quota variables are set to 0, and all other variables are set to their mean across all legislators in the data set.

woman. There is scarcely any difference when the number of parties is large: when N_v is 9.01 (the 95th percentile), there is a 14 percent probability that PR legislators will be female. On the other hand, the effect of the number of parties under SMDs is substantial. When N_v is only 2.12 in a given SMD, all else being equal, there is only a 9 percent probability that legislators will be female, in contrast to the 26 percent chance that a given SMD legislator will be a woman when N_v is 9.01 in the district.

Explanation for the Differences in Women's Representation under PR and SMDs. The combination of (a) societal attitudes toward women as political leaders and (b) the number of parties helps explain differences we see in women's representation across the PR and SMD tiers in different countries – especially between established and postcommunist democracies

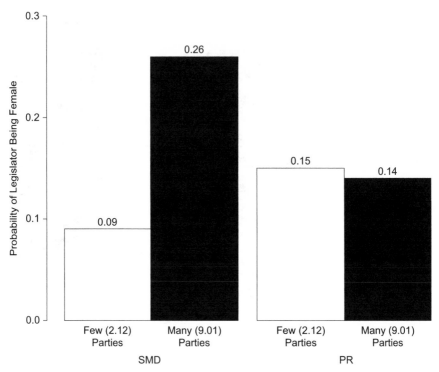

FIGURE 8.6. Number of parties and the probability of legislators being female.

(see Table 8.1). As Table 8.2 illustrates, large numbers of respondents in postcommunist countries believe that men make better political leaders,[10] and there are many more parties in postcommunist countries than in established democracies.[11] On average, in our dataset in Chapter 4, the effective number of candidates at the district level in SMDs is 3.05 in established democracies, as compared to 4.17 in postcommunist systems. In addition, the effective number of parties in the PR tier in established democracies is 4.88, as compared with 5.49 in postcommunist systems.[12]

Figure 8.7 illustrates the combined effect of societal support for women and the number of parties on women's representation in three different types

[10] In the country-level dataset, the correlation between postcommunist states and the continuous measure of agreement with the statement that "Men make better political leaders than women do" is 0.84. The correlation with the dichotomous measure of agreement is 0.66. In the legislator-level dataset, the correlation with the continuous variable is 0.85 and the correlation with the dichotomous measure is 0.66.

[11] The correlation between postcommunist states and the number of parties is 0.56 in the SMD tier and 0.51 when examining both tiers.

[12] Calculated by taking the mean value for each variable for all of the elections in a given country and then taking the mean for all countries.

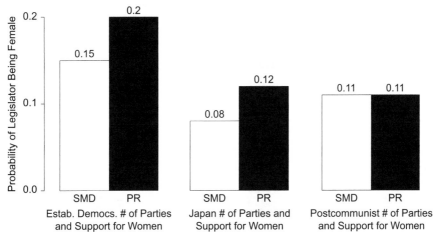

FIGURE 8.7. Combined effect of the number of parties and public attitudes toward women on the probability of legislators being female.

Notes:

- The impact of level of support for women ("Men are better leaders") and the number of parties in the SMD tier are both statistically significant.
- The impact of the number of parties in the PR tier is not statistically discernible from zero.
- In determining the predicted probabilities, we set the number of parties (drawn from Appendix 4A) and "Men are better leaders" variable values at their mean for the type of country in question for all country/elections:
  - Established democracies: 2.82 N in SMDs, 4.41 for N in PR, and 0 for "Men are better leaders"
  - Japan: 2.53 N in SMDs, 4.1 for N in PR, and 1 for "Men are better leaders"
  - Postcommunist: 4.44 in SMDs, 5.84 for N in PR, and 1 for "Men are better leaders"

of contexts: (1) "established democracies" (few SMD candidates/high support for women as leaders), (2) "Japan" (few SMD candidates/bias toward male leaders), and (3) "postcommunist" (many SMD candidates/bias toward male leaders).

High levels of support for women as political leaders mean that women are more likely to hold office under all types of rules in the "established democracies" than in the other types of country cases: all else being equal, there is a 15 percent chance that a given SMD legislator in the "established democracy" scenario will be a woman, and a 20 percent chance under PR – as compared with lower levels under the "Japan" and "postcommunist" scenarios, in which there is a bias toward male leaders.

Differences in the number of parties shape the gap between women's representation under PR and SMD rules. The small number of parties in the "established democracies" and "Japan" scenarios makes it likely that in such

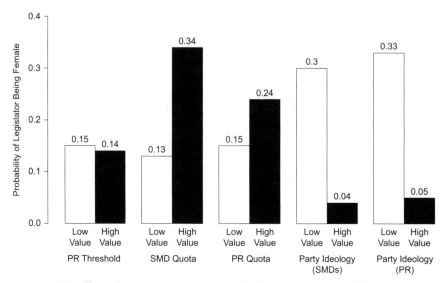

FIGURE 8.8. Effect of institutions and party ideology on the probability of legislators being female.
Notes:

- All the coefficients on the variables listed here are statistically significant at the 0.05 level, except for PR Threshold.
- PR Threshold: Low value is 0; high value is 5%.
- Quota variables: Low Value represents no quota; High Value represents the existence of a quota.
- Party Ideology: Low Value represents Left Party (score of −50); High Value represents Right Party (score of 59.26).

countries women will hold office under PR rather than in SMDs. In contrast, the many candidates in the "postcommunist" scenario increases the likelihood that legislators under SMDs will be female, thus leading to little or no difference between women's representation under SMD and PR rules – and sometimes even greater women's representation in SMDs.

The larger differences between women's representation under different rules in established democracies may be due in part to the fact that so many women (relatively speaking) are elected under PR in "Western" countries, thus creating a greater possibility of substantial differences from the SMD tier. Nevertheless, as our analysis indicates, the number of parties clearly is important as well: when large numbers of contestants compete in SMD elections – as is the case in many postcommunist countries – the difference in women's representation rates between PR and SMD rules disappears altogether.

Impact of Other Factors. Our analysis also provides support for many of the central claims of the literature on women's representation: Figure 8.8 illustrates the impact, all else being equal, of other major factors on women's representation. Interestingly, the figure shows no statistically significant impact of PR thresholds of representation on women's representation, perhaps because we already control for the number of parties in the PR tier. The use of quotas in the SMD tier appears to increase dramatically the likelihood of legislators being female from a 13 percent probability to a 34 percent chance – although this finding may just be a function of politics in Scotland and Wales, the only cases in our sample that use SMD quotas. Quotas also appear to increase the representation of women in the PR tier, from a 15 percent chance of a given legislator being a woman in systems without quotas to a 24 percent probability in systems with quotas. Most striking, party ideology has a major impact on women's representation under both PR and SMDs. All else being equal, there is a probability of 30 percent that an SMD legislator from very left-wing parties will be female; and there is a 33 percent chance that left-wing parties' legislators will be female in PR. In contrast, the probabilities are only 4 (SMD) and 5 (PR) percent that legislators from right-wing parties will be female.[13]

CONCLUSION

This chapter suggests a new view into the relationship between electoral rules and the election of women. Women tend to be grossly underrepresented in national legislatures around the world, but it is widely agreed that closed-list proportional electoral rules offer women a particularly good chance at gaining office. However, the analysis in this chapter suggests significant limits on the usefulness of PR rules to the election of women. In particular, there are differences in how electoral systems affect the election of women in established democracies and postcommunist states. The relative lack of social pressure for women's representation and substantial party fragmentation in postcommunist states work in tandem to (a) reduce women's representation in general and (b) lessen the gap in women's representation between the PR and SMD tiers of mixed systems.

In this way, the dynamic between electoral systems and the election of women can get turned on its head in postcommunist countries, with SMDs becoming more favorable electoral arenas for women because they offer more wide open competition for office. These findings coincide with and extend the conclusions of Matland (1998), who argues that contextual factors influence electoral system effects: there may be a developmental threshold that must be crossed before institutions such as PR have their expected effects promoting the election of women. Matland argues that developing countries that had not

---

[13] Our analysis also examines the impact of tier linkage on the likelihood of legislators being female, but we cannot be confident that there is an effect. When we include Hungary and Italy as systems with unlinked tiers, we find that linkage between the tiers increases the likelihood of legislators being women in both tiers. However, if we categorize either country as a linked system, we find no effect of linked tiers.

yet reached this threshold simply lack the critical mass of women possessing the necessary resources and skills to take advantage of institutional opportunities (1998: 120). Our findings suggest an alternative dynamic in which political conditions, such as party fragmentation, create a different set of incentives and opportunities that then change the impact that electoral rules have on women's representation.

This analysis fits with our larger point in this book that the effects of electoral systems, and perhaps all institutions, are mitigated by the context in which they operate. As with the impact of electoral systems on strategic voting and the number of parties, electoral system effects on the election of women are conditioned by other factors that cannot be presumed to exist in all contexts.

Moreover, our findings about the impact of party system fragmentation on the propensity of women to gain election under PR and SMD rules demonstrates the link between seemingly unrelated effects of electoral rules, and brings us full circle to our earlier focus in the book on how democratic experience and party institutionalization can condition the effects of electoral rules. In post-communist states, weak party system institutionalization reduces the likelihood of strategic defection by voters and elites under plurality rules and produces fragmented party systems, which in turn affects the likelihood of women's representation under different rules.

APPENDIX 8. QUANTITATIVE ANALYSIS OF WOMEN'S REPRESENTATION[14]

Country-Level Analysis

We first run an OLS model (clustering by country) using our data set of 49 elections held in 18 mixed-member systems from 1990 to 2007 (see Table 8.1). The dependent variable is *PR%–SMD%*, the percentage of PR seats held by women in a given country in a given election minus the percentage of SMD seats held by women.

Our most important independent variables relate to (a) whether the country is postcommunist and (b) the number of parties. We include *Postcommunist*, which is coded 1 for the postcommunist cases and 0 otherwise. *PR%–SMD%* should be lower in postcommunist countries, so Postcommunist should have a negative coefficient. In addition, large numbers of parties ought to help increase the number of women getting elected in SMDs, but reduce their numbers in PR, so we include *Effective # of Parliamentary Parties*, the Laakso-Taagepera measure of the number of parties, based on parties' weighted share of all seats in the legislature (N_s Overall from Appendix 4A). We expect Effective # of Parliamentary Parties to have a negative coefficient.

A variety of institutions ought to affect the representation of women: (1) *PR Threshold*, the legal threshold of representation; PR Threshold should have a positive coefficient, because higher thresholds ought to lead to higher party

---

[14] See the online appendix for additional discussion of the quantitative analysis.

magnitude, and, hence, more women elected under PR; (2) *SMD Quota*, which we code as 1 for Scotland and Wales and 0 for all other cases, should have a negative coefficient (i.e., more SMD seats relative to PR);[15] (3) *PR Quota*, which is coded 1 for countries that have legally mandated PR quotas or parties that use them, and 0 for countries that do not have them, should have a positive coefficient; and (4) *Linked Tiers*, a dichotomous variable coded 1 for countries with linked tiers and 0 for those that are unlinked.[16] Linked Tiers should have a negative coefficient: in systems with linked tiers, parties tend to win roughly the same number of seats, irrespective of the number of SMDs that they win. Nominating SMD candidates who may be less likely to win is therefore less "risky," and increases the likelihood that parties might nominate women in the single-seat races.

We also include three controls. First, we create a dummy variable, *Presence of "Women's Party,"* which we code 1 for countries that have a party that was formed explicitly for the purpose of electing women and 0 for all others. Women's parties win most of their seats in PR, so this variable should have a positive coefficient. We also include dummy variables for Bolivia and Lesotho, which are (a) neither established nor postcommunist democracies and (b) both outliers on opposite ends of the spectrum. Bolivia elected many more women in PR, whereas Lesotho elected many more in SMDs.

As shown in Table 8.3, except for Linked Tiers (which is nonsignificant), the signs on the coefficients on all of the variables are in the expected direction and statistically significant.[17] Most important, as expected, Postcommunist and Effective # of Parliamentary Parties both have negative and statistically significant coefficients.

Legislator-Level Analysis

We use an original data set of all 9,306 legislators in 10 countries and 27 lower-house elections that use mixed-member electoral systems.[18] We code the

---

[15] In Wales, twinning was still practiced, but it was done less formally after 1999. In Scotland, it was no longer an official practice of the Labour Party. Nevertheless, twinning had produced so many female SMD incumbents in 1999 in both countries that women were far more likely to continue to win office in SMDs in future elections. If we code Scotland after 1999 as 0 on SMD quota, the magnitude of most of the coefficients change somewhat, but most remain statistically significant as before.

[16] See Chapter 2 for a detailed discussion of the criteria used to code countries as linked or unlinked. In the analysis that we list in Table 8.3, we code Hungary and Italy as unlinked systems. If we code Hungary or both countries as linked, the coefficient on Linked Tiers is in the expected negative direction. However, no matter the coding, the coefficient has a nonsignificant coefficient. In addition, changing the coding of Linked Tiers does not markedly affect the results for the other variables.

[17] We also reran our models with only the last election for each country. Despite the small number of observations, all variables except PR Quota (nonsignificant) have coefficients that remain in the same direction, with the magnitude of the coefficients usually not changing much, and Postcommunist continues to have a negative and significant coefficient.

[18] See the chapter for the specific countries/elections.

TABLE 8.3. *Correlates of the Difference between the Percentage of PR and SMD Seats Held by Women (by Country/Election)*

Postcommunist	−7.218**
	(−3.25)
Effective # of Parliamentary Parties	−1.510**
(i.e., parties winning seats)	(−2.98)
PR Threshold	1.204**
	(2.91)
SMD Quota	−20.05***
	(−4.51)
PR Quota	2.084+
	(1.88)
Linked Tiers	3.183
	(1.53)
Presence of "Women's Party"	11.56**
	(3.70)
Bolivia	5.708***
	(4.95)
Lesotho	−14.68***
	(−7.84)
Constant	9.931***
	(5.29)
N	49
R-Squared	0.79

t statistics in parentheses.
+ $p < 0.1$; * $p < 0.05$; ** $p < 0.01$; *** $p < 0.001$.
• Unit of analysis: country/election
• Dependent variable: percentage of PR seats held by women minus percentage of SMD seats held by women
• OLS, clustering by country (18 country cases)

dependent variable 1 if the legislator is a woman, and 0 if a man. We use a multilevel probit model (generalized linear mixed model run by means of the lme4 package in R) as suggested by Jones (2008). We correct the standard errors by using country as the ID variable (essentially, clustering by country). We include party ideology in our analysis, using the Comparative Manifestos Project (CMP) coding of parties on a left-right ideological scale (Klingemann et al. 2006). Unfortunately, CMP does not provide coding for roughly 1,300 legislators in our data set (in particular, those from women's, ethnic, or regional parties, and those with no party affiliation), so our analysis focuses on the roughly 8,000 legislators for whom we have CMP party coding.

Our core independent variable is *SMD Tier*, which indicates whether the legislator was elected via PR (coded 0) or SMD (coded 1). We expect women to be more likely to gain office through the PR tier, so we expect a negative sign on SMD Tier's coefficient.

In Model 1, we investigate whether, controlling for other factors, women are in fact less likely to hold legislative office in postcommunist countries. *Postcommunist* is a dichotomous variable coded 1 for legislators from postcommunist countries and 0 for others. We also create *SMD*Postcommunist*, an interaction between SMD Tier and Postcommunist. There are fewer female legislators in postcommunist countries, and therefore, even controlling for other factors, we expect Postcommunist to have a negative coefficient. However, compared with PR, there are more female legislators in SMDs in postcommunist countries, so we expect be a positive coefficient on SMD*Postcommunist.

However, focusing on the postcommunist-established democracy divide does not tell us anything about the reasons for the differences between the two types of countries, so, in Model 2, we focus on the effects of societal support for women in political office and the number of parties. As discussed in the chapter, we measure popular attitudes toward women in politics through the WVS question about whether respondents agree with the statement, "Men are better leaders." We code countries where more than 39 percent of respondents agree with the statement as a 1 on "*Men are better leaders,*" and code all other countries as 0. We expect less female representation when more people agree with the statement, so the variable ought to have a negative coefficient.

To test the effect of party fragmentation, we create N, the Laakso-Taagepera measure of the effective number of parties (see Chapter 3). When many parties win seats in PR, few will go beyond the most highly ranked – and usually male – candidates on their PR lists, so analysis of N would best be done if focused on the number of parties winning seats in the PR tier (N_s PR from Chapters 3 and 4). Unfortunately, calculating N_s PR is complicated in linked mixed-member systems, which use the PR tier as compensation, thus making it difficult to create a straightforward measure of the effective number of parties winning seats in such systems. For this reason, for PR legislators, we measure N as the effective number of parties receiving votes in the PR tier (N_v PR).[19] Because larger numbers of parties in PR should lead to fewer women being elected, we expect the coefficient of N to be negative. For legislators elected in SMDs, we calculate N as the effective number of candidates (based on votes) in the SMD legislator's district. To differentiate between PR and SMD legislators, we create N*SMD, which is the interaction between SMD Tier and N.[20]

As we discussed earlier, we use CMP data to code each candidate's *Party Ideology* across a simple left-right dimension. To be able to include elections

---

[19] In countries where the country is divided into multiple PR blocs, for PR legislators we calculate N_v PR for the bloc in which the candidate was elected.

[20] Postcommunist is very highly correlated with popular attitudes toward women as leaders and the number of parties, so we do not include all the variables in a single model.

for which CMP did not yet provide data, for each party we compute the mean ideology score across all the elections in our data set and use this measure for the party's ideology score. The score ranges from -100 to $+100$, with negative scores associated with leftist ideology and positive scores with rightist ideology. Left parties are noted for being more likely to promote women's representation, so we expect a negative sign on the coefficient.

We include a number of institutional variables from the country-level analysis here as well: *PR Threshold* (the size of the legal threshold of representation in the PR tier), which should have a positive coefficient; *Quota*, a dichotomous variable coded 1 for countries and/or parties that have quotas mandating the nomination and/or election of women, which we expect to have a positive coefficient; *SMD*Quota* (an interaction term, so the sum of the coefficients on Quota and SMD*Quota should be positive); and *Linked Tiers*. We are uncertain what effect (if any) tier linkage would have in the PR tier, but we expect linked tiers to increase the probability of the election of women in the SMD tier because of the reduced "risk" of nominating women in SMDs. Therefore, we include the interaction term, SMD*Linked Tiers.

Finally, our aim is to predict how likely it is, given the context, that a legislator will be female. Because incumbents are more likely to be male, we include *SMD Incumbent* and *PR Incumbent*, dichotomous variables coded 1 for incumbents and 0 for non-incumbents. We expect their coefficients to be negative.

We list the results of our two main models in Table 8.4, with most of our expectations borne out. SMD Tier has a consistently negative (and statistically significant) coefficient – that is, in SMDs legislators are less likely to be women. In Model 1, the negative coefficient on Postcommunist indicates that, even controlling for other factors, in postcommunist countries PR legislators are less likely to be women than in established democracies. However, the coefficients for SMD Tier, Postcommunist, and SMD*Postcommunist sum to a smaller negative number than SMD tier by itself: all else being equal, in postcommunist countries SMD legislators are more likely to be women than in established democracies.

In Model 2, the negative coefficient on "*Men are better leaders*" indicates that legislators under any electoral rules were less likely to be women in countries with a bias toward male leaders, which suggests that much of the reason for the low levels of women's representation in countries such as Japan and the postcommunist countries is a general lack of societal support for women as political leaders. As for the number of parties, the coefficient on the uninteracted N variable is roughly zero, suggesting that the number of parties in PR balloting has no effect on the likelihood of a legislator being a woman.[21] However, N*SMD has a positive and statistically significant coefficient: SMD

---

[21] Our lack of a finding of N in PR may be due to the fact that we measure N by votes rather than seats here. Nevertheless, even with alternative measures that seek to incorporate seats rather than votes, our analysis shows no evidence of the impact of the number of parties in PR balloting. (See the discussion in the online appendix.)

TABLE 8.4. *Multilevel Probit Model of Correlates of Legislators Being Female*

	Model 1		Model 2	
	Coef.	SE	Coef.	SE
SMD Tier	−0.278	(0.088)**	−0.552	(0.134)***
"Men are better leaders"			−0.365	(0.107)***
Number of parties				
N			−0.011	(0.017)
N*SMD			0.110	(0.026)***
Postcommunist				
Postcommunist	−0.392	(0.156)*		
SMD*Postcommunist	0.539	(0.129)***		
Type of Party				
Party Ideology	−0.011	(0.001)***	−0.011	(0.001)***
Institutions				
PR Threshold	0.033	(0.025)	−0.011	(0.018)
Quota	0.331	(0.073)***	0.334	(0.071)***
SMD*Quota	0.297	(0.173)+	0.384	(0.161)*
Linked Tiers	0.528	(0.146)***	0.441	(0.125)***
SMD*Linked Tiers	0.332	(0.116)**	0.078	(0.088)
Controls				
SMD Incumbent	−0.102	(0.049)*	−0.079	(0.049)
PR Incumbent	0.007	(0.052)	0.004	(0.052)
Constant	−1.112	(0.115)***	−0.848	(0.148)***
N	7,977		7.975	

+ $p < 0.1$; * $p < 0.05$; ** $p < 0.01$; *** $p < 0.001$.

- Unit of analysis: legislator/election
- Dependent variable: Coded 0 if legislator is male, 1 if legislator is female
- ID Variable: country (10)

legislators in districts with large numbers of candidates have a higher probability of being women than legislators from SMDs with few candidates.

The results for the other variables are largely as expected and do not differ markedly between Models 1 and 2, but a few deserve additional comment. The lack of significance of the coefficient on PR Threshold is probably because we already control for N, which is more directly related to party magnitude. We are uncertain what to make of the significant coefficient on Linked Tiers (and the lack of significance of the coefficient on SMD*Linked Tiers), except that we should probably draw no strong conclusions about the effects of tier linkage because of the relatively small number of countries and which countries we code as Linked. As we explain in Chapter 2, we mostly code Italy and Hungary as Unlinked. If we change these countries' Linked Tiers coding, the coefficients for Linked Tiers and SMD*Linked Tiers become statistically nonsignificant.

9

Conclusion

Why and How Political Context Matters
for Electoral System Effects

In this book, we argue that electoral systems often do not lead to the outcomes that scholars commonly attribute to them because the effects of electoral rules are conditioned by the context in which they operate. We do not suggest that most existing theories about the effects of electoral rules are wrong across all contexts. We also do not claim that we are the first to acknowledge and highlight the impact that political context can have on electoral system effects.[1] However, we do argue that the electoral system literature has tended to emphasize the ability of electoral systems to shape electoral outcomes irrespective of context. Thus, our central point is that many important ideas about the effects of electoral systems are founded on the assumption of particular contextual foundations, and that the effects of electoral rules differ in a predictable and systematic way when the rules operate in a different context.

CONTEXT CONDITIONS INSTITUTIONAL EFFECTS

In the broadest sense, this book offers a different emphasis regarding the interpretation of how institutions and context interact to influence outcomes. In much of the scholarship on institutions, especially work in the rational-choice institutionalist vein, formal rules are expected to impinge on the environments in which they are embedded. The expectation is that institutions channel behavior in consistent ways, and therefore produce relatively uniform outcomes. Much of the distinction between the effects of different electoral rules made by the literature is due to the expectation of a conditioning effect of "restrictive" rules (e.g., FPTP). FPTP is expected to deny representation to parties and candidates who win only a small share of the vote, and therefore leads to outcomes

---

[1] As noted elsewhere in this book, Cox (1997) has been most influential in highlighting how electoral system effects depend on certain preconditions. Among others, Taagepera (2007), Grofman et al. (2009), and Matland (1998) also demonstrate how electoral systems may not have their expected effects under different political conditions.

that are different from what we see under "permissive" rules (e.g., PR with high district magnitude and low legal thresholds of representation), which provide representation even to contestants who win relatively few votes. For example, the most common argument regarding the interaction between context, in the form of social diversity, and electoral systems is that greater social diversity promotes the proliferation of political parties *except* in the presence of (restrictive) single-member district, first-past-the-post electoral rules. Most scholarship argues that FPTP rules place a brake on the effect that social diversity has on party system fractionalization because of the incentives that the rules create for voters to defect from small parties to larger, more competitive alternatives. As a result, irrespective of social diversity, FPTP rules ought to cap the number of viable competitors at two per district.

In contrast, in this book we make the reverse argument: the effects of electoral rules – even restrictive ones – are contingent on conditions found within the contexts in which they operate. For example, we find that the impact of electoral systems on the number of parties depends on specific contextual factors. Most notably, FPTP rules do, in fact, constrain the number of district-level competitors to roughly two when there are well-established parties and homogenous communities. However, in new democracies, especially those with poorly institutionalized party systems, FPTP rules do not reduce the number of competitors as sharply. Moreover, FPTP systems do not suspend the effect of social diversity on the party system. In short, the extent to which we see FPTP rules leading to two viable candidates per district is a function of democratic experience, the relative institutionalization of the party system, and the level of social diversity.

To be sure, we are not arguing that rules do not condition context, but it is important, for a number of reasons, to give great attention to our argument about the importance of context shaping the effects of rules. First, this book certainly finds ample evidence that many voters and elites behave differently under SMD and PR rules, and that there are nearly always fewer parties under FPTP rules than in PR, but such a finding would hardly be surprising to most observers of electoral politics: the view that rules condition context is already well represented within contemporary political science. Second, the reverse argument that we make here receives less attention. Certainly, many observers – including historians, sociologists, anthropologists, and area studies scholars, generally – are likely to state that our argument is obvious: of course context shapes electoral outcomes! However, dismissing our analysis in this way would miss the point that the argument that rules condition context is probably *the* dominant paradigm within contemporary political science. Moreover, the area studies critique about context shaping outcomes would be inclined to argue that each country (or region) is unique, thus making it difficult to make general statements about the effects of rules across a wide array of cases.

In contrast, our argument is a far cry from the view that context simply shapes electoral outcomes. Rather, we argue that differences in context are equivalent to variation in the values of important variables. In other words, our argument is based on generalizable, cross-national social science analysis, and is not a critique based on an occasional unique outlier. We highlight a small number of contextual variables that vary in a limited – but important – set of ways, and, in turn, lead to *systematic and predictable* differences in the effects of electoral rules across different countries, and even between homogenous and more diverse districts within countries.

Understanding the conditionality of the effects of electoral systems is important in part because it helps make outcomes under different electoral rules more predictable. In his path-breaking work on social science mechanisms, Jon Elster highlights how causal explanations are different from predictions (1989: 8–9). That is, even if we demonstrate the causal mechanisms that drive a particular outcome, we cannot predict the outcome unless we know *when* these particular causal mechanisms will operate. In this way, when we draw out the conditions behind different electoral system effects, we, in fact, highlight the factors that make particular causal mechanisms more likely to operate, which in turn improves our ability to make predictions about likely outcomes.

We should highlight that our argument about the conditionality of electoral system effects is not restricted to FPTP rules and the number of parties. For example, in this book we also find evidence of the ways in which contextual factors condition the effects of electoral rules on female representation. Most work on the topic highlights how women are more likely to win office under closed-list PR, as opposed to more restrictive rules, such as FPTP. However, we find that the effect of rules on women's representation depends on the level of party fragmentation: where there are few parties, women's representation is indeed more likely under closed-list PR rules, but where there are many parties, there is little difference in the likelihood of women winning office under closed-list PR and FPTP rules.

This perspective on institutions and their effects can be generalized to other institutions and political outcomes, and, indeed, the idea that context conditions the effects of institutions is hardly new. For example, Dawn Brancati (2009) highlights how the impact of federalism on demands for autonomy or secession depends in large part on whether a country has regionally based parties. Work by Scheiner and his co-authors (Desposato and Scheiner 2008; Milazzo and Scheiner 2011; Scheiner 2005, 2006) indicates how the effect of heavily centralized (or decentralized) government power shapes the party system in different ways depending on the type of voter–politician linkages – that is, whether politics is, first and foremost, clientelistic or programmatic. Moser (2008) shows that the impact of electoral systems on the election of ethnic minorities in Russia is contingent on demographic characteristics of the groups, notably their levels of assimilation, group size, and geographic concentration.

In addition, studies such as those by Matthew Shugart and John Carey (1992), Scott Mainwaring and Shugart (1997), and Jose Cheibub (2007) challenge arguments presuming that certain political outcomes are associated with specific constitutional structures in similar ways to what we have done here concerning electoral systems. In particular, these scholars have argued that effects of presidential and parliamentary systems on political outcomes such as gridlock, interbranch conflict, and, ultimately, democratic stability itself are conditional on other features of political systems, most notably, the nature of the party system – whether there are two or multiple parties, how well parties control their members, and the relative development and cohesiveness of parties. In our view, this book continues a promising vein of research on institutions that sees institutional effects as important but conditional, and thus dependent on the nature of the political context in which these institutions operate.

The central contribution of this book, then, is to show how context can alter systematically the effects of perhaps the world's most widely studied institution – the electoral system, which has been dubbed "the most manipulable instrument of politics" (Sartori 1968: 273). More than most other institutions, electoral rules are often presumed to have relatively uniform effects, regardless of context. Systematic analysis of when electoral systems will and will not have particular effects is important to avoid the mistake of gravitating to the other extreme, which would argue that electoral systems do not have consistent effects across countries. Instead, the analysis in this book suggests that one can see common patterns within broad categories of political contexts found commonly around the world – new versus established democracies, institutionalized versus noninstitutionalized party systems, and diverse versus homogenous districts.

Thus, rather than undermining the idea that electoral systems have important and systematic effects, our book highlights that electoral system effects follow common patterns, but the patterns are less uniform than previously assumed. For example, we do not see a single, universal "law" governing the effects of FPTP rules on the number of parties. Instead, this book suggests the idea that there may be separate "laws" that predict divergent outcomes for established democracies and new democracies, especially those with poorly institutionalized party systems.

MIXED-MEMBER ELECTORAL SYSTEMS AND THE CONTROLLED COMPARISON APPROACH

At the start of the 21st century, Matthew Shugart and Martin Wattenberg (2001c) asked whether mixed-member electoral systems represented the "best of both worlds" by combining elements and effects of PR and SMD electoral rules in one system. Based on a similar idea, in this book we argue that the presence of simultaneous PR and SMD elections within mixed-member electoral systems provides a unique natural laboratory to study the effects of these two electoral systems within the same political environment. Within each country, this "controlled comparison" approach allows us to see what the effect of different electoral rules is, while holding constant the effect of other important features of the country's sociopolitical life, such as social cleavages, socioeconomic development, and culture.

Not everyone agrees that mixed-member electoral systems offer a laboratory to examine the effects of electoral systems. Some scholars argue that mixed-member systems have a "contamination" effect, whereby the simultaneous presence of two different electoral rules in one system can lead to results in each that would be different from those in "pure" PR and SMD systems: the presence of a PR tier might affect behavior in the SMD tier, and the presence of the SMD tier might affect behavior in the PR tier (see, e.g., Clark and Wittrock 2005; Cox and Schoppa 2002; Ferrara et al. 2005; Gschwend et al. 2003; Hainmueller and Kern 2008; Herron and Nishikawa 2001). If so, the contamination scholars argue, controlled comparison is not a useful approach to learning about behavior under PR and SMDs because behavior in the two tiers in mixed-member systems is too different from how actors behave in non–mixed-member systems.

In Chapter 2, we directly address the contamination critique and highlight how controlled comparison offers valuable insights into electoral system effects. We acknowledge that contamination between the PR and SMD tiers of mixed-member systems exists, but we argue that it does not seriously undermine the contributions of our controlled comparison approach. First, we show empirically that outcomes under plurality elections in mixed systems are not systematically distinct from those in pure FPTP elections, undercutting the argument of contamination scholars that results of PR and SMD elections within mixed-member systems bear little resemblance to results in "pure" systems. Second, we argue that contamination, to the extent that it does exist, does not undermine a controlled comparison approach. Indeed, the controlled comparison approach to the study of electoral rules in mixed-member systems creates a harder test of the importance of electoral rules: if we find systematic differences in outcomes between the PR and SMD halves of mixed-member systems that match conventional views of the effects of electoral rules, even despite the potential of contamination, our approach provides even more support for extant theories of electoral system effects. Moreover, if we find that differences in outcomes between PR and SMD tiers vary systematically across different political contexts, such as between new and established democracies or homogenous and diverse districts, the controlled comparison approach can provide insights not available to those who focus exclusively on contamination within these systems.

PARTY SYSTEM FRAGMENTATION, STRATEGIC DEFECTION, AND THE ELECTION OF WOMEN IN MIXED-MEMBER SYSTEMS

Table 9.1 summarizes the major findings of the book.

The central conclusion and theme in this book are that the effects of electoral systems vary depending on the contexts in which they are situated. As presented in Chapter 1, we build this assertion around the idea that common expectations regarding electoral system effects – especially expectations regarding the

TABLE 9.1. *Electoral System Outcomes, Expectations, and Alternative Findings*

Outcome	Usual Expectation	Our Findings
1. The number of parties (Duverger's Law)	FPTP electoral systems promote two-candidate competition at the district level.	In established democracies, FPTP rules reduce the number of parties substantially, but do so to a far lesser degree in new democracies, especially those without institutionalized party systems.
2. Strategic behavior	Voters and elites will shift their support strategically from uncompetitive to competitive candidates in plurality systems, particularly when races are close.	There is strong evidence of strategic defection under FPTP rules, particularly in close races, but only in established democracies. If anything, strategic defection is less common in new democracies with poorly institutionalized party systems when in close races.
3. Diversity/electoral system interaction and the number of parties	More diversity (more groups) leads to more parties, but only under permissive electoral systems.	Social diversity shapes the number of parties under both PR (permissive) and FPTP (restrictive) electoral rules (and the relationship between diversity and the number of parties is often curvilinear – upside-down U-shaped, rather than linear).
4. The election of women	PR leads to more women gaining election than in SMDs.	(a) In established democracies, larger shares of elected representatives are women under PR rules than under SMDs, but in postcommunist states there is little difference in women's representation under PR and SMDs. (b) Party system fragmentation increases female representation under FPTP rules.

number of electoral competitors emerging under different electoral rules – are based on certain assumptions and conditions that do not always hold under all political contexts. Duverger's Law, the expectation that plurality elections will promote two-candidate competition at the district level, is based on the assumption that voters and elites will move away from low-ranking candidates – even if a candidate is their most preferred option – and support just the top two candidates under restrictive FPTP rules. However, strategic defection of this kind requires certain conditions, such as the provision of sufficient information to voters so they can identify candidates who are "out of the running" or differentiate between the candidates in meaningful ways, and then defect from likely losers to more competitive candidates. We argue and demonstrate through our district-level, controlled comparison analysis that this anticipated effect holds rather well in established democracies with well-developed parties, but the conditions that promote such strategic defection are not present in many new democracies, particularly those where parties do not typically help structure the vote. As a result, in new democracies – especially those with poorly institutionalized party systems – the expected winnowing effect of plurality elections may not be realized.

Similarly, arguments about the interactive effect of social cleavages and electoral systems are based on the assumption that most voters and elites will respond to the incentives created by plurality electoral rules to transfer support from likely losers to competitive candidates. When minority groups can gain representation for their own distinct parties, as is likely under permissive rules, they can support such parties without fear of a wasted vote. However, under restrictive rules, work founded on Duverger's Law assumes that minority voting groups will shift their support to one of the large leading contenders. This assumption of strategic defection under restrictive rules is the foundation of the long-held expectation that social diversity affects the number of parties only under permissive electoral systems such as proportional representation. In reality, however, work by scholars such as Cox (1997) and Alvarez et al. (2006) indicates that only a subset of voters in a position to defect strategically actually do so. Furthermore, in contrast to the expectation of Duverger's Law and recent work on the interactive effect of social cleavages and electoral systems (Amorim Neto and Cox 1997; Clark and Golder 2006; Ordeshook and Shvetsova 1994; Singer and Stephenson 2009), our comparisons at the district level of the impact of diversity on the number of parties under permissive (PR) and restrictive (SMD) tiers within mixed-member electoral systems show that there is a remarkably similar effect of diversity under PR and SMD rules. Interestingly, we find that the relationship between diversity and the number of parties (under both sets of rules) often has a curvilinear (upside-down U-shaped) pattern, similar to the expectation of recent work by Heather Stoll (ND).

Finally, we find additional conditioning dynamics in the presumed positive effect of PR on the election of women. The idea that closed-list PR tends to promote the election of women is built on assumptions that (a) parties have an incentive to nominate women in order to attract support from those seeking the representation of women, and closed-list PR gives parties the opportunity to create gender-balanced tickets; (b) closed-list PR provides opportunities to follow these incentives through centralized nomination processes; and (c) plurality electoral systems provide disincentives for the nomination of women, largely because of higher electoral thresholds for gaining representation.

However, as we show in Chapter 8, the experience of postcommunist states suggests that parties do not always have incentives to nominate women owing to a lack of societal support for female politicians, and SMD elections do not always present a higher electoral threshold for representation. Under these circumstances, closed-list PR does not provide a discernible advantage for the election of women.

IMPORTANCE OF SPECIFIC ELECTORAL RULES WITHIN MIXED SYSTEMS

Mixed-member electoral systems are not all the same. Throughout our analyses we also explore the effects of the specific rules that differentiate mixed-member electoral systems from one another. Most notably, mixed systems vary in the ways that outcomes in the SMD and PR tiers affect one another (tier linkage), the choice of rules (FPTP or two-round majority) within the SMD tier, PR district magnitude and the size of legal thresholds of representation in PR, and the relative number of seats available in each tier.

The Devil Is in the Details (but Only Partially So)

In general, our findings show that these details do indeed matter. Probably most important, we find evidence of more strategic defection by voters and elites away from their preferred candidates to more competitive alternatives under SMD rules, and a larger gap in the number of parties between the SMD and PR tiers in unlinked (MMM) systems than in linked (MMP) systems (see Chapters 4 and 6). In other words, SMDs have a stronger constraining effect in unlinked systems in which the SMD tier has a greater impact on the total number of seats that parties win. This result makes sense because a lack of linkage and compensatory seats should increase the incentives for strategic behavior in SMD elections, thus leading to fewer viable contestants in SMDs. Not at all surprising – and totally consistent with previous work – we also find strong evidence that unlinked systems also lead to greater overall system disproportionality. In addition, and also not surprising, we show that women are more likely to be elected under both PR and SMD rules when gender quotas are in place.

We also find some evidence of the importance of other components of mixed-member systems. Most notably, as we had suggested might be the case in Chapters 2 and 3, we demonstrate that on average SMDs have a greater constraining effect under plurality (rather than two-round majority) rules and when there are more seats allocated to the SMD tier than to PR (see Chapter 4). Consistent with previous work, and not at all surprising, we find some evidence that plurality rules lead to lower disproportionality in SMDs than two-round majority rules do, and offer strong evidence that high legal thresholds increase disproportionality under PR. We also provide some evidence that, on average, when a larger share of the seats in a mixed-member system is allocated to SMDs than to PR, disproportionality is higher as well. However, with the exception of our analysis of the impact of tier linkage on strategic defection, the number of parties and disproportionality, our findings remain tentative with respect to the effects of mixed system-specific rules (see Chapter 4).

Nevertheless, although differences between various types of mixed-member system electoral rules affect political outcomes, their influence is typically dwarfed by the effects of contextual factors. In Chapter 4, we show how the degree of democratic experience and party institutionalization seemed to outweigh any effect of more specific rules found within mixed systems. Indeed, we find that countries with poorly institutionalized party systems and a lack of democratic experience were struck by substantial party proliferation at the district level in SMDs, despite the fact that they also employed rules (unlinked tiers and plurality rules in the SMD tier) that should have led to fewer parties (Chapter 4). The stark differences in the number of parties at the district level between established and new democracies, even when controlling for specific rules, strongly suggests that the impact of contextual factors outweighs the effects of specific mixed-member system rules such as linkage.

Similarly, as shown in Chapter 5, the low level of the personal vote in Germany is likely due, in part, to its linked tiers, which increases the importance of candidates' parties in elections, and diminishes the impact of individual candidates' characteristics. However, the much greater incidence of personal voting found in New Zealand, Wales, and Scotland, which also have linked tiers, strongly suggests that electoral rules are not determinative and clearly other contextual factors related to history and the party system also have important effects.[2]

THE MAJOR FINDING OF THE BOOK: THE LIMITS OF DUVERGER'S LAW

Beyond the specific findings of each chapter, we believe that the most general contribution of this book is the emphasis on the importance of context in conditioning the effects of electoral rules. As we argue throughout the book, despite acknowledgment of the impact of contextual factors on the effects of political institutions, the most common emphasis within the literature on formal institutions is that particular rules tend to shape behavior in ways that are relatively consistent across different types of contexts. Nevertheless, as we highlight throughout this book, in many cases electoral rules do not lead to

---

[2] Evidence of the effect of linkage on strategic defection is also tenuous because the statistical significance of the variable changes depending on whether we code the borderline cases of Hungary and Italy as linked or unlinked (see Chapters 4 and 6). Likewise, we found that the effect of tier linkage and PR threshold on the PR–SMD gap in the election of women is limited as well (see Chapter 8).

similar outcomes across all contexts. Instead, context often leads to electoral system outcomes that are very different from what is usually expected.

On this very front, probably the most significant – and potentially controversial – findings in this book suggest the need to revise Duverger's Law: ultimately, one can view our arguments about the ways that context shapes the effects of electoral rules as simply different ways that political conditions limit the uniform application of Duverger's Law.

New Democracies Tend to Experience Different Incentives under FPTP Rules

First, our analysis highlights more systematically something that had been suggested previously by Gary Cox (1997), Mikhail Filippov, Peter Ordeshook, and Olga Shvetsova (1999), and Robert Moser (2001a): For electoral behavior to follow the expectations of Duverger's Law, it is necessary for voters and elites to have significant information about likely outcomes. Numerous features of established democracies – including the presence of established parties that can give voters and elites cues as to the competitiveness of different candidates – make it more likely that such information will be widely available. If it is unclear under FPTP rules who is truly out of the running, voters and elites will have little reason to defect strategically from their top choice to a different (presumably, more competitive) alternative, and – contrary to Duverger's Law – we will not see a winnowing down of competition to two viable candidates. For this reason, in new democracies – especially those in postcommunist countries with poorly institutionalized party systems – FPTP rules regularly produce a large number of candidates in many districts.

This does not mean that voters and elites in new democracies are unwilling to behave strategically. When there are many competitors and high uncertainty over who is likely to win, it is possible for any candidate to capture the seat. It is rational, and not "unstrategic," to support a candidate who is likely to attract only a relatively small number of votes if even a small vote share might allow someone to win the election.

In established democracies, we find clear evidence that voters and elites respond as most commonly expected: under plurality rules in established democracies, it appears that many voters and elites shift their support strategically to candidates other than their own top choice. In this way, the FPTP rules give them an incentive to defect from their true party preferences. In contrast, the incentive appears to be quite different under FPTP rules in new democracies, especially those with poorly institutionalized party systems: in such contexts, because of greater uncertainty over likely outcomes and the possibility, therefore, that "anyone" could win, voters and elites have a strong incentive to support their most-preferred candidate, even under plurality rules that are usually expected to push many political actors toward strategic defection away from their top choice.

In short, FPTP rules have very different incentives under different contexts. When there is substantial information about likely electoral behavior and outcomes, the results under FPTP rules are more likely to match the expectations of Duverger's Law and tend toward two candidates at the district level. But when there is insufficient information to help voters and elites differentiate between different candidates' likelihood of success, incentives under FPTP rules change, and lead to deviation away from Duverger's Law – most notably, leading to many more viable district-level competitors.[3]

Social Diversity Can Promote Divergence from Duverger's Law

Second, our analysis also demonstrates something very surprising: contrary to what Duverger's Law predicts, social diversity (measured as ethnic heterogeneity) conditions outcomes even under FPTP rules.

As we have discussed extensively, the most common expectation of the effect of electoral rules on the number of parties is that PR (or permissive rules in general) promotes party proliferation, but FPTP rules put a brake on the number of parties. Indeed, significant and insightful analyses by Octavio Amorim Neto and Gary Cox (1997) William Clark and Matt Golder (2006), Peter Ordeshook and Olga Shvetsova (1994), and Matthew Singer and Laura Stephenson (2009) offer support for this interactive relationship, demonstrating that increasing social diversity is associated with larger numbers of parties under permissive electoral rules and has no systematic relationship to the number of parties in SMDs. Such analysis is a powerful indicator of the constraining power of electoral rules.

However, our analysis of the relationship between ethnic diversity and party fragmentation in mixed-member systems suggests that diversity appears to shape the number of parties, and does so in similar ways under both FPTP and PR rules. To be sure, under many circumstances FPTP rules lead to smaller numbers of parties than PR – most likely because many voters and elites do follow the incentives of the restrictive rules and defect strategically from their top electoral choice to a more competitive alternative. Still, we find that there is a clear pattern by which the number of parties shifts – even under FPTP rules – in concert with increases in social heterogeneity. This pattern persists across different countries and, within each country that we examine, the pattern is nearly identical under both FPTP and PR rules. In short, although FPTP rules do act as a brake on the number of parties, the rules do not appear to prevent social diversity from shaping party fragmentation.

---

[3] In fact, recent scholarship by Grofman et al. (2009) and Taagepera (2007) suggests that even in established democracies there are regular instances in which district-level electoral results in plurality elections do not match the two-candidate competition expected by Duverger's Law. It should be noted, however, that the degree of party fractionalization at the district level in established democracies such as Great Britain and Canada do not come close to the high level of fragmentation found in new democracies such as Russia or Ukraine.

In other words, social diversity at the district level is another contextual condition that might mitigate the applicability of Duverger's Law. Under conditions of ethnic homogeneity, electoral systems often work as expected by work in the Duvergerian tradition – there are often two (or fewer) candidates per district under FPTP rules. However, as social diversity increases, we see shifts in the effective number of candidates, frequently leading to more than the two candidates per district expected by Duverger.

The Need to Revise Duverger's Law

In these ways, this book suggests that the environments under which Duverger's Law holds are actually limited. First, FPTP rules are unlikely to constrain electoral competition to only two effective parties per district in new democracies, especially those with poorly established parties. Rather, FPTP rules may actually promote party proliferation in such contexts. Indeed, the implication here is that Duverger's Law is unlikely to hold anywhere in which information on likely party support patterns is limited and/or parties do not clearly structure the vote. Second, this book also suggests that social diversity in both established and new democracies tends to promote deviations from the expected two-candidate competition of plurality elections. If, as we find in our analyses, social diversity tends to have roughly the same impact on the number of parties in PR and SMD elections, then socially diverse districts are another environment in which Duverger's Law would not necessarily hold, even in established democracies with well-developed parties.

When we put these two findings together, we come to a conclusion that runs counter to the findings in much of the rest of the literature on electoral systems. Rather than being a relationship that is broadly applicable to most circumstances, Duverger's Law – the expectation that FPTP elections promote two-candidate races at the district level – holds only in relatively homogenous electoral districts within established democracies with well-developed parties. In new democracies, as well as in many socially diverse districts in all democracies, one should not expect plurality systems to constrain electoral competition to two parties at the district level.

Equilibrium and the "Newness" of Democracy?

A reasonable counter-argument to this claim might highlight that theories of electoral system effects are founded on conditions of equilibrium, and that we are overstating the criticism of Duverger's Law by highlighting outcomes in new democracies that are not in equilibrium.

That is, skeptics of our critique might suggest that the principal reason for the outcomes that we find in certain countries that diverge from Duverger's Law is that political actors in these countries have not yet faced a sufficiently stable and certain environment to act as predicted by most theories of electoral rules. Expectations about the effects of electoral rules are based on likely behavior once all actors become accustomed to the system and respond according to the incentives created by it. Once in this equilibrium, few actors have an incentive to change their behavior, thus preventing the sort of "free-for-all" atmosphere we saw in places such as the initial democratic elections in Russia and Ukraine.

Indeed, there is little reason to expect such equilibrium in the initial election under new rules, particularly when the country has little experience contesting democratic elections. Scholars usually assume that political actors need time to understand and adapt to the incentives produced by political institutions (see Horowitz 2003; Reilly 2002). Moreover, our analysis in Chapters 4 through 6 demonstrates that time and learning did play a part in driving electoral system effects, most notably leading to more strategic defection by voters and elites, and, in turn, fewer viable candidates under FPTP rules. If learning is a primary force behind the differences we find in electoral system effects, then the variation in outcomes that we see in this book might be only temporary and will simply fade over time with greater electoral experience.

Nevertheless, it remains important to take into account the systematic differences in electoral system outcomes between new and established democracies for several reasons. To begin with, any polity considering the implementation of a particular electoral system ought to be aware of not only likely medium- to long-term consequences, but those most likely to occur in the short run as well. Indeed, especially in new democracies with little experience with free elections, and potentially great instability, it is important to manage public expectations of the system. In short, it is important to know about likely outcomes of electoral system effects when systems are not in equilibrium.

Moreover, reaching an equilibrium in which restrictive electoral systems produce the expected strategic defection by voters and elites and the resulting Duvergerian two-candidate competition at the district level may be a long process for many new democracies. Even controlling for experience with the electoral system, in this book we still see significant differences between established and new democracies in terms of voter and elite strategic defection and the number of parties. Established democracies typically constrain the number of parties to a greater degree and reach two-candidate outcomes more quickly after the initial mixed-member system elections than new democracies do. It is possible that the differences are due, first and foremost, to different starting points, whereby in the initial elections under new rules outcomes in established democracies match common electoral system expectations better than new democracies do. If so, perhaps such differences will wane over the long term. Future research based on larger numbers of elections for the "new" democracies will be more capable of addressing this question fully than we are at this point.

In addition, it appears likely that for many of the new democracies – especially those, such as Russia and Ukraine, that faced particularly poorly institutionalized party systems – the divergent outcomes occurred in a context of equilibrium, but of a type different from what is usually expected for FPTP elections. That is, as we show in Chapter 6, the most common outcome in SMD races in the poorly institutionalized party systems is what Cox (1997) refers to as a "non-Duvergerian equilibrium": in the poorly institutionalized party systems we examine, there was little difference in the share of the vote won by candidates in second and third place (and often even more poorly ranked candidates). As a result, huge numbers of voters and elites had no reason to defect from their support for any candidate, and learning to differentiate between the likely success of different electoral alternatives was likely to be slow. Only in 2003, the fourth election under Russia's mixed-member system, was there finally significant movement toward greater strategic defection by voters and elites, and a reduction in the number of parties – but, even so, the average effective number of candidates score per SMD was still greater than 3.5 in Russia in that election.

It is possible that with more elections there might have been greater political learning and party institutionalization in Russia, and in Ukraine as well, that might have led to more significant shifts toward Duvergerian outcomes in the SMD tier of their mixed-member systems. Unfortunately for electoral system scholars, in the early 2000s Russia and Ukraine both abandoned their mixed-member systems in favor of pure PR electoral systems. Moreover, beginning in the early 2000s, politics in Russia became markedly less democratic, as the state took control of the media and manipulated the electoral process, creating distorted outcomes. As a result, we are unable to tell whether outcomes in Russia and Ukraine ultimately would have come to match the expectations of Duverger's Law. However, our analysis in this book suggests that in these countries, the transitions to such an outcome would hardly have been smooth – in particular, our discussion in Chapter 6 suggests that electoral experience itself will not lead to a Duvergerian equilibrium. Instead, factors such as weak party institutionalization may produce a stable but different, non-Duvergerian equilibrium that can sustain party proliferation even in plurality elections over the medium- or long-term.

Finally, the issue of equilibrium behavior and outcomes relates only to the differences we find between new and established democracies, but does not play a part in probably our most significant challenge to Duverger's Law: our analysis of social diversity and the number of parties indicates significant divergence from the expected Duvergerian two-candidate configuration per district across different types of democracies. More specifically, we find that social diversity plays a part in shaping outcomes under FPTP rules even in the well-established New Zealand democracy.

AN AGENDA FOR FUTURE RESEARCH

Moving forward, this analysis provides several avenues for future research that build on our findings here, and extend to other elements of electoral systems and even other political institutions.

Laying Bare (and Questioning) Core Assumptions

One of our primary efforts has been to lay bare the core assumptions that we feel have been the basis of current arguments and expectations regarding effects of electoral systems, and question whether and under what conditions these assumptions hold. In the process, we have undoubtedly made our own set of assumptions regarding actors' behaviors, intentions, resources, and incentives. Future work may want to explore and question our assumptions, especially unpacking concepts such as democratic experience and party system institutionalization, and the implications that they have for strategic behavior and electoral outcomes.

District-Level Analysis of "Pure" Electoral Systems

We believe that this book is part of a growing trend that aims to consider electoral system effects at the district level. Acquiring data at the subnational (especially the district) level can be difficult; therefore, much work on electoral systems and their effects examines results that have been aggregated across the entire country. Nevertheless, electoral rules function at the district level, and the logic underpinning most theories of how electoral systems affect politics is based on mechanisms that shape outcomes at the district level. For this reason, to gain an accurate view of how rules shape outcomes, it is important that increasing effort be made to obtain and analyze such data. In the age of the Internet, never-before-imagined data sources have become available. More than ever before, it is becoming possible to collect district-level data on electoral outcomes, as well as sociodemographic characteristics of the residents of districts. As such, future work will have great advantages in being better able to demonstrate empirically the mechanisms underpinning electoral system effects.

In addition, we hope that future work will extend our analysis in this book beyond the mixed-member system setting. We believe that we have made a strong case for the validity of the controlled comparison approach, but the ultimate proof of our arguments will be in analysis of the effects of pure SMD and PR systems. Work by scholars such as Allen Hicken and Heather Stoll (2011), Singer (forthcoming), and Singer and Stephenson (2009) offers important analyses that examine the number of parties at the district level under multiple electoral systems, including principally pure systems. In particular, Singer (forthcoming) and Singer and Stephenson (2009) also consider the extent to which there are different effects depending on, for example, newly democratic and postcommunist contexts. Future work would do well to extend such analysis by continuing to control for contexts of these kinds.

Moreover, the capacity of the literature to make more specific predictions about the effects of FPTP rules would benefit from examining pure FPTP systems in other non-established democratic systems. For example, in contrast to the postcommunist cases we examine in this book, African countries such as

Ghana and Zambia, which use FPTP rules, appear to tend toward single-party dominance, rather than party proliferation. Analysis of such systems would promote greater understanding of the factors that lead to party proliferation under seemingly restrictive electoral rules and what factors undercut party competition altogether.

Future research will be especially welcome in attempting to extend our findings about the impact of social diversity on the party system under different electoral rules. The most surprising, potentially controversial, and important finding in this book is that social diversity affects the number of parties in the same way under FPTP rules as under PR. In Chapter 7, we use district-level data on diversity and party fragmentation to demonstrate the importance of social diversity to the party system even in the pure FPTP system in pre-reform New Zealand. Significantly greater attention to this question ought to be paid using district-level data from other pure FPTP systems. In work we do with Caitlin Milazzo (Moser, Scheiner, and Milazzo, ND), we offer a first cut at such analysis, and demonstrate similar patterns in pure FPTP systems in Canada, Great Britain, India, New Zealand, Papua New Guinea, and the United States. Future research ought to continue that investigation.

Democratic Experience and Party System Development

We give considerable attention to the importance of both democratic development and party institutionalization as contextual factors that shape the effects of electoral rules, but future research would do particularly well to dig more deeply into precisely how democratic experience and party system development condition electoral systems. The third wave of democracy has been at the center of comparative politics for three decades and thus democratic development has received significant scholarly attention. However, we still know relatively little about precisely how – and, more important, why – new democracies differ from more established democracies. Scott Mainwaring and Edurne Zoco (2007) have shown that historical sequences have continued to make party systems within newer democracies that emerged in the late 20th century very different from party systems within more established democracies that emerged earlier. Our book builds on this finding by showcasing that such differences have substantial implications for how institutions affect outcomes. Consequently, more work needs to be done on other differences between new and older democracies and the crucial question of whether these differences will eventually wane, resulting in a convergence in the nature of democratic processes within democracies born during different historical epochs.

The Mechanisms that Underlie the Differences in Democratic and Party System Contexts. In this book, we do not address directly many of the mechanisms underpinning the differences between established and new democracies, especially with respect to party institutionalization, that we claim are important in shaping strategic defection by voters and elites under FPTP rules. Most notably, especially in Chapter 3 we make arguments about the importance of party institutionalization in shaping political system knowledge and the types of relationships between voters, elites, and parties. In particular, we suggest a number of specific ways in which institutionalized parties promote different actors' ability to gain information and, in turn, engage in strategic defection under restrictive electoral rules. Indeed, our analyses in Chapters 4 through 6 indicate significant differences in strategic behavior not only between established and new democracies, but also between institutionalized and noninstitutionalized party systems in new democracies.

However, our variables, which simply indicate into which category we place each country – established democracy, new democracy with institutionalized party system, or noninstitutionalized party system – do not offer more fine-grained distinctions between different countries. For this reason, our analysis cannot indicate precisely which features of established democracies lead to different outcomes under FPTP rules when compared with new democracies, especially those with poorly institutionalized party systems. For example, in Chapter 3, we highlight a number of specific features of strong party systems that help voters and elites who wish to affect the outcome of the race to strategically defect from their most preferred candidate under FPTP rules to more competitive alternatives, but we do not test these specific mechanisms themselves.

A fruitful step in future research on the effects of electoral rules would be to parse out the features that differentiate countries with different levels of democratic and party system development from one another, and investigate how these different features shape behavior under restrictive electoral rules. For example, to what extent are the differences that we find in strategic defection between different contexts a result of differences in the amount of information provided by the party system about the likelihood of candidates from certain parties being competitive (or uncompetitive)? To what extent are differences in voter and elite behavior across contexts due to variation in the amount of information surrounding substantive issues that would allow voters to better rank-order different parties? To what extent is the strength of voters' party identification – or voters' attachment to particular candidates for more personal reasons – a central factor in shaping strategic defection? To what extent do other factors shape the differences we see between established democracies, new democracies with relatively strong party systems, and democracies with poorly institutionalized party systems? Research into questions of these kinds would promote a greater understanding of the conditions under which electoral rules ought to have their expected effects, as well as the importance of parties more generally in the democratic process.

The Importance of Change and Development over Time. From a different perspective, as we note in Chapter 3, countries do not remain "new" democracies forever, and party systems certainly become more institutionalized over time. The literature on democratic development is too rich, detailed, and wide-ranging to give a full accounting here, and there is certainly important work on party institutionalization, most notably by Scott Mainwaring and his co-authors (Mainwaring and Scully 1995; Mainwaring and Torcal 2006; Mainwaring and Zoco 2007). Scholarship on the effects of electoral rules would benefit from additional attention to how changes in democratic development and party institutionalization shape incentives and behavior under different electoral rules.

Our discussion in Chapter 6 of changes in Russia in the early 2000s shows how the development of a new party system can lead to changes in strategic behavior under FPTP rules, but significant work remains to be done on the subject. Unfortunately for scholars (and, even more sadly, for the Russian people), democratic development in Russia came to a grinding halt over the course of the decade. As a result, we cannot know how voter and elite behavior might have continued to evolve under a more democratic and institutionalized Russian party system. Therefore, it is important that scholars continue to explore the relationship between party system development and voter and elite behavior in other countries. Among the most important questions to address would be: At what point in the democratization process, and based on what changes within the system, should we expect outcomes in a democratizing country to match those of more established democracies?

This book highlights the importance of time and learning to the establishment of consistent patterns of behavior and outcomes under particular rules, but our analysis does not differentiate sharply between new and established democracies in terms of the speed and nature of the learning process and change over time. Useful work by scholars such as Tavits and Annus (2006), indeed, shines a light on the learning process in developing contexts over time. However, generally speaking, it remains unclear in what ways the learning process differs between new and established systems, thus suggesting another important area for future work.

Social Diversity, Electoral Systems, and the Number of Parties

Another arena that calls for more research is the interaction between social diversity, electoral systems, and the number of parties at the district level. This book suggests a new interpretation of the effect of electoral rules in channeling social diversity into the party system. In Chapter 7, we find that social diversity tends to affect the number of parties at the district level under both PR and plurality electoral contests within mixed-member systems (and that the relationship between diversity and party fragmentation is often curvilinear – i.e., upside-down U-shaped).

That being said, we leave many questions unanswered regarding why these patterns exist. If the effect of social diversity on the number of parties is not suspended in FPTP systems but rather is similar under both permissive and restrictive electoral systems in all political contexts, then numerous questions arise about the causal mechanisms that undermine strategic defection away from less competitive options in more diverse districts: Who is failing to behave strategically, and why? What other factors, such as other institutions like presidentialism or federalism, may influence this behavior? What type of cleavages can "break through" the constraining effect of FPTP systems, and which cannot? In other words, the argument that social diversity may undermine strategic defection and result in party system fragmentation at the district level despite the constraining effects of FPTP may mean that no countries (except, perhaps, homogenous ones) are immune to the conditionality of electoral system effects.

On this front, survey research or studies using ecological inference analysis (King 1997) could be used to examine which groups – those in the minority, majority, or both – fail to act strategically, and do not defect from uncompetitive parties or candidates. It may also be the case that other contextual factors, such as the presence or lack of ethnic parties, or particular features of ethnic groups' voting behavior, may help explain the effects of diversity on party system fragmentation even under restrictive electoral systems.

Women's Representation

Future work on women's representation would benefit from extending our analysis in Chapter 8 considerably. As we noted earlier, there are more opportunities than ever to collect district-level data for numerous different countries; more data are also becoming available on individual legislators and candidates around the globe. As a result, scholars will increasingly have access to information sources that will make possible a richer understanding of the factors shaping descriptive representation. Most notably, with the generation of public opinion data that are comparable across numerous countries, and the development of multilevel quantitative analysis – whereby we can better combine into models variables relating to individual voters, district characteristics, and national conditions – future research will be able to test more directly the mechanisms posited by the extant literature on the reasons that women do and do not get elected to political office. The more this new research examines representation cross-nationally and focuses, in particular, on differences between new and established democracies, the more we will learn about the conditions that make these mechanisms more likely to be effective.

What Other Areas Merit Further Research?

One of the chief objectives in this book is to reopen fundamental empirical questions regarding electoral system effects that seem largely settled in much of the literature. Other questions not examined here could be explored in the same way.

For example, minority representation – the election of members of minority groups to the legislature – is one area that has strongly asserted hypotheses regarding the effects of electoral systems, but limited direct empirical analyses because of difficulties obtaining data on the ethnic background of individual legislators. Many scholars argue that proportional representation provides greater opportunities for the election of ethnic minorities due to lower electoral thresholds that promote smaller parties, some of which could be ethnic parties (Lijphart 2004; Diamond 1999; Norris 2004; Reynolds 2011). SMD elections are presumed to undermine minority representation because of higher electoral thresholds and, thus, fewer opportunities for minorities to gain election based on ethnic voting. This line of causal logic obviously makes several assumptions regarding how ethnic minorities gain election – the centrality of ethnic voting being the primary one – and the conditions under which ethnic minority groups can mobilize to elect their own members. However, there are reasons to expect that such dynamics may vary depending on key demographic characteristics of minority groups (size, geographic concentration, level of assimilation) and the general political context (such as electoral threshold or the incentives of parties to nominate ethnic minorities). Data on individual legislators' ethnic backgrounds within mixed-member as well as pure electoral systems would go a long way in examining these questions (see Moser 2008).

Our discussion has focused on the conditionality of the effects of electoral rules, but future research would do well to consider the conditionality of other institutions' effects as well. As we noted earlier, there is already work on the conditionality of the effects of the level of government centralization and institutions such as executive regime type (i.e., presidential versus parliamentary structure). As such, the groundwork is now laid for additional analysis of the conditionality of the effects of such institutions.

IMPLICATIONS

Finally, the findings in this book raise several fundamental challenges to common assertions regarding electoral system effects that should prompt a serious rethinking of how political institutions interact with political context to produce certain outcomes. We close by discussing some of the theoretical and practical implications that arise from these findings.

Different Contexts, Different Assumptions, Different "Laws"

Our various arguments and findings suggest that generalized "laws" regarding the effects of electoral systems face serious – and perhaps underappreciated – limitations. At its essence, our argument is that once one relaxes certain assumptions and provides the possibility that certain key conditions may differ across cases, electoral system effects are highly conditional. A single law cannot be generalized to all circumstances. Instead, there need to be different expectations – indeed, different "laws" – for different contexts.

To be sure, scholars such as Gary Cox (1997) and Richard Matland (1998) note that electoral system effects require certain preconditions that, if left unmet, undermine expected effects.[4] However, the unstated assumption in much of the literature has been that these conditions are usually met and the presumed effects of electoral systems on party systems and the demographic characteristics of representatives should usually be realized (see, e.g., Chhibber and Kollman 2004; Clark and Golder 2006). Our analysis, which includes many countries that have recently democratized and have weak party systems, suggests that there are whole categories of states (especially, in our view, new democracies with weak party systems) that are exceptions to commonly accepted rules such as Duverger's Law, and, thus, such exceptions actually diverge systematically from what is usually expected. Moreover, some of the "exceptions" to the rule that we found – most notably, regarding the interactive effect between diversity and electoral systems – are so widespread that they point to a need for a revision or elimination of the rule itself. That is, in the interactive effect of social diversity and electoral rules on the number of parties, it is possible, in fact, that the cases that defy expectations outnumber the cases that reinforce the theory. In these different ways, we believe that the findings in this book call for a rethinking of electoral system effects and a more systematic incorporation of political context into the study of institutions.

Increased Complexity and the Loss of Parsimony

One downside to our analysis is that considering political context as a factor that systematically conditions the effects of electoral systems undermines some of the parsimony of theories, such as Duverger's Law, of the effects of electoral systems. That is, when we add variables and mitigating factors, we make arguments that are more accurate but also more complex. Indeed, some of the power and attractiveness of theories regarding electoral systems comes from the fact that they are not burdened by an excessive number of exceptions, conditions, or additional variables that affect outcomes. Outliers are not necessarily a problem for parsimonious theories such as Duverger's Law or the argument that PR promotes the election of women, especially because such theories are intended to be probabilistic, rather than to determine outcomes in all cases. A few exceptions may "prove the rule," so to speak.

However, key electoral system theories that leave out political context appear to apply poorly to significant numbers of democratic polities, and therefore would benefit from additional clarification. The analysis in this book suggests that divergence from Duverger's Law and the PR advantage for women appears in many new democracies, and significant levels of social diversity can push SMDs away from the expectations of Duverger's Law as well. In this way, more complex models ought to be introduced when institutional effects

---

[4] Moreover, as noted earlier, work by scholars such as Shugart and Carey (1992), Mainwaring and Shugart (1997), and Cheibub (2007) highlights the conditionality of a related institution: executive regime type.

vary across cases in relatively frequent and systematic ways that suggest there is more than one "law" that explains outcomes. Thus, at the most basic level, electoral system studies would generally benefit from explicit acknowledgment of the types of cases to which a given parsimonious theory applies. On another level, when whole categories of states (e.g., new democracies or postcommunist states) defy expected outcomes, theories regarding institutional effects necessarily require additional layers of complexity to address these cases.

The advantages of theoretical clarification are especially likely to outweigh the advantages of parsimony if they do not require markedly greater complexity. Our analysis in this book is a far cry from a claim that, to make accurate predictions, each country must be treated as totally unique. Rather, we highlight a small number of contextual variables, especially democratic experience/party system development and social diversity, that appear to condition the effects of electoral rules. As such, our analysis suggests that outcomes in the areas that we examine can be explained by as few as two or three important factors – hardly a complex series of theoretical models.

Limits on Electoral Engineering?

The conceptualization of institutions as affecting their environment in predictable ways is fundamental to the idea of institutional design. If institutions such as electoral systems are to be reliable instruments of political engineering, it would be beneficial if their effects are relatively uniform across different political contexts. In this way, considering electoral system effects as conditioned by contextual factors would have practical effects for would-be electoral engineers.

On one hand, if electoral systems do not have their expected effects in certain types of countries or in certain types of districts in all countries, then it may be more difficult to use electoral systems to craft specific political outcomes. As Scheiner (2008) argues, observers often expect too much from electoral system reform, especially when striving to promote "distal" effects that are only indirectly influenced by electoral systems, rather than "proximal" effects that are more directly caused by electoral rules. Our analysis pushes a cautionary approach to electoral engineering: the success of attempts to use electoral systems to shape even fairly direct effects of electoral rules, such as the constraining effect on the number of parties or promotion of the election of women, will depend in part on contextual factors. Electoral engineering will not allow a one-size-fits-all type of approach.

On the other hand, the analysis in this book suggests that understanding a small number of contextual factors in a given country can make it possible to predict the effects of electoral rules even more accurately, thus potentially improving the success rate of electoral engineering. The analysis in this book does not suggest that electoral rules are somehow inconsequential or that their effects are ad hoc. Rather, electoral systems have important and systematic effects, but these effects are more variable than is often acknowledged and conditioned by factors that are sometimes neglected and must be taken into consideration – especially by policy makers. Because electoral systems are necessary choices for any democracy – a state must translate votes into seats in some way – such choices should be made with their likely effects firmly in mind. Knowledge of how context alters the effects of electoral systems is essential for such an enterprise.

References

Abramson, Paul, John Aldrich, André Blais, Matthew Diamond, Abraham Diskin, Indridi Indridason, Daniel Lee, and Renan Levine. 2010. "Comparing Strategic Voting under FPTP and PR." *Comparative Political Studies* 43 (1): 61–90.

Aldrich, John. 1995. *Why Parties? The Origin and Transformation of Political Parties in America*. Chicago: University of Chicago Press.

Alesina, Alberto, Arnaud Devleeschauwer, William Easterly, Sergio Kurlat, and Romain Wacziarg. 2003. "Fractionalization." *Journal of Economic Growth* 8 (2): 155–94.

Almquist, Ann and Elizabeth Oakes. 1993. "Women in National Legislatures: A Cross-National Test of Macrostructural Gender Theories." *Population Research and Policy Review* 12 (1): 71–81.

Alvarez, R. Michael, Frederick J. Boehmke, and Jonathan Nagler. 2006. "Strategic Voting in British Elections." *Election Studies* 25 (1): 1–19.

Alvarez, R. Michael, and Jonathan Nagler. 2000. "A New Approach for Modeling Strategic Voting in Multiparty Elections." *British Journal of Political Science* 30 (1): 131–149.

Ames, Barry, Andy Baker, and Lucio R. Renno. 2009. "Split-Ticket Voting as the Rule: Voters and Permanent Divided Government in Brazil." *Electoral Studies* 28 (1): 8–20.

Amorim Neto, Octavio and Gary Cox. 1997. "Electoral Institutions, Cleavage Structures, and the Number of Parties." *American Journal of Political Science* 41 (1): 149–174.

Baker, Andy, Barry Ames, and Lucio R. Renno. 2006. "Social Context and Campaign Volatility in New Democracies: Networks and Neighborhoods in Brazil's 2002 Elections." *American Journal of Political Science* 50 (2): 382–399.

Baker, Andy, and Ethan Scheiner. 2004. "Adaptive Parties: Party Strategic Capacity under Japanese SNTV." *Electoral Studies* 23 (2): 251–278.

Barnes, Samuel, Frank Grace, James K. Pollock, and Peter W. Sperlich. 1962. "The German Party System and the 1961 Federal Election." *American Political Science Review* 56 (4): 899–914.

Bawn, Kathleen. 1993. "The Logic of Institutional Preferences: German Electoral as a Social Choice Outcome." *American Journal of Political Science* 37 (4): 965–989.

Bawn, Kathleen. 1999. "Voter Responses to Electoral Complexity: Ticket Splitting, Rational Voters and Representation in the Federal Republic of Germany." *British Journal of Political Science* 29 (3): 487–505.

Beckwith, Karen. 1986. *American Women and Political Participation*. New York: McGraw-Hill.

Belin, Laura and Robert Orttung. 1997. *The Russian Parliamentary Elections of 1995*. New York: M. E. Sharpe.

Benoit, Kenneth. 1999. "Votes and Seats: The Hungarian Electoral Law and the 1994 Parliamentary Elections." In: Toka, G. (ed.), *The 1994 Election to the Hungarian National Assembly: Analyses, Documents and Data*. Berlin: Edition Sigma.

Benoit, Kenneth. 2001. "Evaluating Hungary's Mixed-Member Electoral System." In Shugart, M. and Wattenberg, M. (Eds.), *Mixed-Member Electoral Systems: The Best of Both Worlds?* Oxford: Oxford University Press.

Bertoa, Fernando. ND. "Sources of Party System Institutionalization in New Democracies: Lessons from East Central Europe."

Bielasiak, Jack. 2002. "The Institutionalization of Electoral and Party Systems in Post-communist States." *Comparative Politics* 34 (2): 189–210.

Birch, Sarah. 2005. "Single-Member District Electoral Systems and Democratic Transition." *Electoral Studies* 24 (2): 281–301.

Birch, Sarah. 2008. "Electoral Institutions and Popular Confidence in Electoral Processes: A Cross-National Analysis." *Electoral Studies* 27 (2): 305–20.

Birnir, Johanna. 2007. *Ethnicity and Electoral Politics*. New York: Cambridge University Press.

Birnir, Johanna and Donna Van Cott. 2007. "Disunity in Diversity: Party System Fragmentation and the Dynamic Effect of Ethnic Heterogeneity on Latin American Legislatures," *Latin American Research Review* 42 (1): 99–125.

Boon, Martin and John Curtice. 2003. "Scottish Elections Research May-June 2003." ICM/The Electoral Commission. http://www.electoralcommission.org.uk/templates/search/document.cfm/8023.

Brancati, Dawn. 2009. *Peace by Design: Managing Intrastate Conflict through Decentralization*. New York: Oxford University Press.

Bratton, Kathleen A. and Leonard P. Ray. 2002. "Descriptive Representation, Policy Outcomes, and Municipal Day-Care Coverage in Norway." *American Journal of Political Science* 46 (2): 428–437.

Cain, Bruce, John Ferejohn, and Morris Fiorina. 1987. *The Personal Vote: Constituency Service and Electoral Independence*. New York: Cambridge University Press.

Carey, John M. and Matthew Shugart. 1995. "Incentives to Cultivate a Personal Vote: A Rank Ordering of Electoral Formulas." *Electoral Studies* 14 (4): 417–439.

Carey, John, and Simon Hix. 2011. "The Electoral Sweet Spot: Low Magnitude Proportional Systems." *American Journal of Political Science* 55 (2): 383–397.

Caul, Miki. 1999. "Women's Representation in Parliament: The Role of Political Parties." *Party Politics* 5 (1): 79–98.

Chandra, Kanchan. 2004. *Why Ethnic Parties Succeed*. Cambridge: Cambridge University Press.

Chandra, Kanchan. 2009. "Why Voters in Patronage Democracies Split their Tickets: Strategic Voting for Ethnic Parties." *Electoral Studies* 28 (1): 21–32.

Cheibub, Jose. 2007. *Presidentialism, Parliamentarism and Democracy*. Cambridge: Cambridge University Press.

Chhibber, Pradeep and Ken Kollman. 1998. "Party Aggregation and the Number of Parties in India and the United States." *American Political Science Review* 92 (2): 329–342.

Chhibber, Pradeep and Ken Kollman. 2004. *The Formation of National Party Systems: Federalism and Party Competition in Canada, Great Britain, India, and the United States*. Princeton, NJ: Princeton University Press.

Clark, William and Matt Golder. 2006. "Rehabilitating Duverger's Theory: Testing the Mechanical and Strategic Modifying Effects of Electoral Laws." *Comparative Political Studies* 39 (6): 679–708.

Clark, Terry and Jill Wittrock. 2005. "Presidentialism and the Effect of Electoral Law in Postcommunist Systems." *Comparative Political Studies* 38 (1): 171–188.

Colton, Timothy and Michael McFaul. 2000. "Reinventing Russia's Party of Power: Unity and the 1999 Duma Election." *Post-Soviet Affairs* 16 (3): 201–224.

Conradt, David P. 2001. *The German Polity*. New York: Addison-Wesley Longman.

Cox, Gary W. 1988. "Closeness and Turnout: A Methodological Note." *Journal of Politics* 50 (3): 768–775.

Cox, Gary W. 1997. *Making Votes Count: Strategic Coordination in the World's Electoral Systems*. New York: Cambridge University Press.

Cox, Gary W. 1999. "Electoral Rules and Electoral Coordination." *Annual Review of Political Science* 2 (1): 145–167.

Cox, Gary W. 2001. "Comment on 'Japan's Multimember SNTV System and Strategic Voting: The "M+1" Rule and Beyond.'" *Japanese Journal of Political Science* 2 (2): 237–239.

Cox, Karen, and Len Schoppa. 2002. "Interaction Effects in Mixed-Member Electoral Systems: Theory and Evidence From Germany, Japan, and Italy." *Comparative Political Studies* 35 (9): 1027–53.

Dahlerup, Drude and Lenita Freidenval. 2005. "Quotas as a 'Fast Track' to Equal Representation for Women: Why Scandinavia in No Longer the Model." *International Feminist Journal of Politics* 7 (1): 26–48.

Darcy, R., Susan Welch, and Janet Clark. 1994. *Women, Elections, and Representation, Second Edition, Revised*. Lincoln, NE: University of Nebraska Press.

Davidson-Schmich, Louise K. 2006. "The Implementation of Political Party Gender Quotas: Evidence from the German Laender, 1990-2000." *Party Politics* 12 (2): 211–232.

Denemark, David. 2001. "Choosing MMP in New Zealand: Explaining the 1993 Electoral Reform." In: Shugart, M. and Wattenberg, M. (eds.), *Mixed-Member Electoral Systems: The Best of Both Worlds?* Oxford: Oxford University Press.

Desposato, Scott and Ethan Scheiner. 2008. "Governmental Centralization and Party Affiliation: Legislator Strategies in Brazil and Japan." *American Political Science Review* 102: 509–524.

Diamond, Larry. 1999. *Developing Democracy: Toward Consolidation*. Baltimore: Johns Hopkins University Press.

Dickson, Eric and Kenneth Scheve. 2010. "Social Identity, Electoral Institutions, and the Number of Candidates." *British Journal of Political Science* 40 (2): 349–375.

Diwakar, Rekha. 2007. "Duverger's Law and the Size of Indian Party System: A District Level Analysis." *Party Politics* 13 (5): 539–561.

Duch, Raymond M. and Harvey D. Palmer. 2002. "Strategic Voting in Post-Communist Democracy?" *British Journal of Political Science* 32 (1): 63–91.

Duverger, Maurice. 1954. *Political Parties: Their Organization and Activity in the Modern State*. London: Methuen.

Duverger, Maurice. 1986. "Duverger's Law: Forty Years Later." In: Grofman, B. and Lijphart, A. (eds.), *Electoral Laws and their Political Consequences*. New York: Agathon Press.

Eckstein, Harry. 1975. "Case Study and Theory in Political Science." In: Greenstein, F. I. and Polsby, N. W. (eds.), *Handbook of Political Science*. Reading, MA: Addison-Wesley.

Economic and Social Research Council (ESRC). 2003. "The Elections in Scotland and Wales: What's at Stake?" Devolution Briefings: Findings from the Economic and Research Council's Research Programme on Devolution and Constitutional Change, Briefing No. 1, April 2003.

Elster, Jon. 1989. *Nuts and Bolts for the Social Sciences*. New York: Cambridge University Press.

Evans, Geoffrey and Stephen Whitefield. 1993. "Identifying the Bases of Party Competition in Eastern Europe." *British Journal of Political Science* 23 (4): 521–548.

Fearon, James. 2003. "Ethnic and Cultural Diversity by Country." *Journal of Economic Growth* 8 (2): 195–222.

Ferrara, Federico. 2004. "Electoral Coordination and the Strategic Desertion of Strong Parties in Compensatory Mixed Systems with Negative Vote Transfers." *Electoral Studies* 23 (3): 391–413.

Ferrara, Federico, Erik S. Herron, and Misa Nishikawa. 2005. *Mixed Electoral Systems: Contamination and Its Consequences*. New York: Palgrave Macmillan.

Fieldhouse, E.A., C. J. Pattie, and R. J. Johnston. 1996. "Tactical Voting and Party Constituency Campaigning in the 1992 General Election in England." *British Journal of Political Science* 26 (3): 403–418.

Filippov, Mikhail, Peter Ordeshook, and Olga Shvetsova. 1999. "Party Fragmentation and Presidential Elections in Post-Communist Democracies." *Constitutional Political Economy* 10 (1): 1–24.

Fish, M. Steven. 2005. *Democracy Derailed in Russia*. New York: Cambridge University Press.

Fisher, Steven. 1973. "The Wasted Vote Thesis." *Comparative Politics* 5 (2): 293–299.

Fitzmaurice, J. 2003. "Parliamentary Elections in Lithuania, October 2000." *Electoral Studies* 22 (1): 161–165.

Franzese, Robert J., Jr. 2007. "Multicausality, Context-Conditionality, and Endogeneity." In: Boix, C. and Stokes, S. C. (eds.), *The Oxford Handbook of Comparative Politics*. New York: Oxford University Press.

Gaines, Brian. 1999. "Duverger's Law and the Meaning of Canadian Exceptionalism." *Comparative Political Studies* 32 (7): 835–861.

Glendinning, Richard and Roger Scully. 2003. "National Assembly for Wales Election 2003: Opinion Research." London: NOP Social and Political, and Aberystwyth: Institute for Welsh Politics.

Golder, Matt. 2006. "Presidential Coattails and Legislative Fragmentation." *American Journal of Political Science* 50 (1): 34–48.

Gorenburg, Dmitry P. 2003. *Minority Ethnic Mobilization in the Russian Federation*. Cambridge: Cambridge University Press.

Grofman, Bernard, Shaun Bowler, and Andre Blais. 2009. "Introduction: Evidence for Duverger's Law in Four Countries." In: Grofman, B., Blais, A., and Bowler, S. (eds.),

Duverger's Law of Plurality Elections: The Logic of Party Competition in Canada, India, the United Kingdom, and the United States. New York: Springer.

Gschwend, Thomas, Ron Johnston, and Charles Pattie. 2003. "Split-Ticket Patterns in Mixed-Member Proportional Election Systems: Estimates and Analyses of Their Spatial Variation at the German Federal Election, 1998." *British Journal of Political Science* 33 (1): 109–127.

Hainmueller, Jens, and Holger Lutz Kern. 2008. "Incumbency as a Source of Spillover Effects in Mixed Electoral Systems: Evidence from a Regression-Discontinuity Design." *Electoral Studies* 27 (2): 213–227.

Hale, Henry. 2004. "The Origins of United Russia and the Putin Presidency: The Role of Contingency in Party-System Development." *Demokratizatsiya* 12 (2): 169–194.

Hale, Henry. 2006. *Why Not Parties in Russia? Democracy, Federalism, and the State.* New York: Cambridge University Press.

Hamilton, Lawrence C. 1998. *Statistics With Stata 5.* Pacific Grove, CA: Duxbury Press.

Harris, Chauncy. 1993. "A Geographic Analysis of Non-Russian Minorities in Russia and its Ethnic Homelands.," *Post-Soviet Geography* 34 (9): 543–597.

Helmke, Gretchen and Steven Levitsky. 2006. *Informal Institutions and Democracy: Lessons from Latin America.* Baltimore: Johns Hopkins University Press.

Herron, Erik S. 2002. "Electoral Influences on Legislative Behavior in Mixed-Member Systems: Evidence from Ukraine's Verkhovna Rada." *Legislative Studies Quarterly* 27 (3): 361–382.

Herron, Erik S. and Misa Nishikawa. 2001. "Contamination Effects and the Number of Parties in Mixed-Superposition Electoral Systems." *Electoral Studies* 20 (1): 63–86.

Hicken, Allen and Heather Stoll. 2008. "Electoral Rules and the Size of the Prize: How Political Institutions Shape Presidential Party Systems." *Journal of Politics* 70 (4): 1109–1127.

Hicken, Allen and Heather Stoll. 2011. "Presidents and Parties: How Presidential Elections Shape Coordination in Legislative Elections." *Comparative Political Studies* 44 (7): 854–883.

Horowitz, Donald. 1985. *Ethnic Groups in Conflict.* Berkeley: University of California Press.

Horowitz, Donald. 2003. "Electoral Systems: A Primer for Decision Makers." *Journal of Democracy* 14 (4): 115–127.

Horowitz, Shale and Eric Browne. 2005. "Sources of Post-Communist Party System Consolidation." *Party Politics* 11 (6): 689–706.

Hough, Jerry. 1998. "Institutional Rules and Party Formation." In: Colton, T. and Hough, J. (eds.), *Growing Pains: Russian Democracy and the Election of 1993.* Washington, DC: The Brookings Institution.

Howard, Marc. 2003. *The Weakness of Civil Society in Post-Communist Europe.* Cambridge: Cambridge University Press.

Inglehart, Ronald and Pippa Norris. 2003. *Rising Tide: Gender Equality and Cultural Change Around the World.* Cambridge: Cambridge University Press.

Iversen, Torben and D. Soskice. 2006. "Electoral Institutions and the Politics of Coalitions: Why Some Democracies Redistribute More Than Others." *American Political Science Review* 100 (2): 165–181.

Iversen, Torben and Frances Rosenbluth. 2008. "Work and Power: The Connection Between Female Labor Force Participation and Female Political Representation". *Annual Review of Political Science* 11: 479–495.

Iversen, Torben and Frances Rosenbluth. 2010. *Women, Work, and Politics: The Political Economy of Gender Equality*. New Haven, CT: Yale University Press.

Jackman, Robert W. 1985. "Cross-National Statistical Research and the Study of Comparative Politics." *American Journal of Political Science* 29 (1): 161–182.

Jesse, Eckhard. 1988. "Split-Voting in the Federal Republic of Germany: An Analysis of the Federal Elections from 1953 to 1987." *Electoral Studies* 7 (2): 109–124.

Johnston, Ron J. and Charles J. Pattie. 1991. "Tactical Voting in Great Britain in 1983 and 1987: An Alternative Approach." *British Journal of Political Science* 21 (1): 95–108.

Johnston, Ron J. and Charles J. Pattie. 2002. "Campaigning and Split-Ticket Voting in New Electoral Systems: The First MMP Elections in New Zealand, Scotland and Wales." *Electoral Studies* 21 (4): 583–600.

Jones, Bradford S. 2008. "Multilevel Modeling." In: Box-Steffensmeier, J., Brady, H., and Collier, D. (eds.), *The Oxford Handbook of Political Methodology*. Oxford: Oxford University Press.

Jones, Mark. 1996. "Increasing Women's Representation Via Gender Quotas: The Argentine Ley de Cupos." *Women & Politics* 16 (4): 75–98.

Jones, Mark. 1997. "Racial Heterogeneity and the Effective Number of Candidates in Majority Runoff Elections: Evidence from Louisiana." *Electoral Studies* 16 (3): 349–358.

Jones, Mark. 2004a. "Electoral Institutions, Social Cleavages, and Candidate Competition in Presidential Elections." *Electoral Studies* 23 (1): 73–106.

Jones, Mark. 2004b. "Quota Legislation and the Election of Women: Learning from the Costa Rican Experience." *The Journal of Politics* 66 (4): 1203–1223.

Jones, Mark. 2009. "Gender Quotas, Electoral Laws, and the Election of Women: Evidence from the Latin American Vanguard." *Comparative Political Studies* 42 (1): 56–81.

Karp, Jeffrey A. 2009. "Candidate Effects and Spill-Over in Mixed Systems: Evidence From New Zealand." *Electoral Studies* 28 (1): 41–50.

Karp, Jeffrey, Jack Vowles, Susan A. Banducci, and Todd Donovan. 2002. "Strategic Voting, Party Activity, and Candidate Effects: Testing Explanations for Split Voting in New Zealand's New Mixed System." *Electoral Studies* 21 (1): 1–22.

Kenworthy, Lane and Melissa Malami. 1999. "Gender Inequality in Political Representation: A Worldwide Comparative Analysis." *Social Forces* 78 (1): 235–269.

Kimball, David C. 2005. "A Decline in Ticket-Splitting and the Increasing Salience of Party Labels." In: Weisberg, H. and Wilcox, C. (eds.), *Models of Voting in Presidential Elections: The 2000 Election*. Stanford, CA: Stanford University Press.

King, Gary. 1997. *A Solution to the Ecological Inference Problem: Reconstructing Individual Behavior from Aggregate Data*. Princeton, NJ: Princeton University Press.

King, Gary, Robert O. Keohane, and Sidney Verba. 1994. *Designing Social Inquiry: Scientific Inference in Qualitative Research*. Princeton, NJ: Princeton University Press.

Kitschelt, Herbert. 1992. "The Formation of Party Systems in East Central Europe." *Politics & Society* 20 (1): 7–50.

Kitschelt, Herbert. 1995. "Formation of Party Cleavages in Postcommunist Democracies." *Party Politics* 1 (4): 447–472.

Kitschelt, Herbert, Zdenka Manfeldova, Radoslaw Markowski, and Gabor Toka. 1999. *Post-Communist Party Systems: Competition, Representation, and Inter-Party Cooperation*. New York: Cambridge University Press.

Klingemann, Hans-Dieter, Andrea Volkens, Judith Bara, Ian Budge, and Michael McDonald. 2006. *Mapping Policy Preferences II : Estimates for Parties, Electors, and Governments in Eastern Europe, European Union, and OECD, 1990-2003.* Oxford: Oxford University Press.

Kostadinova, Tatianna. 2007. "Ethnic and Women's Representation under Mixed Electoral Systems." *Electoral Studies* 26 (2): 418–431.

Krook, Mona Lena. 2010. "Women's Representation in Parliament: A Qualitative-Comparative Analysis." *Political Studies* 58 (5): 886–908.

Krook, Mona Lena. 2009. *Quotas for Women in Politics: Gender and Candidate Selection Reform Worldwide.* New York: Oxford University Press.

Krook, Mona Lena and Judith Squires. 2006. "Gender Quotas in British Politics: Multiple Approaches and Methods in Feminist Research." *British Politics* 1 (1): 44-66.

Krupavicius, A. 1997. "The Lithuanian Parliamentary Elections of 1996." *Electoral Studies* 16 (4): 541–549.

Kunovich, Sheri and Pamela Paxton. 2005. "Pathways to Power: The Role of Political Parties in Women's National Political Representation." *American Journal of Sociology*, 111 (2): 505–552.

Laakso, Markku and Rein Taagepera. 1979. "'Effective' Number of Parties: A Measure with Application to West Europe." *Comparative Political Studies* 12 (1): 3–27.

Lardeyret, Guy. 1991. "The Problem with PR." *Journal of Democracy* 2 (3): 30–35.

Lijphart, Arend. 1971. "Comparative Politics and Comparative Method." *American Political Science Review* 65 (3): 682–93.

Lijphart, Arend. 1984. *Democracies: Patterns of Majoritarian and Consensus Government in Twenty-One Countries.* New Haven, CT: Yale University Press.

Lijphart, Arend. 1991. "Constitutional Design for Divided Societies." *Journal of Democracy* 2 (1): 72–84.

Lijphart, Arend. 1994. *Electoral Systems and Party Systems: A Study of Twenty-Seven Democracies, 1945–1990.* Oxford: Oxford University Press.

Lijphart, Arend. 2004. "Constitutional Choices for New Democracies." *Journal of Democracy* 15 (2): 96–109.

Lindberg, Staffan I. 2004. "Women's Empowerment and Democratization: The Effects of Electoral Systems, Participation, and Experience in Africa." *Studies in Comparative International Development* 39 (1): 28–53.

Lipset, Seymour and Stein Rokkan. 1967. "Cleavage Structures, Party Systems, and Voter Alignments." In: Lipset, S. and Rokkan, S. (eds.), *Party Systems and Voter Alignments: Cross-National Perspectives.* New York: The Free Press.

Madrid, Raul. 2005a. "Indigenous Voters and Party System Fragmentation." *Electoral Studies* 25 (4): 689–707.

Madrid, Raul. 2005b. "Ethnic Cleavages and Electoral Volatility in Latin America." *Comparative Politics* 38 (1): 1–20.

Madrid, Raul. 2008. "The Rise of Ethnopopulism in Latin America." *World Politics* 60 (3): 475–508.

Maeda, Ko. 2008. "Re-Examining the Contamination Effect of Japan's Mixed Electoral System Using the Treatment-Effects Model." *Electoral Studies* 27 (4): 723–731.

Mainwaring, Scott. 1999. *Rethinking Party Systems in the Third Wave of Democratization: The Case of Brazil.* Stanford, CA: Stanford University Press.

Mainwaring, Scott and Timothy Scully. 1995. "Introduction: Party Systems in Latin America." In: Mainwaring, S. and Scully, T. (Eds.), *Building Democratic Institutions: Party Systems in Latin America*. Stanford, CA: Stanford University Press.

Mainwaring, Scott and Matthew Shugart. 1997. "Juan Linz, Presidentialism, and Democracy: A Critical Appraisal." *Comparative Politics* 29 (4): 449–471.

Mainwaring, Scott and Mariano Torcal. 2006. "Party System Institutionalization and Party System Theory after the Third Wave of Democratisation." In: Katz, R. and Crotty, W. (eds.), *Handbook of Political Parties*. London: Sage Publications.

Mainwaring, Scott and Edurne Zoco. 2007. "Historical Sequences and the Stabilization of Interparty Competition: Electoral Volatility in Old and New Democracies." *Party Politics* 13 (2): 155–178.

Mansbridge, Jane. 1999. "Should Blacks Represent Blacks and Women Represent Women? A Contingent 'Yes'." *The Journal of Politics* 61 (3): 628–657.

Massicotte, Louis and Andre Blais. 1999. "Mixed Electoral Systems: A Conceptual and Empirical Survey." *Electoral Studies* 18 (3): 341–366.

Matland, Richard. 1993. "Institutional Variables Affecting Female Representation in National Legislatures: The Case of Norway." *Journal of Politics* 55 (3): 737–755.

Matland, Richard. 1998. "Women's Legislative Representation in National Legislatures: A Comparison of Democracies in Developed and Developing Countries." *Legislative Studies Quarterly* 28 (1): 109–125.

Matland, Richard and Kathleen Montgomery (eds.). 2003. *Women's Access to Political Power in Post-Communist Europe*. Oxford: Oxford University Press.

Matland, Richard and Dudley Studlar. 1996. "The Contagion of Women Candidates in Single Member and Multi-Member Districts." *Journal of Politics* 58 (3): 707–733.

Matland, Richard and M. Taylor. 1997. "Electoral System Effect on Women's Representation: Theoretical Arguments and Evidence from Costa Rica." *Comparative Political Studies* 30 (2): 186–210.

Mayorga, Rene Antonio. 1997. "Bolivia's Silent Revolution." *Journal of Democracy* 8 (1): 142–156.

Mayorga, René Antonio. 2001. "Electoral Reform in Bolivia: Origins of the Mixed Member Proportional System." In: Shugart, M. and Wattenberg, M. (eds.), *Mixed Member Electoral Systems: The Best of Both Worlds?* New York: Oxford University Press.

McFaul, Michael. 1996. *Russia Between Elections: What the December 1995 Results Really Mean*. Washington, DC: Carnegie Endowment for International Peace.

McFaul, Michael. 2001. "Explaining Party Formation and Nonformation in Russia: Actors, Institutions, and Chance." *Comparative Political Studies* 34 (10): 1159–1187.

McKean, Margaret A. and Ethan Scheiner. 2000. "Japan's New Electoral System: La plus ca change." *Electoral Studies* 19 (4): 447–477.

Meier, Petra. 2004. "The Mutual Contagion Effect of Legal and Party Quotas: A Belgian Perspective." *Party Politics* 10 (5): 583–600.

Mickiewicz, Ellen. 1997. *Changing Channels: Television and the Struggle for Power in Russia*. Oxford: Oxford University Press.

Mickiewicz, Ellen. 2008. *Television, Power, and the Public in Russia*. Cambridge: Cambridge University Press.

Milazzo, Caitlin and Ethan Scheiner. 2011. "When Do You Follow the (National) Leader? Party Switching by Subnational Legislators in Japan." *Electoral Studies* 30 (1): 148–161.

Mizusaki, Setsufumi and Hiroki Mori. 1998. "Tokuhyo Deta kara mita Heiritsusei no Mekanizumu" [Examining the mechanism of parallel mixed system from voting data]. *Senkyo Kenkyu* [Japanese Journal of Electoral Studies] 13: 50–59.

Moser, Robert G. 1995. "The Impact of the Electoral System on Post-Communist Party Development: the Case of the 1993 Russian Parliamentary Elections." *Electoral Studies* 14 (4): 377–398.

Moser, Robert G. 1997. "The Impact of Parliamentary Electoral Systems in Russia." *Post-Soviet Affairs* 13 (3): 284–302.

Moser, Robert G. 1999a. "Electoral Systems and the Number of Parties in Post-Communist States." *World Politics* 51 (3): 359–384.

Moser, Robert G. 1999b. "Independents and Party Formation: Elite Partisanship as an Intervening Variable in Russian Politics." *Comparative Politics* 31 (2): 147–165.

Moser, Robert G. 2001a. *Unexpected Outcomes: Electoral Systems, Political Parties, and Representation in Russia*. Pittsburgh: University of Pittsburgh Press.

Moser, Robert G. 2001b. "The Effects of Electoral Systems on Women's Representation in Post-Communist States." *Electoral Studies* 20 (3): 353–369.

Moser, Robert G. 2001c. "Ethnic Diversity, Electoral Systems, and the Number of Parties in Postcommunist States." Prepared for presentation at the Annual Meeting of the American Political Science Association, San Francisco.

Moser, Robert G. 2008. "Electoral Systems and the Representation of Ethnic Minorities: Evidence from Russia." *Comparative Politics* 40 (3): 273–292.

Moser, Robert G. and Ethan Scheiner. 2000. "A Cross-National Study of Strategic Voting in Mixed Electoral Systems." Prepared for presentation at the Annual Meeting of the American Political Science Association, Washington, DC.

Moser, Robert G. and Ethan Scheiner. 2004. "Mixed Electoral Systems and Electoral System Effects: Controlled Comparison and Cross-National Analysis." *Electoral Studies* 23: 575–599.

Moser, Robert G. and Ethan Scheiner. 2005. "Strategic Ticket Splitting and the Personal Vote in Mixed-Member Electoral Systems." *Legislative Studies Quarterly* 30 (2): 259–276.

Moser, Robert G., and Ethan Scheiner. 2009. "Strategic Voting in Established and New Democracies: Ticket Splitting in Mixed-Member Electoral Systems." *Electoral Studies* 28 (1): 51–61.

Moser, Robert G., Ethan Scheiner and Caitlin Milazzo. ND. "Social Diversity Affects the Number of Parties Even Under First-Past-the-Post Rules." Unpublished working paper, UC Davis.

Mozaffar, Shaheen, James Scarritt, and Glen Galaich. 2003. "Electoral Institutions, Ethnopolitical Cleavages, and Party Systems in Africa's Emerging Democracies." *American Political Science Review* 97 (3): 379–390.

Myagkov, Mikhail, Peter Ordeshook, and Dmitri Shakin. 2009. *The Forensics of Electoral Fraud: Russia and Ukraine*. New York: Cambridge University Press.

Nagahisa, Toshio. 1995. "The Electoral Reform That Can Mobilize Japan for Security Cooperation." *Pacific Focus* 10 (2): 73–100.

Niemi, Richard, M. Franklin, and G. Whitten. 1992. "Constituency Characteristics, Individual Characteristics, and Tactical Voting in the 1987 British General Elections." *British Journal of Political Science* 22 (1): 131–137.

Norris, Pippa. 1985. "Women's Legislative Participation in Western Europe." *West European Politics* 8 (4): 90–101.

Norris, Pippa. 1987. *Politics and Sexual Equality*. Boulder, CO: Lynne Rienner Publishers.

Norris, Pippa. 1993. "Conclusions: Comparing Legislative Recruitment." In: Lovenduski J. and Norris, P. (eds.), *Gender and Party Politics*. London: Sage.

Norris, Pippa. 2004. *Electoral Engineering: Voting Rules and Political Behavior*. New York: Cambridge University Press.

Oates, Sarah. 2005. "Where's the Party?: Television and Political Image in Russia." In: Voltmer, K. (ed.), *Mass Media and New Democracies*. London: Routledge

Oates, Sarah. 2006. *Television, Democracy and Elections in Russia*. London: Routledge.

Ordeshook, Peter and Olga Shvetsova. 1994. "Ethnic Heterogeneity, District Magnitude, and the Number of Parties." *American Journal of Political Science* 38 (1): 100–123.

Paxton, Pamela and Sheri Kunovich. 2003. "Women's Political Representation: The Importance of Ideology." *Social Forces* 82 (1): 87–113.

Persson, Torsten. 2002. "Do Political Institutions Shape Economic Policy?" *Econometrica* 70 (3): 883–905.

Persson, Torsten, G. Tabellini and F. Trebbi. 2003. "Electoral Rules and Corruption." *Journal of the European Economic Association* 1 (4): 958–989.

Phillips, Anne. 1995. *The Politics of Presence*. Oxford: Clarendon Press.

Przeworski, Adam, Michael Alvarez, Jose Chiebub, and Fernando Limongi. 2000. *Democracy and Development: Political Institutions and Well-Being in the World*. New York: Cambridge University Press.

Powell, Jr., G. Bingham. 1982. *Contemporary Democracies: Participation, Stability, and Violence*. Cambridge, MA: Harvard University Press.

Putnam, Robert. 1993. *Making Democracy Work*. Princeton, NJ: Princeton University Press.

Rae, Douglas. 1967. *The Political Consequences of Electoral Laws*. New Haven, CT: Yale University Press.

Reed, Steven R. 1990. "Structure and Behavior: Extending Duverger's Law to the Japanese Case." *British Journal of Political Science* 20 (3): 335–356.

Reed, Steven R. 1999. "Strategic Voting in the 1996 Japanese General Election." *Comparative Political Studies* 32 (2): 257–270.

Reilly, Ben. 2002. "Electoral Systems for Divided Societies." *Journal of Democracy* 13 (2): 156–170.

Reynolds, Andrew. 1999. "Women in the Legislatures and Executives of the World." *World Politics* 51 (4): 547–572.

Reynolds, Andrew. 2011. *Designing Democracy in a Dangerous World*. Oxford: Oxford University Press.

Reynolds, Andrew and John Carey. 2012. "Getting Elections Wrong." *Journal of Democracy* 23 (1): 164–168.

Reynolds, Andrew, Ben Reilly, and Andrew Ellis. 2005. *Electoral System Design: The New International IDEA Handbook*. Stockholm: International Institute for Democracy and Electoral Assistance.

Riker, William. 1982. "The Two-Party System and Duverger's Law: An Essay on the History of Political Science." *American Political Science Review* 76 (4): 753–766.

Riker, William. 1986. "Duverger's Law Revisited." In: Lijphart, A. and Grofman, B. (eds.), *Electoral Laws and their Political Consequences*. New York: Agathon Press.

Roberts, Geoffrey K. 1988. "The 'Second-Vote' Campaign Strategy of the West German Free Democratic Party." *European Journal of Political Research* 16 (3): 317–337.

Rosenbluth, Frances, Rob Salmond and Michael F. Thies. 2006. "Welfare Works: Explaining Female Legislative Representation." *Politics & Gender* 2 (2): 165–192.

Rosenbluth, Frances and Ross Schaap. 2003. "The Domestic Politics of Banking Regulation," *International Organization* 57 (2): 307–336.

Rosenbluth, Frances and Michael Thies. 2001. "The Electoral Foundations of Japan's Banking Regulation." *Policy Studies Journal* 29 (1): 23–37.

Rosenbluth, Frances and Michael F. Thies. 2002. "The Political Economy of Japanese Pollution Regulation." *The American Asian Review* 20 (1): 1–32.

Rule, Wilma. 1987. "Electoral Systems, Contextual Factors, and Women's Opportunity for Election to Parliament in Twenty-Three Democracies." *Western Political Quarterly* 40 (3): 477–498.

Rule, Wilma. 1994. "Parliaments of, by, and for the People: Except for Women?" In: Rule, W. and Zimmerman, J. (eds.), *Electoral Systems in Comparative Perspective: Their Impact on Women and Minorities*. Westport, CT: Greenwood Press.

Salmond, Rob. 2006. "Proportional Representation and Female Parliamentarians." *Legislative Studies Quarterly* 31 (2): 175–204.

Samuels, David J. and Matthew S. Shugart. 2010. *Presidents, Parties, and Prime Ministers: How the Separation of Powers Affects Party Organization and Behavior*. New York: Cambridge University Press.

Sartori, Giovanni. 1968. "Political Development and Political Engineering." In: Montgomery, J. and Hirschman, A. (eds.), *Public Policy*. New York: Cambridge University Press.

Sartori, Giovanni. 1976. *Parties and Party Systems: A Framework for Analysis*. New York: Cambridge University Press.

Sartori, Giovanni. 1986. "The Influence of Electoral Systems: Faulty Laws or Faulty Method?" In: Grofman, B. and Lijphart, A. (eds.), *Electoral Laws and their Political Consequences*. New York: Agathon Press.

Sartori, Giovanni. 1994. *Comparative Constitutional Engineering*. New York: New York University Press.

Scarrow, Susan E. 2001. "Germany: The Mixed-Member System as a Political Compromise." In: Shugart, M. and Wattenberg, M. (eds.), *Mixed-Member Electoral Systems: The Best of Both Worlds?* Oxford: Oxford University Press.

Schedler, Andreas. 1998. "What is Democratic Consolidation?" *Journal of Democracy* 9 (2): 91–107.

Scheiner, Ethan. 2005. "Pipelines of Pork: A Model of Local Opposition Party Failure." *Comparative Political Studies* 38 (7): 799–823.

Scheiner, Ethan. 2006. *Democracy Without Competition in Japan: Opposition Failure in a One-Party Dominant State*. New York: Cambridge University Press.

Scheiner, Ethan. 2007. "Clientelism in Japan: The Importance and Limits of Institutional Explanations" In: Kitschelt, H. and Wilkinson, S. (eds.), *Patrons, Clients, and Policies: Patterns of Democratic Accountability and Political Competition*. New York: Cambridge University Press.

Scheiner, Ethan. 2008. "Does Electoral System Reform Work? Electoral System Lessons from Reforms of the 1990s." *Annual Review of Political Science* 11: 161–181.

Scheiner, Ethan and Filippo Tronconi. 2011. "Unanticipated Consequences of Electoral Reform in Italy and Japan." In: Giannetti D. and Grofman B. (eds.), *A Natural*

Experiment on Electoral Law Reform: Evaluating the Long Run Consequences of 1990s Electoral Reform in Italy and Japan. New York: Springer.

Schmidt, Gregory D. and Kyle L. Saunders. 2004. "Effective Quotas, Relative Party Magnitude, and the Success of Female Candidates: Peruvian Municipal Elections in Comparative Perspective." *Comparative Political Studies* 37 (6): 704–734.

Shugart, Matthew. 2005. "Comparative Electoral Systems Research: The Maturation of a Field and New Challenges Ahead." In: Gallagher, M. and Mitchell, P. S. (eds.), *Politics of Electoral Systems*. New York: Oxford University Press.

Shugart, Matthew S. and John Carey. 1992. *Presidents and Assemblies*. Cambridge: Cambridge University Press.

Shugart, Matthew S. and Martin P. Wattenberg. 2001a. "Conclusion: Are Mixed-Member Systems the Best of Both Worlds?" In: Shugart, M. and Wattenberg, M. (eds.), *Mixed Member Electoral Systems: The Best of Both Worlds?* New York: Oxford University Press.

Shugart, Matthew S. and Martin P. Wattenberg. 2001b. "Introduction: The Electoral Reform of the Twenty-First Century?" In: Shugart, M. and Wattenberg, M. (eds.), *Mixed Member Electoral Systems: The Best of Both Worlds?* New York: Oxford University Press.

Shugart, Matthew S. and Martin P. Wattenberg, M. (eds.). 2001c. *Mixed Member Electoral Systems: The Best of Both Worlds?* New York: Oxford University Press.

Schwindt-Bayer, Leslie A. 2005. "The Incumbency Advantage and Women's Election to Legislative Office." *Electoral Studies* 24 (2): 227–244.

Smith, Eric R. A. N. and Richard L. Fox. 2001. "The Electoral Fortunes of Women Candidates for Congress." *Political Research Quarterly* 54 (1): 205–221.

Singer, Matthew. Forthcoming. "Was Duverger Correct? Single-Member District Election Outcomes in 53 Countries." *British Journal of Political Science*.

Singer, Matthew and Laura Stephenson. 2009. "The Political Context and Duverger's Theory: Evidence at the District Level." *Electoral Studies* 28 (3): 480–491.

Spafford, Duff. 1972. "Electoral Systems and Voters' Behavior: Comments and a Further Test." *Comparative Politics* 5 (1): 129–134.

Sperling, Valerie. 1999. *Organizing Women in Contemporary Russia*. Cambridge: Cambridge University Press.

Stoll, Heather. ND. *Changing Societies, Changing Party Systems*. Unpublished book manuscript, UC Santa Barbara.

Stoll, Heather. 2004. "Social Cleavages, Political Institutions, and Party Systems: Putting Preferences Back into the Fundamental Equation of Politics." Unpublished doctoral dissertation, Stanford University.

Stoll, Heather. 2008. "Social Cleavages and the Number of Parties: How the Measures You Choose Affect the Answers You Get." *Comparative Political Studies* 41 (11): 1439–1465.

Taagepera, Rein. 2007. *Predicting Party Sizes: The Logic of Simple Electoral Systems*. Oxford: Oxford University Press.

Taagepera, Rein and Matthew S. Shugart. 1989. *Seats and Votes: The Effects and Determinants of Electoral Systems*. New Haven, CT: Yale University Press.

Tavits, Margit and Taavi Annus. 2006. "Learning to Make Votes Count: The Role of Democratic Experience." *Electoral Studies* 25 (1): 72–90.

Valdini, Melody. 2005. "The Signal of Gender: The Impact of Electoral Rules on the Voters' Use of Information Shortcuts," Paper presented at the annual meeting of the American Political Science Association, Washington, DC.

Valdini, Melody. 2006. *Electoral Institutions and Information Shortcuts: The Effect of Decisive Intraparty Competition on the Behavior of Voters and Party Elites.* Unpublished dissertation, UC San Diego.

Wahman, Michael. ND. "Duverger's Law in Africa: Voter Coordination in 20 African Single Member District Elections." Unpublished manuscript.

World Values Survey 2005 Official Data File v.20090901. 2009. World Values Survey Association (www.worldvaluessurvey.org).

Yoon, Mi Yung. 2004. "Explaining Women's Legislative Representation in Sub-Saharan Africa." *Legislative Studies Quarterly* 29 (3): 447–468.

Index

additional member system, in Germany, 62
Albania, 48
  as new democracy, 81
  women's representation in, 218
alternative vote (AV), xv
  in Australia, 4
Alvarez, R. Michael, 152
Armenia, 48
  disproportionality in, 108
  as new democracy, 81
  non-institutionalized party system in, 82
  party identification in, 82
  SMDs in, 79, 82
  women's representation in, 218
Australia, AV in, 4
AV. *See* alternative vote

Bawn, Kathleen, 122
bias
  in contamination critique, 52–54, 59–61
  in controlled comparison of electoral systems, 59–61
  male leader, 223–224
  against women in electoral systems, 222–223, 224
Blais, Andre, 8, 20
Boehmke, Frederick, 152
Bolivia
  disproportionality in, 108
  mixed-member electoral system in, 48
  as new democracy, 81
  overhang seats in, 65

PR system in, 14
  SF-ratios in, 158
  women's representation in, 218
Bowler, Shaun, 8, 20
Brancati, Dawn, 238
Brazauskus Social Democratic Coalition, 143
Brazil, open-list PR system in, 4, 43
Bulgaria, 48
  as new democracy, 81
  women's representation in, 218

Canada, 52
Carey, John, 238
Carroll, Royce, 106
Cheibub, Jose, 238
Chhibber, Pradeep, 26
Clark, William, 20, 150, 181, 246
closed-list PR systems, xv, 4
  minority representation under, 24
  women as candidates in, 24, 33–34, 208, 209, 211
compensation seats, xv
contamination critique, 50–61, 240
  basics of, 50–51
  biased samples in, 52–54, 59–61
  countervailing evidence and, 54–58
  limitations of, 51–54
  linkage systems and, 55
  longitudinal analysis and, 60–61
  of mixed-member electoral systems, 91
  principal functions of, 59–60
  SMDs and, 51–52
  systematic cross-national analysis and, 56–58, 60–61
context conditionality, 20

controlled comparison, xv. *See also*
    contamination critique
    bias in, 59–61
    criticism of, 45
    cross-national analysis in, 60–61
    Duverger's law under, 49
    female representation in, 47–49
    longitudinal analysis and, 60–61
    mixed-member electoral systems and, 5–6,
        37, 44–46, 239–240
    research applications for, 45–46
    social context and, 51
    validity of, 51
Cox, Gary, 8, 20, 151, 183, 245, 246, 255
Croatia
    disproportionality in, 108
    mixed-member electoral system in, 48
    as new democracy, 81
    PR system in, 66
    women's representation in, 218

decoy party PR lists, 63
democracies. *See also* established democracies;
    new democracies
    differences among/within, 17–19
    party system institutionalization and,
        18–19, 81–85
    political context and, 20–21
disproportionality, xv
    in Armenian elections, 108
    in Bolivian elections, 108
    in Croatian elections, 108
    democratic context and, 113
    district magnitude and, 87–88
    Duverger's law and, 71–72
    effective number of candidates and,
        92
    electoral expectations and, 80
    FPTP system and, 73
    in French elections, 87
    in German elections, 108
    in Hungarian elections, 108
    in Israeli elections, 79
    in Italian elections, 108
    in Japanese elections, 108
    legal thresholds and, 87–88
    LSq measure for, 78, 112–114
    in Macedonian elections, 108
    as mechanical effect, 71, 72, 91–92, 93, 96,
        113
    in mixed-member electoral systems, 77,
        79–80, 91–96
    in new democracies, 76–77

    in New Zealand elections, 108
    number of political parties and, 77–79
    over time, 96
    as psychological effect, 72
    in Russian elections, 2, 93–94, 108
    in Scottish elections, 108
    SMDs and, 92–93
    in Ukraine elections, 108
    in U.S. elections, 80, 87
    in Venezuelan elections, 108
    in Welsh elections, 108
district magnitude, xv, 3
    disproportionality and, 87–88
    Duverger's law and, 71
    in mixed-member electoral systems, 65–66
    number of candidates and, 72, 96–100
    SMDs and, 71
    social cleavage theory of party origins and,
        29–30
    social/ethnic diversity and, 183
    women as candidates and, 209, 211–212
diversity. *See* ethnic diversity; social diversity
Duch, Raymond, 152
Duverger, Maurice, 25
    on social/ethnic diversity, 181–182, 183
Duvergerian, xv
    equilibrium in new democracies, 75–77,
        153, 154, 247–249
Duverger's Hypothesis, 71
    two-round majority electoral systems and,
        71
Duverger's law, xv, 25–27, 37–38, 70–77
    assumption of information under, 73–77
    controlled comparison and, 49
    criticism of, 26–27
    disproportionality and, 71–72
    at the district level, 25
    district magnitude and, 71
    FPTP system and, 25–27, 73, 245–246
    limitations of, 244–249
    mechanical effects and, 70–71
    in new democracies, 73–77, 245–246
    as parsimonious theory, 256–257
    party system institutionalization and,
        83–84
    projection and, 72
    psychological effects of, 71
    revisions to, 247
    SMDs and, 71
    social/ethnic diversity and, 188, 189,
        246–247
    strategic defections and, 38, 151, 242
    strategic voting and, 27, 130

Eckstein, Harry, 59
ecological inference (EI) analysis, 203, 254
effective number of candidates, xvi
  disproportionality and, 92
  district magnitude and, 96–100
  electoral rules as influence on, 98–120
  in established democracies, 97, 98–99
  in Germany, per SMD, 96
  in Hungary, per SMD, 96–97, 105–106
  in Japan, per SMD, 96
  margin of victory and, 142
  in new democracies, 97
  in SMDs, 96–100, 114–115, 117
  in Ukraine, per SMD, 96–97
  in unlinked tiers system, 97
effective number of ethnic groups (ENEG),
    xvi
  in New Zealand, 191
  social/ethnic diversity measures and,
    191–192
effective number of parties (ENEP), xvi
  quantitative analysis of, 203–205
  social/ethnic diversity measures and,
    191–192, 204
effective threshold, xvi
EI analysis. *See* ecological inference analysis
electoral college, in U.S., 78
electoral engineering, 257–258
electoral formulas
  for FPTP system, 65
  in mixed-member electoral systems, 65
  for SMDs, 65, 86–87
electoral rules. *See also* Duverger's law;
    strategic behavior, under electoral rules
  assumptions and, 21–22
  candidate type influenced by, 23
  democratic experience and, 24
  disproportionality and, 72, 91–92, 93,
    113
  effective number of candidates influenced
    by, 98–120
  in established democracies, 8–9
  under FPTP system, 9, 13
  mechanical effects of, 22–23
  in mixed-member electoral systems, 43–44,
    85–88, 108, 243–244
  in new democracies, expected effects of,
    73–74
  non-mechanical effects of, 22, 23
  number of political parties and, 23–24,
    25
  party institutionalization and, 24, 94
  personal voting and, 127

psychological effects and, 100–103
quantitative analysis of, 203–205
SF-ratios influenced and, 157–158
sincere behavior and, 23
SMDs and, 13
social/ethnic diversity influenced by, 23–24,
    195–196, 204
strategic behavior under, 23, 24–25, 32
strategic defection and, 150–152
strategic voting and, 150
theories of, 23–24
underrepresented groups and, 24
women candidates and, 214–216
electoral systems, 2, 3–5. *See also* controlled
    comparison; democracies; minorities, and
    electoral systems; mixed-member electoral
    systems; proportional representation
    system; women, election of
  assumptions about, 22–25
  centralized governments and, 238
  conditionality and, 20–22
  context conditionality and, 20, 35–37
  decentralized governments and, 238
  district-level analysis of, 7, 37–39, 250–251
  effective number of candidates and,
    98–120
  election of women and, 33–35
  engineering of, 257–258
  expectations for, 241
  institutionalized party system and, xvi
  in Japan, 1–3
  non-Duvergian equilibrium within, 75–77
  non-institutionalized party system and,
    xvii
  outcomes for, 241
  party system institutionalization and, xvii,
    18–19
  permissive, xvii, 4, 29
  political context and, 20–21
  pure, xviii
  restrictive, xviii, 4
  in Russia, 1–3
  social/ethnic diversity and, 29–32, 181–184
  strategic voting and, 25–29
  study of, 15
  STV, xviii, 4
  theories about, 22–25
  women's representation and, 210–214
Elster, Jon, 238
endogeneity, and party institutionalization,
    83–84
ENEG. *See* effective number of ethnic groups
ENEP. *See* effective number of parties

established democracies, xvi, 81
　average effective number of candidates in,
　　97, 98–99
　categorization of, 85
　new democracies compared to, 17–18
　psychological effect in, 101–102
　SF-ratios and, 159–161
　social/ethnic diversity in, 32
　strategic defection in, 28, 165
　strategic voting in, 27–28, 150
　women as candidates in, 35, 209, 213–214,
　　215–216
ethnic diversity
　curvilinear models for, 204
　district magnitude and, 183
　district-level analysis of, 180–181, 187–190
　Duverger on, 181–182, 183
　Duverger's law and, 188, 189, 246–247
　Ecological Inference analysis and, 203, 254
　economic cleavages and, 202
　electoral rules as influence on, 23–24,
　　195–196, 204
　electoral systems and, 29–32, 181–184
　ENEG and, 191–192
　ENEP and, 191–192, 204
　in established democracies, 32
　under FPTP system, 21, 184–185, 192–197
　fractionalization measures for, 191
　in Japan, electoral results from, 190–191
　in new democracies, 32
　in New Zealand, electoral results from,
　　190–191, 197–199, 206–207
　number of parties influenced by, 39–40,
　　181–184, 190–191, 204
　party fragmentation and, 32, 34–35, 181,
　　185–190, 192–197
　political entrepreneurship and, 186–187
　presidential elections and, 189
　quantitative analysis of, 203–205
　in Russia, electoral results from, 190–191
　in SMDs, 183, 197–199
　social cleavage and, 180
　strategic behavior influenced by, 24–25,
　　30–32, 203
　strategic voting and, 30–32, 185
　in Ukraine, electoral results from, 190–191
　urbanization levels as measure of, in Japan,
　　191
　in Wales, electoral results from, 190–191
European Union. *See specific nations*

females. *See* women
Ferrara, Federico, 50

Filippov, Mikhail, 245
first-past-the-post (FPTP) system, xvi
　disproportionality under, 73
　Duverger's law and, 25–27, 73, 245–246
　electoral formula and, 65
　electoral rules and, 9, 13
　LSq calculations and, 80
　mechanical effect of, 26
　mixed-member electoral systems compared,
　　56–58
　in New Zealand, 55
　number of political parties under, 29
　psychological effect of, 26
　social/ethnic diversity and, 21, 184–185,
　　192–197
　strategic behavior under, 23
　strategic voting under, 30–32, 123
　in U.S., 54
FPTP system. *See* first-past-the-post system
fragmentation. *See* party system fragmentation
France
　disproportionality in, 87
　electoral system in, 87
Franzese, Robert, 20

gender. *See also* women, election of
　postcommunist states and, 215
Germany
　additional member system in, 62
　average effective number of candidates, per
　　SMD, 96
　compensation seats in, 127
　disproportionality in, 108
　as established democracy, 81
　mixed-member electoral system in, 44, 48,
　　53–54
　MMP system in, 62–63
　overhang seats in, 64–65
　personal voting in, 126, 128–129, 140
　PR tier and, 13, 62
　SF-ratios in, 154, 155, 158
　strategic defection in, 126, 128, 133–134
　strategic voting in, 135
　ticket splitting in, 122, 140
　women's representation in, 218
Golder, Matt, 20, 181, 246
Grofman, Bernard, 8, 20

Herron, Erik, 50
Hicken, Allen, 250
Hungary
　average effective number of candidates, per
　　SMD, 96–97, 105–106

disproportionality in, 108
mixed-member electoral system in, 48
as new democracy, 81
party system institutionalization in, 18–19
unlinked tiers system in, 62–64
women's representation in, 218

incumbency, 212
institutionalized party system, xvi
political context and, 236–239
Israel, disproportionality in, 79
Italy
controlled comparison of electoral system in, 45–46
decoy party PR lists in, 63
disproportionality in, 108
as established democracy, 81
mixed-member electoral system in, 48, 52
PR tier and, 13
scorporo system in, 63
SF-ratios in, 158
unlinked tiers in, 63–64
women's representation in, 218

Jackman, Robert, 16
Japan
average effective number of candidates, per SMD, 96
disproportionality in, 108
electoral systems in, 1–3
mixed-member electoral system in, 1, 48, 52–53
MMM system in, 1
party fragmentation in, from social/ethnic diversity, 192–195
personal voting in, 126, 128–129, 134–135
PR tier and, 13
SF-ratios in, 158
SMDs in, 2
SNTV system in, 128
social/ethnic diversity in, electoral results with, 190–191
strategic defection in, 126
strategic voting in, 135
ticket splitting in, 122, 124
unlinked tiers in, 61, 64
women's representation in, 218
Jones, Mark, 188

Karp, Jeffrey, 55
Keohane, Robert, 59
King, Gary, 59
Kollman, Ken, 26, 150

least-squares index (LSq), xvi
for disproportionality, 78, 112–114
FPTP systems and, 80
leftist political parties, women as candidates in, 213
legal thresholds, xvi
disproportionality and, 87–88
in mixed-member electoral systems, 65–66
in PR systems, 4
women's representation and, 212, 229
Lesotho, 48
women's representation in, 218
Liberal Democratic Party of Russia, 94
Lijphart, Arend, 16, 183
linked tiers, xvi, 62–63. *See also*
mixed-member proportional system
election of women and, 229
in mixed-member electoral systems, 61–65
PR and, xvi, 77–78
SF-ratios and, 158
strategic behavior and, 167
Lipset, Seymour Martin, 183
Lithuania, 48
Brazauskas Social Democratic Coalition in, 143
as new democracy, 81, 97
personal voting in, 126, 128–129
SF-ratios in, 159
strategic defection in, 126
women's representation in, 218
low district magnitude, 72
LSq. *See* least-squares index

M + 1 rule, xvi
Macedonia, 48
disproportionality in, 108
as new democracy, 81
SF-ratios in, 159
women's representation in, 218
Maeda, Ko, 54
Mainwaring, Scott, 238, 251, 253
male leader bias, 223–224
margin of victory
candidate identity and, 142
control variables for, 142–143
in established democracies, SF ratios and, 161, 165–166
independent variables for, 141–143
models for, in mixed-member electoral systems, 141–148
in new democracies, SF ratios and, 161, 165–166
personal voting as influence on, 131–137

margin of victory (*cont.*)
  previous elections as influence on, 136–137, 147
  SF-ratios and, 161, 165–166
  strategic voting as influence on, 125, 131–137
Matland, Richard, 20, 212, 255
mechanical effects, xvi
  of disproportionality, 71, 72, 91–92, 93, 113
  of Duverger's law, 70–71
  of electoral rules, 22–23
  of FPTP systems, 26
  in mixed-member electoral systems, 91–96
  non-mechanical effects compared to, 22, 23
media, in new democracies, 73
minorities, and electoral systems. *See also* ethnic diversity; social diversity; women, election of
  closed-list PR systems and, 24
  representation of, electoral rules as influence on, 24, 254–255
mixed electoral systems. *See* mixed-member electoral systems
mixed-member electoral systems, xvi–xvii, 3–7
  basics of, 42–44
  in Bolivia, 48
  in Canada, 52
  classifications of, 61–66
  contamination effect and, 91
  controlled comparison and, 5–6, 37, 44–46, 239–240
  in Croatia, 48
  definitions of, 43
  disproportionality and, 77, 79–80, 91–96
  district magnitude and, 65–66
  electoral formula and, 65
  electoral rules and, 43–44, 85–88, 108, 243–244
  electoral rules in, 43–44, 85–88, 108, 243–244
  FPTP systems compared to, 56–58
  in Germany, 44, 48, 53–54
  in Hungary, 48
  international expansion of, 5, 44–45, 48
  in Italy, 48, 52
  in Japan, 1, 48, 52–53
  legal threshold and, 65–66
  linked tiers and, 61–65
  MMM, xvii
  MMP, xvii, 1
  in New Zealand, 48, 52

number of parties and, 90–105
personal voting and, 123–124
PR tier and, 66
psychological effects and, 100–103, 117–120
in Russia, 1, 48, 53
SF-ratios and, 155–157
SMD tier and, 44, 66, 68
SMDs and, 44, 66, 68
sociopolitical contexts and, 6–7
strategic voting in, 122–124
subtypes of, 61
ticket splitting in, 151
in Ukraine, 48, 53
unlinked tiers and, 43–44
in Venezuela, 48
women and, 240–243
mixed-member majoritarian (MMM) system, xvii, 1, 61
  in Japan, 1
  in Russia, 1
mixed-member proportional (MMP) system, xvii, 62–63
  in Germany, 62–63
  in New Zealand, 62–63
  overhang seats in, 64–65
MMM. *See* mixed-member majoritarian system
MMP system. *See* mixed-member proportional system
Moser, Robert, 245
multi-member districts, xvii
  SNTV electoral systems and, xviii
  STV electoral systems and, xviii
multiparty electoral systems, xvii

N, 78–79
Nagler, Jonathan, 152
Ncands, 79–80
Neto, Octavio Amorim, 183, 246
new democracies, xvii, 81
  average effective number of candidates in, 97
  categorization of, 85
  definition of, 81
  development of, over time, 76–77, 108, 252–253
  disproportionality and, 76–77
  Duverger's law and, 73–77, 245–246
  electoral volatility and, 18, 73–74
  endogeneity and, 83–84
  established democracies compared to, 17–18

expected effects of electoral rules in, 73–74, 77

margin of victory and SF ratios in, 161, 165–166

media infrastructure in, 73

non-Duvergian equilibrium and, 75–77

non-institutionalized party systems and, 81–83

opinion polling in, 73

party system institutionalization and, 74–75, 251–253

personal voting and, 127, 128–129, 135–136

poorly developed party systems and, 74–75

preference voting in, 152

presidentialism and, 106

projection and, 77

psychological effect in, 24, 101–102

SF-ratios and, 157–158, 159–161, 165

social/ethnic diversity in, 32

strategic defection in, 28, 152, 165

strategic voting in, 152

third wave of democratization and, 81

voter information in, 73–74

women as candidates in, 35, 209, 213–214

new institutionalism, 21

New Zealand

compensation seats in, 127

disproportionality in, 108

ENEG in, 191

as established democracy, 81

FPTP system in, 55

mixed-member electoral system in, 48, 52

MMP system in, 62–63

overhang seats in, 64–65

personal voting in, 126, 128

PR system in, 13

SF-ratios in, 158

SMDs in, 206

social/ethnic diversity and party fragmentation in, 190–191, 192–195, 197–199, 206–207

strategic defection in, 126, 129, 134

strategic voting in, 134, 135

ticket splitting in, 134

women's representation in, 218

Nishikawa, Misa, 50

non-institutionalized party system, xvii, 82

definition of, 81–83

endogeneity and, 83–84

SMDs and, 82

Nparties, 79–80

Ns, 78–79

Nv, 78–79

open-list PR systems, xvii

in Brazil, 4, 43

preference vote in, 4

opinion polling, in new democracies, 73

Ordeshook, Peter, 30, 183, 245, 246

overhang seats, 64–65

Palmer, Harvey, 152

party fragmentation. *See* party system fragmentation

party magnitude, xvii

party system fragmentation, 240–243

assumptions about, 186–187

in Japan, from social/ethnic diversity, 192–195

in New Zealand, from social/ethnic diversity, 192–195

political entrepreneurs and, 186–187

in postcommunist states, 216

in Russia, from social/ethnic diversity, 192–195

social/ethnic diversity as influence on, 32, 34–35, 181, 185–190, 192–197

in Ukraine, from social/ethnic diversity, 192–195

in Wales, from social/ethnic diversity, 195

women as candidates and, 34–35, 214–215, 230

party system institutionalization, xvii

components of, 18

within democracies, 18–19, 81–85

Duverger's law and, 83–84

electoral system effects and, 24, 94

in Hungary, 18–19

multivariable analyses for, 112

in new democracies, 74–75, 251–253

presidentialism and, 106

in Russia, 19

SF-ratios and, 157–158

strategic defection and, 151–152

permissive electoral systems, xvii, 4, 72

social cleavage theory of party origins and, 29

personal voting

analysis of, 129–131

electoral rules as influence on, 127

expectations for, 126–128

in Germany, 126, 128–129, 140

in Japan, 126, 128–129, 134–135

margin of victory and, 131–137

personal voting (*cont.*)
  in mixed-member electoral systems,
    123–124
  national variations in, 128–129
  in new democracies, 127, 128–129,
    135–136
  in New Zealand, 126, 128
  previous elections as influence on, 136–137,
    147
  in SMDs, 125
  under SNTV electoral system, 128
  strategic voting and, 124–125
  ticket splitting and, 123–124
  unlinked tiers and, 127–128
placement mandate, xvii
plurality electoral systems, xvii. *See also*
    first-past-the-post system
political entrepreneurs, 186–187
political parties. *See also* party system
    fragmentation
  in Armenia, party identification and, 82
  disproportionality as influence on, 77–79
  electoral rules as influence on, 23–24, 25
  institutionalized party system and, xvi
  leftist, women as candidates in, 213
  in mixed-member electoral systems, 90–105
  in new democracies, 74–75
  party system institutionalization and, xvii,
    18–19
  rank-ordering preferences and, 75
  in Russia, party identification and, 82
  social cleavage theory, and origins of, 29
  social/ethnic diversity as influence on,
    39–40, 181–184
  strategic voting and, 25–29
  in Ukraine, party identification and, 82
postcommunist states. *See also specific nations*
  gender equality in, 215
  party system fragmentation in, 216
  women as candidates in, 215–216
PR system. *See* proportional representation
    system
preference revelation, 150
  strategic voting and, 150
preference vote, xvii–xviii
  in new democracies, 152
  in open-list PR, 4
presidential elections, social/ethnic diversity
    and, 189
presidentialism, 106
  in new democracies, 106
  party system institutionalization and, 106
projection, 72

Duverger's law and, 72
  in new democracies, 77
  presidentialism and, 72
  in SMDs, to national levels, 104–105, 119,
    120
proportional representation (PR) system, 4.
    See also closed-list PR systems;
    proportional representation tier
  closed-list, 4, 24
  definition of, xviii
  gender quotas and, 220–221
  legal threshold of representation in, 4
  open-list, xvii, 4, 43
  sincere behavior under, 23
  women as candidates under, 33–34,
    209–210, 211–213, 217–218, 221
proportional representation (PR) tier. *See also*
    mixed-member electoral systems;
    proportional representation system
  in Bolivia, 14
  compensation seats and, 43, 86, 127
  in Croatia, 66
  decoy party lists in Italy and, 63
  gender quotas and, 220–221
  in Germany, 13, 62
  in Italy, 13
  in Japan, 13
  legal threshold of representation in, 4
  linked tiers and, xvi, 77–78
  in New Zealand, 13
  in Russia, 14
  scorporo system and, 63
  SF-ratios and, 165
  SMD–PR vote gap and, 144, 145, 146
  in Ukraine, 14
  in Venezuela, 14
  women as candidates in, 33–34, 209–210,
    211–213, 217–221
psychological effect
  of Duverger's law, 71
  of electoral rules, 100–103
  in established democracies, 101–102
  of FPTP system, 26
  in mixed-member electoral systems,
    100–103, 117–120
  variables for, 118
  for voters, xviii
pure electoral systems, xviii
Putin, Vladimir, 163
Putnam, Robert, 45

Rae, Douglas, 183
Reed, Steven, 122

restrictive electoral systems, xviii, 4
Riker, William, 15, 151
Rokkan, Stein, 183
Russia
  campaign financing in, 94
  disproportionality in elections, 2, 93–94,
    108
  electoral systems in, 1–3
  electoral volatility in, 82
  extreme party proliferation in, 94
  Liberal Democratic Party of Russia in, 94
  mixed-member electoral system in, 1, 48, 53
  MMM system in, 1
  as new democracy, 81
  non-Duvergian equilibrium in, 164
  non-institutionalized party system in, 82
  party identification in, 82
  party system institutionalization in, 19
  personal voting in, 126, 128–129
  PR tier in, 14
  SF-ratios in, 154–155, 161–164
  SMDs in, 2, 79, 82
  social/ethnic diversity and party
    fragmentation in, 190–191, 192–195
  strategic defection in, 126
  United Russia Party in, 163, 164
  unlinked tiers and, 61
  Women of Russia Party in, 213
  women's representation in, 218

Sartori, Giovanni, 6, 21
scorporo system, 63
Scotland, 48
  compensation seats in, 127
  disproportionality in, 108
  as established democracy, 81
  personal voting in, 126, 128–129
  SF-ratios in, 158
  strategic defection in, 126, 129
  women's representation in, 218
SF-ratios, xviii, 152–164
  in Bolivia, 158
  Duvergerian equilibrium and, 153, 154
  electoral experience as factor in, 158
  electoral rules as influence on, 157–158
  in established democracies, 159–161
  explanatory variables for, 175–176
  in Germany, 154, 155, 158
  in Italy, 158
  in Japan, 158
  in linked tiers, 158
  in Lithuania, 159
  in Macedonia, 159

  margin of victory and, 161, 165–166
  mixed-member electoral systems and,
    155–157
  multivariate analysis of, 175–177, 179
  in new democracies, 157–158, 159–161,
    165
  in New Zealand, 158
  party system institutionalization and,
    157–158
  patterns in, 159
  PR systems and, 165
  in Russia, 154–155, 161–164
  in Scotland, 158
  strategic behavior and, 155–157
  strategic defection and, 152–158
  in Ukraine, 159
  in unlinked tiers, 158
  in Wales, 158
Shugart, Matthew, 15, 45, 238, 239
Shvetsova, Olga, 30, 183, 245, 246
sincere behavior, under electoral rules, 23
  in PR systems, 23
Singer, Matthew, 30, 67, 183, 246
single nontransferable vote (SNTV) electoral
  system, xviii, 4
  in Japan, 128
single transferable vote (STV) electoral system,
  xviii, 4
single-member districts (SMDs) system, xviii.
  See also SF-ratios; single-member districts
  (SMDs) tier
  constraining effects of, 99–100, 101, 107
  disproportionality and, 92–93
  district magnitude and, 71
  Duverger's law and, 71
  electoral formula, 65, 86–87
  electoral rules and, 13
  FPTP system and, xvi, 3–4, 9
  non-institutionalized party system and, 82
  personal voting in, 125
  projection to national levels for, 104–105,
    119, 120
  two-round majority electoral systems in,
    xix, 4
  in U.S., 54
  women as candidates in, 33, 34–35, 208,
    211, 217–221
single-member districts (SMDs) tier
  in Armenia, 79, 82
  contamination critique and, 51–52
  cross-national analysis of, 67–69
  effective number of candidates in, 96–100,
    114–115, 117

single-member districts (SMDs) tier (*cont.*)
  in Germany, 96
  in Hungary, 96–97
  in Japan, 2, 96
  in mixed-member electoral systems, 44, 66, 68
  in New Zealand, 206
  non-institutionalized party system and, 82
  personal voting in, 125
  PR seats as compensation for, 43, 86
  projection to national levels and, 104–105, 119, 120
  in Russia, 2, 79, 82
  SMD–PR vote gap and, 144, 145, 146
  social/ethnic diversity and party fragmentation in, 183, 197–199
  strategic defection in, 124, 125–129
  ticket splitting in, 123
  two-round majority electoral systems in, xix, 4
  in Ukraine, 79, 82, 96–97
  unlinked tiers system and, xix
  women as candidates in, 218
SMD–PR vote gap, 144, 145, 146
SMDs. *See* single-member districts
SNTV electoral system. *See* single nontransferable vote electoral system
social cleavage theory of party origins, 29
  district magnitude and, 29–30
  permissive electoral systems and, 29
  social/ethnic diversity and, 180
social diversity
  curvilinear models for, 204
  district magnitude and, 183
  district-level analysis of, 180–181, 187–190
  Duverger on, 181–182, 183
  Duverger's law and, 188, 189, 246–247
  ecological inference analysis and, 203, 254
  economic cleavages and, 202
  electoral rules as influence on, 23–24, 195–196, 204
  electoral systems and, 29–32, 181–184
  ENEG and, 191–192
  ENEP and, 191–192, 204
  in established democracies, 32
  under FPTP system, 21, 184–185, 192–197
  fractionalization measures for, 191
  institutional school and, 183
  in Japan, electoral results and, 190–191
  in new democracies, 32
  in New Zealand, electoral results from, 190–191, 197–199, 206–207

number of parties influenced by, 39–40, 181–184, 190–191, 204
  party fragmentation and, 32, 34–35, 181, 185–190, 192–197
  political entrepreneurship and, 186–187
  political expectations from, 191–192
  presidential elections and, 189
  quantitative analysis of, 203–205
  in Russia, electoral results and, 190–191
  in SMDs, 183, 197–199
  social cleavages and, 180
  sociological school and, 182–183
  strategic behavior influenced by, 24–25, 30–32, 203
  strategic voting and, 30–32, 185
  in Ukraine, electoral results and, 190–191
  urbanization levels as measure of, in Japan, 191
  in Wales, electoral results and, 190–191
social norms, election of women influenced by, 214
social sciences, 15–17
  assumptions within, 16
  goals of, 15–16
Soviet Union. *See* Russia; *specific nations*
spoiler effect, 74–75
Stephenson, Laura, 30, 183, 246
Stoll, Heather, 186, 250
strategic behavior, under electoral rules, 23, 24–25, 32
  in FPTP system, 23
  in linked tiers, 167
  SF-ratios and, 155–157
  social/ethnic diversity as influence on, 24–25, 203
strategic defection, xviii–xix, 240–243
  democratic experience as influence on, 167–170
  Duverger's law and, 38, 151, 242
  electoral rules and, 150–152
  in established democracies, 28, 165
  in Germany, 126, 128, 133–134
  in Lithuania, 126
  in new democracies, 28, 152, 165
  in New Zealand, 126, 129, 134
  over time, 167
  party system institutionalization and, 151–152
  political context for, 139
  in Scotland, 126, 129
  SF-ratios and, 152–158
  in SMDs, 124, 125–129

voter information as influence on, 28–29
in Wales, 126, 129
strategic voting, xix
analysis of, 129–131
assumptions about, 27–28
definition of, 150
Duverger's law and, 27, 130
electoral rules and, 150
electoral systems and, 25–29
in established democracies, 27–28, 150
expectations for, 126–128
under FPTP system, 30–32, 123
in Germany, 135
in Japan, 135
margin of victory and, 125, 131–137
in mixed-member electoral systems,
122–124
in new democracies, 152
in New Zealand, 134, 135
number of political parties and, 25–29
personal voting and, 124–125
preference revelation and, 150
previous elections as influence on, 136–137,
147
social/ethnic diversity and, 30–32, 185
Studlar, Dudley, 212
STV electoral system. *See* single transferable
vote electoral system

Taagepera, Rein, 15, 20
threshold-beating voting, 130
ticket splitting
in Germany, 122, 140
in Japan, 122, 124
in mixed-member electoral systems, 151
in New Zealand, 134
personal voting and, 123–124
in SMDs, 123
threshold-beating voting and, 130
twinning, 231
two-party systems, xix
two-round majority electoral systems, xix, 4
Duverger's Hypothesis and, 71

Ukraine
average effective number of candidates, per
SMD, 96–97
disproportionality in, 108
electoral volatility in, 82
mixed-member electoral system in, 48, 53
as new democracy, 81
non-institutionalized party system in, 82
party identification in, 82

personal voting in, 126, 128–129
PR tier, 14
SF-ratios in, 159
SMDs in, 79, 82
social/ethnic diversity and party
fragmentation in, 190–191, 192–195
strategic defection in, 126
women's representation in, 218
United Russia Party, 163, 164
United States (U.S.)
disproportionality in, 80, 87
electoral college in, 78
FPTP rules in, 54
SMDs in, 54
women as candidates in, 211
unlinked tiers, 61. *See also* mixed-member
majoritarian system
average effective number of candidates in,
97
in Hungary, 62–64
in Italy, 63–64
in Japan, 61, 64
in mixed member electoral system, 43–44
personal voting in, 127–128
in Russia, 61
scorporo system and, 63
SF-ratios in, 158
SMDs and, xix

Venezuela
disproportionality in, 108
mixed-member electoral system in, 48
PR tier in, 14
women's representation in, 218
Verba, Sidney, 59
voter defection. *See* strategic defection
voters. *See* strategic behavior, under electoral
rules
voting. *See* preference vote; strategic behavior,
under electoral rules; strategic defection;
strategic voting

Wales, 48
compensation seats in, 127
disproportionality in, 108
as established democracy, 81
personal voting in, 126, 128–129
SF-ratios in, 158
social/ethnic diversity and party
fragmentation in, 190–191, 195
strategic defection in, 126, 129
twinning in, 231
women's representation in, 218

Wattenberg, Martin, 239
West Germany. *See* Germany
women, election of, 33–35
  analysis of, 210–214
  career experience and, 212
  closed-list PR systems and, 24, 33–34, 208,
    209, 211
  controlled comparison of, 47–49
  country-level analysis of, 230–231
  cross-national studies of, 210–211
  developmental thresholds for, 229
  differential correlates for, by nation, 232
  district magnitude and, 209, 211–212
  electoral rules as influence on, 214–216
  in established democracies, as candidates,
    35, 209, 213–214, 215–216
  future research and, 254
  gender quotas for, in elections, xvi,
    220–221, 229
  incumbency reelection and, 212
  leftist political parties and, 213
  legislator-level analysis of, 231–235
  linked tiers and, 229
  in mixed-member electoral systems,
    240–243
  multilevel probit model for, 235
  in new democracies, as candidates, 35, 209,
    213–214

  number of parties as influence on,
    224–225
  party fragmentation as advantage for,
    34–35, 214–215, 230
  party ideology as influence on, 229
  party magnitude and, 212
  placement mandates and, xvii
  in postcommunist states, 215–216
  under PR systems, as candidates, 33–34,
    209–210, 211–213, 217–218, 221
  quantitative analysis of, 230–235
  representation of, electoral rules as influence
    on, 24
  in SMDs, as candidates, 33, 34–35, 208,
    211, 217–218, 221
  social bias and, 222–223, 224
  social norms and, 214
  societal support and, 226–227
  twinning and, 231
  in U.S., 211
  women's parties and, 213
  World Values Survey (WVS) and,
    222
Women of Russia Party, 213
World Values Survey (WVS), 222

Zhirinovsky, Vladimir, 94
Zoco, Edurne, 251